COLONIAL RULE AND CRISIS IN EQUATORIAL AFRICA: SOUTHERN GABON, CA. 1850–1940

ROCHESTER STUDIES in
AFRICAN HISTORY and the DIASPORA

Toyin Falola, Senior Editor
University of Texas at Austin

(ISSN: 1092-5228)

Power Relations in Nigeria: Ilorin Slaves and Their Successors
Ann O'Hear

Dilemmas of Democracy in Nigeria
Edited by Paul Beckett and Crawford Young
(ISSN: 1092-5228)

Science and Power in Colonial Mauritius
William Kelleher Storey

Namibia's Post-Apartheid Regional Institutions: The Founding Year
Joshua Bernard Forrest

*A Saro Community in the Niger Delta, 1912–1984:
The Potts-Johnsons of Port Harcourt and Their Heirs*
Mac Dixon-Fyle

Contested Power in Angola: 1840s to the Present
Linda Heywood

Nigerian Chiefs: Traditional Power in Modern Politics, 1890s–1990s
Olufemi Vaughan

West Indians in West Africa, 1808–1880: The African Diaspora in Reverse
Nemata Blyden

The United States and Decolonization in West Africa, 1950–1960
Ebere Nwaubani

Health, State, and Society in Kenya
George Oduor Ndege

Black Business and Economic Power
Edited by Alusine Jalloh
and Toyin Falola

Colonial Rule and Crisis in Equatorial Africa: Southern Gabon, ca. 1850–1940
Christopher J. Gray

COLONIAL RULE AND CRISIS IN EQUATORIAL AFRICA: SOUTHERN GABON, CA. 1850–1940

Christopher J. Gray

 UNIVERSITY OF ROCHESTER PRESS

First published 2002
by the University of Rochester Press

The University of Rochester Press
668 Mt. Hope Avenue, Rochester, NY 14620, USA
and at Boydell & Brewer, Ltd.
P.O. Box 9, Woodbridge, Suffolk 1P12 3DF, UK
www.urpress.com

ISBN 1-58046-048-8

Library of Congress Cataloging-in-Publication Data
Colonial rule and crisis in equatorial Africa : Southern Gabon, ca. 1850–1940 /
   Christopher J. Gray.
      p. cm.
   Includes bibliographic references and index.
   ISBN 1-58046-048-8
      1. Gabon—History—1839–1960.   2. Gabon—Colonial influence.
   I. Title.   II. Series.

DT546.175.G73 2002
967.21′02—dc21   2002022554

British Library Cataloguing-in-Publication Data
A catalogue record for this book is available from the British Library

Designed and typeset by Straight Creek Bookmakers
Printed in the United States of America
This publication is printed on acid-free paper

CONTENTS

MAPS

Christopher J. Gray

CHRISTOPHER J. GRAY 1958–2000

Chris Gray grew up in Massachusetts. He attended the University of Massachusetts–Amherst, majoring in History and graduating with a B.A. (cum laude) in 1980. As an undergraduate his cross-cultural and social action interests were already marked. During his junior year, he participated in an Overseas Program at Lancaster University, England. While at the University of Massachusetts, he joined the anti-apartheid movement and sought to inform fellow students about the situation in South Africa. He also canvassed Amherst neighborhoods in a campaign for rent control and wrote occasional columns for the university newspaper on pressing social issues.

Following his graduation in 1980, Chris volunteered for service in the Peace Corps. He improved his French and learned how to teach English as a second language, and with these skills, he was sent to francophone Africa (1982–1986). He taught English in a high school in southern Gabon for two years and then volunteered for two more years. He was posted to Senegal where he trained English-language teachers for the Ministry of Education.

From 1986 to 1987, Chris Gray completed an M.A. in Area Studies (Africa) at the School of Oriental and African Studies, University of London. He later revised and published his M.A. thesis, a comparative intellectual history of the works of two notable African scholars (*Conceptions of History in the Works of Cheikh Anta Diop and Théophile Obenga,* London: Karnak House, 1989).

From 1988 to 1995, Chris was a doctoral student in African History at Indiana University; his dissertation research took him back to southern Gabon. During his graduate career, he compiled an impressive academic record and received recognition in the award of several prestigious scholarships: Title VI Foreign Language and Area Studies Fellowships for the study of Lingala, a Social Science Research Council Pre-Dissertation Fellowship to conduct preliminary research in Gabon, and a Fulbright-Hays Doctoral Dissertation Research Grant for research in France and Gabon. He was also a MacArthur Scholar at the Indiana Center on Global Peace and World Change and published the early results of his dissertation research in the center's Occasional Paper series, entitled *Modernization and Cultural Iden-*

tity: The Creation of National Space in Rural France and Colonial Space in Rural Gabon (1994).

A catalog of such academic achievements hardly does justice to Chris Gray as a person, however, for wherever he lived, he established himself as an individual of great integrity—a humane and caring individual, humorous and low-key about his own accomplishments, and passionate about peace and justice. While maintaining a strong academic record, he continued his wider social concerns. This was recognized by Indiana University in the award of the prestigious John H. Edwards Fellowship given for high academic achievement, citizenship, and community service. From 1989 until the time of his death, Chris worked on a volunteer basis for Amnesty International–USA, serving as the coordinator for Gabon and the Democratic Republic of Congo (Zaire). But those who knew him well valued him most for being such a reliable and valuable member of their community. His activities were of the kind that do not appear on a CV but speak volumes for the person. During his years at Indiana University, he was at the center of an African and Africanist community, a good listener, and a resource person to be turned to for advice. He married Kisanga Gray, a Zaïroise, and their home was a meeting place for Africans and their families on the campus.

Chris Gray completed his Ph.D. in 1995 and in the fall of that year received an appointment as an Assistant Professor of African History at Florida International University, where he continued to make the same scholarly and personal contributions that had been the mark of his professional life. While considerably revising his dissertation for publication, he published articles in the *Journal of African History, Africa Today, History in Africa,* and *Islam et Société au Sud du Sahara* (Paris). He also contributed book reviews and film reviews to several scholarly journals. At the time of his death, his manuscript of this publication had been accepted by University of Rochester Press.

At Florida International University, Chris helped to develop the Africa–New World Studies Program and the certificate program in African Studies. He also served as advisor to the Association of People of African Ancestry and Culture, and was the mainstay of the campus chapter of Amnesty International. In 1998, he returned to Gabon as a member of a team sent by the International Foundation for Electoral Systems to conduct a pre-election technical assessment.

Within the history department, Chris devoted his time to teaching and scholarship. He was a caring mentor for undergraduate and graduate students alike. He helped to build the African history curriculum in the department and was largely responsible for the addition of an introductory World History survey course that is part of the general education requirement in the College of Arts and Sciences. He directed several M.A. theses and, at the time of his death, was the chair of the Ph.D. committee of William Allen.

More than anything else Chris was a beloved colleague. His friends in history and other departments throughout Arts and Sciences deeply appreciated his warmth and his unshakeable commitment to justice and fairness. As Provost Mark B. Rosenberg said after a memorial service, "Chris made people around him better." That he did.

Chris Gray died of cancer in October 2000. His death was a terrible loss not only for his wife, Kisanga, his three children, his parents, siblings, and friends, but for his colleagues, students, and professional contacts. He is remembered with admiration, respect, and affection.

Phyllis Martin
Bloomington, 2001
William Walker
Miami, 2001

FOREWORD

This book deals with a topic now receiving a great deal of attention across a range of disciplines: cultural perceptions, uses, and control of space—what is termed "territoriality." While divisions of space in colonial, urban Africa, have attracted some interest, the more difficult task of reconstructing how precolonial societies, often scattered across vast tracts of land, organized space has received less attention from historians. This is especially true for those societies which scholars call "decentralized" and which colonial Europeans dismissed as "chaotic." Focusing on a region of equatorial Africa, Southern Gabon, where he first lived as a Peace Corps teacher and then revisited for fieldwork, Chris Gray here demonstrates the complex cognitive, spiritual, social, and physical experience of space of local populations. Further, he uses the lens of contested space to enhance our understanding of the colonial encounter and to provide new insights into life under colonial rule, which in this region resulted in massive disruption, especially in the first four decades of the twentieth century. The analysis has involved thinking through a complex array of evidence to fathom the complexities of precolonial societies, reconstruct the colonial *mentalité*, and explore the interactions that led to a period of profound crisis, which, Gray argues, still influences the societies of Gabon today. In framing the study, the author draws on a wide range of theoretical and comparative literature, from the celebrated work of Michel Foucault to the studies of the geographer, Robert David Sack; the historian of France, Eugen Weber; the literature specialist, Marie Louise Pratt; and the anthropologists George Dupré and Pierre-Philippe Rey. The study builds in particular on the seminal work on equatorial societies of the African historian, Jan Vansina, and his classic study, *Paths in the Rainforests*.

Preparing this work for publication has been an inspiration and a privilege, but one tinged with great sadness, since Chris died before he could undertake it himself. At the time of his death, the manuscript had been accepted for publication by the University of Rochester Press. In undertaking some editing and minor revisions of the final manuscript, I have been guided by two readers' reports, the 1995 doctoral dissertation, Chris's several publications since that date, and my reflection on our many conversations on the history of West Central Africa. I would emphasize, however, that this publication remains overwhelmingly Chris Gray's work. It stands as a richly researched, innovative, and important achievement.

I should like to thank the following, who have contributed to the publication of the manuscript: the two readers of the University of Rochester Press for their insights, to which I have responded as appropriate and possible; François Ngolet, the Gabonese historian, for his suggestions in updating the bibliography and in finalizing the maps (most of which already existed in rough draft); William Walker, Chair of the History Department at Florida International University, and Kisanga Gray, Chris's wife, for help in the preparation of the biographical sketch, the acknowledgments, and with some practical details; and Toyin Falola, senior editor of the University of Rochester Press's series "Rochester Studies in African History and the Diaspora," and Timothy Madigan, editorial director of the Press, for their suggestions and support.

Phyllis Martin
Bloomington, 2001

ACKNOWLEDGMENTS

Recognizing the people and institutions that have assisted in this work is perhaps the most satisfying aspect of its completion. My debts are many. The project started with my graduate studies at Indiana University where I received support from two Title VI Foreign Language and Area Studies Fellowships. Research in Gabon, Congo, and France was facilitated by a Social Science Research Council Predissertation Fellowship and a Fulbright-Hays Doctoral Dissertation Research Abroad Grant. The year I spent as a MacArthur Scholar at the Indiana Center on Global Change and World Peace allowed me to focus on some of the theoretical approaches which I have further developed since then. I would like to thank the Center's directors, John Lovell and Jack Hopkins, and the publications editor, Victoria Cuffel, for their helpful advice. A John H. Edwards Fellowship from Indiana University allowed for the completion of my dissertation.

My first experience of Gabon came in 1982 as a Peace Corps Volunteer. The desire to continue relationships I established at that time led me to pursue graduate studies in African history. Not surprisingly, a complete list of all who assisted me in Gabon would be far too long. I would, however, like to acknowledge the tremendous debt I owe to the families of Soulounganga Jean-Bruno and the late Mboundou Guy-Joseph for lodging me during my stays in Libreville, Fougamou, and Mussondji. In particular, I would like to thank Baboussa Marie-Louise and Maroundou Annie-Joëlle for their generous hospitality and assistance. In Mouila, I made the home of Tom Prudhomme and his wife, Thérèse, a base for excursions to other towns and villages in the Ngounié province. Over the years I have learned much from Tom's wit and wisdom regarding things Gabonese and life in general. I would also like to acknowledge the aid of several Peace Corps Volunteers who either provided lodging or transportation: John Scheussler in Séka-Séka, Jenny Hamilton in Mimongo, Cindy Brooks in Sindara and John Miller in Mandji. In Libreville, the staffs at the Archives Nationales, the Centre Culturel Français Saint-Exupéry, the Laboratoire Universitaire de la Tradition Orale and the American Cultural Center—in particular Mike Livingston—provided invaluable assistance. Finally, I owe so much to the informants listed in the bibliography. Sadly, two of them have since passed on: Mboundou Guy-Joseph, whose children took me in as family, and Nyonda Vincent de Paul, a key cultural and political figure in independent Gabon, who graciously accorded me two memorable interviews.

In Brazzaville, the staff of the Archives Nationales was helpful as were contacts at the American Cultural Center, the U.S. Embassy, and the Peace Corps, who assisted me in an unplanned trip to Zaire at the end of 1991, where I joined my wife and visited her family. I am particularly indebted to Howard Anderson and Bob Weisflog.

In France, Père Joseph Carrard of the Archives des Pères du Saint-Esprit in Chevilly and the staff at the Archives Nationales, Centre des Archives d'Outre-Mer in Aix-en-Provence were extremely helpful. I also profited from discussions with Catherine Coquery-Vidrovitch, Georges Dupré, Marie-Claude Dupré, François Gaulme, Otto Gollnhofer, and Roger Sillans. Florence Souchet graciously facilitated our acclimation to life in Paris.

In the United States, comparing notes with John Cinnamon, an old Peace Corps colleague and anthropologist of the Fang ethnic group, has been of immeasurable value. Discussions with the art historian, Alisa LaGamma, have been especially stimulating, as we both work in Southern Gabon. François Ngolet, a Gabonese historian based in the United States, kindly gave me a copy of his doctoral thesis on the Bakele and has been a valued interlocutor.

My association with the African Studies Program at Indiana University was one of the most rewarding of my graduate school years. I would like to express my gratitude to Patrick O'Meara, Brian Winchester, Nancy Jacobs, George Brooks, Bill Cohen, John Hanson, Charles Bird, Michael Jackson, and Beverly Stoeltje. Phyllis Martin has been so much more to me and my family than an adviser I hardly know where to begin to express my gratitude. She has been a wise and trenchant critic of grant proposals, dissertation chapters, and conference papers. Our friendship is the most valued possession my wife and I take with us from our stay in Bloomington.

My family has provided tremendous support. My parents, John and Doris Gray, have assisted me in so many timely and numerous ways as have my siblings: Cindy Conena, Charlie Gray, Connie Gray, and Cathy Gray; my grandmother, Dorothy Chaffee, and the memory of my grandfather, Charles Chaffee, have been sources of inspiration. My wife, Kisanga, was somehow able to have a baby and complete her own studies during the three and a half years it took me to write my thesis. Our children, Jeanine, Alex, and Brendan, demonstrated varying degrees of patience but generally understood why we were both so often preoccupied.

No one mentioned above is accountable for what follows; that responsibility is mine and mine alone.

Chris Gray,
Bloomington, 1995

Chris Gray passed away before he was able to update the above acknowledgments that accompanied his dissertation. Many of those mentioned above continued to be important in his personal and professional growth as he established his career as an Africanist scholar and teacher. It seems important, however, that with the publication of this book some more names should be added to cover the years 1995 to 2000, especially those of friends and colleagues at Florida International University. Those close to Chris have suggested that he would want to acknowledge the following with gratitude: Bill Walker, Victor Uribe, and other colleagues in the history department; and John Clark, Jean Muteba Rahier, Terry Rey, Clarence Taylor, and Carole Boyce Davies in the Africa–New World Studies Program. Mohammed Farouk and Edmond Nebaka, both of the University of Miami, worked with Chris in establishing the African Forum for African students, students of African descent, and friends of Africa. Chris's doctoral student, Bill Allen, and his wife, Denise Roth, were close friends who gave important personal support. There are surely others whom Chris might have included; a collective thanks goes to them all. Finally, the dedication of his thesis reads: "To Kisanga with all my love and admiration." He would surely have wanted Kisanga to be acknowledged in similar terms with the publication of this book.

Phyllis Martin
Bloomington, 2001

ABBREVIATIONS

AA	*Annales Apostoliques de la Congrégation du Saint-Esprit*
AEF	Afrique Équatoriale Française
AGG-AEF	Archives de Gouvernement Général de l'Afrique Équatoriale Française
ANC	Archives Nationales du Congo
ANG	Archives Nationales du Gabon
AOM-AEF	Archives d'Outre-Mer—Afrique Équatoriale Française
AP	*Annales des Pères du Saint-Esprit*
APSE	Archives des Pères du Saint-Esprit
BCSE	*Bulletin de la Congrégation du Saint-Esprit*
BDG	Bloc Démocratique Gabonais
BIEC	*Bulletin de l'Institut d'Études Centrafricaines*
BSRC	*Bulletin de la Société des Recherches Congolaises*
CEA	*Cahiers d'Études Africaines*
CICIBA	Centre International des Civilisations Bantu
CFCO	Compagnie Française du Congo Occidental
COGES	Comité Gabonais d'Études Sociales Économiques
CRA	Centre de Recherches Africaines
CPSE	Congrégation des Pères du Saint-Esprit
EPHE	École Pratique des Hautes Études
IJAHS	*International Journal of African Historical Studies*
JA	*Journal des Africanistes*
JAH	*Journal of African History*
JSA	*Journal de la Société des Africanistes*
ORSTOM	Office de la Recherche Scientifique et Technique Outre-Mer
PUF	Presses Universitaires de France
PUNGA	Parti d'Union Nationale Gabonaise
RG	*Réalités Gabonaises*
RGSH	*Revue Gabonaise des Sciences de l'Homme*
SAFIA	Société Agricole, Forestière et Industrielle pour l'Afrique
SAO	Société Agricole et Commerciale du Bas-Ogooué
SFN	Société des Factories de Ndjolé
SHN	Société de la Haute-Ngounié
SHO	Société du Haut-Ogooué
UDSG	Union Démocratique et Sociale Gabonaise
UOB	Université Omar Bongo

A NOTE ON SPELLING

The spellings of Gabonese geographical and cultural terms have not been sufficiently standardized. Thus, researchers are obliged to justify those adopted in their work. For rivers, lakes, lagoon, massifs, and towns, I have relied upon the national map, *Gabon: Carte au 1:1,000,000* produced jointly in 1987 by the Institut Géographique National in Paris and the Institut National de Cartographie in Libreville. Cultural terms have proven a more tangled affair. As discussed below, the ability to name through writing is an expression of power; the naming and spelling of Gabonese ethnic groups continues to be a subject of intense political negotiation. For example, intellectuals from Southern Gabon have rejected the French rendering of their ethnic group, *Bapounou,* for *Bapunu,* and in the process have asserted control over their identity. They have also sought to rid the spelling of names and terms in the Punu language of French distortions: for example *mutéti* (a kind of basket) for *moutette,* or "Mbumb-Bwas" (the name of a Gabonese historian) for "Mboumba-Bouassa." A team of linguists and anthropologists has recently brought these developments to their logical conclusion by producing a table of "ethnoscientific" spellings for Gabonese ethnic groups and languages (see Raymond Mayer and Michel Voltz, "Dénomination ethnoscientifique des langues et des ethnies du Gabon," RGSH 2 (1990): 43–53). Although this was a very important development and an interesting comment on the state of Gabonese national identity, as most of the scholars who worked on the project were French, the characters employed to render certain sounds made these spellings too awkward for my purposes. I instead relied on the common-sense approach adopted by David Gardinier in his *Historical Dictionary of Gabon* and my own sense of appropriate usage. Still some problems remained: for example, the term "Eshira" is still employed in administrative contexts to refer to an ethnic group and language of Southern Gabon, even though the people themselves tend to use the terms "Gisira" and "Gisir" for their ethnic group and language. I discuss "Eshira" in terms of colonial invention but will use "Gisira" when referring to the contemporary ethnic group. Below is a list of the spellings I employ for the ethnic groups and languages of Southern Gabon:

Ethnic Group	*Language*
Bapunu	Punu
Gisira	Gisir
Mitsogo	Tsogo
Apindji	Apindji
Bakele	Kele
Simba	Simba
Eviya	Eviya
Nkomi	Nkomi
Balumbu	Lumbu
Bavungu	Vungu
Bavarama	Varama
Massango	Sango
Nzabi	Nzabi
Galwa	Galwa
Ajumba	Ajumba
Enenga	Enenga
Okandé	Okandé
Vili	Vili
Ngowé	Ngowé
Orungu	Orungu
Mpongwe	Mpongwe
Fang	Fang

In rendering clans and lineages there are even greater problems, as no attempts at standardization have been undertaken. My only guidance has been to avoid linguistic spellings; this was merely for stylistic convenience.

INTRODUCTION

The origins of this book can be traced to two encounters I had while trekking through the hilly equatorial forests of south-central Gabon in August of 1983. A friend and I had spent the night in Massima, an old gold-mining camp that had turned into a village. As we left Massima to plunge into an uninhabited part of the forest, we came across a French geologist prospecting for gold. He was equipped with a compass and maps and boasted that he had no need of guides since he was able to calculate his exact position by using his measurement instruments. In the meantime, we had just made arrangements with a hunter from the Babongo[1] people to bring us to a nearby village, where we would find guides to make the two-day trek over difficult terrain to Mount Iboundji. This Babongo hunter had no use for maps, yet he, too, knew just where he was going when hunting in the forest.

At the time, I casually remarked upon this interesting contrast between the French geologist and the Babongo hunter and their methods of moving about the forest. It was only years later when I was thinking through my research findings that the juxtaposition of the geologist and the hunter resurfaced and assumed a deeper significance. It symbolized the different dichotomies that have often defined the colonial encounter: precision versus fluidity; abstract versus concrete knowledge; literate versus non-literate ways of knowing; modern versus premodern; colonial versus precolonial. A proverb shared among the peoples of Southern Gabon—"the clan knows no boundary"—pushed me to consider the colonial encounter between the French and the peoples of Southern Gabon in terms of differing conceptions of space. The proverb implies the flexibility and non-territorial nature of clan identity, this in contrast to bounded nineteenth-century Western conceptions of social identity determined by attachment to ethnic or national territory.

In reading through the considerable literature on space, I came upon a theory of human territoriality developed by the geographer Robert David Sack, where territoriality is described as "a powerful geographic strategy to control people and things by controlling area."[2] By thinking in terms of space and employing Sack's theory of territoriality, the present study effectively blurs the above dichotomies and yields a more subtle historical analysis. Throughout human history, all societies have organized themselves in physical space; all societies have produced cognitive maps that facilitate this ordering in space; all societies have practiced territoriality. Physical spaces and cognitive maps are historical products that interact with each other in dialectical fashion; the particular forms they take vary with historical context.

In the second half of the nineteenth century, two very different cognitive maps confronted each other in Southern Gabon. Clan and lineage relationships were most important in the local cognitive map and the manipulation of kinship crucial to controlling people and things by controlling area; territory was thus socially defined. The French cognitive map, in contrast, was defined by a territorial definition of society that had emerged with the rise of the modern nation-state and industrial capitalism. This modern territoriality exploited an array of bureaucratic instruments—such as maps and censuses—unknown to the peoples of Southern Gabon in the mid-nineteenth century. Accessing and employing these territorial instruments are essential elements of modernity. The ability of these instruments to deny the existence of locally created territories first in the space of the text and subsequently in real physical space was fundamental to the exercise of colonial power. As European explorers, missionaries, and colonial administrators attempted to impose modern territoriality, they named and categorized peoples and things to correspond to a European logic and to meet the needs of a European project.

Thus modern or colonial (the two are used interchangeably in the book) territoriality involved the imposition of categories and institutions foreign to the peoples to whom they were applied. Before the 1920s, colonial ethnic categories and institutions did not reflect the lived reality of Gabonese peoples subject to French rule. But with a more effective colonial presence, these institutions started to become "real" as cultural elites negotiated their meanings in reference to their own traditions. The result was not the neat denial of precolonial practice denoted in the texts of the map or census but a strongly ambiguous condition. This ambiguity left its imprint on the new colonial territories and cognitive maps, which have since been appropriated by the postcolonial Gabonese state.

This encounter between different practices of territoriality has been played out in all the inhabited regions of the globe over the last three centuries. The territorial analysis employed in this study may be fruitfully applied beyond Southern Gabon to the historical experience of modernity generally.

The book starts in the early decades of the nineteenth century, a point when the impact of the Atlantic trade was already introducing new spatial orientations in Southern Gabon but before the advent of the French colonial presence. It ends around 1940, by which time a modern territoriality had obtained an ambiguous triumph, and space had been effectively delimited along colonial lines with concommitant transformations for local cultural and social identities.

There are seven chapters. Chapter 1 introduces the analytical and theoretical concepts employed in the study. Spatial analysis in precolonial equatorial Africa begins by thinking about regions; there were no formal regions organized around urban centers in Southern Gabon, but there were relations of long-distance trade and dependent exchange that constituted dynamic functional regions. Due to its ecological diversity and the patterns of clan migrations occurring within its space, Southern Gabon is of particular interest to the historian. The elements of Jan Vansina's equatorial political tradition[3]—House, village, and district—are introduced and their unique evolution in Southern Gabon described. Central here is the development of matrilineal clans and lineages from about the thirteenth century. Their role in the precolonial social order is discussed, the analysis building upon the insights of Vansina as well as the French scholars Pierre-Philippe Rey and Georges Dupré. Clans in precolonial Southern Gabon were aterritorial social entitites sufficiently flexible to accommodate the complex trade and dependent exchange practiced within and across Southern Gabon's districts and functional regions. The proverb "the clan has no boundary" (as the Nzabi version, *Ibanda pange vé,* translates) attests to this adaptability and to the social definition of territory that operated in these societies.[4] Sack's theory of human territoriality is introduced to close the chapter; I argue that the application of this theory to Southern Gabon's experience of French rule results in a deeper understanding of the colonial encounter.

Chapter 2 describes the practices of territoriality among the peoples inhabiting Southern Gabon in the mid-nineteenth century. It summarizes the impact of the Atlantic slave trade and then describes the patterns of district settlement and the contexts of district territoriality. The precolonial long-distance trade networks of the Southern Gabon functional regions are then traced out. From the mid-nineteenth century, the boundaries and nodal points of these functional regions were constantly shifting due to a boom in trade opportunities brought on by an influx of European goods and a demand for forest products. A people known as the Bakele were particularly active in exploiting these openings, and their experience is analyzed to illustrate changing settlement patterns and district structure. Following this discussion, Chapter 3 considers the relationship between cognitive kinship maps and territorial practice. The shifting nature of alliances and the creative flexibility of relations is emphasised. The chapter closes with a discussion of the men's initiation society most commonly known as *mwiri,* the central instrument of precolonial territoriality at the village level.

Chapter 4 opens with a discussion of the initial impact of European presence in Southern Gabon in the second half of the nineteenth century. Most dramatic were the introduction of diseases like smallpox to the region, resulting in a number of traumatic epidemics that undermined precolonial territoriality. The establishment of European factories and the consequences of the ever-accelerating pace of commerce are also examined. An argument is then elaborated which posits that vision in the form of an appropriating gaze was a fundamental instrument of European colonial power, and that this power was expressed through writing in the texts of travellers, missionaries, and colonial administrators. The power of writing and its availability to Europeans allowed colonial agents to name the spaces and physical features of Southern Gabon according to a modern logic. Maps are then shown to be especially powerful instruments of territoriality. A final section traces the textual and cartographical history of the term "Eshira" through to its use as a category in colonial census-taking and its appropriation as a modern ethnic identity. The census is described as perhaps the most powerful tool of modern territoriality.

Chapter 5 examines the ambiguous impact of colonial territoriality in Southern Gabon. An opening section analyzes the territorial ambitions of the different colonial spaces established in Southern Gabon between 1870 and 1910: commercial factory, Christian mission, concession holding, and administrative post. Their power for disruption and chaos is demonstrated through the difficult period of food shortage and famine that affected much of the region between 1910 and 1920. Chapter 6 then examines the subsequent transformation of Southern Gabon as a functional region through the building of roads and the development of a timber industry. The consequences for the evolution of modern ethnic identities are examined. Finally, it is argued that the imposition of colonial territoriality was a singularly ambiguous triumph given weak long-term infrastructural investment particular to the timber industry and a lack of resources available to the colonial state.

The final chapter considers Vansina's pronouncement of the death of the equatorial tradition during the colonial period in conjunction with J.-F. Bayart's "politics of the belly" analysis of African political continuity, this in light of the ambiguous situation reigning in Gabon in the 1920s and 1930s. The spate of "Leopard men" killings in the 1910s and 1920s is discussed as a pathological response by clan leaders to the crisis of their declining power and of the equatorial tradition in general. With the establishment of colonial chieftaincies in the 1920s and 1930s, *canton* chiefs were asked to assume modern functions like tax collection and the organization of labor with limited access to the bureaucratic instruments of colonial territoriality. They remained largely dependent upon the brute force of the Regional Guard. Fully colonial creations, these *canton* chiefs were for the most part unsuccessful in integrating aspects of precolonial "big man" authority with opportunities provided by modernity. The 1930s also witnessed a proliferation of healing societies in which women played predominant roles, and I argue for a more nuanced view of the "death of tradition" where these healing societies represent important survivals of precolonial practice. The conclusion reaffirms the main arguments of the study and considers some recent developments such as the continuing reconfirmation of spatial and ethnic identities under the postcolonial Gabon state.

Notes

1. "Babongo" is one of a number of terms used by the Western Bantu peoples of Gabon to designate local hunter-gatherers, popularly known as "pygmies."

2. Robert David Sack, *Human Territoriality: Its Theory and History* (Cambridge: Cambridge University Press, 1986), 5.

3. Jan Vansina, *Paths in the Rainforests: Toward a History of Political Tradition in Equatorial Africa* (Madison: University of Wisconsin Press, 1990).

4. The Punu version of the same proverb is : "Ifumba àgá panga"; see Monique Koumba-Manfoumbi, "Les Punu du Gabon, des origines à 1899: Essai d'étude historique," (Thèse de doctorat, Université Paris I, 1987), 253.

1

DEVELOPING A SPATIAL APPROACH TO HISTORICAL CHANGE IN EQUATORIAL AFRICA

Regions: Formal and Functional

Neither Gabon nor Congo contain "regions" in the full sense of the word where "regions" are consecrated by a traditional name, historical antecedents, solid economic structures, or long term historical domination by an urban center. Where, then, are we to mark down the necessary articulations without falling into the arbitrary?

Gilles Sautter[1]

The African equatorial forest, long a source of mystery and wonder to the Western outsider, is neither so monolithic nor intimidating to the peoples who live in it. The myth of impenetrable jungle hostile to human habitation must be tossed in the dust bin with other quirky Western notions about Africa. Since the publication of Jan Vansina's *Paths in the Rainforest*,[2] scholars interested in the past of the Bantu peoples of equatorial Africa no longer have to worry about "falling into the arbitrary." Using evidence drawn from historical linguistics, archaeology, and precolonial ethnographic accounts, Vansina methodically argues for the existence of an equatorial political tradition dating back to the arrival of Western Bantu speakers in the forest zones of Gabon some three thousand years ago. This endured as the core tradition of the area up to the colonial conquest at the end of the nineteenth century. Vansina's exposition is compelling, one that will long remain the primary reference point for the study of the past of peoples one scholar labeled "any historian's nightmare."[3]

The ambition of the present work is to extend and refine insights made by Vansina (and others) concerning the impact of the colonial experience on the peoples of Southern Gabon and the central components of their precolonial equatorial tradition. In so doing a particular argument concerning the nature of modernity is put forward, the implications of which reach beyond Gabon to the experience of modern European colonialism in general. This is accomplished through analysis informed by a spatial conception of historical change. Recently, a group of Africanist scholars has come together to exploit innovative work produced on space by geographers and to share research findings on precolonial and colonial African history. A particular concern has been to apply concepts of "region" to historical developments on different parts of the continent.[4]

The quotation opening this chapter from French scholar Gilles Sautter's massive 1966 geography of Gabon and Congo reveals a "formal" concept of region. A formal region from the perspective of political geography would display clearly defined boundaries, a single authority, and uniformly applied laws; from the perspective of economic geography a formal region would contain an urban center serving a recognized hinterland. Thus on the basis of his stated criteria, Sautter's remarks are accurate: there were no formal political or economic regions in precolonial Gabon.

But neither were the spaces of the equatorial forest arbitrary; regions can also be conceptualized in terms of function. Functional regions are structured systems formed from spatial interactions generated by the movement of persons, goods, services, and information. The boundaries of functional regions are fluid and undergo considerable change over time.[5] The spatial analysis of functional regions facilitates the study of precolonial long-distance trade and population movements in Southern Gabon.

Southern Gabon refers to an area whose northern boundary follows the course of the Ogooué River to the mouth of the Offoué River, a tributary on the Ogooué's left bank. The Offoué defines the eastern limit with its headwaters in the Du Chaillu Massif approaching the southern limit which is roughly defined by the headwaters of the Nyanga River and this river's descent to the Atlantic Ocean. The Atlantic coast from the mouth of the Ogooué to the mouth of the Kouilou corresponds to the western boundary of this region (see Map 1; latitude 0°N, 4°S; longitude 9°E, 12°E encompasses the region).

This geographic space has historically been the site for a myriad of functional regions created by the local population to provide networks for

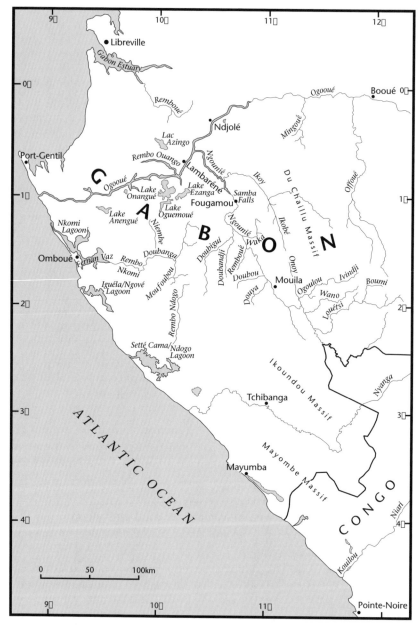

Map 1. Southern Gabon

political, economic, and cultural exchange. The boundaries of these regions shifted continually from the mid-nineteenth to the mid-twentieth
century, and networks often extended across the delineations indicated
above. Even the name "Southern Gabon" is an imposition, first inscribed
by Europeans and now reflecting more contemporary developments. Today it is emerging as a formal political region within the context of the
Gabonese nation-state; in the mid-nineteenth century the peoples inhabiting this space claimed no such regional identity.[6] Yet Southern Gabon, as I
have sketched it, remains a suitable unit for historical study.[7]

First, the area is ecologically diverse. Five types of tropical rainforest
cover close to ninety percent of Southern Gabon. There are the small areas
of mangrove forest near the mouths of the Ogooué River and the Nkomi
Lagoon and marshy and inundated forests stretching along the banks of
the Ogooué and the southern lagoons. The coastal plain forests and the
mountain forests of the massifs, however, dominate the landscape. A kind
of forest vegetation resulting from deforestation for agriculture has become
more prominent in the last fifty years but also existed in precolonial times.
Slim strips of savannah are found along the Nyanga and Ngounié Rivers,
scattered on the coastal plain and at the Ogooué-Offoué confluence.[8]

Thick ferrous soils of a clay texture and yellow-ochre color dominate
the region but are poorly suited for agriculture, despite luxuriant forest
growth. A coastal plain of marsh and lagoons extends east along the Ogooué
to the town of Ndjolé, encompassing the chain of lakes near the town of
Lambaréné, and then heads south to include the Nkomi (Fernan Vaz),
Ngové (Iguéla), and Ndogo (Setté Cama) Lagoons and their tributaries
(most notably the Rembo Nkomi and the Rembo Ndogo). Just to the south
and east of this coastal plain one encounters a series of hilly areas split apart
by the Nyanga and Ngounié Rivers and their surrounding savannah. These
include the small Koumounawali Massif near the town of Fougamou, the
northern stretch of the Mayombe Massif, and the Ikoundou Massif. The
area between the Ngounié and Offoué River basins is dominated by the
Du Chaillu Massif, whose thickly forested hills rise to heights of nearly
1000 meters. The Ngounié River, the second most important tributary of
the Ogooué, and its tributaries have their headwaters in the Du Chaillu
Massif and, in terms of physical geography, serve as an axis for Southern
Gabon.[9]

The climate is equatorial, with temperatures ranging between 21°
and 28° centigrade over a given year. The lowlands in the interior are the
warmest spots; the hills of the Du Chaillu Massif are significantly cooler.

There are four distinct seasons: a long dry season that generally begins in June and lasts until September; a rainy season that goes from September to January; a short dry season of a few weeks straddling January and February; and then another rainy season that lasts from February until June. There is some variation as to the length of these seasons within the Southern Gabon region: along the Ogooué and in the Du Chaillu Massif the short dry season is simply a slowing down of the rains while in the littoral region and the Ikoundou Massif the long dry season can last up to five months.[10]

This ecological diversity is significant in that the peoples who have historically inhabited Southern Gabon developed a variety of material skills and cultural practices to adapt to their physical surroundings. As a consequence, peoples of the "coast" came to distinguish themselves from peoples of the "forest," peoples of the "savannah" from those of the "river," and so on. These diverse skills and practices provided the basis for the various functional regions. In Southern Gabon, the relationship between a people and its environment was never static, and population movement in precolonial times was constant. Migrations of relatively short distance resulted in "coastal" peoples becoming "forest" peoples or "forest" peoples becoming "river" peoples, these movements often necessitating a shift in material and cultural practices which in turn altered the boundaries of the functional regions. An example is found in the oral traditions of the Ngové (or Ngowé) people; the stories relate that prior to their arrival on the Ngové (Iguéla) Lagoon some five hundred years ago the Ngové were a "savannah" people ignorant of net fishing, a skill they acquired after settling on the lagoon and becoming a "river" people.[11]

Gabonese and Western historians have sought to reconstruct patterns of population movement in the area of the equatorial forest that is now the Republic of Gabon. By weaving oral traditions of population movement together with the observations of early European explorers, they have been able to discern the broad outlines of the migrations occurring over the past several centuries. The most recent cartographic synthesis of these findings shows that Southern Gabon served as point of convergence for population movements from the south, east, and north during the seventeenth, eighteenth, and nineteenth centuries.[12] Thus, the resulting contacts and exchanges between peoples moving through the area are of particular interest to the historian. What is more, Vansina suggests that the peoples settling in Southern Gabon during this period developed a particular variation of the equatorial tradition, and that this provided a shared framework for political and cultural practice across the region.[13]

Equatorial Political Tradition

Vansina posits that in its ancestral form Western Bantu equatorial tradition contained three interconnecting social groups: the House, the village, and the district. Relations between these three groups were very flexible, and the contours of each varied according to region and historical period.[14] In the common base tradition, the House was the domain of the big man and the basic unit of social organization; it was also a spatial unit within a village and clearly marked off from its companion Houses. Since villages relocated every ten to fifteen years, there was a continual flux of big men coming together and moving apart with their House membership in tow. Even prior to the impact of the Atlantic trade in the sixteenth century, there existed a hierarchy of social statuses, as lingusitic analysis reveals Western Bantu terms for "slave, client, protected/adopted person or group, serf (hunter and gatherer group), friend and cadet in the sense of junior member."[15] Slaves and other dependents were not traded as commodities but used more as pawns to cement relationships between Houses.

The exchange of women was of fundamental importance for relations between big men as well as for the reproduction of the House. Through a whole range of possible marriage arrangements,[16] a big man sought to increase the number of women in his House not only to bring their children under his control but also to attract younger men as members. Control over matrimonial exchange was the key instrument of power within a House and a major source of its inequality.[17] Sources of power and wealth in precolonial equatorial Africa resided in control over *people*—wives and dependents—and not ownership of land or goods. Prestige goods or parcels of land were accumulated not for their inherent value but for their potential value in obtaining future adherents to the House. This notion of "wealth in people" was a defining characteristic of the precolonial and precapitalist societies in Southern Gabon until the end of the nineteenth century.[18]

The village was a group of Houses and the basic unit of settlement. Generally, the physical layout of a village was defined by two parallel lines of rectangular private dwellings which enclosed a plaza. Public buildings were found in the plaza; these were often spaces for artisans and for public assembly. There was at least one men's clubhouse in each village but sometimes there were several, each belonging to a particular House.[19] A village was led by the big man who founded it, but he consulted with the big men of the other member Houses in making decisions.

Collective institutions played a crucial role in creating solidarity across the Houses of a village. In Southern Gabon, following the introduction of matrilineal descent from the Congo basin in about the twelth or thirteenth century, two new social groups came into existence: the local matrilineage and the clan.[20] Yet though the creation of the matrilineage meant descent was now traced from the female "belly," a married woman still continued to live at her husband's place of residence. Her children thus lived apart from their mother's brother. This lack of congruence between residence and lineage resulted in a spatial dispersion of the members of a given matrilineage. One's identification with a matrilineage, then, was determined by matrilineal kinship ideology and not by residence within a particular village or district. Clans developed in an effort to bridge this discordance between residence and descent as different matrilineal relatives separated in space sought to formalize their kinship. Further formalization came with recognized clan heads drawn from the most powerful known matrilineages. A clan head sought to legitimate his position by claiming that his matrilineage descended from the first-born daughter of the original female clan ancestor. Through the clan ideology, chains of alliances such as that of the powerful Bumwele were created.[21] The authority of a clan head extended beyond the territorial authority wielded in his own village and was expressed through the aterritorial ideology of matrilinearity.[22]

In the Congo River basin—in regions that were to accommodate the Kongo, Tio, and Loango Kingdoms—centralization and hierarchy became the defining characteristics of matrilineages and clans. However, Vansina posits that in Southern Gabon matrilinearity was put to a different use. Here powerful village associations, notably what is most often referred to as *mwiri,* were the essential governing bodies and the village the most prominent social unit. With the adoption of the matriclan, the peoples of Southern Gabon resisted the centralizing tendencies that occurred further south. As Vansina has noted, they:

> claimed that each local clan was equivalent to other clans elsewhere and derived from a common ancestor. Thus they built up a network of regional alliances by inventing lists of correspondences between the names of different clans. In this way they overcame the lack of common overarching institutions between districts and perhaps villages. Soon the whole area formed a single social whole, even while it remained strongly decentralized.[23]

The district was the largest social organization of space known in the equatorial tradition. Districts were clusters of villages whose inhabitants grouped together for security and to facilitate matrimonial and economic exchange. A district, then, served as a functional region for its constituent villages. The area of Southern Gabon in the mid-nineteenth century was marked by these district village clusters, which were separated from each other by "dead" or uninhabited zones. The first European explorers re-marked upon this, but their observations were not emphasized in later ac-counts; as a result anthropologists often mistakenly referred to districts as "maximal lineages" or "subtribes."[24]

A district did not have a leader nor was there necessarily a principal village. In Southern Gabon following the introduction of matrilinearity, the district was a matrix of bilateral alliances between village and clan lead-ers; these latter met together only in times of war when a common defense was required. Though the physical life of a village was relatively short, that of a district could be quite long. As villages broke apart and member matrilineages regrouped, the founding matrilineages usually remained within their district to create new villages and new functional regions. In this way a sense of shared heritage based on district identity developed over time.[25]

Given shifting boundaries and physical settings, it is more accurate to view the district as an alliance of matrilineages rather than villages. Clans were the ideological form of these district alliances. By the nineteenth cen-tury, membership in a particular clan could be indicated by a common name or origin story, a shared food taboo, similar tattoos, or a claim to the same symbolic totem.[26] When a clan member from a different matrilineage arrived in a village, it was the duty of his clan brothers residing in the village to provide him with hospitality. Shared clan membership also facili-tated long-distance trading contacts; members of clans separated in space liv-ing in different districts and sporting different names were able to identify one another as kin and enter into commercial exchange. The belief in a single founding ancestor gave each clan a sense of permanence; each matrilineage within a clan was said to descend from the progeny of the founding ancestor. No sibling was considered superior to another, just as each of the matrilineages was in theory the equal of the other. The historical reality, however, was one of continual shifts in clan affiliation and unequal relationships between different clans and between the matrilineages within a single clan. Even so, the ide-ology of clan permanence and equality remains influential to this day.[27]

Thinking about Clans and Kinship

Clearly, an understanding of the functions of clans and the "calculus of kinship"[28] is central to an analysis of precolonial Southern Gabon. The ethnic groups and regional groupings of contemporary usage are recent developments stemming from the imposition of the colonial and postcolonial Gabonese state. Indeed, the ethnic classifications produced by Hubert Deschamps and Marcel Soret in early attempts to write about Gabon's past need to be seen as the culmination of a colonial project. This project sought to name and classify the peoples of Gabon on the basis of shared language and cultural practice and an attachment to a formal region.[29] The requirements of modern bureaucratic administration demanded that such formal regions be found, or if not found, invented. Even an astute and encyclopedic observer like Sautter, after having delineated the artificiality of Gabonese ethnic designations and demonstrating their analytical weakness, argued that, for lack of anything better, they were necessary to an understanding of the history of Gabonese population movements.[30]

But there is indeed something better. Early works by the French administrator Georges Le Testu and the Gabonese priest André Raponda-Walker pointed to the fundamental importance of clans to precolonial cultural identity and social structure.[31] Yet because French colonial anthropology had no equivalent to the postwar British school of social anthropology influenced by descent theory, there exist rather few ethnographic monographs focusing on the the function of clans and kinship structures among the various African peoples living in France's colonies. It was only with the rise of French Marxist anthropology in the 1960s that there developed serious analysis of the position of matrilineages and clans in the precolonial societies of Southern Gabon.[32] Two doctoral dissertations written in France by Gabonese scholars, Pierre-Louis Agondjo-Okawe and Joseph Ambouroue-Avaro, were also integral in shifting the focus away from ethnic groups as a unit of analysis.[33]

Studies from the French Marxist school by Pierre-Philippe Rey and George Dupré are of particular significance for Southern Gabon. Rey's attempt to describe the workings of a precolonial lineage mode of production practiced by Tsangui, Punu, and Kuni peoples who inhabited the hinterland between Mayumba and Loango provides a number of important insights into the past functions of clans and lineages. He categorically asserts that the clan needs to be the appropriate focus for historical study of precolonial social structure.[34] For Rey the lineage mode of production in precolonial and precapitalist equatorial Africa was a mode of exploitation where a class of elders—the clan and lineage heads—expropriated the surplus derived from the labor of a class of dependents—namely women and junior male members of the clan or lineage.

The keystone to these structures among the Tsangui, Kuni, and Punu peoples was the concept of *mukuna*. *Mukuna* is often mistranslated as "terre" in French (or "land" in English) and thus has been misinterpreted as simply referring to the unit of land belonging to a particular lineage. Rey, however, describes it as the whole complex series of obligations and duties owed to lineage heads by their dependents, and as such it expresses the relations of production for these societies. Given that the members of a particular matrilineage or clan were dispersed in space, Rey argues that clans and lineages existed only in political and economic terms through the actual lineage heads themselves, past and present, and not in the group of individuals who at any one time were its members. The only visible, concrete social grouping was the *mukuna* where one found residing in relative proximity "not only the paternal sons and descendants of the matrilineal landholders (living and deceased) but also slaves, client lineages, pygmies if there were any, and allies come to establish themselves on this land or their descendants."[35]

The *mukuna*, then, was the actual unit that produced the surplus for the elders/lineage heads while the matrilineage and clan provided the ideological instruments on which their authority was based. There is an important distinction regarding territory and social identity to be made from Rey's analysis of the *mukuna*; namely claims upon territory were realized through the *mukuna*, a process that was separate from the construction of cultural and social identity based on an aterritorial kinship ideology.

Dupré, an anthropologist who at one time collaborated with Rey, also adopts a "modes of production" approach in his rich study of the Nzabi clans located in the Upper Nyanga River basin.[36] He sets out to describe the "order" of Nzabi precolonial society. In his analysis, the forest itself becomes a fundamental means of production, as all aspects of Nzabi material production drew from its resources. Hunting and agriculture were the most important activities and Dupré argues that the fluid settlement practices of the Nzabi and other peoples inhabiting the equatorial forest were the result of a contradiction between the hunter's need for mobility and the farmer's need for permanence. They were not simply due to exhaustion of the soil through farming. The cyclical movement of villages was then "a necessity organically inscribed" in the reproduction of the forest, the essential means of production in Nzabi society.[37]

In discussing relations of exploitation, Dupré posits that no exploitable surplus resulted from the precolonial production of subsistence goods and that the focus should be on the process of social production. Fundamental in this regard was the dependent position of women. Though their agricultural labor was responsible for much of the produce required for subsistence, women had little input in decisions related to the production process such as where to cultivate, preservation of the forest, and the timing and place of village resettlement. Due to exogamous marriage practices, women resided in the villages of their husbands and thus only used the fields to which their husbands had access. It was the labor of women issuing from their role in production as farmers and their role in reproduction as mothers that created a "time surplus" for men. Unencumbered by the tasks of raising food and children, men employed this "surplus" of free time to negotiate the circulation and exchange of women. In the process the conditions for women's exploitation were perpetuated.[38]

Dupré sees women and the forest as holding identical positions in Nzabi cosmology, where only the actions of men upon nature were capable of bringing about the fertility of the soil or fecundity of women. The dependent position of women would have been but a single manifestation of the efforts of men to possess and dominate nature. Marriage, in this view, was "the transfer of possession of a natural entity that conferred upon the beneficiary a certain autonomy in terms of subsistence, thus helping him down the path to elder status and control over social production."[39] Dupré insists that the dependent position of women was the only form of exploitation that existed within precolonial Nzabi society. In so doing, he denies the significance given to the "elder/cadet" relationship by Rey and others.

Dupré, in another departure from Rey, considers the problem of space in his description of the Nzabi precolonial order. He argues that the mobility and weak population density required for Nzabi material production determined the spatial limits and constraints on the production of Nzabi society. In reckoning the fundamental role of the circulation of women for social production with the mobility required for material production, Nzabi political organization was required to "define itself without reference to space"; as a consequence, "the units between which women circulated were *aterritorial* units."[40] From this situation and the need to generalize the practice of circulating women across the geographical space inhabited by the Nzabi, the clan system developed. Although Dupré's analysis is presented in an almost timeless and ahistorical manner, it does serve to delineate an essential historical characteristic of clan identity: its aterritoriality. Dupré notes that "abstracted from space, the clan cannot be apprehended in the visible" and that "any attempt to do so will end in failure." The system of clans in the precolonial order, then, was "a struggle against space," an effort to provide a sense of permanence among peoples who were not only mobile and dispersed but at times willing to switch allegiances.[41]

"The Clan Has No Boundary": The Social Definition of Territory

This proverb nicely conveys the fundamental incongruity between matrilineal conceptions of descent and actual residence in space. The clan's lack of boundary suggests its aterritoriality as well as its flexibility. This flexibility provided a social network capable of negotiating contacts across the sometimes considerable expanse of Southern Gabon's functional regions. Historically, societies of this kind—premodern, non-literate, wealth in people, absence of economic classes and class conflict, politically decentralized—relied upon a *social definition of territory* where "group membership and political action revolved around kinship linkage rather than residence in a particular territory."[42] Rey's discussion of the role of *mukuna* among the Tsangui, Punu, and Kuni demonstrates this relationship in two ways. First, it shows the lack of connection between the residential unit of production—the *mukuna* with its variable constituants belonging to different lineages—and the institutions of social identity—the aterritorial matrilineages and clans. Second, it demonstrates that authority derived from these aterritorial institutions facilitated access to land. One worked or obtained land by appealing to the *mukuna* lineage head who drew upon authority not from the ownership of territory but from a matrix of past and current kinship obligations.

Gabonese clan leaders did not consider the spaces of premodern districts as territory; districts were alliances of clans, social expressions of aterritorial kinships links. Another proverb further illustrates the unboundedness and aterritorialty of the clan by contrasting this quality with the boundary and observable reality of the cultivated field. The Nzabi version is *Panga niungi butala mépanga ibanda utala vé* or "One sees the boundaries of the field, one does not see those of the clan."[43]

The kinship calculus that defined clan and matrilineage affiliation was actually a malleable instrument upon which actors negotiated relationships of power and influence. Vansina argues that social anthropologists tended to reproduce the "folk models" of the peoples they were studying and thus overlooked those characteristics dominating the process of actual social organization: inequality and irregularity. Kinship structures were ideology and did not reflect the real workings of precolonial politics where "rank was more often determined by the fluctuations of power politics."[44] Though Rey and Dupré stressed inequality, Vansina posits that "it was much more pronounced, and much more irregularly distributed than their model implied."[45] Competition for power and influence left ample room for individual initiative and it was the messiness of this process that passed right through the sieve provided by models based on lineage. For Vansina, it is the historian's task to confront the messiness of the past and reconstruct its particularity as much as available evidence will allow.[46]

History and the Theory of Human Territoriality

Though not concerned with developing widely applicable models for the social sciences, Vansina's equatorial tradition does rest upon a particular theory of the "nature of reality." There are two types of reality, he argues, one physical or phenomenological, and the other cognitive. It is in the interaction of the cognitive and physical that one can discern "the relations between habitat, society and culture."[47] I adopt this basic "physical/cognitive" distinction—and the dialectical relationship Vansina posits between the two—but replace "reality" with "space." In my conception, all societies in all places have organized themselves in space according to ideologies or "cognitive maps"[48] peculiar to their habitat and historical experience. Indeed, Vansina indicates the spatiality embedded in his "cognitive reality" through a reference to the "cognitive *landscapes* of peoples in the forests."[49] The cognitive map spatializes ideology and can be defined as a collective expression of the ways a particular people perceives and interprets its existence in physical space. Changes in the physical space of people will stimulate innovation in its cognitive map; likewise innovation in a society's cognitive map will bring about change in physical space.[50] The interaction between the two is in the form of a continual dialectic.

Cognitive maps are historical products, and their varied transformations among the peoples of the globe have been determined by such things as habitat, migration, commercial opportunity, production sites, sacred space, and contact with other peoples bearing different cognitive maps. In Southern Gabon, Vansina's equatorial tradition provided the fundamental grid for both the cognitive maps and the functional regions established in Southern Gabon from the arrival of Western Bantu-speakers in the equatorial forest up until the end of the nineteenth century. Topographical features, the production and marketing of salt, and centers of spiritual power might, for example, contribute to local cognitive maps.[51] The imposition of French colonial rule, however, marked the historical moment when modernity and its accompanying instruments of power were introduced to the area. As has occurred across the globe since the rise and spread of industrial capitalism, the consequences of modernity in Southern Gabon were dramatic and profound, transforming the cognitive maps of its peoples, altering its physical landscape, and reorienting its functional regions.

I argue that the crucial transformation resulting from this colonial encounter is linked to the assumption that humanity has experienced a long-term spatio-historical development where *social definition of territory* has evolved towards a *territorial definition of society*. Edward Soja first posited this broad evolution some thirty years ago: "One of the most important developments in human social and political organization comes about when localized kinship or residence groups become territorial units within a political system."[52] The *social definition of territory* was a key feature in the cognitive map of the Western Bantu-speaking peoples living in nineteenth-century Southern Gabon; the *territorial definition of society* was a key feature in the cognitive map of the French who sought to order the spaces and peoples of Southern Gabon according to the needs of modern bureaucratic administration and European industrial capitalism. The clash between the two has left an ambiguous legacy to the leaders and institutions of the post-colonial Gabonese state.

In terms of global history, the spatio-historical shift from the "social" to the "territorial" is connected to other long-term historical processes such as the rise of the state and the development of economic classes as well as to the commodification of land and labor occurring under modern capitalism. Scholars have engaged in intensive debate on the mechanisms and the specifics as to how, when, and where these integral transformations took place and will continue to do so. I adhere to an interpretative model that has applications beyond Southern Gabon to the spread of modernity generally. For the purposes of this study, however, we need only admit that in the historical moment of the latter half of the nineteenth century, when the various clans of Southern Gabon encountered the agents of French colonialism, the former were not under the authority of a modern territorial state while the latter had access to instruments of power capable of imposing modern territoriality.

The intellectual origins of this distinction between the social definition of territory and territorial definition of society are clearly found in the "blood to soil" evolutionary transition developed in the work of Henry Sumner Maine and Lewis Henry Morgan during the latter half of the nineteenth century. Their work led two generations of social anthropologists to focus on kinship as the defining characteristic of "primitive" societies. This sharp distinction between kinship and territory as two incompatible and mutually exclusive types of social organization has rightfully been criticized for creating the illusion of an ahistorical typology and for neglecting the territorial aspects of pre-modern societies.[53] But historical analysis based upon this fundamental insight need not be so ham-handed or tied to rigid evolutionary stages.

The work of the geographer Robert David Sack brings the necessary subtlety to this mode of inquiry. Sack develops a theory of human *territoriality* that yields important insights to the changes that occurred in Southern Gabon during the period of French colonial rule and to the experience of modernity generally. For Sack, "territoriality" is "a particular kind of behavior in space" and "forms the backcloth to human spatial relations and conceptions of space";[54] it is defined "as the attempt by an individual or group to affect, influence, or control people, phenomena and relationships by delimiting and asserting control over a geographic area. This area will be called 'territory.'"[55]

Territoriality points out that human spatial relationships are not constructed in a power vacuum. Indeed, the practice of territoriality "is the primary spatial form power takes."[56] Spatial analyses of functional regions *describe* how a particular group of people uses the land, how they organize themselves in space, and how they give meaning to place and are connected to territoriality but, as Sack suggests: "What geographers call nodal regions, market areas, or central place hinterlands are not necessarily territories. They can be simply descriptions of the geographic extent of activities in space. They become territories though if the boundaries are used by some authority to mold influence, or control activities."[57]

Sack argues that territorial uses of space have a history incorporating the evolution from "social" to "territorial." In this schema, less sophisticated forms of territoriality in what he terms "classless-primitive" societies developed into the more complex practices of "pre-modern civilizations" and finally to the full exploitation of territorial techniques found in "modern capitalist" society. He further posits that the exploration of how and why modern capitalist society employs the complete range of territorial effects can help "to unravel the meanings and implications of modernity."[58]

The idea of evolution that Sack's model proposes, the notion of a progressive march from "classless/primitive" to "pre-modern civilizations" to "modern capitalist" societies, must be approached cautiously. It is certainly cause for unease given its implied theory of increasing complexity through a process akin to natural selection. In the past, this supposed linear progression and the accompanying notion of progress in human civilization has served as an effective and pernicious ideology for the oppression and suffering imposed upon large portions of the world's population. Sack has made the unfortunate choice of using the terms "primitive" and "civilization" to distinguish different societies' relationships to territoriality. Yet he is fully aware of the pejorative connotations associated with "primitive" and wants the term to refer back to its original meaning of "primary or original in time or even rank" which "is in no sense pejorative."[59] In this he certainly seems guilty of a certain political and historical naïveté or a desire to provoke. Sack, however, is at pains to distance himself from the value-laden past of the terms he employs. The conception of sequential changes "must be divorced from the notions that they were somehow inevitable, necessarily for the better, and in one direction only."[60]

Indeed, the utility of his model resides in the flexibility it brings to the explanation of complex historical developments and in the rejection of exclusive "either/or" divisions implied in the rigid application of "primitive" and "civilized." It allows for the influences of kinship to exist in modern capitalist society and those of territoriality to be operative in premodern decentralized societies such as those found in equatorial Africa in the mid-nineteenth century. The colonial encounter, or "different societies facing each other at the same Time,"[61] became a transformative experience for the inhabitants of Southern Gabon as more and different instruments of territoriality were introduced into the region by Europeans. Thus the capacity to control people and things by controlling area was greatly enhanced as Southern Gabon became more thoroughly connected to the networks and rhythms of global capitalism. Further, the identities of those exercising territoriality shifted as clan elders whose kinship authority was based on the social definition of territory were marginalized by colonial agents—European and African—who sought to impose a modern authority based on the territorial definition of society. The results, as this study demonstrates, were decidedly ambiguous.

It must be emphasized that to admit that humanity's power to control its environment has increased exponentially with the rise of modern industrial capitalism over the last three centuries does not entail adherence to a particular kind of human progress, evolution, or superiority. Theodor Adorno captures this nicely in the following aphorism: "No universal history leads from the savage to humanity, but there *is* one that leads from the slingshot to the megabomb."[62] No one, I would think, would want to deny the reality of humanity's increased power over nature. It does, however, require from the historian possible explanations as to how, where, and why this process, generally called "modernity," first occurred and then spread itself over the whole of the globe. The particular episode of this process that occurred in Southern Gabon from the mid-nineteenth century to the beginning of World War II is especially revealing, as it shows both the power and limitations of modernity's ability to impose itself on the pre-modern spaces of the African equatorial forest: an awesome and at the same time humbling project.

Notes

1. Gilles Sautter, *De l'Atlantique au fleuve Congo: Une géographie du sous-peuplement* (Paris: Mouton, 1966), 1:118.

2. Jan Vansina, *Paths in the Rainforests: Toward a History of Political Tradition in Equatorial Africa* (Madison: University of Wisconsin Press, 1990).

3. See Finn Fuglestad, "The Trevor-Roper Trap or the Imperialism of History: An Essay," *History in Africa* 19 (1992): 317.

4. Allen Howard has been the guiding force behind this group, and his work a key reference point; see Allen M. Howard, "The Relevance of Spatial Analyis for African Economic History: The Sierra Leone–Guinea System," *JAH* 17, 3 (1976): 365–88; and his "Big Men, Traders, and Chiefs: Power, Commerce, and Spatial Change in the Sierra Leone–Guinea Plain, 1865–1895" (Ph.D. diss., University of Wisconsin–Madison, 1972). Richard Shain, Charles Ambler, John Cinnamon, Eli Bentor, Jan Bender Shetler, and I are among the scholars who have presented papers for conference panels organized around spatial themes.

5. Howard, "Relevance of Spatial Analysis," 369; see also the entry on "Region" in Robert P. Larkin and Gary L. Peters, *Dictionary of Concepts in Human Geography* (Westport: Greenwood Press, 1983), 199–205; and Edward W. Soja *The Political Organization of Space* (Washington D.C.: Association of American Geographers, 1971), 1–6. Related discussions include Carol A. Smith, "Regional Economic Systems: Linking Geographical Models and Socioeconomic Problems," in *Regional Analysis,* ed. Carol A. Smith, vol. 1: *Economic Systems* (New York: Academic Press, 1976), 3–59; Mary Beth Pudup, "Arguments within Regional Geography," *Progress in Human Geography* 12, 3 (1989): 369–91; J. Nicholas Entrikin, "Place, Region and Modernity," in *The Power of Place: Bringing Together Geographical and Sociological Imaginations,* ed. John A. Agnew and James B. Duncan (Boston: Unwin Hyman, 1989), 30–43; and Claudio Lomnitz-Adler, "Concepts for the Study of Regional Culture," *American Ethnologist* 18, 2 (1991), 199–214. For an application of a similar formal-functional distinction to West African history, see Akin L. Mabogunje and Paul Richards, "Land and People—Models of Spatial and Ecological Processes in West African History," in *History of West Africa,* ed. J.F.A. Ajayi and Michael Crowder (London: Longman, 1985), 1:5–47.

6. See discussion of the "Bajag" of Southern Gabon in Christopher Gray, "In the Shadow of the Rainforest: What History for Which Gabon?" in *Culture, Ecology, and Politics in Gabon's Rainforests,* ed. J. F. Barnes and M. C. Reed (Boulder, Colo.: Westview, forthcoming). Also, W. Magang-Ma-Mbuju and F. Mbumb Bwas, *Les Bajag du Gabon: Essai sur l'étude historique et linguistique* (Paris: Imprimerie Saint-Michel, 1974).

7. François Gaulme adopts a similar rationalization in his historical study of the region around the Fernan Vaz Lagoon. See his *Le pays de Cama: Un ancien état côtier du Gabon et ses origines* (Paris: Karthala/C.R.A., 1981), 84–85.

8. See section "Végétation" in Ministère de l'Education Nationale de la République Gabonaise, et al., *Géographie et cartographie du Gabon: Atlas illustré* (Paris: EDICEF, 1983), 34–37.

9. See map in Sautter, *De l'Atlantique,* 1:144–45; and also the "Oro-Hydrographie" map in *Géographie et cartographie,* 11.

10. *Géographie et cartographie,* 22–25.

11. The tradition is reported by Hilaire Aleko in Hilaire Aleko and Gilbert Puech, "Note sur la lagune Ngové et les Ngubi," *Pholia* 3 (1988): 261–63. For a similar process among the Nunu on the Zaire River, see Robert Harms, *Games against Nature: An Eco-Cultural History of the Nunu of Equatorial Africa* (Cambridge: Cambridge University Press, 1987), 4–6.

12. See the "Migrations historiques" map in *Géographie et cartographie,* 43.

13. See Vansina, *Paths,* 158–60.

14. Ibid., 73.

15. Ibid., 76; see also 278–79 for the relevant lexical items. For a description of these different kinds of dependency among Punu-speaking clans, see Georges Le Testu, *Notes sur les coutumes Bapounou dans la circonscription de la Nyanga* (Caen: J. Haulard la Brière, 1918), 7–12; and the discussion in Pierre-Philippe Rey, *Colonialisme, néo-colonialisme et transition au capitalisme: Exemple de la "Comilog" de Congo-Brazzaville* (Paris: François Maspero, 1971), 81–106.

16. Vansina notes that by the nineteenth century there existed "sister exchange, delayed exchange (preferential marriages: various possibilities), marriage by capture, marriage by payment of compensation (bridewealth), marriage by gift to conclude peace, and cicisbeism (the gift of a wife by a man who had married her before)"; Vansina, *Paths,* 77.

17. Ibid., 74–77.

18. Ibid., 251; for similar observations about "wealth in people," see John Thornton, *Africa and Africans in the Making of the Atlantic World, 1400–1680* (Cambridge: Cambridge University Press, 1992), 74–76; Joseph C. Miller, *Way of Death: Merchant Capitalism and the Angolan Slave Trade 1730–1830* (Madison: U. of Wisconsin Press, 1988), 43–50; Igor Kopytoff, "The Internal African Frontier: The Making of African Political Culture," in *The African Frontier: The Reproduction of Traditional African Societies,* ed. Igor Kopytoff (Bloomington: Indiana U. Press, 1987), 40–46; Igor Kopytoff and Suzanne Miers, "African Slavery as an Institution of Marginality," in *African Slavery: Historical and Anthropological Perspectives,* ed. Kopytoff and Miers (Madison: U. of Wisconsin Press, 1977), 1–81; and for a sophisticated rethinking, see Jane Guyer, "Wealth in People and Self-Realization in Equatorial Africa," *Man* 28 (1993): 243–65; Guyer, "Wealth in People, Wealth in Things: Introduction," *JAH* 36, 1 (1995): 83–90; and Guyer and Samuel M. Eno Belinga, "Wealth in People as Wealth in Knowledge: Accumulation and Composition in Equatorial Africa," *JAH* 36, 1 (1995): 91–120.

19. These would be the various forms of the reflex "*-bánjá": *nganza* in Apindji and *ébandza* in Tsogo refer to religious temples. See Vansina, *Paths,* 271–72; Stanislaw Swiderski, "Le Bwiti, société d'initiation chez les Apindji au Gabon," *Anthropos* 60 (1965): 557; and Otto Gollnhofer, Pierre Sallée, and Roger Sillans, *Art et artisanat tsogho* (Paris: ORSTOM, 1975), 38–39.

20. Vansina, *Paths,* 152–53.

21. See the case of the Bumwele in chapter 2.

22. Vansina, *Paths,* 153–54.

23. Ibid., 159.

24. Ibid., 81. For use of the term "sous-tribu," see Marcel Soret, "Introduction," in Raponda-Walker, *Notes d'histoire du Gabon* (Montpellier: Imprimerie Charité for the Institut d'Études Centrafricaines, 1960), 8–9; for an example of districts being confused as clans in

a description of the "Sangou" (Massango) ethnic group, see Hubert Deschamps, *Traditions orales et archives au Gabon: Contribution à l'ethno-histoire* (Paris: Berger-Levrault, 1962), 48.

25. Vansina, *Paths,* 82.

26. John and Jean Comaroff argue that "totemic consciousness" was prevalent in much of precapitalist Africa, and that it emerged "with the establishment of symmetrical relations between structurally similar social groupings" such as those that developed between clans in Southern Gabon. See John and Jean Comaroff, "Of Totemism and Ethnicity," in *Ethnography and the Historical Imagination,* ed. John and Jean Comaroff (Boulder, Colo.: Westview Press, 1992), 54–55. For shared totems in Southern Gabon, see George Dupré, *Un ordre et sa destruction* (Paris: ORSTOM, 1982), 162–64, and the "Appendix: Clan List and Correspondences" in Christopher Gray, "Territoriality, Ethnicity and Colonial Rule in Southern Gabon, 1850–1960" (Ph.D. diss., Indiana University, 1995).

27. Vansina, *Paths,* 82. The origin accounts of Nzabi-speaking clans demonstrate this ideology of equality; see versions collected by Gérard Collomb, "Les sept fils de Nzèbi: Un mythe cosmogonique des Banzèbi du Gabon," *JA* 49, 2 (1979): 91–120; and Suzanne Jean, "Organisation sociale et familiale et problèmes fonciers des populations Bandjabi et Bapunu de la Ngounie-Nyanga: Étude préliminaire" (Unpublished report: Bureau pour le Développement de la Production Agricole, Paris, 1962), 3–5.

28. The phrase is from Paul Richards, "Spatial Organisation and Social Change in West Africa—Notes for Historians and Archaeologists," in *The Spatial Organisation of Culture,* ed. Ian Hodder (Pittsburgh: University of Pittsburgh Press, 1978), 271.

29. Deschamps, *Traditions orales,* 17–18; Soret, introduction to Raponda-Walker, *Notes d'histoire,* 5–10.

30. See Sautter, *De l'Atlantique,* 157–72.

31. Le Testu, *Notes sur les coutumes Bapounou,* 21–24; Raponda-Walker, *Notes d'histoire,* 21–23; and "Une curieuse coutume gabonaise: La parenté entre clans familiaux de tribus différentes," *Liaison* 69 (1959): 45–48.

32. See Adam Kuper, *The Invention of Primitive Society: Transformations of an Illusion* (London and New York: Routledge, 1988), 190–209; and see his "Lineage Theory: A Critical Retrospect," *Annual Review of Anthropology* 11 (1982): 71, for a critique of lineage theory and the continuity between British social anthropology and French Marxist anthropology.

33. Pierre-Louis Agondjo-Okawe, "Structures parentales gabonaises et développement," (Thèse de doctorat, Faculté de Droit et des Sciences Économiques de Paris, 1967); and Joseph Ambouroue-Avaro, "Le Bas-Ogowé au dix-neuvième siècle," (Thèse de doctorat, Paris, Sorbonne, 1969). Avaro's thesis was published as *Un peuple gabonais à l'aube de la colonisation* (Paris: Karthala-C.R.A., 1981). A portion of Agondjo's dissertation appears as "Les droits fonciers coutumiers au Gabon (Société Nkomi, Groupe Myene)," in *Rural Africana* 22 (1973): 15–29.

34. "Let us state at the outset that the clan is a more solid and constant unit of reference than the ethnic group"; Rey, *Colonialisme,* 80; for an earlier statement of the same view, see Rey, "Articulation des modes de dépendances et des modes de reproduction dans deux sociétés lignagères (Punu et Kunyi du Congo-Brazzaville)," *CEA* 9, 3 (1969): 415.

35. Rey, "L'esclavage lignager chez les Tsangui, les Punu et les Kuni du Congo-Brazzaville: Sa place dans le système d'ensemble des rapports de production," in *L'esclavage en Afrique précoloniale,* ed, Claude Meillassoux (Paris: Maspero, 1975), 512.

36. See Dupré, *Un ordre,* 10–11, 407–9; also Dupré and Rey, "Réflexions sur la pertinence d'une théorie de l'histoire des échanges," *Cahiers Internationaux de Sociologie,* 133–62.

37. Dupré, *Un ordre,* 111.

38. Ibid., 128–30.

39. Ibid., 131.

40. Ibid., 145 (emphasis added).

41. Ibid.

42. Soja, *The Political Organization of Space,* 13; see also the discussion in Robert David Sack, *Conceptions of Space in Social Thought: A Geographic Perspective* (Minneapolis: U. of Minnesota Press, 1980), 167–82.

43. Dupré, *Un ordre,* 160.

44. Vansina, "The Peoples of the Forest," in *History of Central Africa,* ed. David Birmingham and Phyllis M. Martin (London: Longman, 1983), 1:85.

45. Ibid.

46. See Vansina, "The Power of Systematic Doubt in Historical Enquiry," *History in Africa,* 1 (1974): 109–28.

47. Vansina, *Habitat, Economy and Society in the Central African Rain Forest* (Providence, R.I.: Berg, 1992), 5; see also his *Paths,* 71–73.

48. For the idea of "cognitive maps," see Ervin Laszlo and Ignazio Masulli, eds., *The Evolution of Cognitive Maps: New Paradigms for the 21st Century* (New York: Gordon and Breach Science Publishers, 1993); and Paul Richards, "Kant's Geography and Mental Maps," *Transactions, Institute of British Geographers* 61 (1974): 1–16; for a somewhat different conception of cognitive maps informed by Marxism and the rise of capital, see Fredric Jameson, "Cognitive Mapping," in *Marxism and the Interpretation of Culture,* ed. Cary Nelson and Lawrence Grossberg (Urbana and Chicago: U. of Illinois Press, 1988), 347–57.

49. Vansina, *Habitat, Economy and Society,* 5.

50. Lefebvre posits a similar relationship between modes of production and space, where "the shift from one mode to another must entail the production of a new space." See Henri Lefebvre, *The Production of Space,* trans. Donald Nicholson-Smith (Oxford: Blackwell, 1997), 46.

51. Chapters 2 and 3 provide several specific examples of how such cognitive maps might be constructed. For example, see p. 41 for a cognitive view of landscape and pp. 79–80 for an example of how landscapes and cemeteries might orientate notions of space.

52. Edward W. Soja, *The Political Organization of Space* (Washington, D.C.: Association of American Geographers, 1971), 8.

53. See Kuper, *Invention of Primitive Society,* 2–9; and Robert J. Thornton, *Space, Time, and Culture among the Iraqw of Tanzania* (New York: Academic Press, 1980), 8–16.

54. Sack, *Human Territoriality,* 23, 26.

55. *Ibid.,* 19.

56. *Ibid.,* 26.

57. *Ibid.,* 19.

58. *Ibid.,* 6, 53–91, for the full development of this argument; see also Sack, *Conceptions of Space,* 170–85.

59. Sack, *Human Territoriality,* 53; for a similar defense of the use of "primitive," see C. R. Hallpike, *The Foundations of Primitive Thought* (Oxford: Clarendon, 1979), v–vi; for a critique of these views mentioning Sack, see Michael J. Casimir, "The Dimensions of Territoriality: An Introduction," in *Mobility and Territoriality: Social and Spatial Boundaries among Foragers, Fishers, Pastoralist and Peripatics,* ed. Michael J. Casimir and Aparna Rao (Oxford: Berg, 1992), 1–3; and for an earlier discussion of related issues that defines "primitive society" as "all those societies that historians and economists *neglect,*" see Maurice Godelier,

"Territory and Property in Primitive Society," *Social Science Information,* 17, 3 (1978), 399–426.

60. Sack, *Human Territoriality,* 54.

61. As opposed to "the same societies at different stages of development"; see discussion in Johannes Fabian, *Time and the Other: How Anthropology Makes Its Object* (New York: Columbia University Press, 1983), 155.

62. Quoted in Fabian, *Time and the Other,* 159.

2

TERRITORIALITY IN THE FUNCTIONAL REGIONS, DISTRICTS, AND VILLAGES OF SOUTHERN GABON TO THE 1880S

Impact of the Atlantic Slave Trade

For the peoples of Southern Gabon, participation in the creation of an Atlantic trade system dominated by a commerce in slaves marked the critical first step of their integration into the expanding global capitalist system. Though the equatorial forest regions of West Central Africa sent far fewer captives to the Americas than savannah regions to the north and south, the slave trade had a profound impact nonetheless.[1] From the mid-sixteenth century to the mid-eighteenth century the Loango Kingdom was the dominant power on the equatorial coast. The network of clans that formed this kingdom came to be known as the Vili people, and caravans organized by Vili traders extended their reach into Southern Gabon. Throughout the eighteenth century Loango Bay and the Malemba and Cabinda ports to the south were important centers for slaves acquired from the interior and key conduits for the established Portuguese and Dutch trade as well as newly active French and English interests (see Map 2). Between 1685 and 1705 about 6,000 slaves per year were exported from the Loango Coast; this dropped to 2,000 per year over the next ten years but by 1750 had increased to 5,000. The period between 1755 and 1793 witnessed the peak as 13,500 slaves

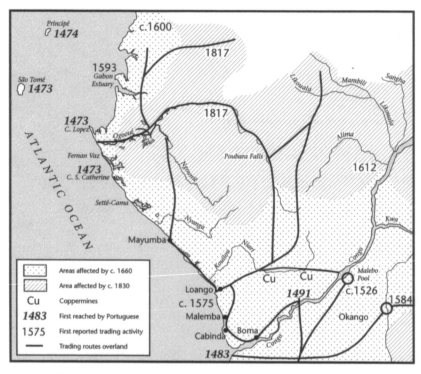

Map 2. The Atlantic Slave Trade before 1830. Based on Jan Vansina, *Paths in the Rainforest* (Madison: University of Wisconsin, 1990), p. 199.

per year left the Loango coast ports. All told, nearly one million slaves were exported from the Loango coast between 1660 and 1793.[2]

The economic influence of the Loango Kingdom was in decline from the mid-eighteenth century, being pushed aside by the rise of entrepreneurial families.[3] However, its impact on the clan structures and cognitive maps of many peoples in Southern Gabon endured. The titles of the kingdom's political offices were adopted by developing trading polities such as that created by the Orungu at Cape Lopez. Further, a particular conception of clan hierarchy and interrelationships originating from the Loango Kingdom's Chilongo district spread throughout much of the region.[4] Vili trade caravans were responsible for spreading Loango's influence into Southern Gabon. In the eighteenth century, the leaders of Vili caravans exploited and extended the networks of Southern Gabon's functional regions. Their influence was based not upon direct governance but a system of alliances created with clan leaders of the interior. Vili caravans did not generally undertake systematic slave raids—though they did of course resort to such measures—but rather tried to negotiate for captives through existing channels attuned to "wealth in people" exchange. The *Mubiri*, or caravan leader, made use of trade charms and esoteric powers rather than force to maintain leverage among the peoples with whom he traded. Caravan leaders had to be talented negotiators not only to procure slaves but also to ensure the caravans' safe passage as clan heads occupying villages along trade routes exercised their territoriality through tolls and other tribute.[5]

The expansion of the slave trade in Southern Gabon added a new element to the commercial strategies of village and clan leaders who henceforth sought to position themselves at sites most favorable to profiting from this commerce. The increased competition to control key sites along the caravan routes likely resulted in a growing number of armed conflicts between clan leaders. With the authority of the Loango ruler (Maloango) in decline from the mid-eighteenth century, coastal brokers and entrepreneurial families worked with clan leaders in the interior to coordinate their transactions across the existing networks of trading and clan alliances. Cognitive maps were altered to accomodate functional regions geared to the coastal trade; clan ideologies of common origin were created to solidify a close trading relationship. The history of the Bumwele clan is noteworthy in this regard.

The Gabonese historian Monique Koumba-Manfoumbi notes that branches of the Bumwele clan are found in the contemporary Bapunu, Gisira, Nzabi, and Balumbu ethnic groups.[6] Oral traditions collected by Koumba-Manfoumbi have the ancestors of the Bumwele living near the present Congolese town of Divénié at the end of the sixteenth century (see Map 3). They further indicate that some time in the seventeenth century the Bumwele founding ancestor, Mueli-Ngeli, with the assistance of his hunter-gatherer dependents, led his people on a northwest trek into the savannah region on the left bank of the Upper Ngounié River, establishing several villages along the way. By the beginning of the eighteenth century, they were settled in villages found between the Ngounié savannah and the forested hills of the Du Chaillu Massif, thus controlling access to the peoples living in the latter area. These peoples—the ancestors of the contemporary Nzabi, Massango, and Mitsogo ethnic groups—sent significant numbers of slaves to the coast. Through the eighteenth and into the nineteenth century, the Bumwele clan came to control key points along the trade route to Loango. They even developed a kinship relationship with the ruling clan of the Loango Kingdom and in this way assumed the top slot in the ideological clan hierarchy that spread from the Loango coast into the interior. However, Bumwele efforts to build up a new kingdom along the Kouilou River did not materialize, and the decentralized power of shifting coalitions of clan leaders remained the rule in the villages and districts under its influence.[7]

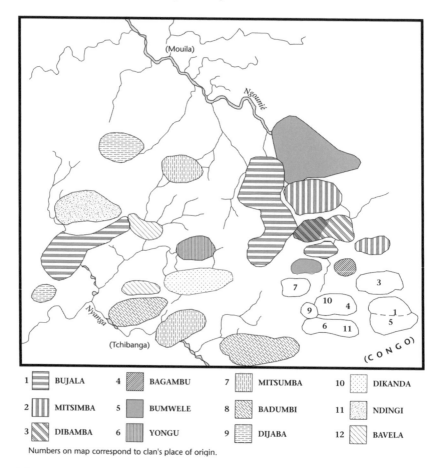

1	BUJALA	4	BAGAMBU	7	MITSUMBA	10	DIKANDA
2	MITSIMBA	5	BUMWELE	8	BADUMBI	11	NDINGI
3	DIBAMBA	6	YONGU	9	DIJABA	12	BAVELA

Numbers on map correspond to clan's place of origin.

Map 3. Location of Punu-Speaking Clans. Based on Monique Koumba-Manfoumbi, "Les Punu du Gabon, des origines à 1899: Essai d'étude historique" (Thèse de doctorat, Université de Paris, I, 1987).

Not all clans experienced the success of the Bumwele. Numerous clans were losers in the competition for control over trade routes, and some became more victims than players. There were clans that sought to flee the trade altogether by moving from the vulnerable savannahs into the relative protection of remote sections of the forested massifs. This was the case with members of the Dijaba clan, whose traditions indicate a migration west from Divénié towards the Mayumba coast, where they settled in a village called Igoci. Here they developed close relations with the Lumbu-speaking peoples who traded with the Vili at Mayumba. But at some point (perhaps toward the end of the seventeenth century), the Dijaba pushed back into the interior in flight from slave raiders, possibly Lumbu or Vili caravans seeking to supply the Loango market via the Mayumba route. In their retreat they crossed the hills of the Ikoundou Massif and came down to a savannah district controlled by the Bujala clan. The Bujala barred the way to the Dijaba, and this led to a battle which resulted in the dispersal of the Dijaba clan throughout the surrounding forests (see Maps 2 and 3).[8]

It is essential to realize that the prosperity enjoyed from the "middleman" role in trade to the coast was experienced only by powerful clans like the Bumwele, who created chains of alliances stretching from the coast to the furthest edges of the trading zone and claimed the largest number of dependents at their disposal.[9] It has been estimated that a maximum of one hundred lineageheads, who were almost always members of the largest clans, participated in the slave trade in the area from the Loango coast to the hinterland along the Kouilou and Niari Rivers.[10] Most other clans played either minor roles as sources of supply or sought to keep their distance by settling far from the trade routes.

By the beginning of the nineteenth century new coastal outlets were developing, and the Loango axis was being overtaken by several axes reaching into the interior from places like Mayumba, the Fernan Vaz, Cape Lopez, and the Gabon Estuary. The decline of the Loango Kingdom coincided with major developments in the Atlantic slave trade as a whole, as Portuguese, Brazilian, and Spanish traders stepped in to replace the departing Dutch, French, and British.[11] Mayumba emerged as an important slave port in the nineteenth century. By the 1840s, Mayumba had a population of about 1000 and was home to seven or eight slave barracoons belonging to Portuguese, Brazilian, and Spanish interests. From the 1840s European slavers had to deal with British anti-slave patrols, and as a result created collecting points away from the major centers; Banda was one such place south of Mayumba. At Banda one could find between 700 and 800 captives awaiting shipment, while at Mayumba the barracoons usually held 500 to 600.[12]

Further up the coast other minor eighteenth-century trading centers began to grow in importance. The most noteworthy in this regard was the centralized kingdom created at Cape Lopez by Orungu clans. To the north of Cape Lopez in the Gabon Estuary, various Mpongwe clans started to play a more active in the Atlantic trade.[13] In 1788, Cape Lopez and the Gabon Estuary were estimated to be exporting five hundred slaves per year; this in contrast to 13,500 per year from the Loango Coast (see Map 2). This annual estimate of five hundred may have tripled in the early years of the nineteenth century as Portuguese and Brazilian slavers began to import slaves to the islands of São Tomé and Principé. As was the case along the Loango coast and its hinterland, commerce was conducted through the interlocking trade and clan alliances which spread from the southern bank of the Gabon Estuary and the coastal area around Cape Lopez out along the Ogooué basin and into the Du Chaillu Massif.[14]

To the south of Cape Lopez lies the Fernan Vaz Lagoon; at the beginning of the nineteenth century this region supplied important numbers of slaves to the Orungu. The Nkomi clans inhabiting this region sought to imitate the Orungu success and created a centralized kingdom of their own.[15] With the rise of the Orungu and Nkomi Kingdoms, the Ogooué River and the Rembo Nkomi (Nkomi River) developed into key conduits in the slave trade (see Map 1). The confluence of the Ngounié and the Ogooué Rivers became the site of intense competition between middlemen, since it served as the gateway to the trading communities of the Middle Ogooué; Enenga- and Galwa-speaking clans came to control this nodal point.[16] Access to the Rembo Nkomi was controlled by the alliance of two Nkomi clans, the Avogo and the Abulia. Dominion over this route was essential to the titular head of the kingdom, the *rengondo,* who was also the Avogo clan head. The centralizing power of the Nkomi *rengondo* was dependent upon the maintenance of an equilibrium between the most powerful Nkomi clans: the Avogo, the Abulia, the Asono, the Avandji, and the Avemba. Each of these clans had corresponding branches among peoples in the interior with whom economic and cultural exchange was conducted.[17]

The competition to supply the coastal markets stimulated population movement in the interior as the traditional competition for control over strategic commercial nodal points intensified. The magnitude of these developments increased in exponential fashion after 1830 as the European Industrial Revolution flooded equatorial trade routes with manufactured goods. Opportunities for middlemen traders were plentiful, and clan leaders sought to exploit them by moving into commercially active areas. For example, the opening decades of the nineteenth century witnessed the exodus of numerous Kele-speaking clans from the Estuary region to positions along the Ogooué, the Lakes region, the Rembo Nkomi, and eventually into the Du Chaillu Massif as they sought to supply the market for slaves and later the growing markets for ivory, ebony, and rubber. These Kele-speaking clans are usually portrayed in the oral traditions of their neighbors as slave-raiders provoking conflict wherever they went. It was around 1840 that the much-discussed "Fang migration" from the Woleu and Ntem Rivers down to the Ogooué and into the Gabon Estuary began, with trading opportunities foremost in the minds of the leaders of these Fang-speaking clans. And to the south of the Ogooué there was a less dramatic drift of Nzabi- and Tsangui-speaking clans to the south and west who sought more lucrative contacts with the coastal trade.[18]

By the mid-nineteenth century, the coastal trading entrepôts along the Gabon Estuary, the Ogooué Delta, and the Fernan Vaz Lagoon had

peaked in terms of their economic dominance and degree of political centralization.[19] Due to the effective closing of the Brazilian market in 1851,
the 1850s witnessed a real decrease in the numbers of slaves leaving the
equatorial coast. However, by 1860, activity in the Cuban slave market,
with the aid of American finance, allowed for a continued flow of captives.[20] Spanish and Portuguese slavers plied the hidden nooks and crannies
of the swampy Gabonese coast to avoid detection by British and French
squadrons. In addition to the Cuban market, the growth of coffee and
cocoa plantations on nearby São Tomé and Principé created a need for
slave labor. The 1860s actually witnessed an increase in the slave trade as
the small boat traffic between Cap Lopez and the Portuguese islands allowed the Orungu Kingdom to maintain its influence on the Ogooué into
the 1870s. In the mid-1860s it was estimated that seven hundred to a
thousand slaves were being exported annually from Orungu-controlled
barracoons; in 1875 the number was estimated at three to four thousand.[21]

The majority of these slaves came down to the coast through the
complex system of trading and clan alliances that had developed along the
Ogooué River. Others arrived from the Fernan Vaz after descending a similar network of alliances that extended from the Rembo Nkomi overland to
the Du Chaillu Massif on the right bank of the Ngounié River. The pock-
ets of relatively dense population found in the forested mountains of this
region were also served by overland routes to the Rembo Ndogo, which
flows into the Setté Cama Lagoon, and by several other overland routes
terminating at the Iguéla Lagoon, Mayumba and Loango (see Map 4).

Control over commercial nodal points was again key for those leaders
seeking entrance into networks of alliances that sent slaves, ivory, redwood,
and raphia cloth down to the coast in exchange for salt and European goods
like cloth, machetes, bells, empty bottles, gun powder, flintlock rifles, knives,
axes, iron bars, brass wire, and copper basins known as "neptunes." The
most successful ventures resulted in the rise of clans which became specialists in supplying goods and people from the source regions in the Du Chaillu
Massif to the networks controlling the coastal markets. Along the routes
heading northeast from Loango and Mayumba, these were most often Punu-
speaking clans, with the Bumwele and the Bujala being the most important. Further north Gisir-speaking clans plying the trade routes to the Fernan
Vaz, Iguéla, and Setté Cama Lagoons were the most influential. The Ogooué
River trade in the Lakes region and at the confluence with the Ngounié
was, at the outset of the nineteenth century, dominated by a complex configuration of Gisir-, Enenga-, Galwa-, Ajumba-, and Kota-speaking clans.[22]

As European demand for commodities like rubber, ebony, and ivory
grew in the closing decades of the nineteenth century, previously marginal

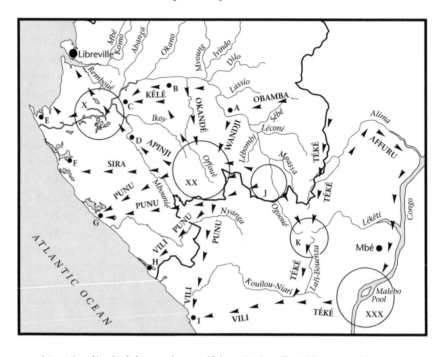

X   Intersection of Lambaréné area trade routes (Galwa-, Ajumba-, Vili-, and Enenga-speaking clans).
XX   Intersection of Du Chaillu Massif area trade routes (Nzabi-, Sango-, and Tsogo-speaking clans).
XXX   Intersection of Congo (Bobangi-Téké) and Niari-Kouilou (Téké-Kongo) area trade routes.

A   Dumé nodal point (Duma-speaking clans; Ogooué commerce).
B   Lopé nodal point (Okandé-speaking clans; Ogooué commerce).
C   Samkita nodal point (Kélé-speaking clans; interior trade routes).
D   Samba nodal point (Vili and Eviya-speaking clans; Ngounié commerce and interior trade routes).
E   Maritime nodal points at Cap-Lopez, Apomandé, and Sangazanga (Orungu-speaking clans; Ogooué and Ngounié commerce).
F   Fernan-Vaz nodal points (Nkomi-speaking clans; Rembo Nkomi and interior trade routes).
G   Setté-Cama nodal point (Ngové-speaking clans; interior trade routes).
H   Mayumba nodal point (Vili-speaking clans; interior trade routes).
I   Loango nodal point (Vili-speaking clans; interior trade routes, Niari-Kouilou and Malebo Pool commerce).
J   Area containing Téké-Tsaayi and Tsangui markets.
K   Area containing Téké-Lali markets.

Map 4. Trade Routes in Southern Gabon in the 1870s. Based on Annie Merlot, *Vers les plateaux de Masuku (1866–1890)* (Libreville/Paris: Centre Culturel Français Saint-Exupéry-Sépia, 1990), p. 150.

areas often located in uninhabited dead zones were integrated into the larger commercial network, and access to rubber vines, ebony trees, and elephants became sources of wealth as well as foci for territorial practice. The latter half of the nineteenth century witnessed the setting up of factories in the interior to collect forest products and distribute European goods. This led to the entrance of novel kinds of players into the Southern Gabon network of trading and clan alliances. Notable in this regard were leaders of Kele- and Fang-speaking clans who carved out new niches in the system by aggressively asserting control over strategic points along trade routes and exploiting those newly important geographic areas rich in rubber vines, elephants, and ebony wood.

By the 1880s, European traders and their subordinates—who were often Senegalese or from the coastal Mpongwe clans—were asserting territorial control over strategic nodal points. Despite extraordinary pressure, precolonial functional regions and territoriality held sway up until 1900 and the introduction of concession companies. Europeans and their agents had to adapt to existing commercial practices if they were going to succeed. Thus, despite the accelerated population movement, the increased economic opportunity, and the growing insecurity, the peoples inhabiting Southern Gabon over the whole of the nineteenth century were able to negotiate their entry into the modern world through the institutions of a political equatorial tradition several thousand years old. Clan and lineage heads remained the leaders of social groupings who drew their identity from an aterritorial kinship ideology. Districts continued to be occasional coalitions of clan leaders residing in a loosely defined geographical space. The exploitation and distribution of male and female dependents, of prestige and trade goods, and of products for the European market were still under the control of clan leaders, and accomplished through the complex system of clan and trading alliances that had been operating for centuries. Decentralization of power remained the defining characteristic of the equatorial tradition in Southern Gabon in the nineteenth century. Loosely constructed districts made up of physically mobile villages inhabited by representatives of spatially dispersed matrilineal clans persisted as the main social building blocks of this precolonial order.

District And Functional Regions in the Nineteenth Century

In describing the districts and functional regions of nineteenth-century southern Gabon one is not necessarily referring to territoriality. The district functioned only as a territory under certain circumstances, most notably in grouping villages together for self-defense from an outside aggressor and in regulating the movements of traders and their goods. The functional regions enclosing the long-distance trade networks that connected the clans and villages of districts separated in physical space by uninhabited dead zones did not conform to our definition of territory under any circumstances in the nineteenth century.

The actual physical arrangement of districts in the space of Southern Gabon was due to ecological factors and positioning for participation in trade. Historically, ecologically diverse areas providing access to forest, savannah, and water resources were most desirable for settlement; there were also districts specialized in the techniques of metallurgy that developed around copper and iron ore deposits at the southwestern edges of Southern Gabon.[23] With the coming of the Atlantic trade, district settlement shifted to exploit the flow of commerce and new trade routes to the coast.

Waterways furnished an essential means of transportation, and it follows that easily recognizable and long-standing districts developed at key positions on rivers and lakes. For example, the Okandé-speaking clans, who controlled the confluence of the Ogooué and Offoué Rivers from at least the opening decade of the nineteenth century and whose trading partners were the Enenga- and Galwa-speaking clans situated more than one hundred kilometers downstream at the mouth of the Ngounié, were organized into three distinct districts in the 1870s: "Ngambé," encompassed by the Mokékou Mountains, and "Lopé" and "Achoum" located in the savannah.[24] The geographical boundaries defining these districts were clearly marked as mountains separated Ngambé from Lopé, and the extent of Achoum was determined by the mouth of the Offoué (see Map 5).

Districts were often named according to their location in local conceptions of geographic space. A name might correspond to residence on a specific river or more generally in terms of residence "upstream" as opposed to "downstream"; or it might indicate a contrast between residence on a river as opposed to inland, or in the forest as opposed to the savannah. The names of individual rivers and streams provided essential landmarks for local cognitive maps and their enunciation in migration accounts traced a people's past movements. "Upstream" and "downstream" appear to have had cosmological signficance as well, and the image of the river and its movements functioned as a cardinal axis in the initiation visions of the male *bwété* society practiced by a number of peoples in Southern Gabon.[25]

The predominance of geographical district names—as opposed to an ethnic name or the name of a founding clan leader—seems to indicate a people's relatively recent movement into a region. For example, the traditions of Eviya-speaking clans—who were active traders clustered at Samba

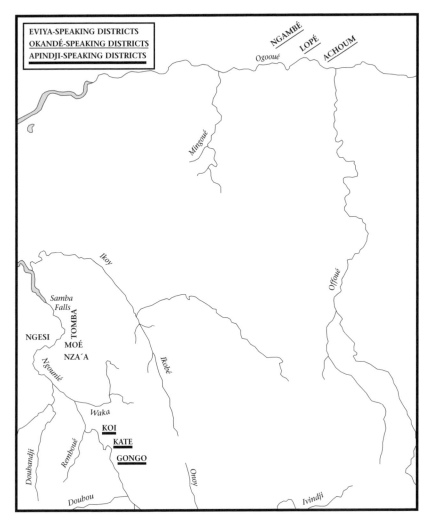

Map 5. Districts: Okandé-, Eviya-, and Apindji-Speaking Clans.

Falls on the Ngounié in the mid-nineteenth century—indicate migrations of short distance into surrounding areas to exploit the growing commercial opportunities. By the end of the century, they were grouped into four districts: the "Eviya Ngesi" (those of the river), "Eviya Tomba" (those of the mountain), "Eviya Moé" (those above), and "Eviya Nza'a" (those of the savannah) (see Map 5).[26]

Just to the south of the Eviya districts, Apindji-speaking clans residing along the Ngounié in the nineteenth century organized themselves into loosely defined districts based on geographical position: "asi-gongo" (those upstream) and "asi-koï" (those downstream) but also "asi-mbéï" (those of the river) and "asi-mósényè" (those of the interior). In the oral traditions of the Apindji, there is mention of a middle district, "kate," whose most powerful chief, Nzondo-Momba, mediated disputes between the chief Dibiti of the asi-gongo and the chief Kinga of the asi koï. These seem to have been the three most powerful big men among Apindji-speaking clans in the latter half of the nineteenth century; the traditions also employ the names of these clan leaders to refer to the districts themselves, suggesting the fluidity of naming practices. The boundaries between these districts were not clearly marked, all this indicating instablity and the recent arrival of these Apindji-speaking clans on the Ngounié. Lending further credence to their recent arrival, the explorers Compiègne and Marche reported that a few Apindji-speaking clans lived along the Middle Ogooué in the 1870s, suggesting that the Ngounié-based Apindji probably migrated from this area a generation or so earlier. By 1908, the configuration of Apindji districts along the Ngounié had taken a somewhat different form.[27]

Overland trade routes also provided axes for the establishment of districts. As with the Apindji-speaking clans, where districts were fluid and blended into one another, such was the case of the nineteenth-century trade route on the right bank of the Ngounié, commencing near what is now the town of Mouila, then heading east into the hills of the Du Chaillu Massif and cutting across the Onoy, Ogoulou, and Wano Rivers (see Map 1). The explorer Paul Du Chaillu traveled these trails in 1865 and noted the frequency with which he encountered villages along his march. He was further impressed by the extensive cultivation of peanuts along the Ogoulou, taking this as evidence of a considerable population. The villages he passed through were inhabited by Punu-, Tsogo-, Sango-, and Nzabi-speaking clans; Du Chaillu described these villages as grouped into "districts." In beginning his march east on the right bank of the Ngounié, he noted:

> We left the banks of the river at a quarter past six a.m. Shortly afterwards we passed through an Apono [Bapunu] village and at half-past eight a.m. came to three Ishogo [Mitsogo] villages close together. All three probably belonged to the same clan, and they contained a considerable population. It was no new feature to find a settlement of a tribe living in the middle of a *district* belonging to another tribe. The Ishogos had been driven by war from their own territory, and have thus intruded on unoccupied lands within the territory of their neighbors.[28]

The fluid nature of these districts and the undeveloped sense of a modern ethnicity allowed clans whose primary language was different from the district's original inhabitants to settle within its bounds and even share residence in the same village. On arriving at a stream that he referred to as the "Ogidanga" and which he posited as a boundary between the "Ishogo" (Mitsogo) and the "Ashango" (Massango) peoples, the explorer noted that:

> The two tribes are curiously intermixed in the Ishogo villages; on the one side of the street Ishogos dwell, and on the other side Ashangos; they are probably related by marriage, and thus live in company; or it may be that the various clans, which are fast diminishing in numbers, unite together in order to form a large and populous village.[29]

Du Chaillu, in focusing on intermarriage and clans, was on the right track as to how districts came into being. In relatively densely populated regions like the trade route travelled by Du Chaillu, districts flowed imperceptibly into one another, and it was even possible that a single village could claim membership in two different districts. However, most of Southern Gabon was not so densely populated and district village clusters were more often separated by large expanses of unoccupied lands described as "desert" or "dead" zones.

Du Chaillu, in the final weeks of his first trek in Southern Gabon at the close of 1858, vividly describes a dead zone which at the time separated the Waka district of Tsogo-speaking clans from districts of Sango-speaking clans further east in the Du Chaillu Massif;[30] this was some fifty kilometers to the north of the route he would take in 1865.

> A party of Isogo [Mitsogo] and Apingi [Apindji] agreed to accompany me as far as the Ashango [Massango] villages, which they said lay in the mountains, about three days' journey off. . . . We started on the 29th [December 1858]. The way was somewhat rocky, and the forest dense. Roads there were not, and my companions did not even know the country. . . . The majestic forest through which we travelled seemed to be quite devoid of life, except indeed insect life. Once in a while I ran against the web of the great yellow spider, and occasionally we heard the cry of some little birds. But no larger animals had left their traces in our sight. My gun seemed a useless encumbrance. Not even a monkey showed himself. . . . The gloom of the woods was something quite appalling to the spirits. It seemed a fit place for the haunt of some sylvan monster, delighting in silence and the shades of night.[31]

Dead zones were found not only in mountainous forest but also on the savannah. Du Chaillu, once again, noted during his 1865 exploration along the trade route on the right bank of the Ngounié that "away from these main pathways there were vast tracts of prairie and some wooded

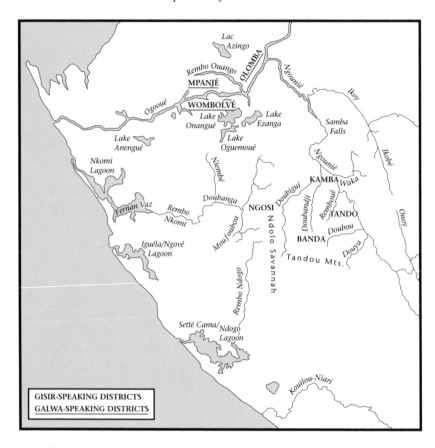

Map 6. Districts: Gisir- and Galwa-Speaking Clans.

land remaining in their original desert condition."[32] In 1858 Du Chaillu travelled across the uninhabited Tandou Mountains which functioned as a dead zone between the Ngosi and Tando districts inhabited by Gisir-speaking clans. Forested hills also served to divide the cluster of Gisir-speaking villages found in the numerous savannahs of the Ngosi district from the districts of Kele- and Nkomi-speaking clans on the Rembo Nkomi and Doubanga River (see Map 6). In 1893, thirty-five years after Paul Du Chaillu first described these deserted zones, Joachim Buléon, a French missionary priest, tramped through the same region and spoke of "the dead forest lying dormant in eternal rest."[33]

Given relatively stable conditions over time, the members of a particular district could develop something like a shared ethnic identity and even recognize the leader of an important clan as a centralized authority.

This was the case with the Nkomi-speaking clans of the Fernan Vaz and the creation of the titled position of *rengondo*. Perhaps functioning even prior to the impact of the Atlantic trade, the *rengondo* served as a mediator between the powerful clan heads of a large district that may have included the Iguéla Lagoon as well as the Fernan Vaz, parts of the Ogooué, and Lake Anengué, as well as the Rembo Nkomi. The existence of this position served to regulate the rapid growth in commercial activity brought by the trade in slaves. However, by the mid-nineteenth century this centralized authority was in decline and effective only among the Nkomi-speaking clans of the Fernan Vaz district. Those Nkomi-speaking clans residing just to the north on the Ogooué River now formed a different district and did not share in the Nkomi identity of the lagoon. As a consequence, they were not signatories of an 1868 treaty with French authorities.[34]

A similar process occurred among the Gisir-speaking clans of the Ngosi district (see Map 6). By the mid-nineteenth century, a term for district leader, *mata*, was in use, and there existed a central meeting place named "Gikulu-Gindzaka" in the Ndolo savannah for the various clan leaders to come together and conduct their business.[35] When Paul Du Chaillu first entered the plains of the Ngosi district in 1858 he noted that "the villages were so scattered at random that I could not make an accurate count of them, but there are between 150 and 200."[36] The estimate may be too high but this and other observations suggest that the Ngosi district was quite large and enjoying a period of relative prosperity due to its middleman position in the slave trade. Du Chaillu's main contact during his time in the district was the old chief Olenda (Ademba clan) who was said to rule along with "other chiefs" over the "Ashira Ngozai."[37]

The different accounts of how the term "Ngosi" came to refer to the district of Gisir-speaking clans reveal much about the fluid process of naming in nonliterate, premodern societies. Raponda-Walker suggests that the district was named after a powerful chief, Ngossi-Guitsola (Pugura clan), a successor to Olenda and active in the latter half of the nineteenth century; this is doubtful, though, as the district term was in use before the chief came upon the scene.[38] Others argue that "Ngosi" comes from a Kele term for a particular bird that inhabits the savannah and was used by the neighboring Kele-speaking clans to refer to the Gisir-speaking clans of the area. Another view is that it refers to a kind of grass found in the savannah. Finally, there is the suggestion that it is an imposed label and that the members of the district called themselves "Bisi Tandu Dubigi" ("those of the upper Doubigui River"). Whatever its origin, the district defined by the savannah of the upper Doubigui River has been, along with those labeled "Kamba" and "Tando," a key building block in the construction of a modern Gisira ethnic identity.[39]

In the nineteenth century, there existed no overarching ethnic identity to integrate these districts. Kamba, which Du Chaillu labeled "an outlying district of Ashira-land" (an "Ashira-land" that only existed in the mind of the explorer), was a cluster of villages located on the lower Doubigui River near its mouth with the Ngounié (see Map 6). He noted that "these Ashira Kambas consider themselves a distinct people from the Ashira of the prairie."[40] Du Chaillu also visited "Otando country," or the Tando district, separated from the Ngosi district by the forested Tandou Mountains. This Tando district was located in the savannah along the left bank of the middle Ngounié, with the Doubou River apparently marking its nineteenth-century southern extension.[41] Mayolo was the principal chief or *mata* of the Tando district in the 1860s. Du Chaillu considered the inhabitants of this district "a branch of the Ashira nation" but they likely saw themselves as members of a distinct district and certainly did not consider themselves part of a functioning "Ashira nation."[42]

These three districts became "fixed" in the administrative classifications of the colonial period and are most readily mentioned when considering contemporary Gisira regional distinctions today. It is important to realize, though, that colonial maps of the 1890s continued to designate the "Kamba" as a separate people from the "Eshiras" and included a district of Gisir-speaking clans not visited by Du Chaillu known as "Banda."[43] Cyprien Guipieri, a Gisira notable, suggests that there were only two districts of Gisir-speaking clans at the end of the 19th century, that of the "Gisir-gi-Tandu" and the "Gisir-gi-Banda," the "Tandu" being the upstream district on the Doubandji and the "Banda" the downstream one. Vincent de Paul Nyonda, another Gisira notable, states there were four: "Kamba, Banda, Tandou and Tandou Doubigui," the latter one called "Ngose" by neighboring Kele-speaking clans. Clearly, the Gisira ethnic identity operating today in the modern state of Gabon was not effectively operating a century ago, and identification with one's district took precedence.[44]

Further complicating the arrangement of districts among Gisir-speaking clans in the nineteenth century is a list of *bisa* compiled by Raponda-Walker corresponding to more modest tracts of land than the Ngosi, Tando, and Kamba districts mentioned above. These appear to have been earlier smaller districts that resulted from the fissioning of the matrilineages making up the first villages established by Gisir-speaking clans at the mouth of the Doubigui; the village of Kamba, which supplied the name for the larger district, was among these earlier settlements, probably established sometime in the eighteenth century. On the lower Doubigui and Doubandji, according to Raponda-Walker, the villages of "Yombi, Ngubi, Ndugu, Gilunga, Gisambi, Girandu, Mulamba, etc. . . . gave their names to diverse fractions of territory or *bisa.*"[45]

In the final weeks of 1864, Du Chaillu visited the village of Dihaou, a few miles south of the confluence of the Doubigui and Doubandji Rivers and said to be "the chief town of the Ashira Kambas." The explorer noted that "Dihaou is a cluster of three or four little villages each containing about fifteen houses."[46] The *bisa* listed by Raponda-Walker must have been of a similar composition. The chief's name was "Dihaou Okamba" and Du Chaillu and his party were obliged to spend some time there in order to obtain permission to continue on to the neighboring district of Eviya-speaking clans on the Ngounié River. Just over a year later, in 1866, the British trader Robert Bruce Walker visited a similar cluster of Eviya-speaking villages; "Buali" was "a group of five or six villages rather than a single town" containing "about five hundred huts."[47]

One manifestation of how districts functioned as territories can be seen with these smaller clusters of villages. The leaders of these smaller districts were certainly more capable of controlling people and things by controlling area than the *mata* of the Gisira-Ngosi, for example. Whether invested in a single individual or in a council of clan leaders, the leadership of districts the size of Ngosi was informal and fragile, specializing in mediation rather than effective territoriality. These larger districts had developed to meet the needs of growing trade at commercial nodal points and were constructed according to a "continuity of conception"[48] that mirrored the structures of the smaller districts and continued to stress decentralization.

Lacking the literate instruments of administration, classification, communication, and enforcement required for control over large geographical spaces, precolonial territoriality could only be effectively exercised within the smaller geographical districts like the Dihaou cluster of villages encountered by Du Chaillu. In this particular case, what was controlled was access to the next district, Du Chaillu's passage forming a single link in the chain of relations that travellers had to work through to penetrate the Southern Gabon interior in the mid-nineteenth century. Trade, of course, was also conducted along this chain of relations; indeed, Du Chaillu's whole journey traces out a network of "trading friends," or *bakanga* in Punu, as the explorer was passed on from one *mukanga* to another much like a *mùtétì* (a special woven basket) of salt heading from the coast to the interior.[49]

The long distance trading contacts cultivated by the clan leaders of a particular district often led to the development of favored relationships with other districts. This was the case with the Galwa-speaking clans in the

Wombolyè district (located on the left bank of the Ogooué at Lake Onangué) and the Mpanjè district (located on the right bank of the Ogooué where the Ouango branches off from the main stream), whose trade contacts in the latter half of the nineteenth century were strictly with the Vili- and Eviya-speaking clans at Samba Falls on the Ngounié. The Galwa-speaking clans of the Olomba (upstream) district traded solely with the Okandé-speaking clans of the Middle Ogooué (see Map 6).[50]

Districts formed along axes provided by waterways and overland trade routes; their spatial distribution was further determined by nodal points in the long-distince trade. The most important nodal point in the Southern Gabon interior was located just downstream from where the Ngounié flows into the Ogooué near the site of present day Lambaréné. Here Galwa- and Enenga-speaking clans controlled the flow of goods from the districts of Okandé-speaking clans upstream on the Ogooué as well as those goods coming down the Ngounié from Samba Falls. There were designated areas within villages where trade was conducted (most often in the men's public house) but there were no organized markets serving the local districts. Coastal traders, usually Orungu but also Spanish and Portuguese, arrived in those villages within the various districts where they had trading friends. They would either provide goods on credit with the hope of obtaining a payment in slaves at a later date or seek payment for goods that they had left earlier. Traders from Galwa- and Enenga-speaking clans also travelled to the coast to conduct business. Negotiations were drawn out and very complex affairs requiring considerable diplomatic skill. A trader might stay within a district several months attempting to strike new deals or conclude old ones.[51]

The most powerful clan leaders benefited from either inherited or newly won privileges that helped to assure their commercial position. For example, the blind chief Ranoké, the leader of the Enenga-speaking Azyondo clan from at least the 1850s to the early 1890s, had considerable control over access to the Okandé districts further up the Ogooué. In the mid-1860s, members of Enenga-speaking clans other than the Azyondo could trade only as far as the district of the Apindji-speaking villages on the banks of the Ogooué just downstream from the confluence with the Mingoué.[52] To go further, they had to be accompanied by members of the Azyondo clan. During this period, Ranoké allowed his trading friends from the Galwa-speaking clans of the Olomba district to trade at Okandé; however, he had recently withdrawn this privilege from members of Ajumba-speaking clans. These latter were then obliged to focus their commerce on the Ngounié.

By the 1870s, the most powerful figure of the Galwa-speaking clans was a chief and trader named Nkombé. The son of an Enenga woman and adept at exploiting the esoteric power of trade charms and accompanying rituals, Nkombé obtained wives from all the surrounding peoples, even from as far up the Ogooué as the Okandé districts, where he travelled twice a year to buy slaves. He had come to rival Ranoké in terms of influence and was widely respected if not feared throughout the region until his death from poisoning at the end of 1873.[53]

Although neither Ranoké nor Nkombé ruled out the use of violence to enforce their influence, both relied heavily on their esoteric or "invisible" powers to maintain and enhance their positions. For example, Ranoké's Azyondo clan owned powerful trading charms that functioned in a territorial fashion to control access to the districts further up the Ogooué. Notable in this regard was the sacred "fetish point" found on the right bank of the Ngounié as it empties into the Ogooué; rituals had to be performed and offerings made at this site, which was also a cemetery for Azyondo clan elders, in order to assure a safe and successful voyage up the Ogooué.[54]

Powerful clan leaders like Ranoké and Nkombé spent several months of the year conducting trade in the Okandé district of Lopé, another key nodal point for the Middle Ogooué (see Map 5). In the mid-1870s, Lopé was described as the "general rendezvous" for the Okandé-speaking clans of the area, where they came to exchange "bananas, goats, slaves and little ivory" for salt brought from the coast by the Enenga and Galwa middlemen who obtained it from the Orungu at Cape Lopez. All observers note the ardent desire to trade for salt among the peoples of the Southern Gabon interior. Lopé in and of itself was of no importance, and there was no permanent village on its site. Indeed, it functioned like a market and remained empty until a convoy of *pirogues* (canoes) arrived from downstream. This occurred in February during the short dry season and again during the long dry season from June to September. Being able to organize and successfully complete a long-distance trading caravan was an important step to obtaining power and influence; only the most able clan and lineage heads could pull it off. Participation in these caravans as a young boy served as an initiation into the responsibilities of manhood.[55]

By the mid-1870s, the Ogooué was no longer the sole trade route supplying the Okandé districts as the aggressive tactics of Osyéba- and Fang-speaking clans, seeking to carve out their niche in the network of trading alliances, greatly disrupted the river traffic.[56] As a consequence, salt made its way to the middle Ogooué overland from Mayumba, where it

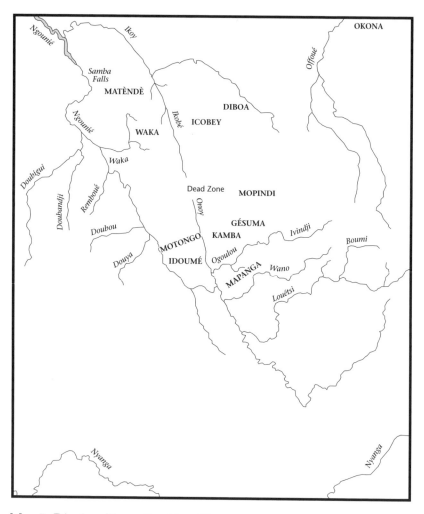

Map 7. Districts: Tsogo-Speaking Clans.

passed through a commercial nodal point at the village of Idoumé on the right bank of upper Ngounié (close to where Du Chaillu had passed in 1865) and continued along the "chemin du sel (salt trail)"[57] to a second nodal point on the upper Offoué known as "Okona" (see Map 7).

The explorers Marche and Brazza mistakenly believed that "Okona" referred to an ethnic group.[58] However, an August 1885 report from Alfred Fourneau, a member of Brazza's West African Mission, showed that it was a nodal point in the long-distance trade network. Travelling among the villages of Simba-speaking clans on the lower Offoué, Fourneau noted that all the able men of the district had made their annual dry season visit upstream to Okona to trade.[59] Idoumé was described at the end of the nineteenth century as being:

> the contact point of the five principal tribes from which slaves are exported to the coast: Apindji, Tando, Bapounou [Bapunu], Mitchogo [Mitsogo] and Matchango [Massango], all of whom use this point as a base.[60]

Functioning as a port and a market site, it was controlled by members of the Dibur-Simbu, the Punu-speaking branch of the powerful Bumwele clan, whose influence in the savannah of the Ngounié basin expanded rapidly in the nineteenth century. Idoumé was one of the first villages established by the Dibur-Simbu when, according to Punu traditions collected by Koumba-Manfoumbi, they expanded into an unoccupied "no man's land" and created districts on the right bank of the Ngounié. They also moved along the left bank to establish villages near what is now the town of Mouila.[61] Sometimes these new zones were not unoccupied, as other Punu traditions relate that Idoumé had once been part of a district of Mitsogo-speaking clans until "the members of Simbu's lineage (*bisi Simbu*) imposed themselves over it."[62]

The Gabonese researcher Hygnanga-Koumba translates *bisi* into French sometimes as "clan," sometimes as "lineage," though Vansina's lexical gloss indicates a link to geographical place. In this particular instance *bisi* (or *bissi*) can mean "member of" or "those of" a specific lineage such as those founded by the children of the female ancestor Simbu. According to Micheline Koumba's study of the Dibur-Simbu, these were *Bissi Mikulu mi Simbu*; *Bissi Ntsumb-Simbu*; *Bissi Kumb-Dibamb* or *Kumb-Simbu*; and *Bissi Badjinn ba Simbu*. Yet these lineages were also associated with a particular geographic area; the *Bissi Mikulu mi Simbu* established themselves on land that is now part of Mouila while the other three established themselves on land further away. This is an illustration of the subtle intersection between kinship ideology and claims to geographical space, where the ideological creation of lineages from a clan ancestor takes on a territorial element as the cluster of villages settled by matrilineal descendants over time forms a small district.[63]

Further down the Ngounié River at the terminus of a series of falls and rapids beginning where the town of Fougamou is presently located was found the important nodal point of Samba Falls. Like its trading partner downstream at the mouth of the Ngounié, Samba was not the province of any one district or clan but the site of a series of village clusters whose clan leaders sought to profit from the much-desired role of middleman. In the 1860s and 1870s, in the immediate vicinity of the actual "falls"—which in reality are not much more than rapids—Vili-speaking clans formed the villages of "Ikanga" and "Kongo-Mboumba" while three miles upstream there was the small district of Eviya-speaking clans clustered around the villages of "Buali" and "Etambé."[64] During this period, trade contacts downstream were severely disrupted by Kele-speaking clans who robbed and pillaged river traffic on the lower Ngounié. The flow of goods and people downstream to the nodal point at the confluence of the Ngounié and Ogooué slowed, and the slack was taken up by Nkomi-speaking clans of the Fernan Vaz who brought much-desired salt, salted fish, and European goods to Samba to exchange for ivory, slaves, and raphia cloth.[65]

Just as Galwa- and Enenga-speaking clan leaders did all that they could to prohibit the coastal Orungu traders from penetrating beyond their districts further up the Ogooué, the Vili- and Eviya-speaking clan leaders at Samba Falls exercised district territoriality in seeking to keep their trading partners, whether African or European, from traveling into the forested mountains on the right bank of the Ngounié where they obtained ivory, slaves, and raphia cloth from districts of Tsogo- and Sango-speaking clans. A British trader in the 1870s remarked that "nobody was allowed to pass Samba Falls" and that anyone using the main road to the east

> paid Ibango or toll to the Evili [Vili] king and this toll amounted to quite one sixth of the value of the produce. No native coming from the interior was allowed to sell without coming into the town and must be accompanied by one of the citizens whilst selling and the toll was handed over immediately the purchase was made.[66]

Districts established near the most active nodal points had rather different experiences in the latter half of the nineteenth century than those located in the source areas at the end limits of the trading network. As the struggle for control over strategic nodal points became more intense during the period between 1850 and 1880, the practices of the equatorial political tradition came under increasing pressure. In the short period between Du Chaillu's 1858 visit to the Ngosi district of Gisir-speaking clans and his 1864 return, the explorer noted some revealing changes:

> A few rambles about the Ashira prairie showed me that the population had much diminished, since my visit six years previously. Many of the villages which then studded its grassy slopes and hollows had disappeared. It is true that some of the head men had removed their people to new villages in the

woods, which surround the prairie; nevertheless, I believe the total number of people had been much reduced. The tribe was once superior to all their neighbors in industry and cleanliness, and in the quality of their clothing and ornaments. A deterioration was now plainly visible. The well-woven dengui which people used to wear had almost disappeared, and in its stead I saw only garments of thin, dirty, cotton cloth. A few of the older women alone were decorated with copper rings round the neck. The young people had also abandoned the practice of filing their front teeth, and I noticed a total change of fashion in the dressing of their hair, increasing commerce with the Rembo [Nkomi] having had the result of their adopting Commi [Nkomi] fashions. The tribe have now constant intercourse with the Commi, and of late years the warlike Bakalai [Bakele] have married many of their women and of course taken them away.[67]

The Ngosi district's strategic middleman position and consequent further integration into the Atlantic commercial network had in the matter of a few years undermined a number of material and cultural practices. The desire to get closer to the source of European goods stimulated a series of movements by Gisir-speaking clans down the Rembo Nkomi and toward the Iguéla Lagoon where in the latter area the "Gisir-Ngosi" mixed with "Loango" to create a new district during the colonial period called "Gisir-mue-Luangu" (see Map 6).[68] The move of villages into the forest may have been the consequence of conflicts with Kele-speaking clans or simply an effort to get closer to the sources of ebony, ivory, and rubber that European factors were demanding in ever greater quantities.[69]

The increase in commercial opportunities as a result of being close to a nodal point also led to an increase in competition and jealousy between clan and lineage heads. Witchcraft accusations, poison ordeals, and the poisoning of rivals were on the rise as ambitious leaders sought new heights of wealth and power, thus creating fear and mistrust among each other and their dependents. The consequence was an atmosphere of paranoia where village settlements broke into smaller units and often moved to a different location when the death of a member unleashed suspicion and accusations. At the turn of the century, Gisir-speaking clans recalled once having lived in large villages containing six to ten *ebandja* corresponding to the number of lineages residing there; however, in the span of a generation these large villages had been split into "an infinity of tiny hamlets scattered here and there."[70]

This was not the case with the districts of Tsogo-speaking clans lo-cated in the forested hills to the east of the Ngounié (see Map 7). In the latter half of the nineteenth century, these districts were not located near the most active nodal points and thus were not yet fully drawn into the whirlwind of commerce happening just to the west. Their villages were large and stable,[71] and there appear to have been no overly ambitious leaders trying to dominate the districts for themselves. Local material culture was still flourishing; in 1865 Du Chaillu was impressed by the beautifully carved doors on all the dwellings of the village.[72] Unlike the villages of the Gisir- and Kele-speaking clans who abandoned residence upon death of a member, Du Chaillu

> was pleased to find that the people here were not so much afraid of death as the tribes nearer the sea; they do not abandon a village when a death occurs. Indeed, the villages are so large that this custom would be very difficult to keep up.[73]

Even the names of these districts of Tsogo-speaking clans suggest a stability not found at the commercial nodal points. Of the eight districts listed by Raponda-Walker only two, Waka and Okobi (or Icobey), are geographical terms named from rivers. The other six, Matèndè, Dibuwa (or Diboa), Gésuma, Kamba, Mapanga, and Mopindi, are "ethnic appellations" according to Raponda-Walker, suggesting long-term establishment.[74] Otto Gollnhofer notes that for the districts of Tsogo-speaking clans, "each of these *mabiya* (districts) enjoyed total internal autonomy."[75] Since there existed no overarching authority ruling over the different Tsogo-speaking clans nor was there a leader of a particular clan powerful enough to assert authority over the others, each district was an independent economic and judicial unit. Clan members seeking to hunt, fish, start a plantation, or bury a relative in a district other than their own were obliged to seek permission from that district's leaders. Gollnhofer further remarks that there existed "a solidarity between members of a particular *ebiya* (district) in situations of conflict with representatives of another *ebiya* (marriages, adultery, fights, deaths, etc.)."[76]

In the mid-nineteenth century, Tsogo-speaking clans held slaves but not so many as to have separate slave villages, nor was slavery central to their society when compared to peoples closer to the coast.[77] Local hunter-gatherers were in a dependent relation to the clans of the interior but their movements were contained within the district of their clan's residence. Du Chaillu observed in 1864 that the "Obongos," though "eminently a migratory people." did not "wander very far":

> that is, the Obongos who live within the Ashango [Massango] territory do not go out of that territory—they are called the Obongos of the Ashangos—

those who live among the Njavi [Nzabi] are called Obongo-Njavi—and the same with other tribes.[78]

These districts had accepted boundaries and frontiers, usually rivers, mountains, or dead zones.[79] Interestingly, oral traditions report that the dependent hunter-gatherers who guided their clans into new areas were also responsible for establishing the boundaries of districts. An account of the Dibur Simbu move into the districts of Tsogo-speaking clans on the right bank of the Ngounié in the late eighteenth century is revealing. The brothers of Simbu, the founding woman ancestor of the Dibur Simbu, were accompanied in their migration by "their pygmy."[80] After crossing over to the right bank of the Ngounié, using trees that he felled as bridge, the hunter-gatherer killed an elephant. He then returned to the members of his clan and informed them of his activities. The clan members also crossed the Ngounié and killed an elephant. While on the right bank,

> The pygmy found a sign made by a pygmy belonging to the Tsogo peoples. He also met a pygmy belonging to the Apindji people. The three then fixed a boundary on the Dusama River. It is the pygmies who fix the territorial boundaries of peoples, and this according to both ethnic groups and clans.[81]

Signs communicating boundaries could take the form of charms. Such charms also served to protect the inhabitants of a village or the crops of a plantation. Their territorial efficacy was linked to their consecration by a ritual specialist.[82] Along narrow river passages, fences, like the one described by Du Chaillu on the Doubanga, a branch of the Rembo Nkomi, were constructed to control the flow of traffic and establish authority within a district:

> The Bakalai [Bakele] had made a fence across the river to bar the passage, leaving only a gap near the shore for small canoes to pass. This had been done on the account of some petty trade-quarrel which the people of this tribe had had with their neighbors.[83]

The explorer was traveling with Quengueza, the head of the Abulia clan which controlled trade on the Rembo Nkomi. The latter was furious at coming across such an affront to his authority and the fence was quickly destroyed.

In the forest, boundaries were communicated by the tieing together of vines or plants and placing them along a path; this was often the work of the men's initiation society, *mwiri,* of which more will be discussed below.

In another account of the Dibur Simbu's move onto the right bank of the Ngounié, it is noted that even though the clans of the existing Tsogo-speaking districts "had clearly marked off their territory," the Punu-speaking Dibur Simbu "did not pay attention to this demarcation, they tore down all the possible warning signs to outsiders and then entered Tsogo property."[84] This act of destruction precipitated an aggressive reaction from the inhabitants of the Mitsogo district.

Southern Gabon as functional region in the mid-nineteenth century can be envisioned as a patchwork of districts and dead zones with more fluid districts near commercially active nodal points and more stable clusters in the supply areas. The influx of European goods and the creation of global markets for tropical products greatly accelerated the pattern and volume of trade in the latter half of the century. Southern Gabon as a functional region took on new forms as new players in the network of trading alliances established new districts and integrated previously neglected spaces into the commercial activity of the region. These new clan leaders and their adherents could accomplish this in a number of ways: they could establish new districts close to existing commercial nodal points; they could attempt to work the dead zones in a semi-nomadic fashion by collecting rubber, cutting ebony, or hunting elephants; they could operate on the periphery of existing districts by seizing women and children for slaves; or they could attempt to reroute trade flows by disrupting waterways, thus creating opportunities on previously underused overland routes. These developments brought more land under the influence of the intermittant territoriality practiced in precolonial Southern Gabon and resulted in the exploitation of previously untapped resources. In the mid-nineteenth century, the disparate activities of Kele-speaking clans best illustrate these new opportunities.

Bakele[85] and Growing Trade Opportunities

Descendants of Kele-speaking clans are spread out over much of what is now Gabon (see Map 8) and scholars have on occasion been tempted to lump them into a hunter-gatherer category. This, however, would be misleading, as the movements of hunter-gatherers in nineteenth-century Southern Gabon were restricted to the district in which they resided and determined by their dependent relationship within a clan.[86] Though Kele-speaking clans were very mobile, their motivations for moving were connected to trade; thus they had access to wealth generated from commerce not

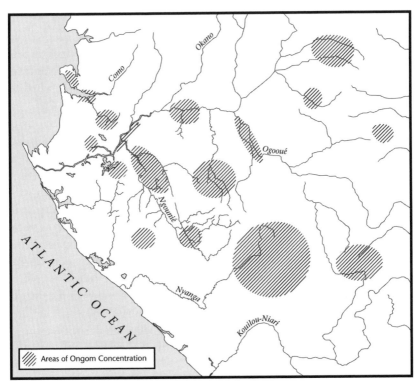

Map 8. Distribution of Kele-Speaking Clans. Based on François Ngolet, "La dispersion Ongom-Bakele en Afrique Centrale: Esquisse d'anthropologie historique (origines–vers 1900)" (Thèse de doctorat, Université Paul Valéry, Montpellier III, 1994).

available to hunter-gatherers. These latter did participate in the trading network, most notably in the gathering of rubber or in the hunting of elephants, but this activity was conducted in service to the head of their clan. Many Kele-speaking clans became specialists in these hunting and gathering phases of trade but they also could settle down along trade routes and establish villages and districts in ways that hunter-gatherers could not. Indeed, Kele-speaking clans, like the other clans of Southern Gabon, were aided in their migratory movements by dependent hunter-gatherer guides.[87]

The British explorer Bowdich, from information gathered in 1818, mentions the "country of the Kaylee (sometimes called Kaylay)" lying in the area between the Gabon Estuary and Ogooué River. He also mentions "Samashialee" as being the "capital" and "residence of King Ohmbay."[88] By the 1840s, Kele-speaking clans were acting as key middlemen in the network supplying the Asiga clan of the Mpongwe leader King Denis, who ruled the left bank of the Estuary. They functioned as a connecting link between the Mpongwe-speaking Agulamba clan located on the Estuary at the mouth of the Remboué River and the Ajumba who were established on Lac Azingo.[89]

In the decades between 1820 and 1850, Kele-speaking clans began to skirt the periphery of the commercial nodal points developing at the Ngounié-Ogooué confluence and along the Rembo Nkomi and started to carve out a space for themselves in the growing commercial network. Though it has been argued that these movements were a consequence of pressure applied by the Fang-speaking clans forcing them out of their positions in the region of the Gabon Estuary,[90] they might just as easily be seen as stemming from the desire of Kele-speaking clan leaders to gain a foothold in the more dynamic trade further south. Not powerful enough to oust the Galwa- or Enenga-speaking clans from their districts, they established themselves upstream on the Middle Ogooué in the 1840s most notably in the district called Samkita.[91] They also moved into the lake region downstream and from there began to establish themselves on the left bank of the Ngounié.[92] The French explorer Griffon du Bellay described their territorial practice in 1862:

> Not interested in navigation, they have hardly settled on the riverbanks, but they seem, on the other hand, very jealous of the possession of their lands in the bush and do not willfully allow peoples of other races to pass through them. There they monopolize the transit of ordinary commercial products: captives, elephant teeth, wax and finally mats, baskets and other woven objects in whose fabrication the Bakele have acquired considerable expertise.[93]

The leaders of these Kele-speaking clans worked the periphery of the commercial nodal points and ranged further into the dead zones separating districts as the demand for rubber, ivory, and ebony grew in the latter half of the nineteenth century. Specialists of forests as opposed to waterways, they used this expertise to gain access to resources in southern Gabon in the mid-nineteenth century. Control at nodal points along rivers required the labor of clan dependents adept at rowing and manipulating a *pirogue* along the treacherous waterways of rivers like the Ogooué. One of the reasons Okandé-speaking clans were so influential stemmed from their unparalleled ability to navigate the Ogooué between Lopé and its confluence

with the Ngounié. Successful exploitation of the new commercial opportunities often required the adaptation and learning of new skills associated
with settlement in a different ecological zone. These transformations are often
indicated in oral traditions; for example, Bakele traditions indicate that some
Kele-speaking clans became adept boatmen after settling on waterways.[94]

The extreme mobility of Kele-speaking clans allowed them to move
into the spaces between the established districts set up on the key waterways. Du Chaillu noted that:

> one of the peculiar traits of the Bakalai [Bakele], which distinguishes them
> from other tribes with whom they are intermixed, is their roving character.
> They never stay long in one place. A Bakalai village is scarce built—often
> plantations have not borne fruit the first time—when they feel impelled to
> move. Then everything is abandoned; they gather up what few stores of
> provisions they may have, and start off, often for great distances, to make
> with infinite pains a new settlement, which will be abandoned in turn some-
> times after a few months, though occasionally they remain a year or two, and
> even more, in the same place.[95]

Given this mobility and the fact that they usually settled on the fringes of
existing districts, Kele-speaking clans did not always establish districts themselves. An exception would be Samkita, which formed when Kele-speaking
clans assumed positions on the Ogooué and then maintained the existing
network they had established inland from the river's right bank. Yet even
within the space of the district itself these clans practiced an almost constant movement of village sites.[96]

Du Chaillu was witness to the beginnings of a district of Kele-speaking clans on the Doubanga River (see Map 6). With the Nkomi chief
Quengueza, he visited the Bakele chief, Obindji,[97] at his village. The explorer noted:

> It is a recent settlement, and not very large. The family is quite powerful; but
> when their chief wished to remove to the river from his inland settlement,
> most of his people refused. These Bakalai are reputed to be very war-like,
> and various circumstances show that they are so. They are much dreaded by
> other tribes; and I find that these others have left all the right side of the river
> to their fighting neighbors. Those who live on the river-bank, however, are
> in some sort bound to keep the peace; for they have no right near the water
> but with the leave of Quengueza, and this they get only on premise of peace-
> able behavior.[98]

Obindji's clan had probably been in the area less than twenty years and was most likely among those Kele-speaking clans who moved down from the Lakes area and then spread south to the Rembo Nkomi and east to the left bank of the Ngounié, no doubt fighting among themselves as well as with the Galwa-, Gisir-, Vili-, and Eviya-speaking clans they encountered along the periphery of established districts.[99] However, when Obindji wanted to establish himself on the Doubanga River he was obliged to develop a "trading friendship" with Quengueza, the leader of the clan who controlled the waterway. This was a matter for negotiation, not force, which was most often the case when clans moved in to assume existing positions along the trade routes. Violence was resorted to in the form of hostage-taking or murder, but these acts were not undertaken in an effort to conquer and subsequently destroy a people. Rather they were strategies adopted in the never-ending series of "palavers" through which power and authority were negotiated.[100]

Obindji's efforts to gain a solid foothold on a key waterway of the trading network were halted by the smallpox epidemic of 1864–65 that took not only his life but wiped out his entire village.[101] However, three decades later the missionary Buléon collected a Bakele legend which attributes the establishment of permanent districts of Kele-speaking clans along the Rembo Nkomi to two wise "kings," "Koumou," and "Abwali." These two figures became the *ombwiri,* or spirits, of the two main peaks of the Koumounawali Massif that watch over the fortunes of the Bakele districts below. These peaks also function as a dead zone boundary with the Kamba district of Gisir-speaking clans to the east. In the legend the two kings seek to stop the extreme nomadism of the Kele-speaking clans. They ask, in effect, that the Kele-speaking clans create a district:

> for as long as the months of the dry season will last, you will gather together by families, you will hunt in the thick bush, and you will return to the dwellings you have built loaded down with the spoils of elephant hunting. You will sell the ivory to passing tribes and to the Whites coming from the shores of the setting sun, you will be rich. You will not move from your settlements but rather wait here for their arrival.[102]

When the dry season ended and the rains made commercial travel untenable, the two kings told the Kele-speaking clans to settle on the two banks of the Rembo Nkomi and live off the fish in the river and the game of the forest. They gave the following commands to their people:

> Leave no longer; be always united and live on your river between your two mountains. Cursed be the one among you who will like a foreign soil; cursed

the one who will be a subject of discord and violate the traditions of his family. Children, we demand from you the oath that you will no longer leave this region. . . . That it be thus! cried the crowd; by *Omwiri*, we swear it.[103]

This legend, though filtered through a Biblical missionary style, does reflect the actual development of a stable Bakele district on the Doubanga and Rembo Nkomi between the years 1850 and 1890. Ironically, the small-pox epidemic that killed Obindji also devastated Quengueza's village. The latter's Nkomi-speaking Abulia clan, which had controlled this important river commerce, suffered serious losses, and there thus opened up an op-portunity for the creation of a district of Kele-speaking clans.

Still, as late as the 1890s, other Kele-speaking clans further east con-tinued the old practices of nomadism and general disruption of trade routes. In the 1850s, Kele-speaking clans had moved in among the Gisir-speaking clans of the Banda district on the upper Doubandji, creating a good deal of tension there. They also occupied the left bank of the Ngounié near Samba Falls, thus prohibiting the movement of Apindji-speaking clans established downstream who had previously travelled to the districts at the mouth of the Ngounié to trade with Enenga-speaking clans.[104] Throughout the 1860s, they attacked and pillaged the *pirogues* of Vili- and Eviya-speaking clans descending from Samba and by the 1870s controlled the left bank of the Ngounié from Samba Falls to the Ogooué as well as the strategic position where the Ikoy flows into the Ngounié on the right bank.[105]

During the next two decades, they pushed into the Du Chaillu Mas-sif from the Ngounié and the Ogooué; their positions on the Ogooué were being pressured by the arrival of Fang-speaking clans from the north. Inci-dents of Kele-speaking clans disrupting trade on the Ngounié are numer-ous in the colonial archives from 1877. The end of the long dry season in August when water levels were lowest and *pirogues* were obliged to pass close to the banks to avoid the now exposed fallen trees, sand banks, and rocks in the middle of the river became the preferred time for Bakele shore-based attacks.[106] With the disruption of river trade, the use of overland trails assumed greater importance; these were often controlled by Kele-speaking clans generally more adept in the forest than on the water. Con-trol and knowledge of the trails connecting Samkita with the Ngounié were a crucial element in Bakele efforts to increase their influence as middlemen. By 1900, unstable conditions on the Ogooué and Ngounié had considerably aug-mented commercial traffic on these alternative overland routes.[107]

As they moved in the classic fashion of skirting established districts and working the dead zones, Kele-speaking clans invariably came into conflict with those clans already resident in the area. In the 1890s they forced Tsogo-speaking clans of the Matèndè, Dibuwa, and Waka districts off the Ikoy River (see Map 7), sparking a series of conflicts that have left a considerable imprint upon Tsogo oral traditions. These traditions state that the Kele-speaking clans (who are referred to as "Mbangwe," meaning "rapid" and reflecting their incessant migrations) attacked the villages of Tsogo-speaking clans to make off with women and children so as to increase their numbers and counter the sterility of their own women. These battles were caricatured in a masque performed at dawn following a nocturnal public dance organized by the members of *bwété*, one of the central initiation societies for men. One consequence of these Bakele incursions was the dispersal to the west of a number of Tsogo-speaking clans who ended up establishing villages in districts inhabited by Punu- and Apindji-speaking clans.[108]

The latter half of the 1890s witnessed the most intense period of conflict as Mangunde-ma-kuze, head of the Kele-speaking Sa-buka lineage, led a series of successful attacks against Mitsogo districts. Mitsogo traditions relate that district organization for self-defense in the face of Bakele aggression was a total failure until the belligerents made contact with the Tsogo-speaking clans of the Kamba district. It was only after several of the clans—most notably the Motoka, the Ghasanga, and the Pogheo—concocted a war charm able to subdue the Bakele that the conflict ended.[109] In 1907, probably not much more than a decade after the actual events, Raponda-Walker was travelling through the villages of the Waka district where he obtained an account of the Bakele-Mitsogo conflict from Mbagna, a leader in the village of Ndougou:

> Among those of us who put an end to the Bakele incursions were the Mitsogo-Kamba.—The Bakele wanted to give chase to our tribe while it emigrated but the Kambas resolved to stand firm and wait for them. In order to give themselves courage, they organized a huge fetish dance, known as *Epoboué*, and thus hardened, they attacked the Bakele near Mount Motendè. The combat was long and bloody. Finally, the Bakele, not used to experiencing such a strong resistance from the Mitsogo, took flight and no longer desired to reappear on our territory unless it was to conduct commerce there.[110]

The Bakele incursions among the Tsogo-speaking clans demonstrate how districts exercised territoriality in organizing a defense against an outside aggressor. If prominence within Mitsogo oral traditions is any indication, these conflicts were of a scale and intensity previously unknown in Mitsogo experience. It may be that this external aggression stimulated the development of broader notions of district and ethnic solidarity among the Tsogo-speaking clans. It is often the case that the process of identifying with a newer and larger "we" is first aroused by outside intervention. The exposure to grave external threats and the crystallization of ethnic identity was greatly amplified during the colonial period when the French attempted to impose an hegemony through modern territoriality.

The French scholar Annie Merlet employs the term "hegemony" to describe the impact of Kele-speaking clans throughout Southern Gabon in the nineteenth century. I would argue, however, that the use of this term exaggerates the extent of Bakele power and presents a distorted view of their movements, much in the same way that the Fang were originally seen as aggressive conquerors. It is important to realize that leaders of Punu- and Gisir-speaking clans, for example, also did very well during this period.[111] Kele-speaking clans came to control key bits of the interior commercial network by their aggressive, disruptive strategies, but their territoriality was neither continuous nor rigorously maintained. Oral traditions reveal a pattern of initial aggression where Kele-speaking clan leaders would abduct members of other clans, but within a generation these same clans would be conducting matrimonial exchanges.[112]

Violence in precolonial Southern Gabon was most often a tactic used to solve trading disputes and even to create trading alliances.[113] A resourceful Kele clan leader could within his lifetime forcibly abduct a woman from, for example, a Gisir-speaking clan, thus instigating a short period of violent confrontation followed by protracted negotiations ending in an agreement with the woman's clan head regarding the damages owed. A trading alliance with this clan would be established and the new tie continually cemented through the mutual exchange of female dependents and other kinds of transactions.

Since Kele-speaking clans determined descent patrilineally while most peoples in Southern Gabon traced descent matrilineally, exchanging women and determining the clan membership of their children was problematic. When men from Galwa-speaking clans first started marrying women from Kele-speaking clans (probably in the first half of the nineteenth century), the children of the union at first sought to exercise their clan rights in their fathers' clans as would have been the practice among the Kele. But their Galwa father's clan treated them as slaves, thus greatly annoying the Kele side of the family. It was eventually decided that, if a Kele woman married a Galwa man, descent would be determined matrilineally.[114]

These kinds of complications were simply tacked on to the already complex system of negotiations, gifts and counter-gifts, obligations, and disputes that occurred in the process of matrimonial exchange between clans. The population movements and incursions stimulated by the rapid growth of trade in the latter half of the nineteenth century brought about a disruption in the exchange practices within districts where patterns and obligations between clans and lineages had been developed during a more stable period.[115] This resulted in new opportunities opening up within the networks of alliances; Kele-speaking clans and then Fang-speaking clans moved rapidly to take advantage of the instability. The cognitive map provided by clan ideology proved a malleable and effective means of socially incorporating and encoding new trading partners and relationships.

Notes

1. See Vansina, *Paths*, 197–237, for a useful summary.

2. See Phyllis M. Martin, *The External Trade of the Loango Coast, 1576–1870: The Effects of Changing Commercial Relations on the Vili Kingdom of Loango* (Oxford: The Clarendon Press, 1972), 73–94.

3. See Phyllis M. Martin, "Family Strategies in Nineteenth-Century Cabinda," *JAH* 28, 1 (1987): 65–86.

4. For the commercial practices of the Loango Kingdom, see Martin, *External Trade*, 97–101; for the influence of the Loango Kingdom on the Southern Gabon coast, see K. David Patterson, *The Northern Gabon Coast to 1875* (London: Oxford University Press, 1975), 74; Ambouroue-Avaro, *Un peuple gabonais*, 145; François Gaulme, *Le pays de Cama*, 92–128, 226; Annie Merlet, *Autour du Loango (14e–19e siècle)* (Paris/Libreville: Sépia/Centre Culturel Français Saint-Exupéry, 1991), 46–48. For the notion of clan hierarchy, see R. P. Meyer, "Hiérarchie des clans (*bifumba*), tribus (*malongo*), ethnies, peuples," (Unpublished document, Mayumba, ca.1960), 2–4; and for the role of clans in general in the Loango Kingdom, Frank Hagenbucher-Sacripanti, *Les fondements spirituels du pouvoir au Royaume de Loango: République populaire du Congo* (Paris: ORSTOM, 1973).

5. Martin, *External Trade*, 117–26; see also Hagenbucher-Sacripanti, *Les fondements*, 19–20; for a fascinating study of an important trade charm whose influence spread to some Punu-speaking clans, see John M. Janzen, *Lemba, 1650–1930: A Drum of Affliction in Africa and the New World* (New York: Garland Publishing, 1982).

6. Among the Gisira, the Bumwele are called "Bumwedi," among the Nzabi "Bavonda," and among the Lumbu "Imondu"; see Koumba-Manfoumbi, "Les Punu," 254. Rey notes branches of the Bumwele exist among the Kuni Nzanda and Tsangui ethnic groups in the Congo; see Rey, *Colonialisme*, 105–6 (see "Appendix: Clan List and Correspondences," in Gray, "Territoriality," for a full listing).

7. See Koumba-Manfoumbi, "Les Punu," 79–83, for Bumwele clan origins and migration; also Rey, *Colonialisme*, 105, 189, 197–99, 514; and Vansina, *Paths*, 222, for development of its influence; Meyer, "Hiérarchie des clans," 4, for the Bumwele position in the clan hierarchy. Of course, as this and the next chapter go on to demonstrate, other factors apart from trade might also be responsible for shifting clan affiliations, and, as Map 4 indicates, migrations were in multiple directions.

8. Koumba-Manfoumbi, "Les Punu," 90–94.

9. See Rey, *Colonialisme,* 224–31.

10. Ibid., 224, 231.

11. Martin, *External Trade,* 136–40; Martin, "Family Strategies," 71–80; and Miller, *Way of Death,* 505–31. See also Norm Schrag, "Mboma and the Lower Zaire: A Socioeconomic Study of a Kongo Trading Community c. 1785–1885" (Ph.D. diss., Indiana University, 1985).

12. Martin, *External Trade,* 140–43; E. Bouët-Willaumez, *Commerce et traite des noirs aux côtes occidentales d'Afrique* (Geneva: Slatkine Reprints, 1978, orig. ed. Paris, Imprimerie Nationale, 1848), 162–63.

13. T. Edward Bowdich, *Mission from Cape Coast Castle to Ashantee* (London: J. Murray, 1819; reprinted London: Frank Cass, 1966), 431–32; Patterson, *Northern Gabon Coast,* 2–3; 27–28; Ambouroue-Avaro, *Un peuple gabonais,* 98–99, 102–5, 123–24, 143–47; Vansina, *Paths,* 232–33; and Gaulme, *Le pays de Cama,* 170–71.

14. Ambouroue-Avaro, *Un peuple,* 130; Patterson, *Northern Gabon,* 34–43 for São Tomé trade and figures; on the Mpongwe, see Henry Bucher, "The Atlantic Slave Trade and the Gabon Estuary: The Mpongwe to 1860," in *Africans in Bondage,* ed. P. Lovejoy (Madison, 1986), 136–54, and "The Mpongwe of the Gabon Estuary: A History to 1860," (Ph.D. diss., University of Wisconsin–Madison, 1977, 120–92).

15. Gaulme, *Le pays de Cama,* 174–75, 184–86.

16. For geographers, a nodal point is the "center or node" that interacts with "a surrounding hinterland" thus providing the basis for a formal or nodal region. In precolonial Southern Gabon, as we have seen, clearly delineated formal *regions* did not exist but one can discern a number of commercial nodal *points* in the functional regions of the long-distance trade network; see "Region" in Larkin and Peters, *Dictionary of Concepts in Human Geography,* 199–205.

17. Ibid., 217–19, 245; see Gray, "Appendix: Clan List and Correspondences," in Gray, "Territoriality."

18. For the Kele-speaking clans, see René Avelot, "Notice historique sur les Bakalè," *L'Anthropologie* 24 (1913): 197–240, and François Ngolet, "La dispersion Ongom-Bakele en Afrique Centrale: Esquisse d'anthropologie historique," (Thèse de doctorat, Université Paul Valéry-Montpellier, 1994); for the "Fang migration," see Nicolas Metegue N'Nah, "Le Gabon de 1854 à 1886: Présence française et peuples autochtones," (Thèse de doctorat, Université de Paris I, 1974); Christopher Chamberlin, "The Migration of the Fang into Central Gabon during the Nineteenth Century: A New Interpretation," *IJAHS* 11, 3 (1978): 429–56; Anges Ratanga-Atoz, "L'immigration Fang, ses origines et ses conséquences," *Afrika Zamani* 14/15 (1984): 73–81. For the Nzabi and Tsangui-speaking clans, see Dupré, *Un ordre,* 31–39.

19. See Bucher, "The Mpongwe," 274, 354; Patterson, *Northern Gabon Coast,* 48; Elikia M'Bokolo, *Noirs et blancs en Afrique Équatoriale: Les sociétés côtières et la pénétration française (vers 1820–1874)* (Paris: Éditions de l'E.H.E.S.S., 1981), 90–98; Gaulme, *Le pays de Kama,* 185–90; Ambouroue-Avaro, *Un peuple,* 146–56, 180–84.

20. Martin, "Family Strategies," 79–80; and Martin, *External Trade,* 146–48.

21. See Patterson, *Northern Gabon Coast,* 132–36, for a general discussion of the São Tomé trade and the American missionary sources for the 1860s figures; see Roger Sillans, "L'apport des explorations à la connaissance du milieu ethnique gabonais de 1843 à 1893: La rencontre de deux civilisations," (Thèse de Doctorat d'État, Université de Paris I, 1987), 251, for the 1875 estimates from the French marine; for mention of Spanish slave ships and

the São Tomé trade earlier in the century, see T. Edward Bowdich, *Mission from Cape Coast Castle to Ashantee* (London: John Murray, 1819; reprint London: Frank Cass, 1966), 452. See also, for trade between Gabon and São Tomé, François Gaulme, *Le Gabon et son ombre* (Paris: Karthala, 1989), chapters 3 and 4.

22. Bowdich, *Mission from Cape Coast*, 427–34, provides the earliest mention of the "Adjoomba," "Gaelwa," "Eninga," "Okota," "Asheera," and "Okandee" as being active in the Ogooué River trade. Bowdich spent two months in the Gabon Estuary in 1817 and obtained information about the interior from slaves and traders. A number of French studies mistakenly claim that he actually visited the Ogooué. For Bowdich's description, see *Mission from Cape Coast*, 424–25; for the chain of errors, see Avelot, "Recherches sur l'histoire," 369; Raponda-Walker, *Notes d'histoire*, 10, 60, 106, 144; Annie Merlet, *Légendes et histoires des Myéné de l'Ogooué* (Paris/Libreville: Sépia/Centre Culturel Français Saint-Exupéry, 1989), 15, 22, 35; *Vers les plateaux de Masuku*, 24, 56, 181. For the role of the Punu-speaking Bujala and Bumwele clans in the slave trade, see Koumba-Manfoumbi, "Les Punu," 117–21, 150–52, 162–65; for Gisir-speakers as middlemen, see L. Girod, "L'esclavage chez les Eshiras," *AA* (1907): 9–10; for the controversial question of precolonial relations between Gisir- and Galwa-speaking clans in the Lakes region, see Pasteur Ogoula-M'Beye, *Galwa ou Edongo d'antan,* trans. Paul-Vincent Pounah (Fontenay-le-Comte: Imprimerie Loriou, 1978), 61; Paul-Vincent Pounah, *Carrefour de la discussion* (Coulonges sur l'Antize: Imprimerie Reynaud, 1971), 17–20, 72–74; for the Kota-speaking clans, see J. J. Eckendorf, "Une curiosité ethnographique: Les O-kota du bas-Ogooué," (Unpublished document, n.d.); for relations between Galwa-, Enenga-, and Ajumba-speaking clans in the 1860s, see Walker, "Relation d'une tentative d'exploration," 70–73.

23. See Gérard Collomb, "Métallurgie du cuivre et circulation des biens dans le Gabon précolonial," *Objets et mondes* 18, 1/2 (1978): 59–68; and Collomb, "Quelques aspects techniques de la forge dans le bassin de l'Ogooué (Gabon)," *Anthropos* 76, 1/2 (1981): 50–66.

24. The explorer Brazza used the term "district" in reference to these geographical areas; see "Rapport de P. Savorgnan de Brazza sur son expédition dans l'Afrique équatoriale (août 1875 à novembre 1878)," in Henri Brunschwig, *Brazza explorateur: L'Ogooué 1875–1879* (Paris: Mouton, 1966), 113–15.

25. For the cosmological signficance of "upstream" and "downstream" among the Fang people of northern Gabon, see James Fernandez, *Fang Architectonics* (Philadelphia: Institute for the Study of Human Issues, 1977), 1–3; for the mythic upstream river voyage in Mitsogo *bwété*, see Roger Sillans, "*Motombi* mythes et énigmes initiatiques des Mitsogho du Gabon central. Route de la vie," (Thèse du troisième cycle, EPHE, Paris, 1967).

26. For Eviya districts, see Sebastien Bodinga-bwa-Bodinga, *Traditions orales de la race Eviya* (Paris: T.M.T., 1969), 11; also Mathias Mbigui, "Recherche sur l'histoire de Sindara (1858–1946)," (Mémoire de maîtrise, UOB, Libreville, 1984), 17; Léonard Diderot Moutsinga Kebila, "Contribution à l'histoire Eviya" (Mémoire de maîtrise, UOB, Libreville, 1989), 14–15. "Ngesi" was the earliest cluster, its central commercial role indicated by villages named "Bwalè" and "Galoa" and by a folk explanation suggesting that the term "Ngesi" is derived from the English "yes" illustrating contact beginning in the 1860s with English-speaking agents of Hatton-Cookson. Raponda-Walker reports that in 1900 the "Ngossi" ("Ngesi") district of Eviya-speaking clans was on the left bank of the Ngounié between the Samba and Fougamou falls; "Moé" was on the right bank of the Ngounié above Fougamou falls; and "Tomba" was inland from the river on the right bank. He also

notes that the "Eviya Moé" were integrated into a district of Gisir-speaking clans named "Gisira gi Mosonga" which also appears to have been established at the end of the nineteenth century; see Raponda-Walker, *Notes d'histoire,* 103; *Contes Gabonais* (Paris: Présence Africaine, 1967), 220; Archives CPSE, Boîte 1019, Fonds Pouchet, I. *Notes d'histoire,* Raponda-Walker, "Villages de la Basse Ngounié vers 1900"; Bodinga-bwa-Bodinga, Interview Notes I, Fougamou, May 21, 1991.

27. For speculation on the boundaries between the nineteenth-century districts, see Hortense Togo, "La tradition orale des Apindji (Ngounié, Gabon): Origines de peuple, mode de vie, médecine, religion et ethique," (Mémoire de maîtrise, UOB, Libreville, 1988), 26; also Raponda-Walker, *Notes d'histoire,* 126; Stanislaw Swiderski, "Histoire des Apindji d'après la tradition," *Anthropologica* 18, 1 (1975): 91, 105; Joseph Pombodié, Interview Notes XXIV, Mouila, September 30, 1991. For Apindji-speaking clans along the Middle Ogooué, Alfred Marche, *Trois voyages dans l'Afrique Occidentale: Senegal-Gambie-Casamance-Gabon-Ogooué* (Paris: Librairie Hachette, 1879), 197, and Le Marquis de Compiègne, *L'Afrique Équatoriale: Okanda-Bangouens-Osyéba* (Paris: Plon, 1875), 91–92. In 1908, the colonial administrator Georges Bruel listed four districts—which he mistakenly labels "clans"—of Apindji-speaking clans: "Migabi" named after a river; "Diono" also named after a river ("Dioumou" on contemporary maps); "Tando" which means "upstream" in Punu and Gisir; and "Mossimé" whose villages were inland; see Bruel, "La boucle de l'Ogooué," *Revue Coloniale* 96 (1911): 190.

28. Paul B. Du Chaillu, *A Journey to Ashango-Land* (New York: D. Appleton and Company, 1867), 242 (my emphasis). Actually, the reverse was true as throughout the nineteenth century the Dibur-Simbu, a Punu-speaking branch of the powerful Bumwele clan, was moving into the unoccupied space of a Mitsogo district known as Motongo on the right bank of the Ngounié in an effort to obtain slaves and act as middlemen in the flow of people and goods to the coast; see Gollnhofer, "*Bokudu,*" 62.

29. Du Chaillu, *Journey to Ashango-Land,* 296–97, map endpiece; what Du Chaillu refers to as the "Odiganga" was more than likely the Ogoulou and not the Boumi as suggested in E. Jobit, "Mission Gendron au Congo Français, Explorations de la brigade Jobit," *La Géographie,* 3 (1901), 187. For a similar mixture of "Ashango" (Massango) and "Njavi" (Nzabi) in a single village, Du Chaillu, *Journey to Ashango-Land,* 300.

30. Gollnhofer, "*Bokudu,*" 62–63.

31. Paul B. Du Chaillu, *Explorations and Adventures in Equatorial Africa* (London: T. Werner Laurie, 1861), 460–61.

32. Du Chaillu, *Journey to Ashango-Land,* 258.

33. See R. P. Buléon, *Voyage d'exploration au pays des Eshiras* (Lyon: Bureaux des Missions Catholiques, 1895), 21, 68.

34. See Gaulme, *Le pays de Cama,* 223–29.

35. This would be an example of the "confederal regime" described by the Gabonese historian Metegue N'Nah; see Nicolas Metegue N'Nah *Economies et sociétés au Gabon dans la première moitié du 19e siècle* (Paris: L'Harmattan, 1979), 18–20; for discussions of position of *mata,* see Deschamps, *Traditions orales,* 23; Christian Mamfoumbi, "Évolution des sociétés secrètes chez les Gisir du Gabon," (Mémoire de maîtrise, Université Paris Val-de-Marne, 1981), 35–40; N'Dimina Mougala, "Les Gisir," 47–50; Antoinette Goufoura Offiga, "Recherches sur le rôle de la chefferie indigène Gisira dans l'administration coloniale française de la Ngounié," (Mémoire de maïtrise, UOB, Libreville, 1985), 28; Walker, *Notes d'histoire,* 21.

36. Du Chaillu, *Explorations,* 413.

37. Du Chaillu, *Journey to Ashango-Land,* 95.

38. Raponda-Walker, *Notes d'histoire,* 22. This may be the same "Ngossé" or "Ngossi" who was arrested by the colonial administration in 1915; see AOM-AEF (Aix), D 4D 4(1)D13 1915, "Resumés des rapports mensuels, Circonscription des Eschiras, avril-mai 1915".

39. Mbigui, "Histoire de Sindara," 23; N'Dimina Mougala, "Les Gisir," 36; Vincent de Paul Nyonda, *Autobiographie d'un Gabonais: Du villageois au ministre* (Paris: Harmattan, 1994), 104. I would like to express my deep gratitude to the late Mr. Nyonda for sharing with me a portion of his unpublished manuscript during our meetings in July 1991.

40. Du Chaillu, *Journey to Ashango-Land,* 90, 95–96.

41. Raponda-Walker, *Notes d'histoire,* 104; Mbigui, "Histoire de Sindara," 23. When I travelled on the Ngounié in 1991, the Douya, five kilometers upstream from the Doubou, marked the ethnic boundary on the left bank of the river between the Gisira-Tando and the Bapunu though Bapunu villages had recently been established further downstream in the Gisira-Tando district; Interview Notes XI, Jean-Christophe Mabende, Ngounié River, June 17–June 25, 1991.

42. Du Chaillu, *Journey to Ashango-Land,* 158, 210.

43. "Eshira" is the French colonial term for "Gisira." See the maps in Auguste Forêt, "Le Lac Fernan-Vaz," *Bulletin de la Société de géographie* 19 (1898), 309; and R. P. Le Scao, "Autour de Setté-Cama," *Annales de la Propagation de la Foi* (1903), 382.

44. Guipieri interviewed in Mbigui, "Histoire de Sindara," 23; Nyonda, *Autobiographie,* 104.

45. Raponda-Walker, *Notes d'histoire,* 106; Raponda-Walker, "Le sorcier et son oeuvre dans la Ngounié," *AA* (1911): 337.

46. Du Chaillu, *Journey to Ashango-Land,* 94–95.

47. Buali would soon be known as "Ngesi" because of its contact with English traders; Walker, "Relation d'une tentative d'exploration," 76.

48. See discussion in Kopytoff, "Internal African Frontier," 51–52.

49. For the role of *bakanga* among Punu-speaking clans, see Rey, *Colonialisme,* 220–23; for a description of *mùtètì* (appears as "moutette" in French documents) and the salt trade, see Koumba-Manfoumbi, "Les Punu," 244–48.

50. See Raponda-Walker, *Notes d'histoire,* 65–66; Paul-Vincent Pounah, *Notre Passé, Étude historique* (Paris: Société d'Impressions Techniques, 1970), 22; Ogoula-M'Beye, *Galwa,* 174–75. Robert Bruce Walker refers to the "Mpanja" in 1866 as "a fraction of the Igalua (Galwa)" indicating that they considered themselves distinct from other Galwa districts; see Walker, "Relation d'une tentative d'exploration," 79.

51. For a rich description of nineteenth-century trading practices, see Ogoula-M'Beye, *Galwa,* 173–87.

52. Although contemporary Apindji ethnic traditions attest that those Apindji-speaking clans residing on the Ogooué in the nineteenth century remained in contact with those who established districts on the Ngounié, the French explorer, Léon Guiral, who travelled on the Ogooué in 1881, noted that the Apindji-speaking clans with whom he came into contact were "greatly astonished" to learn of "their brothers on the Ngounié"; see Léon Guiral, *Le Congo Français du Gabon à Brazzaville* (Paris: Plon, 1889), 24; for Apindji migration accounts, see Togo, "La tradition orale," 11–18; Swiderski, "Histoire des Apindji," 93–102; and Joseph Pombodié, Interview Notes XXIV, Mouila, October 4, 1991.

53. Walker, "Relation d'une tentative d'exploration," 71; on Nkombé, see Du Quilio, "Voyage dans l'Ogoway," *Revue maritime et coloniale,* 41 (1874), 17–19; Le Marquis de Compiègne, *L'Afrique Équatoriale: Gabonais-Pahouins-Gallois* (Paris: Plon, 1875), 209–43; *Okanda-Bangouens-Osyéba,* 54–70; Alfred Marche, *Trois voyages,* 122–30; 179; Annie Merlet, *Légendes et histoires,* 119–56; and Ogoula-M'Beye, *Galwa,* 199–214.

54. For details on the Azyondo "fetish point," see Walker, "Relation d'une tentative d'exploration," 121–25; M. Aymes, "Résumé du voyage d'exploration de l'Ogooué entrepris par le *Pionnier,* en 1867 et 1868," *Bulletin de la Société Géographique* 17, 27 (1869): 426–29; Compiègne, *Gabonais-Pahouins-Gallois,* 227; *Okanda-Bangouens-Osyéba,* 79. For the story of Ranoké's blindness and its connection to his esoteric power, see Robert Hamill Nassau, *My Ogowe, Being a Narrative of Daily Incidents during Sixteen Years in Equatorial West Africa* (New York: Neale Publishing Company, 1914), 124; and Compiègne, *Okanda-Bangouens-Osyéba,* 83. For descriptions of similar rituals performed by Galwa-speaking clans before the sacred islands of Lake Onangué, see Griffon du Bellay, "Exploration du fleuve Ogo-Wai, Côte Occidentale d'Afrique (juillet et août 1862)," *Revue maritime et coloniale,* 9 (1863): 80–88.

55. For information on Lopé, see Compiègne, *Okanda-Bangouens-Osyéba,* 109–37; Brazza, "Rapport," 112–15; Marche, *Trois voyages,* 206–8; for examples of the salt trade, Compiègne, *Okanda-Bangouens-Osyéba,* 123, 132; Etherelda Lewis, ed., *Trader Horn: Being the Life and Works of Alfred Aloysius Horn* (New York: Simon and Schuster, 1927), 126–27; for the composition and social functions of trading caravans, Ogoula-M'Beye, *Galwa,* 182–83; Charles Bonzon, *À Lambaréné: Lettres et souvenirs de Charles Bonzon, Missionnaire au Congo Français 16 juillet 1893–20 juillet 1894* (Nancy: Berger-Levrault, 1897), 58.

56. See Brazza, "Rapport," 114–15; Avelot, "Recherches sur l'histoire," 375; and discussion in Dupré, *Un ordre,* 28–30, for impact upon the movements and trading practices of Nzabi-speaking clans.

57. As it was still known in 1916 when the missionary Martrou passed through the area; see M. Martrou, "Gabon, Le secret de l'Ofoué, Journal de voyage de Monseigneur Martrou entre Mouila et Boouè (Novembre-Décembre 1916)," *AA* (1923): 60.

58. Marche, *Trois voyages,* 261; Brazza, "Rapport," 114.

59. "Lettre de Fourneau à Dutreuil de Rhins, Booué, 28 août 1885," in Catherine Coquery-Vidrovitch, *Brazza et la prise de possession du Congo: La Mission de l'Ouest Africain 1883–1885* (Paris: Mouton, 1969), 266.

60. Joachim Buléon, "La Mission de Sainte-Croix en face de l'esclavage," *AA* 14 (1899): 79.

61. See Koumba-Manfoumbi, "Les Punu," 79–83, 115, 118.

62. "Texte No. 4, Pierre Koumba-Mamfoumbi, Corpus des Traditions Orales," in Francis-Bernadin César Hygnanga-Koumba, "Recherches sur l'histoire des villages du Canton Ngounié Centrale du début du 18e s. au milieu du 20e s." (Mémoire de maîtrise, UOB, Libreville, 1989), 99.

63. See "Texte No. 3, Norbert Diramba-Moussiali; Texte No. 4, Pierre Koumba-Mamfoumbi, Corpus des Traditions Orales," in Hygnanga-Koumba, "Villages du Canton Ngounié Centrale," 95, 99; Vansina, *Paths,* 224; Micheline Koumba, "Le Dibur-Simbu et la naissance de Mwil-Bapunu" (Rapport de license, UOB, Libreville, 1985), 15.

64. Walker, "Relation d'une tentative d'exploration," 75–76; Compiègne, *Okanda-Bangouens-Osyéba,* 24–35; Marche, *Trois voyages,* 169–73.

65. For a description of travel on the Ngounié between Samba and the districts downriver, see Ogoula-M'Beye, *Galwa,* 184–85; for Nkomi trade at Samba, see Lewis, *Trader Horn,* 80.

66. Ibid., 72, 127–28, 133.

67. Du Chaillu, *Journey to Ashango-Land,* 116.

68. N'Dimina Mougala, "Les Gisir," 8.

69. Du Quilio noted that this was a reason for village movement among Galwa-speaking clans in 1873; Du Quilio, "Voyage dans l'Ogoway," 20.

70. Raponda-Walker, *Notes d'histoire,* 104. *Mboundou,* or *mbundu,* was the name of the most widely practiced poison ordeal. There are a number of descriptions by early explorers; see Du Chaillu, *Explorations,* 256–58; Compiègne, *Okanda-Bangouens-Osyéba,* 69–70; Marche, *Trois voyages,* 158–59; also Raponda-Walker and Roger Sillans, *Rites et croyances des peuples du Gabon* (Paris: Présence Africaine, 1962), 100–101; and more generally, Anne Retel-Laurentin, *Sorcellerie et ordalies, l'épreuve du poison en Afrique noire: Essai sur le concept de négritude* (Paris: Éditions Anthropos, 1974).

71. Du Chaillu counted 191 dwellings in the village of Igoumbié; see Du Chaillu, *Journey to Ashango-Land,* 262–64.

72. See illustration in ibid., opposite 264; also the drawings done by Roger Sillans from the personal notebooks of Alexandre Le Roy's 1893 travels in the area in Raponda-Walker and Sillans, *Rites,* 11, 37, 99, 171, 183, 225, 239.

73. Du Chaillu, *Journey to Ashango-Land,* 380.

74. Raponda-Walker, *Notes d'histoire,* 113; Gollnhofer provides meanings for some of the district names: "Mapanga" translates as "the first"; "Ghesuma" ("Gésuma") is "who goes down"; "Mopindi" is "forest" or "wood"; "Matèndè" is reported to have a more geographical meaning, "in the Louga River basin," which follows in that it was the district furthest west and closest to Samba Falls; "Waka" and "Okobi" are also further west thus suggesting that the geographical names refer to the latest arrivals and the non-geographic names are older districts; see Gollnhofer, "*Bokudu,*" 62–63.

75. Ibid., 63.

76. Ibid., 63–64.

77. This was the case with the Nzabi-speaking clans as well; see Dupré, *Un ordre,* 191–92; "Le commerce entre sociétés lignagères: les Nzabi dans la traite à la fin du 19e siècle (Gabon-Congo)," *CEA* 48 (1972): 641–45.

78. Du Chaillu, *Journey to Ashango-Land,* 322; hunter-gatherers provided services to particular clans not to Du Chaillu's invented ethnic categories.

79. On the difference between "frontiers" and "boundaries," see Ladis K. D. Kristof, "The Nature of Frontiers and Boundaries," *Annals of the Association of American Geographers* 49 (1959): 269–82.

80. "It was this pygmy who sought sites for them so they could establish themselves." This pygmy belonged to the members of the Bumwele clan"; see "Texte No. 3, Norbert Diramba-Moussiali, Corpus des Traditions Orales," in Hygnanga-Koumba, "Villages du Canton Ngounié Centrale," 97.

81. Ibid., 98.

82. See Raponda-Walker and Sillans, *Rites,* 88–95, for some examples.

83. Du Chaillu, *Journey to Ashango-Land,* 80.

84. Koumba, "Le Dibur Simbu," 17.

85. The Gabonese historian François Ngolet argues that *Ongom* is the more fundamental term harking back to an original homeland at the sources of the Ogooué in what is now the Republic of Congo; the term *Kele* (from the verb *u-kelekwé* meaning "those who are suspended or without roots") came to refer to those lineages who migrated furthest to

the west settling along the Gabon Estuary, in the Lakes region and along the middle Ogooué and Ngounié rivers; see Ngolet, "Dispersion Ongom-Bakele," 321–25, and his article "Inventing Ethnicity and Identities in Gabon: The Case of the Ongom (Bakele)," *Revue française d'histoire d'outre-mer* 85, 321 (1998): 5–26.

86. See Deschamps, *Traditions orales,* 128 and Vansina, *Paths,* 91, 325 n 64.

87. See "Annexe II, Migrations anciennes, Abwene Gabriel et Olondo Marcel, Legiembwe, Mai 1989," and "Annexe IV, Migrations Ntombolo, Makobie Louis et Bedone Gustave, Lembunga, Avril 1989," in Ngolet, "Dispersion Ongom-Bakele," 582, 602.

88. Bowdich, *Mission from Cape Coast,* 427; Raponda-Walker suggests that "Samashialee" refers to "Samkita" or "Sambekita" (also rendered "Samquita"), an important district of Kele-speaking clans on the Middle Ogooué in the mid-nineteenth century, though 1818 may be too early to place them on this river; see Raponda-Walker, *Contes Gabonais,* 33, and Avelot, "Recherches sur l'histoire," 373.

89. Bucher, "The Mpongwe," 133–34; also J. Leighton Wilson, *Western Africa: Its History, Condition and Prospects* (New York: Harper, 1856), 258–59, 300–301.

90. R. Avelot, "Notice historique," 216–18; Ngolet, "Dispersion Ongom-Bakele," 456–83.

91. For descriptions of Samkita in the 1870s, see Compiègne, *Gabonais-Pahouins-Gallois,* 232; Compiègne, *Okanda-Bangouens-Osyéba,* 80; Marche, *Trois voyages,* 243–44; Brazza, "Rapport," 102–4. There were probably several districts named "Samkita," as the American missionary Nassau noted in 1874 that the term is from the Kele "Osamu-Kita" meaning "affair of the trade"; twenty years earlier in 1854 another American missionary, William Walker, came across an island further downstream named "Esimbi-akita" (translated as "he stops traders") and François Ngolet, who is Bakele, notes that the term comes from "Sa-okita" (translated as "those of commerce"); clearly the term corresponds to a district and not a clan as indicated in the annotations provided by Raponda-Walker and Roger Sillans to Brazza's account of his first expedition. See Nassau, *My Ogowe,* 112; K. David Patterson, "Early Knowledge of the Ogowe River and the American Exploration of 1854," *IJAHS* 5, 1 (1972): 86; Ngolet, "Dispersion Ongom-Bakele," 393; Brunschwig, *Brazza Explorateur: L'Ogooué,* 102 n 2.

92. See Griffon du Bellay, "Exploration," 79, and Aymes, "Résumé du voyage," 431, for descriptions of Bakele on Lake Onangué.

93. Griffon du Bellay, "Exploration," 79.

94. See Ngolet, "Dispersion Ongom-Bakele," 331–33; also Du Chaillu, *Exploration and Adventures,* 383. It is interesting to note that in the 1880s, Brazza, having determined that members of Fang-speaking clans were more "dynamic" and more likely to work effectively with the colonial administration than other peoples, sought to employ the experienced Okandé to train the Fang in the techniques of *pirogue* navigation along the Ogooué; see "Rapport Général du Commandant Pradier (1886)," in Coquery-Vidrovitch, *Brazza et la prise de possession du Congo,* 442.

95. Du Chaillu, *Explorations,* 384.

96. Brazza, "Rapport," 129; Guiral, *Le Congo Français,* 200–201.

97. "Obindji" seems to have been a titular name that one assumed upon becoming the leader of a Kele-speaking clan. Robert Bruce Walker met an "Obinji" among the Kele-speaking clans on the Ogooué in 1866. The assumption of a new name accompanied the new identity a person took on as he/she went through initiation into the various stages of human existence. Ogoula-M'Beye notes that among Galwa-speaking clans a person obtain-

ing the position of "oga" chose a new name for himself and dropped the old one; from then on no one had the right to refer to their "oga" by his real name. See Walker, "Relation d'une tentative d'exploration," 123; and Ogoula-M'Beye, *Galwa,* 53.

98. Du Chaillu, *Explorations,* 265.

99. Virtually all the peoples of Southern Gabon refer to conflicts with Bakele in their traditions; see Raponda-Walker, *Notes d'histoire,* 114–15, 125; Raponda-Walker, "Les tribus du Gabon," *BSRC* 4 (1924): 83–87, 92; Deschamps, *Traditions orales,* 21–22, 42, 47, 109, 129–30; Gollnhofer, "*Bokudu,*" 198–99, 247–77; N'Dimina, "Les Gisir," 38; Mbigui, "Histoire de Sindara," 19–24; Moutsinga Kebila, "Histoire Eviya," 15; Goufoura Offiga, "Chefferie Indigène Gisira," 19; Jerôme Nziengui Moukani, "Histoire des implantations Bavungu dans la région du sud-ouest du Gabon: Des origines à 1968," (Mémoire de maîtrise, UOB, Libreville, 1988), 39; Moulengui-Mouele, "Esquisse d'étude monographique sur une ethnie Gabonaise: Le cas des Sangu dans la première moitié du XIX siècle," (Mémoire de maîtrise, UOB, Libreville, 1983), 32. In reciting his identification slogan to Du Chaillu in 1859, Olenda, the elderly leader of the Gisir-speaking Ademba clan, referred to the Doubanga ("Ovenga") and Niembe ("Niembai") rivers to the west of his 1859 district which were then occupied by Kele-speaking clans; this suggests that the Ademba may have been pushed out of the area in Olenda's lifetime; see Du Chaillu, *Explorations,* 411.

100. For a description of a fortified Bakele village and mention of trade palavers, see Du Chaillu, *Journey to Ashango-Land,* 91–93; see Ogoula-M'Beye, *Galwa,* 91–92, for the role of hostage-taking; for a general description of "*palabres*" from the perspective of a French missionary priest, see R. P. Maurice Briault, *Dans la forêt du Gabon: Études et scènes africaines* (Paris: Bernard Grassat, 1930), 31–40.

101. Du Chaillu, *Journey to Ashango-Land,* 397–401.

102. Buléon, *Au pays des Eshira,* 8.

103. Ibid., 9–10.

104. Du Chaillu, *Explorations,* 436, 458.

105. Walker, "Relation d'une tentative d'exploration," 75; Compiègne, *Okanda-Bangouens-Osyéba,* 37.

106. AOM-AEF (Aix), B 2B Correspondence Ancienne 1848–1912, "Commandant du Gabon à M. le Ministre de la Marine, le 18 mars 1877"; "Commandant du Gabon à M. le Ministre de la Marine, le 20 juillet 1882"; "Commandant du Gabon à M. le Ministre de la Marine, le 10 décembre 1885"; "Rapport sur la situation politique de la Colonie du 15 juin au 15 juillet 1892"; see also Henri Brunschwig, "Expéditions punitives au Gabon (1875–1877)," *CEA* 2, 3 (1962): 358–59.

107. Nassau, *My Ogowe,* 121–22; René Avelot, "Dans le boucle de l'Ogooué, *Bulletin de la Société de Géographie de Lille* (1901): 240.

108. See Gollnhofer, "*Bokudu,*" 196, 246–70; and his "Les rites de passage de la société initiatique du Bwété chez les Mitsogho: La manducation de l'iboga," (Thèse de doctorat, Université René Descartes-Paris V, 1974), 198–201; Joseph Moukandja, Interview Notes XX, Mimongo, June 6, 1991. Du Chaillu remarked in 1859 that "few Bakalai women have many children"; Du Chaillu, *Explorations,* 388.

109. See Ngolet, "Dispersion Ongom-Bakele, 504–7; Gollnhofer, "*Bokudu,*" 252–54; Raponda-Walker, *Notes d'histoire,* 22, 114.

110. Raponda-Walker, "Au pays des Ishogos, simple récit de voyage," *Le Messager du Saint Esprit* (1910): 177.

111. Merlet, *Vers les plateau de Masuku,* 63.

112. Sebastien Bodinga-bwa-Bodinga, Interview Notes I, Fougamou, May 21, 1991; "Annexe VI, Okoya Charles et Bekote Jean-Louis, Nombakele, Avril 1989," in Ngolet, "Dispersion Ongom-Bakele," 623.

113. On the general function of violence in exchange practices, see Ogoula-M'Beye, *Galwa*, 91–92, 193–94; and Rey, "L'esclave lignager," 520; for a general theoretical discussion, Rey, "Guerres et politiques lignagères," in *Guerres de lignages et guerres d'États en Afrique*, ed. Jean Bazin and Emmanuel Terray (Paris: Éditions des Archives Contemporaines, 1982), 33–72.

114. Ogoula-M'Beye, *Galwa*, 80–81; see also Raymond Mayer, *Histoire de la famille gabonaise* (Libreville: Centre Culturel Français Saint-Exupéry, 1992), 69–84; and Nicolas Metegue N'Nah, "L'Origine du système de filiation matrilinéaire chez les Ngwemyènè," in Metegue N'Nah, *Lumière sur points d'ombre: Contribution à la connaissance de la société gabonaise* (Langres: Imprimerie Guéniot, 1984), 33–52.

115. See discussion in Rey, *Colonialisme*, 90–91.

3

"THE CLAN HAS NO BOUNDARY": COGNITIVE KINSHIP, MAPS, AND TERRITORIALITY

Flexibility and Shifting Clan Alliance

A revealing anecdote from documentation compiled early in this century by the Galwa Protestant pastor Ogoula M'Beye clearly illustrates the primacy of clan allegience (as opposed to "ethnic groups") and demonstrates the flexibility of clan ideology. It concerns the alliance between the Fang-speaking Ebiveny clan and the Galwa-speaking Avanji clan. Fang-speaking clans had moved into the Galwa district of Olombo (Lambaréné) in the 1870s; in order to facilitate exchange with the resident Galwa-speakers the outsiders sought to establish special friendships between clans.[1] Thus in the short span of a decade the Fang-speaking Ebiveny and the Galwa-speaking Avanji were able to establish a clan alliance entailing a number of mutual obligations such as the Ebiveny collaborating with the Avanji in a dispute with another Fang-speaking clan in the mid-1880s. Ogoula-M'Beye provides this account:

> In 1884, in the region of Njambyalika, district of Lambaréné, a Fang from this village killed an Avanji named Okèlè. During this period, despite the presence of the French administration which ruled the region, tribal killings persisted. The Avanji thus went to avenge their brother among the Fang of Njambyalika. The Ebiveny of Kongwè—Andèndè today—were not to be

outdone, they allied themselves with their fellow Avanji in order to massacre the Fang of Njambyalika in spite of their tribal "brotherhood."[2]

Trading friendships could thus be established within a lifetime, and clan correspondence could take a mere generation.

Rey provides a detailed instance of how a trading alliance was established at the beginning of this century in a district of Lumbu-speaking clans located in the savannah stretching southeast from the left bank of the upper Nyanga. It is instructive in that the story begins with initial tension between the two main actors. Ndende was the most influential clan head in the district and Nzungu an ambitious trader whose matrilineal descent was traced from a Tsangui-speaking clan (the Mutsinga branch of the Dikanda) but whose mother was married into a Lumbo-speaking clan. Nzungu, having recently profited from the opportunities open to middlemen in the slave and ivory trade between the coast and interior,[3] sought to impose his authority over the members of his father's clan. These latter resisted and turned to the chief Ndende to block this move. Tensions persisted for a time (Ndende sending spies to stake out Nzungu's village) until Nzungu, after obtaining a powerful charm from a Tsangui-speaking trading friend at Mossendjo,[4] made a dramatic visit to Ndende's village. Differences were worked out over several demijohns of palm wine; Ndende was so impressed with Nzungu's courage that he expressed the desire to take a woman from Nzungu's Dikanda clan as his wife. Nzungu arranged that his niece, Dubondo, marry Ndende. Ndende then arranged it so that Nzungu could trade for ivory among the former's trading contacts at Mossendjo and provided him with the necessary goods: 30 rifles, 30 pieces of cloth, 30 matchets, 30 bags of salt, 30 boxes of powder, 30 blankets, 30 demijohns, 30 forks, 30 spoons, 30 plates and 30 drinking goblets. The caravan was to be drawn from Nzungu's people and when, due to a misunderstanding, they arrived armed at Ndende's village, the latter quickly forgave the affront, citing this newly created alliance. He even provided one of Nzungu's sons, Masafuku Mombo, with a wife from among his dependent women after the young man performed a particularly difficult athletic feat. This new alliance of trading friends was consecrated with a festive meal.[5]

A ritual meal was also the central event in the series of rites (*si nyagane mangè*) undertaken to establish a kinship alliance with the members of a Galwa-speaking clan. As with the Ebiveny and the Avanji clans cited above, the alliance of "two families on good terms with each other" forbade resorting to violent conflict in the case of a dispute. The two clans would rather agree to a defensive alliance in case of an attack from nearby neighbors. To consecrate the alliance, a goat was killed and then prepared with plantains. After the delicious meal, the table companions cut themselves and exchanged blood. They then took out anvils and hammers so as to confirm the act by making incantations to the gods and asking them to wreak vengeance upon all who would violate this freely consented alliance. Henceforth these two families became one, they could no longer intermarry, they became sisters.[6]

As trading opportunities increased in the nineteenth century so did these kinds of alliances. Though Rey justifiably insists upon the distinction between "trade-friends" and "clan alliances,"[7] it does appear to be the case that a trading friend could become incorporated as a clan member in a relatively short period of time. The mutual exchange of female clan members was the key to cementing these relationships.

Between clans who resided within the same district for an extended period of time, patterns of preferential marriage between individual clans developed where the original alliance was renewed through "grandfathers marrying their granddaughters"; that is "a given marriage was only the repetition of an earlier marriage and the continuation of an alliance."[8] The ideology of preferential marriages created a pool of classificatory granddaughters that was actually quite extended; this was then used to determine which women were "marriageable" for the "grandfather/lineage head" but also for the whole male membership of the matrilineage. The marriage of classificatory granddaughters to classificatory grandfathers was an ideal not often accomplished in practice; more often these women were married to nephews of grandfathers within the matrilineage. The knowledge of which lineages and clans could provide eligible candidates for marriage was restricted to male elders and a key source of power in the precolonial order of Southern Gabon.

In the latter half of the nineteenth century, these types of alliances between clans could be maintained only in stable districts like those found among Tsogo-speaking clans and Nzabi-speaking clans located in the commercial source areas of the Du Chaillu Massif. The cultivation of trading friends was not such a prominent concern for clan leaders in the hinterland. A different situation held for those clan leaders established in districts close to the increasingly unstable commercial nodal points to the north along the Ogooué and to the west toward the coasts. Here the growing commercial traffic and the accompanying influx of Kele- and then Fang-speaking clans dramatically expanded opportunities for participation in long-distance trade leading to an increase in the number of trading friends, relationships that in many cases evolved into clan alliances.[9]

What was the relationship between clan authority and precolonial territorial practice? How did clans or clan leaders attempt to affect, influence, or control people, phenomena, and relationships by delimiting and asserting control over a geographic area? The clan leader's authority, it has been argued, rested upon a social definition of territory as opposed to a territorial definition of society. This social definition of territory was expressed in the particular cognitive kinship maps that took form in Southern Gabon.

As Kele-speaking clans opened new spaces for exploitation or as the clans of the Gisira Ngosi left the savannah to be closer to the primary sources in the forest, they established what Igor Kopytoff has labeled "frontier communities." Though they may have physically moved away from the clans in their village of origin, perhaps as the result of a dispute of some kind, the leaders of these frontier villages did not break from the cognitive maps of clans and lineages, and thus recreated in their new settings the particular variety of equatorial tradition developed in Southern Gabon.[10] As these clan and lineage leaders moved through physical space they took with them the cognitive kinship maps through which they affected, influenced, or controlled people, phenomena, and relationships. These cognitive kinship maps provided the idiom through which the movements of clan dependents and trade goods were negotiated. The intertwining journeys of people and objects across the complex web of continual palavers linking the villages within a single district or connecting powerful clan leaders to each other in long-distance trade across savannah and forest were the articulation of a dialectical relationship between the "cognitive" and the "physical" fundamentally different from that derived from the modern capitalist territoriality introduced by the French colonial administration.

The cognitive kinship maps for much of Southern Gabon were marked by a hierarchy of clans modeled on the ideological specializations of the four main clans found in the Chilongo district of the Loango Kingdom.[11] The French missionary priest Meyer reports that these four main clans controlled access to land in the area of what is now the Nyanga province in the independent Republic of Gabon. Their original appellations and ranking in Chilongo were: the Imondo clan, whose totem symbol is the leopard and is in terms of hierarchy the "king," the clan of the Maloango royalty; the Ukonge clan, whose totem symbol is the partridge and represents the "first wife" position; the Bayengi clan, whose totem symbol is the parrot and represents the "second wife"; and the Badumbi clan, whose totem symbol is the "hummingbird" and represents the "younger brother."[12]

Throughout Africa and the world, the idiom of kinship has been used as a metaphor to express political relations and the structure of authority. This is clearly what is occurring above. As the influence of the Loango Kingdom extended into Southern Gabon during the period of the Atlantic slave trade so, too, did this cognitive map of clan hierarchy. It spread north along the coast and into the interior to the east as frontier areas were provided with a "continuous 'feeding'" of these "metropolitan" Loango cultural patterns.[13] This explains why branches of the royal Imondo clan are found occupying positions of importance as far north as the Fernan Vaz.[14]

In the interior among the Punu-speaking districts, the Bumwele—whose most important leader in the 1860s, Mayenge Numbu, enjoyed "a dominant position over a vast zone"—occupied the slot of the "king" clan.[15] It is interesting to note that the "eagle" (*aigle-pecheur*) is a totem symbol for the Bumwele, a clan who rose to prominence by trading slaves, and that the same bird serves as symbol for the abduction of slaves in some of the migratory accounts of the region.[16] Clan correspondences were able to draw from a rich pool of cultural symbols to create and cement their relations. The "parrot" totem has proven to be an effective symbol in this regard. For example, generations of exchange among Tsogo and Sango speakers have resulted in the close relationship between the Pogheo and Sima (both parrot clans), a relationship that was first stimulated by the trade in slaves according to Tsogo tradition.[17]

There are numerous examples of branches of clans, which at an earlier time were probably lineages within clans, that have established alliances with clans speaking other languages. For example, the Gisir-speaking Dibura-Masamba are allied with the Punu-speaking Dibur-Simbu, both branches of larger clans (Bumwedi or Mombi for Dibur-Masamba; Bumwele for Dibur-Simbu) whose affiliations then bring them kinship with the various Gimondu (Imondo) clans found among speakers of Vungu, Varama, Vili, and Lumbo. As Raymond Mayer points out in his history of the Gabonese family, these clan correspondences are dynamic, and their simple delineation is a shorthand for the complex series of scissions and population movements that are the historical stuff of the functional region.[18] They form an intricate web where intermarriage and alliances slip imperceptibly into one another paying no heed to the ethnic categories through which Europeans later sought to understand social relations.

Though the names might change, the cognitive maps of clan hierarchy were continually renewed, manipulated, and ultimately maintained by the elders who established tradition. The example of the Dibur-Simbu is instructive. The collected versions of the origins of the Dibur-Simbu relate that it is a branch of the Bumwele clan and that Simbu was either the niece or the sister of the founding Bumwele ancestor.[19] The stories tell of her marrying and leaving her kin; the original migration of the Bumwele to the right bank of the Ngounié is sometimes telescoped into being contemporary with the movements of the Dibur-Simbu onto the site of the present-day town of Mouila though these events most likely occurred at different periods. The identity of Simbu's husband remains a point of dispute, sometimes reported to be a member of the Punu-speaking Dibamba-Kadi clan or from a Tsogo-speaking clan or from a Nzabi-speaking clan or that he was a dependent hunter-gatherer.[20] In addition, the term *dibur* has historically indicated a dependent relationship to a larger, more powerful clan: in this case the Dibur-Simbu would have been in a dependent relationship to the Bumwele, though in its modern derivation it can simply mean "family" as among Gisir-speakers.[21] These bits of evidence suggest that the Dibur-Simbu were probably at one time in a dependent relationship to the Bumwele but, as a consequence of the actions of Simbu and her descendants—no doubt aided by the opportunities available in the growing slave trade during the last half of the eighteenth and first half of the nineteenth centuries—the Dibur-Simbu were able to establish themselves as a powerful clan and assume the "king" position in the ideology of clan hierarchies allotted to the Bumwele. That the Dibur-Simbu are said to correspond to the various Gimondu clans further supports this scenario.[22] It is in focusing on the ambiguities and silences of the oral traditions as well as the cognitive map in which they are embedded that we can glimpse how through the initiative of talented leaders, even those of dependent status, a lineage was able to impose its influence and thus initiate its incorporation into the patterns of clan hierarchy.

Cognitive kinship maps also posit that certain districts "belong" to particular clans. This is clearly seen at those commercial nodal points where trade had been most fully developed. In the Fernan Vaz, Nkomi-speaking clans controlled well-defined districts which were then further parcelled out according to lineage and village.[23] As described by Agondjo-Okawe:

> The clan leader has powers relative to the granting of individual or temporary rights on the land as concerns authorization to build, plant, fish, hunt, etc. These precarious rights do not concern the ownership of the land but rather its use; this is why the clan leader can by himself decide the granting of these rights and delegate his powers to the lineage or village heads.[24]

When it came to the transfer of land ownership a clan head could not act alone but was obliged to consult a clan council. Usufruct rights were, of course, accorded to members of clans other than one's own and even to clans speaking different languages.

This was certainly the case further in the interior where, for example, Koumba-Manfoumbi has been able to map the districts of Punu-speaking clans in the eighteenth and nineteenth centuries. She notes that "strangers," or *bényi,* who came to these districts through matrimonial alliance or dependent exchange did not have the rights of full clan members and owed tariff obligations in service or in kind (*pahu*) to the clan chief whose charge they were under.[25] But as was seen in the above case concerning the Lumbo-speaking clan leaders Nzungu and Ndende, wealth obtained in trade allowed a powerful "big man" to impose his authority despite being born into the fringes of the clan hierarchy.

What is more, when a wealthy clan leader was particularly active in the exchange of women and dependents, it was not uncommon in the nineteenth century to find the members of the "ruling" clan in a minority to the non-clan members actually resident in the clan's district or village. The Catholic missionary Lejeune noted that in 1890 the blind chief Ranoké was "alone with two or three wives, the only free member of his village. But forty dwellings surrounded his: these are the huts of his slaves, the sons of his slaves and the slaves of his slaves."[26]

These kinds of situations are what led European observers, searching for "pure" members of their invented ethnic categories, to predict the disappearance of those peoples most corrupted by trade, such as the Orungu and the Mpongwe on the coast.[27] Commercial peoples of the interior were not exempt either, as Fourneau claimed that Okandé-speaking clan members of "pure race" were declining in 1885 due to their mixing with Kele- and Simba-speaking clans as well as to the birth-spacing and abortion practices of Okandé-speaking women.[28] Though one would not wish to deny the very negative impact of alcoholism, venereal disease, and other vices of Western civilization, certainly the fictional assumptions of a prior ethnic purity, promoted in many cases by the local clan members themselves, resulted in the invention of categories that significantly distorted the actual situation. For the norm was, and always had been, "mixing" through the exchange of women across the network of clan and trading alliances. Thus identities and their corresponding units were, and always had been, fluid and dynamic.

Given that matrilineal clans were aterritorial and their membership dispersed spatially, it was quite often the case that members belonging to the clan of the ruling elder were the minority in residential units, whether district or village. This situation was exacerbated at the commercial nodal points. First on the coast and later in the interior, those clan leaders most active in the slave trade controlled a number of villages composed entirely of non-clan dependents who often worked plantations and provided the clan leader's main village with food. In 1864 Du Chaillu visited the village of Mouendi, whose chief Nchiengain controlled an important crossing on the left bank of the Ngounié just upstream from the Douya River near what is now Mouila. He noted that Nchiengain was "the leading chief of the Apono (Bapunu) tribe in these parts; but his clan is now, I hear almost extinguished. . . . The people of Nchiengain's village are all Bambais or Bambas—that is, the children of slaves, born in the country."[29] As the trade in rubber, ivory, and ebony created opportunities for greater numbers of clan leaders to participate in commerce, the labor obtained from these dependents became even more essential as they gathered the products from the forest, carried loads, and sometimes even led trade caravans.

The villages where they resided were often called *mpindi*, a general term referring to numerous types of temporary settlements erected in the "bush" for purposes of agriculture, hunting, or fishing. Du Chaillu visited one such village in 1864:

> A march of about a mile beyond the river brought us to a large plantation, the chief slave settlement of the late King Olenda. It comprised a large extent of land cleared from the forest, and contained a village inhabited by the slaves, three or four hundred in number. I was greatly astonished to find the houses better built than in the town of Olenda, and the whole village more neat and orderly. . . . The slave village had its chief, himself a slave, and all called themselves the children of Olenda. He was an Ashango (Massango) man, a chief in his own country, and probably sold into slavery on account of witchcraft. He was a savage of noble bearing, and apparently of good disposition. He had several wives and a large family of children. The other slaves called him father, and he exercised quite a patriarchal authority over them. These plantations supply the household of the chief of the clan with food, and his wives have also small patches of clearing in the same place, which they cultivate themselves with the help of others. The majority of the slaves were inherited by old Olenda, and a great number had known no other master. This village was not the only slave-farm owned by the late chief, but it was the largest of them.[30]

This *mpindi* under the authority of Olenda's Ademba clan was in the forest several miles distant from Olenda's main village on the savannah. It was among the cluster of villages that made up the loosely structured district over which Olenda and the Ademba clan could exercise their authority. But it was not through the delimitation or assertion of control over the

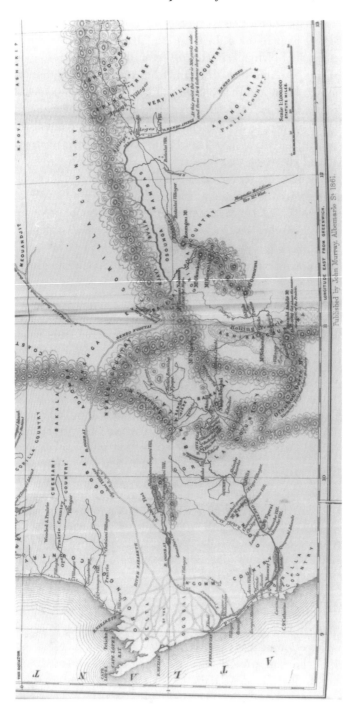

Map 9. Part of the "Map of Western Equatorial Africa showing the Country explored by P. B. Du Chaillu during the Years 1856, 57, 58, & 59." From Paul B. Du Chaillu, *Explorations and Adventures in Equatorial Africa* (London: J. Murray, 1861), endpiece.

geographic area that Olenda had attempted to influence or control the activities of his dependents residing in the forest settlement. It was through the cognitive map of clan ideology that this was accomplished. The Sango-speaking chief of the *mpindi* did not derive his identity from his residence in the physical space of an Ademba territory (in the way any one born in the physical space of the United States can claim American citizenship) but from his position within the cognitive map of Olenda's Ademba clan. His children born to dependent women would assume the identity of the Ademba clan and Olenda's particular lineage—even though he himself had been born into the clan of Sango-speaking women who lived two hundred kilometers to the east. For whatever reason, he was removed from the cognitive kinship map of his mother's clan, and as he moved through the physical space of the forest he likely passed through the cognitive kinship maps of either Eviya-, Vili-, or Apindji- speaking clans before settling among the Gisir-speaking Ademba of which his children would henceforth be adherents. The interaction and exchange between clans was constant, and the Sango-speaking chief's case no doubt reflected innumerable other stories just like it. The knowledge that his offspring had descended from a dependent lineage would be maintained by clan elders and referred to in future situations of marital exchange or intra-clan disputes. The maintenance of the clan's social boundaries—usually the prerogative of a specialized secret society open only to mature adult males[31]—was a much greater priority than the maintenance of the territorial boundaries of the clan's districts.

The cluster of villages over which the Ademba clan had some control certainly had recognizable and accepted boundaries, but in the mid-nineteenth century these were constantly changing as Kele-speaking clans sought to infiltrate districts from their fringes. Clans often consecrated their connection to a particular geographical area by establishing cemeteries where they buried their leading members.[32] The death of an important clan leader and the accompanying rites and negotiations provided one of the rare occasions that the significant members of a matrilineal clan actually came together to physically meet and resolve problems of succession, inheritance and other long-standing disputes.[33] There are even examples within the oral tradition when clan leaders feigned serious illness in order to bring clan members together to deal with a particular crisis.[34]

When the old chief of the Gisira Ngosi, Olenda, died in 1864, Du Chaillu noted that he

> was buried in the cemetery of the chiefs of the Ademba clan, the clan of Ashira over which he had been the head. I say buried, although this term

hardly applies to the custom followed by these people of exposing the corpse above-ground. The cemetery was in a little grove of trees just outside the village.[35]

Olenda's clan was fortunate in that they remained in such close proximity to their cemetery, this despite the fact that Kele-speaking clans may have moved them off the Niembe and Doubanga Rivers at some point in Olenda's long life. Three decades later in 1893, the missionary Le Roy noted that Gisir-speaking clans now traveled great distances to bury their dead, possibly due to the fact they had been physically separated from their clan cemeteries by the incursions of Kele-speaking clans. This is given further credence by Raponda-Walker, who noted in a 1954 article that the names of three cemeteries belonging to the Gisir-speaking Musanda, Puguru, and Buyombu clans were also the names of Bakele villages that had recently been abandoned.[36]

These clan cemeteries do not represent a territorial relationship to a geographic area but a symbolic and ideological one. In addition to cemeteries, individual clans honored the *ombwiri*, or spirits, that inhabited natural wonders such as waterfalls or caves found within their districts; each clan established a connection with a particular site.[37] But when the members of a clan were moved out of a particular district or an established clan absorbed outsiders, these rights could either be transferred, just like dependents, in order to develop alliances, or maintained according to the ideology of clan hierarchy, or re-created in the context of a move into a frontier zone where new sites would be chosen to make these symbolic connections.[38]

The basic cognitive concept operating in the relationship between clan and access to land was that of "firstcomer."[39] At its most fundamental level, this was expressed through the respect afforded hunter-gatherers, the inhabitants of Southern Gabon prior to the arrival of the Western Bantu, and the privilege they wielded in leading clans to settlements and establish boundaries. In terms of a hierarchy between clans, it was always the proclaimed firstcomer to a district who enjoyed the special privileges of distributing land parcels and collecting tribute. In the traditions of the Tsogo-speaking clans of the Du Chaillu Massif, it was the Motoka clan who, with the aid of their hunter-gatherer guide Motsoi, discovered the forest they now inhabit, distributed the land to other clans, and instituted the practices of clan exogamy.[40] Mondadi-Aghetombo, a Mitsogo *evovi* (judge), explained to the anthropologist, Otto Gollnhofer, in the 1960s that:

[T]he whole of the forest was divided into sections by the Motoka clan: That part there is for the Osembe clan; this one here for the Pogheo; that one for the Nzobe; this one for the Ghasanga. . . . These sections of the forest, it's not that we have given them out because of disputes or the resolution of palavers: the cause of this partition is marriage and friendship.[41]

From this position as firstcomer, the Motoka claim an ideological primacy and a particular ritual significance within the practices of the various initiation societies. Due to intermarriage, each Mitsogo district contained representatives of all the Tsogo-speaking clans, though that clan to which the district had been assigned in the original distribution retained certain special rights. Mondadi-Aghetombo gives an idea of how this clan territoriality functioned:

If you pass through the forest of other clans, you must first give something to the people who live there. You must not climb up the fruit trees as they have their owners, they were planted by the "Elders."[42]

However, this was not "ownership" in the modern capitalist sense. Du Chaillu noted in the 1860s that "a man is more respected for his trading goods than for the territory or land he possesses."[43] Control over territory was exchanged in the same manner as goods and dependents in order to solve disputes or advance palaver negotiations. The value of the goods one held and the value of the strategic land positions one controlled were determined by their potential for obtaining adherents.

Oral traditions provide numerous examples. From the Sango-speaking Sima clan[44] living along the Ivindji River in the Du Chaillu Massif it is reported that

a woman named Bilengui from the sub-clan Sima-Kombe na Madoume died due to drowning in the Ivindji River when she was pregnant. This river used to belong to the Motoka clan and was originally called "Diwouwou." As damage payment to compensate for the dead drowned girl, the Motoka clan ceded Diwouwou river to the sub-clan Kombe na Madoume; henceforth the Diwouwou river was called "Ivinzi" [Ivindji] which means: in replacement.[45]

A similar incident was related to Gollnhofer by Ghebonzesekwae, an elder of the Tsogo-speaking Pogheo clan. A female member of the Pogheo sister clan, the Benge, had been married into a Kele-speaking clan and she had two children. Though Kele-speaking clans were patrilineal, the Benge considered these children members of their clan, and when the mother and children drowned along the Ikoy River while fishing, the Tsogo-speaking Benge clan demanded compensation from the Kele-speaking clan as this stretch of the river belonged to the latter.

> Since the river which caused the death of three persons belongs to you, then you, the Bakele, give us another person in compensation (or another thing). As at that time there was no merchandise available, the Bakele responded to the Benge we don't have any merchandise so take the river. And that river was the Ikoy.[46]

The shrewd manipulation of marriage alliances could also be employed to gain access to land. In the mid-nineteenth century, the most numerous and powerful of the Punu-speaking clans controlled the key districts along the trade route to the coastal outlet of Mayumba. These were: the Dibur-Simbu branch of the Bumwele, who oversaw the district on the right bank of the Ngounié where the commercial nodal point Idoumé was located; the Bujala, who operated on the left bank and who were said to be "as numerous as the seeds of gourd"; and the Jungu-pasi branch of the Mitsumba clan, who profited from having a number of hunter-gatherer dependents and residing in a district close to Idoumé. Indeed, the Bumwele and the Bujala had become so numerous from their accumulation of dependent female adherents and the incorporation of their children into the clan that intra-clan marriage came to be practiced and exogamy restricted only to lineages within the clan. Less numerous clans were generally found at less advantageous positions in the trading network unable to claim "first-comer" status in the more lucrative districts. This was the case of the Badumbi and Bagambu. Yet these clans, by contracting marriages with branches of the Bumwele, Bujala, and Mitsumba, were thus able to transfer control of districts to their own members. In giving their female dependents in marriage to the Jungu-pasi branch of the Mitsumba, Badumbi clan leaders were able to obtain control over districts previously under Jungu-pasi jurisdiction. The Bagumbu operated in a similar fashion to impose their authority over districts previously under control of the Bujala.[47]

Territoriality in precolonial Southern Gabon could be exercised only over small strategic chunks of land. Territory was socially defined from cognitive maps drawn from aterritorial clans and lineages; "ownership" in the modern capitalist sense did not exist. Territoriality was merely a strategy among others used to enhance the wealth of one's lineage or clan. Attempts by clan leaders to influence people and phenomena by delimiting and asserting control over districts were intermittent and contextual, and certainly not the predominant concern they are in modern capitalism. It was wealth in people that mattered, and this was obtained through the manipulation of clan and lineage relations, often entailing esoteric knowledge of charms and rituals that would act to assure success. Territory or territorial behavior, to paraphrase Paul Bohannan and Sir Henry Maine, was "an aspect of the group, but *not* the basis of grouping."[48] Precolonial clans and lineages were social groups with territorial dimensions but were not territorial entities in themselves.

We have examined the district, the largest spatial unit found in precolonial Southern Gabon, and have shown that it was a loosely defined cluster of villages uniting the various clans living within its bounds in obligations of self-defense in case of outsider attack. Clan leaders could exercise territoriality in the name of a district by attempting to control the movement of traders and trade goods across district boundaries, an intermittant territoriality extended over a relatively small cluster of villages. It will be recalled that the village was the most prominent unit within the equatorial tradition that developed in Southern Gabon. Thus, it follows that territoriality was most thoroughly exercised at this level; a series of male and female initiation societies were the institutions responsible for controlling people and things within the area of the village and its immediate environs. The most effective of these was a male initiation society most often referred to as *mwiri*.

Mwiri and Territoriality

Mwiri is the most widely used term to describe a masculine association or secret society which during the precolonial era was the most important authoritative body in the life of the clan and village. Early observers described it as an institution of public order that "intended to keep the women, children and slaves in subjection."[49] It was known as *mwiri* among speakers of Gisir, Sango, Varama, Vungu, Punu, Lumbu, Nzabi, Ngowé and Eviya; *omwétsi, mwétsi,* or *mwetyi* among speakers of Mpongwe or Séké; *mwéli* or *mwélé* among speakers of Kele or Benga; *mwédi* among speakers of Nzabi; *mwéé* or *ya-mwei* among speakers of Tsogo; *omwèli* among speakers of Apindji; and *omwiri* among speakers of Nkomi and Orungu. Associations performing similar functions were called *yasi* among Galwa speakers, *indo* or *ukuku* among the Mpongwe, and *ungala* among speakers of Kele and peoples of the upper Ogooué.[50]

As usual, the naming process is fluid. One reason for this diversity was the "tradition of renewal" that existed in precolonial cultural practice where members of a particular initiation society periodically sought to ritually regenerate its authority.[51] This sometimes involved the renaming of the association in order to incorporate attractive new practices introduced by outsiders. Thus it follows that the coastal Mpongwe, who were exposed to and absorbed the traditions of numerous interior peoples during the Atlantic trade, had by the mid-nineteenth century three different societies— *mwetyi, ukuku* and *indo*—performing similar functions.[52]

A second source for the proliferation of terms was due to the series of gradations *mwiri* initiates passed through as they gained maturity in the precolonial world. Each gradation had a different name that could have been used interchangeably with *mwiri*; for example, among Punu-speaking clans, entrance to *idieri* was a first step to initiation into *mwiri* and *ngoji* was a society with similar goals.[53] *Mwiri*-type initiation societies were also adapted to meet specific and immediate needs. This seems to have been the case with the *kono* society created by Tsogo-speaking clans in order to ward off the aggressions of Kele-speaking clans at the end of the nineteenth century. A man already had to be initiated into *ya-mwei* (the Tsogo name for *mwiri*) in order to become a member of *kono*. Members of *kono* were responsible for inflicting the punishments and fines that were required when the precepts of *ya-mwei* were violated. These types of roles have led to speculation concerning the relationship between *mwiri* organizations and the infamous "leopard men" active in the early decades of colonial rule.[54]

Initiation into *mwiri* occurred most often as a boy was entering puberty; it involved a period of isolation, physical hardship and abuse, and the revelation of the secular identity of the *mwiri* masque. This masque had terrorized the initiate as a young boy as it groaned ominously from the forest and rampaged through the village calling out those who had violated its many edicts against theft, adultery, and other behavior deemed detrimental to the public order. The initiate then received a series of tatoos on the left arm just above the elbow and on the left wrist which represented the mark left by the *mwiri* spirit (often called *mangongo*) who sometimes took the form of a crocodile. *Mwiri* initiates, who included all adult men, would take an oath to *mwiri* by tapping the tatoo on the upper left arm with the fingers of their right hand and pronouncing words swearing their allegiance to the *mwiri* spirit.[55] These oaths were often noted by early observers and were used in a solemn fashion to demonstrate sincerity in trade or other kinds of palavers. Flouting a *mwiri* oath could result in death. In the 1840s an American missionary noted that

When a covenant is about to be formed among the different tribes, *Mwetyi* is always invoked as a witness, and is commissioned with the duty of visiting vengeance upon the party who shall violate the engagement. Without this their national treaties would have little or no force. When a law is passed which the people wish to be especially binding, they invoke the vengeance of *Mwetyi* upon every transgressor, and this, as a general thing, is ample guarantee for its observance.[56]

Indeed, as foreign traders sought to establish themselves in the interior in the latter half of the nineteenth century, both African and European found it to their advantage to become members of *mwiri.* Aloysius Smith, better known as "Trader Horn," active along the Ogooué and Ngounié Rivers in the early 1880s, related that some of his African assistants were eager to become members of *Yasi,* the form of *mwiri* practiced by the Galwa-speaking clans and that he himself "had the pleasure of being initiated" in "a special ceremony . . . necessary for a white man." Once a member he "could *Ranga Yasi* (swear by saying *Yasi*) which meant calling *Yasi* to witness what I said, and I would be believed by all members of the fraternity."[57] At the turn of the century, a Senegalese, "Dioconda or Dongonda Cisogo" (probably "Cissoko"), in service to the colonial administration with years of experience trading among the Kele-speaking clans in the area of Samba Falls, was able to facilitate the travels of the colonial official René Avelot due to his having been "initiated into a kind of secret society presided over by Bakele fetishers."[58] This secret society was most likely *mwiri.*

Ironically, as the growing commerce in rubber, ivory, and ebony drew more participants into the trading networks and led to the creation of commercial nodal points where European factories were the primary attraction, the role played by *mwiri*-type associations in trade diminished. This occurred first in Libreville where *ukuku,* whose Mpongwe-speaking members had once been able to effectively boycott foreign traders, "early lost its position, for the population was too heterogeneous and there were too many diverse interests."[59] Similarly, as Lambaréné developed into a European commercial nodal point from the first half of the 1870s, *yasi* started to lose its influence. The establishment of Protestant and Catholic missions and their Christian teachings further undermined the power of *yasi.* Already in 1879 Mengila-Nguva, a young Galwa student at the Protestant mission run by the American Presbyterian R. H. Nassau dared to publicly mock *yasi.* He was accused of revealing its secrets to the missionaries and to Galwa women and was abducted by Galwa members of *yasi* from the Wombolyé district. Nguva was to be put to death but Nassau learned of this plan and sent a group of missionaries and traders to rescue the boy.[60] The Catholic priest Lejeune tells of a similar episode that occurred in the mid-1880s and, by 1895, he boasted that in and around Lambaréné "le *Yaci* est mort."[61] This pronouncement was a bit premature, as a revival of *yasi* among the Galwa in Lambaréné, organized by a chief named Rigondja, took place at the turn of the century.[62]

Mwiri was central to much of the economic, political, and religious order of precolonial Southern Gabon, and its members were responsible for important ritual functions in ceremonies organized around the birth of twins, in the preparation of the poison ordeal *mbundu,* and in conducting the postmortem autopsies on persons believed to have harbored in their bodies a kind of evil substance related to witchcraft.[63] A masculine society whose goal was to regulate the behavior of its members' female dependents, *mwiri* served as a kind of surveillance force that watched over the wives of men whose trading activities took them from their village for months on end. For a nineteenth-century Galwa-speaking trader whose activities took him to Samba Falls on the Ngounié, information regarding his wives' infidelities could be used to explain an unsuccessful journey or, in the case of a successful journey, used to vaunt his trading abilities since he had succeeded in spite of his wives' behavior.[64]

Mwiri had its feminine counterpart, which is most usually known as *njembe* or *nyembe*. This latter association also sought to maintain the public order (it was particularly effective in discerning the identity of thieves) and commanded a good deal of respect from men.[65] In the myths accounting for the origin of *mwiri,* it is usually women who discover the *mwiri* spirit while out fishing at a river; when they return with it to the village (the spirit is often said to be in the form of fish or crocodile), the women either neglect it or do not realize the significance of their discovery and the men take the spirit for themselves and organize a society to venerate it.[66]

In terms of territoriality, *mwiri* represented the most prominent attempt by a group to affect, influence, or control people, phenomena, and relationships by delimiting and asserting control over a geographic area. It has been described as a "kind of league for the protection of Nature and the maintenance of public places, doubling as a secret police meant to search out and punish guilty parties whoever they may be."[67] The geographic area over which *mwiri*'s authority extended included the public space of the village where the cavernous call of the *mwiri* spirit from the forest at night would signal to the women of the village to begin cleaning the plaza and surrounding paths of any unwanted overgrowth the following day.[68]

But also coming under *mwiri*'s jurisdiction were those areas used by the village for hunting, fishing, gathering, and agriculture. This could cover a considerable expanse and usually encompassed the former sites of the village, which often served as secondary plantations. The *mwiri* society determined whether a particular area's resources were at risk of depletion and created "local nature reserves," where for a period of several years it was forbidden to hunt, fish, cut down trees, or gather fruits; infractions resulted in sanctions.[69] The paths leading to these restricted areas were cordoned off by a rope of banana leaves or by vines suspended from two trees. Charms were also used to communicate these boundaries; these could consist of:

> magic plants wrapped in a black or red tissue or placed in a bottle containing water and other ingredients. These "medicines" were generally dangled from a fruit tree, a felled palm tree, or simply hung in the field, this preventing anyone from laying waste to a field or picking fruits that were not yet ripe.[70]

Violating these charms could bring on illness and even death. The offending party might also be sold into slavery. The Catholic missionary Joseph Coignard relates that: "In 1908, in the Tandou mountains along the Remboé River, an affluent of the Ngounié, I succeeded in setting free an Eshira [Gisira] woman, sold as a slave with her three children, due to a theft of pineapples protected by the Mwiri taboo."[71]

François Gaulme notes the similarity in function of *mwiri* associations and their maintenance of the trade routes leading into villages with those associations that maintained the physical and sacred character of the roads leading out of the Loango capital of Buali in the seventeenth and eighteenth centuries.[72] The *lemba* association, so brilliantly analyzed by John Janzen, seems to be a related association as well. It served to monitor the public space of the markets that developed in the districts along the Niari and Kouilou Rivers. Membership in *lemba* was limited to the growing sector of wealthy traders, and its influence extended into the Punu-speaking clans of the upper Nyanga. Like *mwiri*, *lemba* provided an alternative—well adapted to trade—to the centralizing forces resulting from booming commerce. Indeed, its formation was an effort to cope with the development of wealthy traders and permanent markets, features not present in much of Southern Gabon which was less intimately connected to the more active commercial regions of the Pool and the lower Congo. Thus, *lemba* was not practiced in the source areas of the Du Chaillu Massif inhabited by Nzabi-speaking clans.[73]

Though virtually all adult males were members of a *mwiri*-type organization (without this pedigree one remained classified a child or a women), its territorial practices were limited to locally defined geographical areas and resisted centralization. Members of different clans residing in different districts could recognize themselves as members of similar organizations but *mwiri* provided neither a cultural identity nor political structure superseding clan affiliation. In fact, it was initiation into *mwiri* that prepared a young man for the acquisition of knowledge about his clan and lineage history and their relationship vis-à-vis other clans and lineages.

This transfer of knowledge was often the province of a separate society, or perhaps grade of *mwiri*, known as *nzeo, nzegho,* or *tsieno*. It was here that a man learned which lineages had dependent origins, which lineages had exchanged women between them, and which lineages offered possibilities for marriage. This was restricted information and open only to mature males who had fathered children. A particular class of judge, called *evovi* among Tsogo-speaking clans, was usually the holder and the dispenser of this body of knowledge, known as *bokudu* (or *bukulu* among Gisir-speaking clans). Here was contained the "stuff" of the cognitive kinship maps and it was available to only a limited sector of the population: elder men. Along with the fabrication of charms and the ability to use them, this knowledge formed the "symbolic capital" that matched the "wealth in people" represented by a powerful big man's accumulation of adherents and prestige goods.[74]

By the second half of the nineteenth century, *mwiri*, however, was coming into more intimate contact with territorial practices of a modern capitalist society, where territory defined society and the tools available to expand territory were exceptionally powerful. The gradual development of new nodal points centered around European factories and Christian missions led to confrontation and the undermining of the basis of *mwiri's* authority. It is not at all surprising that the battle lines should have been so clearly drawn with *mwiri* and its related associations on one side, and the factories and the missions on the other. The next chapter examines the impact of early European penetration into Southern Gabon and the modern instruments of territoriality that facilitated this process.

Notes

1. Nassau, *My Ogowe*, 101; Ogoula-M'Beye, *Galwa*, 100.
2. See Ogoula-M'Beye, *Galwa*, 100; Metegue-N'Nah uses this anecdote to argue for the relatively recent development of Gabonese "tribalism." In the rural regions of Gabon today one can still witness the predominance of clan connections over ethnic identity as I

did in 1991 when I accompanied a Massango hunter seeking to trap game on "foreign" Apindji territory; the hunter used his matrilineal membership in the Massango Sima clan (which has the parrot for a totem) to link with the corresponding Apindji clan and thus facilitate his trapping activity. At one point in the negotiations an Apindji elder exclaimed, "This Massango/Apindji thing, it's not important." See Metegue N'Nah, "Les relations inter-ethniques au Gabon au XIXe siècle," in Metegue N'Nah, *Lumière*, 24–26; Jean-Christophe Mabende, Interview Notes XI, Saint-Martin, June 25, 1991.

3. Koumba-Manfoumbi notes that the booming commercial opportunities of the nineteenth century saw the rise among Punu-speaking clans of a new social category based on recently accumulated wealth, *bandumba*. Blacksmiths, weavers, and even foreign outsiders successful in commerce, such as Nzungu, could become *bandumba*; Koumba-Manfoumbi, "Les Punu," 162.

4. Tsangui-speaking clans were important producers of iron and controlled access to the ore deposits in and around Mossendjo. The other peoples of Southern Gabon believed that the Tsangui possessed incredible esoteric powers due to their smelting expertise. For example, Raponda-Walker reports that upon the passing of Haley's Comet in May 1910, "the Bavili, Mitsogo, Evia and other populations of the Ngounié maintained that it was a new weapon of war fabricated by the Batsangi (a talented race of blacksmiths) in order to kick the Europeans out of the country"; see Raponda-Walker, "Dénominations astrales chez les Mpongwè de Libreville et autres tribus de langue *omwènè*," *BSRC* 24 (1937): 199. For the role of Tsangui precolonial metallurgy, see G. Dupré, *Un ordre*, 31–43; 98–105; Collomb, "Métallurgie du cuivre," 59–60; and Collomb, "Quelques aspects techniques," 64–66.

5. Rey, *Colonialisme*, 221–22.

6. Ogoula-M'Beye, *Galwa*, 165–66.

7. Rey, *Colonialisme*, 220.

8. See discussion concerning this practice among the Nzabi in G. Dupré, *Un ordre*, 169–70.

9. Rey notes that the rubber trade incorporated far more lineage heads into the networks of long-distance commerce than slavery ever did; Rey, *Colonialisme*, 283–84.

10. Kopytoff, "Internal Frontier," 22.

11. See Map 2 in Martin, *External Trade*, 12.

12. Meyer, "Hiérarchie des clans," 1–2; Meyer also notes that this hierarchy is symbolized in the features of the famous white masks of the region. For an excellent study of these "white masks" and the related *mukudj* masquerade, see Alisa LaGamma, "The Art of the Punu *Mukudj* Masquerade: Portrait of an Equatorial Society," (Ph.D thesis, Columbia University, 1995); for features of masks as an expression of political relationships among the nearby Téké-tsayi people, see Marie-Claude Dupré, "Masques de danse ou cartes géopolitiques? L'invention du Kidumu chez les Téké tsayi au XIXe siècle (République populaire du Congo)," *Cahiers des Sciences Humaines* 26, 3 (1990): 447–71.

13. Kopytoff, "Internal Frontier," 75.

14. "Appendix: Clan List and Correspondences," in Gray, "Territoriality," 512–25.

15. Rey, *Colonialisme*, 106.

16. Bodinga, *Traditions orales de la race Eviya*, 10; Bodinga, Interview Notes I, Fougamou, May 21, 1991.

17. See Gollnhofer, *"Bokudu,"* 193–95. According to Tsogo traditions, intermarriage with all their neighboring peoples was originally stimulated by the trade in slaves; see also, "Appendix: Clan Lists and Correspondences," in Gray, "Territoriality," 512–25.

18. Mayer, *Histoire de la famille gabonaise,* 65.

19. Koumba-Manfoumbi, "Les Punu," 79–83, 110–11; Koumba, "Dibur-Simbu," 11–16; Hygnanga-Koumba, "Villages du Canton Ngounié-Centrale," 37, 95.

20. Koumba-Manfoumbi, "Les Punu," 79; Koumba, "Dibur-Simbu," 13.

21. Rey, *Colonialisme,* 102–3; Koumba-Manfoumbi, "Les Punu," 143; Raponda-Walker, *Notes d'histoire,* 103.

22. See Gray, "Appendix I: Clan List and Correspondences," in Gray, "Territoriality," 512–25.

23. Agondjo-Okawe, "Représentations et organisations endogènes de l'espace chez les Myene du Gabon (Nkomi et Mpongwe)," in *Enjeux fonciers en Afrique Noire,* ed. E. Le Bris, E. Le Roy, and F Leimdorfer (Paris: ORSTOM/Karthala, 1982), 103–4.

24. Agondjo-Okawe, "Les droits fonciers," 22–23.

25. Koumba-Manfoumbi, "Les Punu," 161; see also Rey's discussion of *pahu* (which he spells *pawu*) in Rey, *Colonialisme,* 108–10.

26. R. P. Lejeune, "L'esclavage au Gabon," *Annales de la Propagation de la Foi* (1891): 339–40.

27. See K. David Patterson, "The Vanishing Mpongwe: European Contact and Demographic Change in the Gabon River," *JAH* 16, 2 (1975): 217–38.

28. "Lettre de Fourneau à Dutreuil de Rhins," in Coquery-Vidrovitch, *Brazza et la prise de possession du Congo,* 267. On the Okandé, see also Sautter, *De l'Atlantique,* 755, and Payeur-Didelot, *Trente mois au continent mystérieux: Gabon-Congo et côte occidentale d'Afrique* (Paris: Berger-Levrault, 1899), 174.

29. Du Chaillu, *Journey to Ashango-Land,* 231–34; *yibamba* is the term presently used among Punu-speakers to refer to white people.

30. Ibid., 141. In 1895, Mary Kingsley visited the "slave villages" belonging to Galwa-speaking clans near Lambaréné; see Mary H. Kingsley, *Travels in West Africa: Congo Français, Corisco and Cameroons* (London: Macmillan, 1897), 219; for a general discussion of the role of *mpindi* settlements, see Sautter, *De l'Atlantique,* 779–80.

31. Among Sango and Nzabi speakers this society was known as *nzewo* and among Punu speakers, *tsieno;* see Biwawou-Koumba Manonza, "Histoire, ethnologie et clans des peuples du Sud Gabon" (Unpublished document, Libreville, 1974), 1; and Rey *Colonialisme,* 124.

32. For descriptions of burial practices reserved for lesser personages such as slaves, see Robert Hamill Nassau, *Fetishism in West Africa: Forty Years' Observation of Native Customs and Superstitions* (London: Duckworth & Co., 1904), 231–35; and Raponda-Walker and Sillans, *Rites,* 103–8.

33. For a detailed discussion of the negotiations that are conducted at funerals, see Simon Augoueli-Matoka, "Sur les institutions funéraires chez les Gisir du Gabon," (Mémoire de maîtrise, Université de Caen, 1979).

34. See "Texte No. 10 and Texte No. 11, Hubert Moukaga, Corpus des Traditions Orales," in Hygnanga-Koumba, "Villages du Canton Ngounié-Centrale," 117, 122.

35. Du Chaillu, *Journey to Ashango-Land,* 132.

36. Raponda-Walker and Sillans, *Rites,* 107; Raponda-Walker, "Les cimetières de familles au Gabon," *RG* 4 (1959), 7.

37. For examples, Raponda-Walker and Sillans, *Rites,* 126; and Pascal Mboumba, "Contacts historiques et culturels entre Mitsogo et Fang au Gabon," (Mémoire de maîtrise, Université de Paris I, 1981), 61. For a dispute between the Punu-speaking Dibur-Simbu and Mussand clans over the sacred *Mangondu* forest (next to the main cemetery in Mouila)

and the *Mugumi* water spirit of the Ngounié, see Koumba, "Le Dibur-Simbu," 18, and LaGamma, "Art of the Punu," 60–67.

38. See Pierre Bonnafé, *Histoire sociale d'un peuple congolais, Livre II: Posseder et gouverner* (Paris: ORSTOM, 1988), 31–34, for a pertinent discussion of the symbolic nature of the links between Kukuya lineages and their sacred woods. Also Rey's discussion of the Punu institution of *mukuna* demonstrates that precolonial territorial practices were in a complex relationship with non-territorial concerns, such as access to the esoteric power of the ancestors, and not the dominant practices found under modern capitalism; see Rey, "L'esclavage lignager," 512–15; Rey, *Colonialisme,* 151–54.

39. Kopytoff, "Internal African Frontier," 52–61.

40. Gollnhofer, *"Bokudu,"* 243–45.

41. Ibid., 244.

42. Ibid., 245; see also the discussion in Alain Maclatchy, "Monographie de la subdivision de Mimongo," (Unpublished document, Layoulé, 1936), 71–76.

43. Du Chaillu, *Journey to Ashango-Land,* 17; for useful discussions of attitudes toward land and conceptions of wealth, see Paul Bohannan, "Africa's Land," in *Tribal and Peasant Economies,* ed. George Dalton (New York: Natural History Press, 1967), 51–60; and Guyer, "Wealth in People," 243–65.

44. See "Appendix: Clan List and Correspondences," in Gray, "Territoriality," 512–25.

45. Biwawou-Koumba Manonza, "Histoire," 5.

46. Gollnhofer, *"Bokudu,"* 198.

47. Koumba-Manfoumbi, "Les Punu," 118–22; Alisa LaGamma has collected an account of the Djungu clan's transfer of land to the Badumbi at Moabi; Alisa LaGamma, personal communication.

48. Bohannan, "Africa's Land," 57.

49. Wilson, *Western Africa,* 395

50. Raponda-Walker and Sillans, *Rites,* 226; Ngolet, "Dispersion Ongom-Bakele," 356.

51. See John Janzen, "The Tradition of Renewal in Kongo Religion," in *African Religions: A Symposium,* ed. Newell S. Booth, Jr. (New York: NOK Publishers, 1977), 69–115, for a discussion of the continuity provided by this practice during the colonial period among a neighboring people. More generally on religious ritual and renewal, see Mircea Eliade, *The Myth of the Eternal Return or, Cosmos and History,* trans. Willard R. Trask, (Princeton, N.J.: Princeton University Press, 1974).

52. Nassau, *Fetishism,* 248. Certain practices associated with *mwiri,* such as a spirit speaking from underground and ritual scarification on the upper arm, were observed by Andrew Battell at the end of the sixteenth century; see E. G. Ravenstein, ed., *The Strange Adventures of Andrew Battell* (London: Hakluyt Society, 1901), 49, 56–57.

53. Koumba-Manfoumbi, "Les Punu," 172, 180, 285–86; see also Père Lejeune, "Superstitions africaines: Le Ntilo et le Yaci au pays des Galoas," *AA* 10 (1895): 32, for mention of the advanced "Yaci" (*yasi*) grades of "Epowé," "Eyoga," and "Konou."

54. Gollnhofer, *"Bokudu,"* 95–99, 257–70; Raponda-Walker and Sillans, *Rites,* 236; leopard men are discussed in chapter 7.

55. See Raponda-Walker and Sillans, *Rites,* 227–32; Raponda-Walker, "Les tatouages au Gabon," *Liaison* 65 (1958): 36–39; Stanislaw Swiderski, "Les agents éducatifs traditionnels chez les Apindji," *Revue de psychologie des peuples* 2 (1966): 204–7; Mamfoumbi, "Evolu-

tion des sociétés secrètes," 99; Ngolet, "Dispersion Ongom-Bakele," 240–42; Otto Gollnhofer and Roger Sillans, "Phénoménologie de la posséssion chez les Mitsogho, Aspects psycho-sociaux," *Psychopathologie Africaine* 10, 2 (1974): 189–92; Gollnhofer and Sillans, "Cadres, éléments et techniques de la médecine traditionnelle Tsogho: Aspects psychothérapiques," *Psychopathologie Africaine* 11, 3 (1975): 305–8; Gollnhofer and Sillans, "Aperçu sur les pratiques sacrificielles chez les Mitsogho: Mythes et rites initiatiques," *Systèmes de Pensée* 5 (1979): 167–74; Gollnhofer and Sillans, "Le mythe de la découverte du génie de l'eau chez les Mitsogho," *L'Ethnographie* 1 (1981): 37–46.

56. Wilson, *Western Africa*, 392.

57. Lewis, *Trader Horn*, 56; for further less credible details, 71–72. Merlet is not accurate in thinking that Horn was initiated into *bwiti*; Merlet, *Légendes et histoires des Myéné*, 67; for Aloysius Smith's experiences in Southern Gabon, see also Tim Couzens, *Tramp Royal: The True Story of Trader Horn* (Johannesburg: Raven Press, 1992), 91–191.

58. Avelot, "Dans le boucle," 252; "Notes sur les pratiques religieuses des Ba-Kalè," *Bulletins et mémoires de la Société d'anthropologie de Paris*, 2 (1911), 287–88.

59. Nassau, *Fetishism*, 147.

60. Nassau, *My Ogowe*, 322; Lewis, *Trader Horn*, 192–93; Couzens, *Tramp Royal*, 154–55; Paul-Vincent Pounah, *Concept Gabonais* (Monaco: Société des Éditions Paul Bory, 1968), 53–54.

61. Lejeune, "Superstitions africaines," 32–35.

62. See "Cte. de St. François de Lambaréné," *BCSE* 8 (1901–1902): 591.

63. Raponda-Walker and Sillans, *Rites*, 115–21; Gollnhofer, "*Bokudu*," 115–17; Mamfoumbi, "Évolution des sociétés secrètes," 99; Stanislaw Swiderski and Marie-Laure Girou-Swiderski, *La poésie populaire et les chants religieux du Gabon* (Ottawa: Éditions de l'Université d'Ottawa, 1981), 66–78; Cécile Balouki-Moussa-Manzanz, "Tradition et modernité chez les Punu du Gabon: La santé de la femme enceinte et celle du nouveau-né de l'ère coloniale à nos jours," (Mémoire de l'EHESS, Paris, 1983), 133.

64. Ogoula-M'Beye, *Galwa*, 187.

65. Wilson, *Western Africa*, 396–97; Du Chaillu, *Explorations and Adventures*, 293–94; Fleuriot de Langle, "Croisières à la côte d'Afrique," *Le Tour du Monde* 31 (1876): 277; Compiègne, *Gabonais-Pahouins-Gallois*, 139; Avelot, "Pratiques religieuses," 294; Nassau, *Fetichism*, 247–62; Raponda-Walker and Sillans, *Rites*, 239–53; Mamfoumbi, "Evolution des sociétés secrètes," 104–5.

66. For versions of the myth, see Archives CPSE, Boîte 1010, Dossier B (IV), Fonds Pouchet, "P. Joseph Coignard, Étude sur les principaux fétiches et sociétés occultes des pays Eshiras-Apindjis-Isogo (Hte. Ngounyé-Gabon-A.E.F.), le 7 juin 1926"; P. Le Scao, "Au Pays de Sette-Cama," *Le Messager du St. Esprit* (1908), 255–56; Gollnhofer, "*Bokudu*," 228; Gollnhofer and Sillans, "Le mythe," 37–46; Pounah, *Concept Gabonais*, 50; N'Dimina Mougala, "Les Gisir," 58; Pierre Sallée, "L'arc et la harpe: Contribution à l'histoire de la musique du Gabon," (Thèse de doctorat, Université de Paris X, 1985), 181–84; and Anselme-Moïse Orendo Sossa, "Recherches sur l'histoire des Pové: De la période ante-coloniale à l'aube de la colonisation," (Rapport de recherches, UOB, Libreville, 1985), 34. An account from Marcel Guebenda collected by Moutsinga Kebila in 1988 suggests a symmetry between *mwiri* and *nyembe* as the *bolo* spirit in *nyembe* originally belonged to men but was given to women when the former obtained the *mwiri* spirit; see Moutsinga Kebila, "Histoire Eviya," 85–87; this is also indicated in Père Coignard's 1926 study.

67. Raponda-Walker and Sillans, *Rites*, 232.

68. Ibid., 233–34.

69. Ibid., 232; see also discussion in Maclatchy, "Sub-division de Mimongo," 77–78.

70. Charles Mombo Maganga, "Un siècle d'histoire varama: Seconde moitié du XIXe s., première moitié du 20e s.," (Mémoire de maîtrise, UOB, Libreville, 1986), 91.

71. P. Joseph Coignard, "Étude sur les principaux fétiches."

72. Gaulme, *Le pays de Cama,* 110; also Martin, *External Trade,* 22–23.

73. Janzen, *Lemba,* 54–79; Rey, *Colonialisme,* 133.

74. Biwawou-Koumba, "Histoire," 1; Rey, *Colonialisme,* 124; Orendo Sossa, "Histoire des Pové," 35; Moulengui-Mouele, "Le cas des Sangu," 28; Mamfoumbi, "Évolution des sociétés secrètes," 31; Gollnhofer, *"Bokudu,"* 5.

4

THE INSTRUMENTS OF COLONIAL TERRITORIALITY

The Impact of Early European Penetration

Throughout the latter half of the nineteenth century, the territorial practices of the various clans inhabiting Southern Gabon remained dominant. The decentralized patchwork of districts held together by the intricate weave of clan and lineage ideology still held sway over most of the region though more uniform cloth was already being sewn over districts along the Ogooué.[1] However, much had occurred in the fifty years between 1850 and 1900. In 1850, there were no European factories located in the Southern Gabon hinterland. By the turn of the century a series of commercial waves had flooded the region with European products, and in their wake factories run by Europeans and their African agents dotted the major trade arteries.[2] A steadily accelerating absorption of the functional regions of Southern Gabon into the networks of global capitalism through the exploitation of rubber, ivory, and ebony placed great strain on the existing social definition of territory and laid the foundation for the modern capitalist territorial definition of society imposed by French colonialism.

In the latter half of the nineteenth century, the penetration of Europeans and their agents undermined the territorial practices of the Southern Gabonese clans at several levels. First, the movements of European and African traders from the coast into the interior in ever increasing numbers from the 1860s altered the disease environment of Southern Gabon and resulted in a number of deadly smallpox epidemics. Smallpox had existed on the coast of West Central Africa from at least the sixteenth century, and epidemics periodically occurred at trading settlements servicing the Atlantic slave trade.[3] An especially deadly outbreak began at the Angolan port of Ambrizette early in 1864; by June a French steamer had spread it to Libreville and the Estuary, decimating the local population.[4] Due to precolonial territorial practice where clan leaders controlled a single link in the commercial chain of relations and were thus able to restrict access further inland to their trading partners, the outbreak of smallpox epidemics had remained a coastal phenomenon until the mid-nineteenth century.

One of the first European treks into Southern Gabon, that of Paul Du Chaillu and his entourage of Fernan Vaz Nkomi-speakers, was most likely responsible for spreading the 1864 epidemic from the coast to the hinterland. Not only did this early European penetration prove a harbinger for the colonial domination that was to come but it also established the pattern—disease carriers from the coast moving along trade routes in the interior—by which syphilis and sleeping sickness later spread.[5] Du Chaillu first learned of the outbreak in January 1865 while staying with the old chief Olenda in the Gisir-speaking Ngosi district where one of the chief's nephews was taken ill with an unknown disease. The explorer recognized the symptoms described to him as smallpox and the nephew died the following day.[6]

In less than a week, the smallpox had infected most of the village. Olenda himself became sick and died. It soon spread throughout the Ngosi district:

> The once cheerful prairie of Ashira had now become a gloomy valley of the dead; each village was a charnel-house. Wherever I walked, the most heartrending sights met my view. The poor victims of the loathsome disease in all its worst stages lay about in sheds and huts; there were hideous sores filled with maggots, and swarms of carrion flies buzzed about the living but putrid carcasses. The stench in the neighborhood of the huts was insupportable. Some of the sick were raving, and others emaciated, with sunken eyes, victims of hunger as well as of disease. Many wretched creatures from other villages were abandoned to die in the bush.[7]

By the middle of 1865, the epidemic had spread east to the Tsogo-speaking districts on the right bank of the Ngounié. Du Chaillu was perceived by the local population as being responsible for its dissemination.[8]

After a series of misadventures among Sango-speaking clans in the hills of the Du Chaillu Massif stopped his eastward trek, the explorer retraced his steps and passed through the devastated Ngosi district in September 1865 before arriving at the Rembo Nkomi, where the smallpox epidemic had hit particularly hard. Quengueza, the leader of the Nkomi-speaking "Abouya" (Abulia) clan that controlled trade along the river, lost his entire family and was forced to abandon and relocate his village. Many of the Kele-speaking clans established on the Rembo also suffered losses and had abandoned their villages; the influential leader Obindji was one of the victims.[9]

> Almost every one we met bore traces on his or her face of the ravages of the small-pox; and there was not one who had not lost a near relative during these unhappy times. In fact, the Abouya clan of the Commi (Nkomi) is almost destroyed; in a few years there will be nothing left of this people, once the most important clan of the Rembo.[10]

The smallpox epidemic did indeed lead to the decline of the clan's dominance as by the 1890s Kele-speaking clans had established districts and controlled trade on the Rembo.[11] Similar shifts in district configuration certainly occurred in other areas affected by the outbreak.

The epidemic of 1864 and 1865 had a profound impact among the peoples of Southern Gabon who justifiably associated the spread of disease with the arrival of Europeans in their districts. Both the British trader R.B.N. Walker in 1866 and the French Lieutenant Aymes in 1867 pointed to the fear of smallpox as a reason for their not being allowed to penetrate further into the interior.[12] A second major outbreak occurred in 1877 along the middle Ogooué and appears to have been spread by Savorgnan de Brazza and his entourage during the explorer's first expedition. Albert Schweitzer, writing in the 1930s, was told by "old people" living in Lambaréné that in 1886 on the lower Ogooué "an epidemic of smallpox . . . destroyed nearly half the population."[13]

Sporadic outbreaks occurred throughout the 1890s: 1892 in the Fernan Vaz and at the end of 1896 in the Ngosi District. These culminated in another serious epidemic in and around the commercial nodal point of Samba on the Ngounié in 1897 and 1898.[14] Vili-speaking clans, who had been active participants in the flow of trade to the Ogooué, were decimated. Raponda-Walker reported that all families suffered losses and that there were "cadavers everywhere, sometimes two or three in the same hut." The important village of Mubu, an hour's walk from Samba Falls and nearly one kilometer in length, had to be abandoned, and by 1899 all that remained was "a pile of rubble." Indeed, the number of Vili-speaking clans was reduced to four.[15]

These Vili-speaking clans never recovered from the losses sustained during this epidemic and quickly became marginal players in the commerce of the area. Their experience illustrates how the introduction of new epidemic diseases undermined precolonial territoriality. Vili-speaking clans were key middlemen traders in the 1860s and 1870s, established as they were at the commercial nodal point at Samba. But beginning at this same period they were being challenged by Kele-speaking clans assuming strategic positions on the left bank of the Ngounié and thus disrupting their river connection to the Ogooué. In the 1890s, the Bakele clan leader Ndimba terrorized Vili villages, leading raids to obtain slaves and dependent women. Though he was finally killed in an attempt to attack the village of Mubu in 1898, the power and influence obtained by Ndimba indicate an atmosphere of aggression and growing insecurity that undermined territorial practices associated with stable districts and accepted clan status.

The smallpox epidemic of 1897 and 1898 further accelerated this process as the number of deaths forced a reconfiguration of the kinship system; whole clans disappeared and then regrouped under the four main survivors. Drastic alterations regarding the claims and enforcement of "first-comer" clan status no doubt occurred as Kele- and, in the 1890s, Fang-speaking clans (most notably the Esindok from which the colonial post of Sindara derived its name) moved into strategic locations in and around Samba.[16] The abandonment of an important village like Mubu, a strategy often resorted to in times of crisis, resulted in the dispersal of members of Vili-speaking clans to villages of Eviya-, Gisir-, or even Kele-speaking clans and the return of Vili clan dependents to their villages of origin.

At the occurrence of an epidemic a period of chaos ensued where the elements of precolonial territoriality—control over access to neighboring districts and resources, the claims of "first-comer" status within a district by various clans, the ritual functioning of initiation societies like *mwiri,* and the loose functioning of districts themselves—were tossed to the wind to be sorted out once a semblance of stability returned. The trouble was that from the 1890s until well into the 1920s there would be very few moments of stability over much of Southern Gabon. Precolonial territoriality, a fragile and circumstantial practice to begin with, would have little opportunity to reconstruct itself once the instruments of modern territoriality effectively appeared and altered the landscape.

The establishment of factories and the introduction of small river steamers (the first travelling up the Ogooué in 1862) signaled the permanent entry of Europeans as participants in the struggle for control over the commercial nodal points of the network. From 1867, the British firm Hatton and Cookson was established at the key nodal point at the confluence of the Ngounié and Ogooué Rivers (See Map 1). By the mid-1870s, they were joined by several other British and German firms; French factories generally played a marginal role in European commercial activity until the creation of the concession system at the turn of the century. The explorer Compiègne noted in 1874 that the European factories had already carved out their niche and that "the blacks from all the tribes at present know perfectly well where the factories are located, and come there themselves, often from very great distances, to bring their ivory and their rubber."[17] The presence of European factories stimulated a considerable increase in the volume of trade in Southern Gabon; the American Protestant missionary Nassau noted a large increase in traffic on the Ogooué above Lambaréné between 1875 and 1876.[18]

The earliest European explorers of Gabon recognized that the complex chains of middlemen traders and the practice of giving advances for products to be obtained months in the future were unacceptable obstacles to capitalist-style commerce; it was hoped that the creation of European factories would undermine this system.[19] Though the European traders would continue to provide credit for future goods into the twentieth century, the increased trade from the presence of factories did alter the system of clan and commercial alliances almost immediately as Kele- and Fang-speaking clans accelerated their movements into strategic commercial areas. By 1882 Fang-speaking clans, active in the area of Lambaréné since 1875, were capable of cutting off river access to the Ngounié in order to express their dissatisfaction with European trading practices.[20]

Trade continued to increase on the middle Ogooué throughout the 1880s, with the European factories further adding to the instability through the ruthless behavior of their agents (more than six hundred were active on the lower and middle Ogooué in the mid-1880s) and the introduction of guns and gunpowder on a scale hitherto unknown. Thus at the outset of De Brazza's famous West African Mission in 1883, much of the Ogooué was already in turmoil.[21]

The West African Mission lasted two years, from 1883 to 1885, and though De Brazza exaggerated its accomplishments—claiming to have definitively broken the chain of clan and trading alliances operating on the Ogooué—he did sever some links, and this aided the growing influence of Fang-speaking clans. Rubber exploitation above the Kele-speaking district of Samkita had been unknown in the mid-1870s, but a decade later Fang-speaking clans, in classic fashion, were exploiting previously neglected areas and establishing new overland trade routes on the periphery of existing districts. They then took over strategic nodal points and created Fang-speaking districts on the Ogooué itself, successfully competing against the Okandé-speaking clans of the Lopé district. The latter exploited their experience in river transport and provided the wage labor required to move goods and personnel between the newly established colonial posts. These developments created a chain reaction where Kele-speaking clans and others previously active on the Ogooué sought to strengthen their control over secondary water and overland routes on the southern left bank between the Ngounié and Offoué. The resulting tensions were certainly a factor in the series of conflicts that occurred between Kele- and Tsogo-speaking clans during the 1890s in the Du Chaillu Massif.[22]

Members of Fang-speaking clans were not the only ones to profit from the new opportunities provided by the burgeoning trade. Mpongwe-speaking traders from the Gabon Estuary were for a time able to exploit successfully their historical commercial links to Southern Gabon. In 1877, a certain Ngeza, in the employ of Hatton and Cookson, ran a small factory and traded for rubber among Vili-speaking clans near Samba. In 1873, Compiègne met a Mpongwe trader named Digomi, who collected rubber, ivory, and ebony from Kele-speaking clans established on Lake Oguemoué. A decade, later, in 1882, this man had apparently extended his activities further east as the Catholic missionary Bichet came across a "Dégoma" whom he described as enjoying a certain influence on the Ngounié. In 1895, Mary Kingsley met a Mpongwe merchant named Mr. Glass who had been active on the Ngounié. An important consequence of these traders' endeavors was the spread of the Mpongwe language as the commercial lingua franca used by those operating along the middle Ogooué and lower Ngounié.[23]

Further south on the commercial networks extending out of Mayumba and the Ndogo Lagoon, Portuguese and Afro-Portuguese traders were more active with a Portuguese pidgin often functioning as a commercial lingua franca in many districts.[24] In the 1880s, Aloysius Smith travelled up the Ngounié to Samba and heard that south of the Tando district of Gisir-speaking clans, "Portuguese convicts who had large quantities of slaves cut a large quantity of rubber" and that due to their aggressive tactics "the country was in a state of ferment."[25] As the British firms began to dominate more and more of the Southern Gabon trade in the 1880s and 1890s, English came to be widely used, much to the annoyance of the new French colonial administration.[26]

Mpongwe and Portuguese commercial influences were vestiges from the period of the Atlantic slave trade, but the growing importance of

Senegalese traders in Southern Gabon was a more recent development. First arriving as auxiliaries in the French military garrison established on the Gabon Estuary in 1843, Senegalese were active in trade on the lower Ogooué by 1867.[27] Hatton and Cookson employed a certain "Youssouf" to collect ebony from Fang- and Ajumba-speaking clans on Lake Azingo in the 1870s; the firm also benefited from the services of "Mané" at their factory in Lambaréné. The most influential Senegalese trader in the lakes region was certainly Kerno Mahmadou-Seydiou. Sent as a political exile to Gabon by the French, Kerno had a factory in Lambaréné in 1874 and had been trading on the Ogooué for a number of years. From 1877, the French benefited from his services as a mediator in trade disputes between Senegalese and Fang- or Kele-speaking clans, noting that "his influence had become considerable" on the middle and lower Ogooué.[28]

The Senegalese took advantage of the rapidly growing volume of trade and its consequent disruptions by exploiting the violent and aggressive tactics traditionally used in commerce such as confiscating *pirogues* and taking hostages to force the payment of debts. Though Senegalese usually took wives from the clans with whom they traded, their insertion into the kinship exchange networks associated with stable districts was only partial, this allowing them to operate with a greater ruthlessness. By 1881, as agents for the German Woermann firm, they had broken the Enenga-speaking Azyondo clan's control over access to the Okandé-speaking districts. They were also credited with introducing the practice of hostage-taking to this region. In the previous decade Senegalese traders had been in continual conflict with Kele- and Vili-speaking clans further down the Ogooué. Whereas within the local networks of commercial and clan alliance violence was resorted to in order to advance a palaver, Senegalese and European traders took to burning down entire villages in the pursuit of their interests. Local clan leaders were quick to adopt these techniques, the shift from control over people to the destruction of property aptly symbolizing the confrontation between different conceptions of wealth. The newly created colonial administration occasionally despaired of the chaos and disruption resulting from Senegalese trading activity—which included middlemen roles in the clandestine slave trade—but De Brazza, for one, appreciated their role in breaking the links of the precolonial trading system along the Ogooué.[29]

It was through the growing influence of these foreign outsiders that modern territoriality came to confront the precolonial practices of Southern Gabon. Senegalese or Mpongwe traders lived in villages, married local women, and became members of influential initiation societies; in this way they wielded power in the manner of a traditional clan leader. Yet they were different in that they were often agents connected to a European factory, a newly established outpost of the modern capitalist system. The rubber, ebony, and ivory that they collected were sent off to a world where transactions were recorded in writing and where the literate instruments of modern territoriality were employed to ensure the efficient organization of labor, transport, and communication. The growing trade brought the peoples of Southern Gabon a step closer to direct contact with these modern instruments. Senegalese factory agents, by obtaining positions of power in the network of commercial and clan relations, helped to undermine existing practices and to open the way for the imposition of modern ones.

Until his death in 1902, a Senegalese named Sada-Ndiaye was "the most feared and the most obeyed" figure along the trade routes in the Punu-speaking districts inland from Mayumba. The colonial administrator Le Testu remarked:

> Sada-Ndiaye abducted women or had them handed over to him, sold children, appointed himself the heir of his friends, and, if necessary, used his firearms as far as the banks of the Ngounié at Dilolo. He had "soldiers" and knew how to use them. Yet he was a foreigner. Chiefs from earlier times did not hold onto their authority, when they had any, by means any different from those employed by Sada-Ndiaye.[30]

But there was a difference and this was observed at the village level in the commercially active Ngosi district in 1893 by the Catholic missionary R. P. Joachim Buléon. In earlier days, clan leaders had controlled trade within their districts, but in districts like Ngosi their authority was being superseded by outsiders who temporarily established themselves in villages to participate in commerce. Arriving in the village of Mbia-ni-Shongo on a branch of the Moufoubou River, Buléon was met by a Nkomi-speaking trader from the Fernan Vaz. Though an outsider, it was the trader, in the chief's absence, who provided hospitality to the missionary. A generation earlier it had not been uncommon for a trader to spend several months in a village or district a considerable distance from his home to negotiate or collect debts. However, with the introduction of European factories and the boom in rubber and ivory, traders, now agents often in European employ, settled for longer periods in villages and assumed new positions of authority. Buléon remarked that

> during his stay in the interior, (the trader) cuts a grand figure. As he is rich, he has many friends, and they often rely upon his arbitration. Sometimes the

trader knows how to read and write a little: then he can quickly pass for an oracle, and his prestige, if he knows how to maintain it, knows no bounds.[31]

From Appropriating Gaze to Naming Space

Rivers without names and countries without maps. . . ."
—Aloysius Smith (Trader Horn)[32]

To govern territories, one must know them . . . unless a region is first conceived of and named, it cannot become the specific subject of a map.
—Matthew Edney[33]

It is significant that Buléon mentioned the ability of traders to read and write, as literacy is central to the exercise of modern territoriality. The instruments of modern territoriality are products of what the geographer David Harvey has labeled the "Enlightenment project," in which a European "totalizing vision of the globe" sought to order knowledge according to universal categories.[34] For the critic Mary Louise Pratt, these categories are the expression of a "planetary consciousness" that emerged in the first half of the eighteenth century "marked by an orientation toward interior [geographical] exploration and the construction of global-scale meaning through the descriptive apparatuses of natural history."[35] The upshot of this "Enlightenment project," or European "planetary consciousness," was that by the end of the nineteenth century, according to Harvey, " the world's spaces were deterritorialized, stripped of their preceding significations, and then reterritorialized according to the convenience of colonial and imperial administration."[36]

The first stage of this process was the possession of space in the "appropriating gaze" of the European observer. By the middle of the nineteenth century, vision had long since become the dominant sense in European bourgeois modes of perception, and when explorers such as Du Chaillu or De Brazza ventured into unchartered areas like Southern Gabon they did so with "imperial eyes" capable of incorporating the specificity of all they surveyed into the universalizing categories of the Enlightenment.[37] Indeed, a study on the creation of colonial space in German South West Africa suggests "there is a certain sense in which vision amounts to colonization."[38]

In 1858, Du Chaillu visited the Apindji-speaking clans of the Koï district on the Ngounié; his account reveals several key elements of the

European appropriating gaze. First, the explorer viewed their labor in terms of capitalist notions of productivity and remarked that the "Apingi are, for Africans, a very industrious people" as "the men do some *work* here" making a fine quality raphia cloth. Second, he interpreted clan-controlled access to fruit trees as evidence of private property, this showing "that the Apingi have made a very important step in advance of the Bakalai and Shekiani, and all the other tribes I have met." Finally, he presaged the colonial concern of controlling population movement and fixing the peoples of Southern Gabon in colonial territory by noting these Apindji-speaking clans "are a settled people, and need only flocks and cattle to make them a prospering nation." Du Chaillu contrasted this to the mobility of villages found in districts closer to the commercial nodal points on the coast.[39]

Pratt suggests that Du Chaillu's gaze was somewhat ambiguous, a less confident version of the "monarch-of-all-I-survey" trope employed by contemporary travelers such as Richard Burton. The passage she selects from *Explorations and Adventures in Equatorial Africa* contains the elements of imperial mastery and envisions the transformation of the equatorial forest through its contact with Christian and capitalist civilization. But in the passage Du Chaillu's musings are interrupted by the presence of a "serpent" hanging from a branch above him, and as a consequence his vision "of forests giving way to plantations of coffee, cotton, spices; of peaceful negroes going to their contented daily tasks; of farming and manufactures . . . vanished in a moment."[40]

Du Chaillu's threatening serpent was significantly symbolic of a European vision that had long been disturbed by the unknown mysteries of the forest.[41] Indeed, the equatorial forest of Gabon presented an acute challenge to the appropriating gaze of those explorers, missionaries, and colonial administrators who sought to bring order to its perceived chaos. The perspective required for the "landscape discourse" of the "seeing-man" was simply unobtainable from within such closed quarters.[42] The dense equatorial forest served as a formidable obstacle to the visual dominance of space and effectively disoriented the European gaze. Mary Kingsley noted that spending a night in the Gabonese forest was "like being shut up in a library whose books you cannot read all the while tormented, terrified and bored."[43] The French administrator George Bruel equated the impossibility of grasping the fullness of the forest landscape to the condition of a myopic "who, without his glasses, can see only details."[44]

Thus it took a man of extraordinary vision and energy to see beyond the details and conjure up the images required to carve a colony out of the daunting environment of the equatorial rain forest. Such a man arrived on the scene in the form of Pierre Savorgnan de Brazza. De Brazza was an Italian-born aristocrat who became a French citizen as a consequence of his service as an officer in the French navy. The three voyages he undertook to the interior of Gabon between 1875 and 1885 culminated in the formation of the colony of French Congo in 1886. De Brazza's dreams of transforming into productive colonies what for Europeans were underpopulated, impenetrable, and unhealthy equatorial environments have been rightly labeled "visionary." His was a passionate gaze bordering on obsession as he often wildly exaggerated the impact of his missions and the commercial potential of the regions he explored. The explorer Stanley thought he was crazy when they met at Malebo Pool in 1882. Yet it was from De Brazza's vision that the physical form of Gabon the colony took shape. Thus he has been referred to as "a prodigious 'inventor of space.'"[45]

Writing served to mediate the impact of the gaze. De Brazza's vision was expressed through his travel accounts, maps, and bureaucratic reports; these existed in a textual space which prefigured the changes in physical space that occurred as colonial rule became more effective.[46] Different "explorers" might depict aspects of their individual "gaze" as well as the times in which they travelled. As a naval officer, De Brazza was keenly interested in cartography, for example. But Du Caillu and De Brazza shared similar views of the untold wealth and promise of power that lay in the equatorial regions as they sketched in regions along their routes while leaving blank spaces for the "unknown."

The act of Europeans writing about the nonliterate peoples and the hitherto "unseen" environment of Southern Gabon in the mid-nineteenth century had two important consequences. First, it initiated an ongoing dialogue between textual and physical space through which the territorial units of colonial and independent Gabon were forged. This is the same dialectical relationship outlined above that exists between a society's cognitive map and physical reality; the distinction resides in the textual elements of the nineteenth-century European cognitive map which were not found in the cognitive maps of the precolonial equatorial tradition. It was the power afforded by writing that ultimately allowed the French to spread the modern practice of territoriality to Southern Gabon.

Second, writing provided the European gaze with the ability to negate the spaces and practices of the nonliterate peoples of Southern Gabon. The ability to write gave European explorers, missionaries, and colonial administrators the power "to classify and supplant existing *unwritten* meaning."[47] One of the objectives of De Brazza's West African Mission of 1883 to 1885 was to break up the complex network of trade relations that controlled commerce on the Ogooué so as to clear space for the unhindered long distance trade of the recently established European factories. Although he was only partly successful in this regard, the passage below, referring to the practice of providing advance credit to a series of middlemen in lieu of future compensation (not at all appreciated by European traders), clearly reveals his goals: "It was necessary to clear the ground before this state of affairs could pass out of the practices of these primitive peoples; and then it was necessary to organize the commerce of the region on another basis."[48]

"Clearing the ground" was first accomplished in the travel account and accompanying maps before it became a reality in the physical space of Southern Gabon. It would not be until the 1920s that the commerce of the region was effectively organized along the lines envisioned by Brazza. However, the ability of the written text and other literate tools (such as mapping) to empty space of its local, unwritten significance was a clear expression of "a real inability of the European eye to look at the world and see anything other than European space—a space which is by definition empty where it is not inhabited by Europeans.[49] This point is neatly illustrated by the map Brazza used in public lectures given in France early in 1886; much of Southern Gabon is simply blank; empty because it had yet to come under the full force of the European appropriating gaze (see Map 10).[50]

Writing was quickly perceived by the peoples of Southern Gabon as being the source of European power. Nearly all travel accounts describe the attitudes of awe and respect inspired by the European acts of reading, writing, or sketching.[51] Du Chaillu related that when Apindji-speaking villagers saw him "write they at once exclaimed that I was about to make cloth, and this was the pattern."[52] While stopping in a village of Kele-speaking clans near the mouth of the Ngounié in 1876, Nassau noticed on the wall in one of the dwellings an "alphabet card" that had been taken from his mission:

> I did not demand it, but asked for it. They would not give it up. They said they had bought it, paying a gun for it! That was lying. The chart was worth perhaps 5 cents: a gun cost $3. . . . The preposterous falsehood was only a high bid, they thinking I would pay for my white-man's "book," which was knowledge, which was therefore power.[53]

Paper and writing paraphernalia soon entered into the store of symbols employed in the myths and legends of local oral traditions. Marche wrote of a legend that circulated among Galwa-speaking clans in the late 1870s where a women had appeared among them to predict a short dry

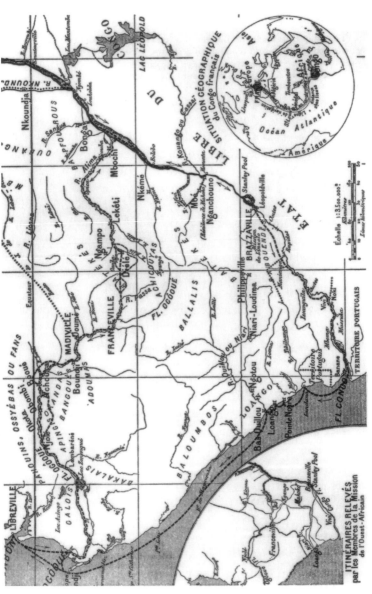

Map 10. Part of the Map used by De Brazza for a public address, Paris, 1886. From the Minutes of the Meeting of the *Société de Géographie*, Bibliothèque Nationale, Paris, p. 112.

season and consequent food shortage; Marche was told that this woman was "carrying a child on one arm, and in the other hand was holding a *paper* that we were not able to read since we are not white."[54] The colonial encounter with writing also altered the various origin myths of the region as the instruments of power of the French administration had to be incorporated and explained. In the *bokudu* traditions of Tsogo-speaking clans, this was accomplished by explaining humanity's separation into three distinct "races": "Pygmies," "Whites," and "Blacks." The myth relates that Motsoï, the progenitor of all humanity, offered to the representatives of the White and Black races two trunks, one large and one small. The blacks chose first and picked the large one containing machetes and axes. The whites waited and opened the second trunk which contained pencils and paper. This particular version, told by the Mitsogo elder Otakambamba in the early 1960s, concludes: "This is why you (whites) are left with wealth, because you are left with the medicines, the medicines needed for writing; this is why we do not know how to write."[55]

The appropriating gaze and the ability to write that which was previously unwritten allowed European colonial agents to impose their practice of "naming space."[56] At its most pompous level, this process saw explorers naming natural wonders like lakes and falls after European royalty; Du Chaillu, for example, named the series of rapids on the middle Ngounié "Eugénie Falls" in honor of the French Empress.[57] The production of a name in the textual space of a travel account or on a map was the first step to its entering into local parlance. Some geographical terms, such as Eugénie Falls, never made it beyond a textual reality; others, such as the "Du Chaillu" massif and the "Ngounié" River, came to be widely used as the colonial state and practices of modern territoriality became effective.

As we have seen, the naming practices of the peoples of Southern Gabon during the precolonial period were fluid and reflected a different perception of space than that employed by Europeans. The "bird's-eye view" perspective provided by map-making was not available to the local inhabitants, who gave names to rivers, streams, lakes, savannahs, and mountains but who did not have names for vast expanses of space like the forested mountains that came to be known as the "Du Chaillu Massif." Districts, of course, had names but were not larger than 500 square kilometers, and their boundaries not known to be depicted graphically in masks or sculpture. Indeed, it would have been virtually impossible to identify these types of geographical features without the perspective gained from mapping.[58]

The naming of the key waterway in Southern Gabon further illustrates this confrontation between fundamentally different conceptions of space and the power of writing. What has come to be known as the "Ngounié" River on the maps of the colony and independent nation of Gabon is known to Gisir- and Punu-speakers as "Durèmbu-du-Manga," to Apindji-, Eviya-, and Tsogo-speakers as "Otèmbo-a-Manga" and to Kele-speakers as "Mèlèmbyè-a-Manga." The first part of each of these names is a generic term for "body of water" while *manga* refers to a species of dwarf palm abundant along the river's banks. "Ngounié" is the French deformation of "Ngugni," a term used by the Vili-speaking clans settled around Samba in the mid-nineteenth century to refer to the northern frontier of their district ("Nsina-Ngugni"). This term "Ngugni" was then employed to refer to the river by the Galwa-, Enenga-, Ajumba-, Orungu-, Nkomi-, and Mpongwe-speaking traders who came to the Samba nodal point for commerce. When Du Chaillu and R.B.N. Walker reached the river with guides speaking the above languages, they initiated the name appropriation process by writing down "Ngouyai" or "Ngunyé" on their maps and in their text.[59]

On the map of Du Chaillu's 1856 to 1858 travels, the Ngounié is inaccurately depicted, as the explorer believed he had penetrated 200 kilometers further into the interior than he had actually gone. In addition, the middle and upper segments of the river are labeled "Rembo Apingi" (Apindji) and "Rembo Apono" (Punu), this reflecting local conceptions of space where naming was limited to segments of large rivers and determined by the identity of those inhabiting its banks (see Map 9). The more precise conception of a single, all-inclusive name for a European geographical feature called "river" was not known. Indeed, among Tsogo-speaking clans, the branches of a large river are considered the latter's "children" and the great rivers like the Ogooué are viewed as being "born" from the sea. Thus the notions of "river mouth" and "source" are the reverse of European conceptions.[60]

Maps and Mapping

Du Chaillu, having received a good deal of criticism for the many inaccuracies found in his first map, sought to develop a more refined appropriating gaze on his return to Europe and thus learned how to take positions through astronomical observation and compass bearings before going back to Southern Gabon in 1864. His efforts resulted in a more accurate map for European purposes and one in which the term "Ngouyai" effectively replaced local river terms in textual space. In this he initiated the process of emptying the space of Southern Gabon of its specificity and clearing the ground for the imposition of modern territoriality.[61]

Maps were particularly effective instruments in this regard. Recent work in the history of cartography seeking to insert the map and process of its creation into social and cultural history have been of considerable assistance in understanding these developments. From this new vantage point, "maps constitute a specialized graphic language, an instrument of communication that has influenced behavioral characteristics and the social life of humanity."[62] Firmly ensconced in the tide of historical events, maps and mapmaking lose their innocence and are no longer viewed as neutral, objective representations of physical space. They embody instead a form of knowledge subject to the manipulation and control of those who exercise, or seek to exercise, territoriality. European explorers, missionaries, and colonial administrators arriving in Southern Gabon shared in the cognitive map of the West where "mapmaking was one of the specialized intellectual weapons by which power could be gained, administered, given legitimacy and codified."[63] The geographer J. B. Harley plainly states that "as much as guns and warships, maps have been the weapons of imperialism."[64] The ability to map, as with the ability to write, allowed for the creation of a textual space where the physical space of the real world was abstracted, reified, and emptied of its autochthonous unwritten meaning. Thus, "while the map is never the reality, in such ways it helps to create a different reality."[65] The Portuguese had begun the naming and mapping of the coastal space of Gabon in the fifteenth and sixteenth centuries but virtually nothing was known about the interior until the second half of the nineteenth century.[66] The mapping of the Ogooué was begun in 1862 and grew in sophistication as explorers travelled further upstream toward its source. Yet its complex delta system was not accurately drawn until a colonial hydrographic mission was undertaken in 1911.[67] Du Chaillu's maps remained the principal sources of information for the Ngounié until the creation of the French Congo colony in 1886, though Père Bichet published a rough map of the lower Ngounié in 1882, indicating villages and factories between the Ikoy and Samba as well as affixing ethnic designations (see Map 11).[68] At around the same time, Aloysius Smith, in service to the trading firm of Hatton and Cookson, tells of making a "navigation chart" of the Ngounié and of a map he "drew of the big slave roads" to the coast servicing Samba and the middle portion of the river.[69] These maps were privileged information, as maps so often were throughout history, and as trade secrets specific to the concerns of Horn's firm they were not meant for publication.

De Brazza's West Africa Mission of 1883 to 1885 had as one of its tasks the correction of cartographic errors and the filling in of blank spaces. A good deal was accomplished along the Ogooué although, as previously

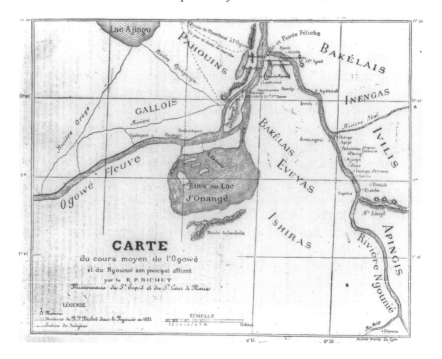

Map 11. The Middle Reaches of the Ogooué and Ngounié. From R. P. Bichet, "Quelques jours dans l'Ogowé (Afrique Occidentale)," *Les Missions Catholiques*, 1882, p. 583.

noted, the map distributed to the Parisian public at the *Cirque d'Hiver* early in 1886 left much of the space of Southern Gabon blank (see Map 10).[70] It would be the task of the new French Congo colony to map this area. Missions cutting across the Du Chaillu Massif from the colonial post of Lastoursville (created in 1885) on the Ogooué to Samba on the Ngounié were organized in 1890 and 1893. It is significant that in 1893 the colonial administrator Godel was accompanied by Monseigneur Le Roy and Père Bichet of the Holy Ghost Fathers' mission.[71]

Inventing Ethnic Identity: Naming through Text, Map, and Census

> Until a collective cultural identity receives a proper name, it lacks, in an important sense, a recognizable sense of community (both by members and outsiders).
>
> —Anthony D. Smith[72]

Just as the rivers and hills of Southern Gabon were named and thus appropriated for European purposes, so were the area's populations. Peoples had to be named and then fixed in the bureaucratic textual spaces of the map and census so that their movements and activities could then be controlled within the physical space of the French colonial territory. The policies of village "regroupements"—first undertaken in Southern Gabon in 1911 so as to facilitate tax collection—and recruitment of labor for the timber industry and colonial projects, resulted in a different kind of population mobility than that which marked the precolonial period.[73] The modern territorial practices of the French administration sought to fix the populations in the spaces under its jurisdiction, first on paper and then in physical reality, so as to facilitate their movements and activities within the new economic and political nodal points developing in Southern Gabon. This "fixing" required an ethnic classification whose "controlling image was of a natural situation where society was composed of discrete, territorially bounded units whose inherent clarity was muddied by migrations and "endemic tribal warfare."[74]

The assumptions behind colonial ethnic names like "Eshira," "Mitsogo," or "Bapounou" were that they corresponded to well-defined territorial units, shared a common homeland from which they migrated and then split or mixed with other groups, and that a unique cultural identity was anchored in their different languages. Herein was expressed the logic of the map and census, a territorial logic where a population's fixed position in space determined its ethnic identity.

This was a fundamentally different logic than those precolonial notions that found identity rooted in the aterritorial ideology of kinship. As was argued in chapters 2 and 3, clan and lineage formed the basic units of precolonial identity. Though there did exist a sense of otherness stemming from language difference and place of settlement that distinguished "Eshira" from "Mitsogo" from "Bapounou" in the mid-nineteenth century, there did not exist corresponding political institutions or leaders that spoke for these "invented" colonial constituencies. Indeed, when these distinctions were made by the local populations they were based upon the same logic that differentiated clans and lineages. Slogans recalling the founding or noteworthy ancestors of a particular group were often the vehicle for the expression of these differences.[75]

A slogan used by Tsogo- and Apindji-speakers, whose languages are very similar, harkens back to an account from the *Bokudu* traditions indicating a close historical relationship between their various clans and a split resulting from the violation of a *mwiri* precept; the result is that Apindji-speakers refer to the Mitsogo as the "Kange," the name of the ancestor's lineage responsible for the violation. For Apindji-speakers, the term "Mitsogo" would only be operative in the invented colonial context as they already had their own ethnic appellation for their neighbors. A similar situation held for Tsogo-speakers when they referred to the Bapunu ethnic group in the early 1960s; instead of using the term "Bapunu" in discussing their historical contacts they used "Ndinga," the name of a founding ancestor. These practices indicate that the cultural identities that the colonial administration wanted to fix lacked, for their purposes, proper names.[76]

Thus, it is very revealing to examine the transformation of those terms that have come to represent modern Gabonese ethnic groups. "Bapunu," for example, presently corresponds to the largest ethnic group found in Southern Gabon whose members are dominant in the towns of Mouila, Ndende, Moabi, and Tchibanga. However, it may be that the term comes from "bapuni" meaning "killers" and refers back to the aggressive role of Punu-speaking clans in the nineteenth-century slave trade, presumably a term applied by outsiders (and even if this was not the case, the belief in this derivation could be powerful at a later date). What's more, up through the 1930s ethnic maps distinguished "Apounous" found in the areas of Ndende and Mouila from "Yakas" inhabiting Moabi and Tchibanga. Le Testu hesitantly suggested that the "Bapounou" were a branch of the "Bayaka" and pointed out that "yaka" was a term meaning "savage" and used by the coastal peoples to refer to inhabitants of the interior. This would seem to be similar to the colonial adoption of the Vili "Ngounié" for the river; coastal peoples from Mayumba and Loango were among the first to serve as interpreters and employees in the colonial administration and thus provided the terms that would become fixed on colonial maps and census forms.[77]

Determining the names and spellings for the ethnic units Europeans needed to find and ultimately had to invent was recognized early on as a problem. Pourtier credits Du Chaillu for spatially delineating the ethnic zones of Southern Gabon "with a remarkable accuracy"[78] but in so doing denies the fundamental position of local notions of identity based on clan and lineage. What Du Chaillu really did was to set in motion the European project of finding appropriate names and spellings for the modern ethnic groups that later developed under colonial rule. In 1890, the colonial official Berton made the next move, as he claimed that Du Chaillu's names for the peoples of Southern Gabon were incorrectly noted. He also insisted upon the "rigorous exactitude of the names of tribes"[79] used in his own text and map.

Yet the problem was not resolved, as in 1931 Raponda-Walker noted that, " In a general fashion, the names under which we designate the tribes of Gabon are not their real names because most of the time we get them from neighboring tribes."[80] He then provides a table of the terms for "A Single Individual," "The Tribe," and "The Language" according to the usage of each people known to him.[81] However, by this time the colonial administration had greatly improved its census-taking capability, and certain spellings had already become fixed by bureaucratic routine. The determination of which spellings to adopt continues to be a source of debate down to the present day.[82]

The census, even more than the map, was the most powerful instrument in the colonial naming repertoire. Census-taking is a very powerful instrument of modern territoriality, and it is always a significant historical development when those individuals or groups seeking to control people and things by controlling space gain access to it.[83] A map could fix a term in space that was meant to correspond to an invented ethnic group, whereas a census reached down to the level of individuals who were named and categorized according to age, sex, village residence, and membership in an ethnic group. The process of collecting census information left vivid memories among the local population. An elderly informant's remembrance of an early colonial official was this: "It was he who recorded me in the census: he looked at my face then gave the age."[84] One could not ask for a better example of the colonial gaze.

The decision to implement a per capita tax in 1900 obliged the French Congo administration to conduct information-gathering activities so as to determine the rolls eligible for taxation. In Gabon, tax collection became the gauge of colonial hegemony for the French, a symbol of submission for the Gabonese, and a focus of resistance. So powerful was this symbol that it was integrated into the origin myths of the Mitsogo to explain the relations between the "white," "black" and "Pygmy" races of humanity. In these myths, "Pygmies" are seen as the older brothers of the "whites" because the colonial administration did not force them to work or pay taxes.[85]

At the turn of the century, the period of concession company influence was just getting underway. The bold lines delineating concession holdings on maps drawn up in Paris betrayed an ignorance of the actual terrain (see Map 12). A number of geographic expeditions were required to effectively apply the "textual reality" to real physical space. Several brigades were organized in 1899 to provide the "geodesic canvas" on which the concessions could work out the precise boundaries of their holdings and the administration could determine the contours of its administrative units.[86] Further data was obtained by the administrator Georges Bruel during his

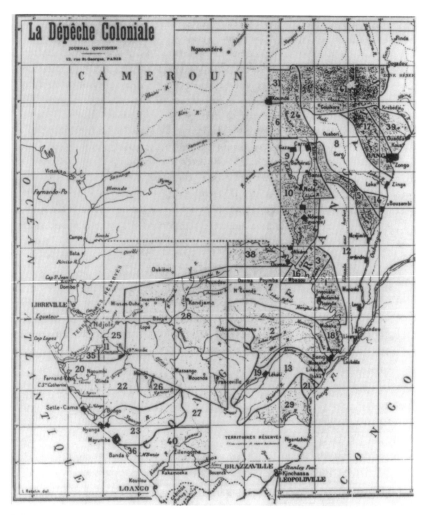

Map 12. Concessionary Companies in French Congo. Part of a map published in *La Dépêche Coloniale*, 1900.

1907–1908 assignment to draw the boundaries between the Société du Haut-Ogooué (S.H.O.), the Société des Factories de Ndjolé (S.F.N.), and the Société de la Haute-Ngounié (S.H.N.) concessions. All of this information was put together to produce the kind of detailed and accurate map required for modern administration.[87]

Bruel was also the first to attempt a systematic census in Southern Gabon. The connection to tax collection was clearly made in 1909 by Merlin, the Governor-General of the French Congo, who stressed that:

tax collection should always be preceded by a census of taxpayers and that this census be undertaken with the greatest care but not to the extent that there is established in the mind of the native a link of cause and effect between the information we ask of him and the use made of it against him.[88]

Merlin was quite naive in thinking that this link would not be made, and a suspicion of the quantitative techniques of census-taking immediately developed and remains strong to this day in Gabon.[89] Not only did the census help to perform the practical work of collecting revenue in Southern Gabon, but it also played an important part in further objectifying fluid notions of local ethnic identity along lines convenient to the colonial administration. It is in the ethnic categories printed on census forms that we find the clearest expression of the colonial invention of modern ethnic identity. Yet one can trace this "invention" through the textual spaces of explorers' accounts and maps which were the essential precursors to the colonial administration's power to name and make statements about the populations of Southern Gabon.[90]

Precolonial naming practices did not lend themselves to the establishment of the lists and tables required by a census. At the beginning of the twentieth century, an individual's name in Southern Gabon generally consisted of a first name followed by the father's name. For example, the leader of the resistance of the Punu-speaking clans in the Mokab district from 1907 to 1912 was "Mavurulu ma Nziengi," or "Mavurulu son of Nziengi." But he was also known with a different first name as the son of his mother, "Nyonda-man-Kit." The latter practice may have been predominant in an earlier period, but an individual could have one name within his or her matrilineage and another within the patrilineage. When an individual became a member of a male or female initiation society, the event marked a break with previous identities and often required the assumption of a new name. What is more, most of the peoples of Southern Gabon obliged newly married women to take on a new name reflecting the circumstances of the marriage arrangement. As already noted, when a man became the head of his clan he assumed a titular name and his former name became taboo. Finally, Le Testu noted that when members of Punu-speaking clans moved from the interior to the coast at Mayumba in the opening decades of this century, they assumed the names of the Vili-speaking clans to avoid the stigma of being labeled "Yaka" or "savage."[91] This adoption of a dominant ethnic identity, effectively imagining oneself into the colonial categories, happened time and again during the colonial period as the population of Southern Gabon began to cluster around the new centers of colonial influence.

An influential "scientific" study—there was even an English transla-tion—by a French colonial official, Adolphe Louis Cureau, suggested that "naming" people was

> one of the greatest difficulties which European civilization has encountered in Equatorial Africa, for as there are no distinctive names, no public records are possible, and one is in the presence of a confused mass in which float individu-alities which are like phantoms and as changeable and fleeting as mist.[92]

In order to properly fix an individual's name for bureaucratic purposes such as the census, Le Testu was adamant that officials drawing up tax rolls insist on getting a first name with a father's name along with the name of the individual's clan; in this way there could be no confusion as it was very rare for the same individual to have the same first name, the same father's name, and the same matrilineal clan name. Stressing the importance of precision in naming, Le Testu argued that it was "the essential condition of a good police."[93]

Though Le Testu was one of the few observers to recognize the cen-trality of clan and lineage in Southern Gabon, his decision to use the French word *tribu* to correspond to "clan" (*tribu Boumouellé* for Bumwele clan) and *race* for "ethnic group" (*race Mitsogho*) compounded an already con-fused terminological practice. For example, Bruel had earlier used the term *tribu* for "ethnic group" (*tribu* Mitsogho) and *clan* for "district" (*clan des Mitsogho Matende*). A very influential attempt at synthesis published in 1914 by L. Poutrin used *tribu* for "ethnic group" (*tribu Eshira*) and *groupe ethnique* or *famille* for a broader grouping based largely on linguistic simi-larity (*groupe ethnique Eshira-Ashango*). Cureau remarked that the "ethnog-raphy" of the French colonies in Central Africa "appears to be all disorder and confusion" and commented that "the races, nations, tribes and families which share the soil of the Dark Continent are innumerable." He never made clear what these categories corresponded to though with some hesita-tion he did refer to "races" of "Pygmy" and "Bantu." Ethnic categories did not figure in the first colony-wide censuses as population estimates were given according to *circonscription,* the colonial administrative unit. How-ever, tables drawn up for various purposes within the *circonscriptions* used the rubric *race* for "ethnic group" (*race Eschira*). This confusing situation continued well into the 1940s.[94]

The difficulty in settling upon accepted categories betrayed the on-going process of ethnic invention. In the same way that the dense equato-rial forest challenged the appropriating gaze, the decentralized and nonliterate societies defied colonial attempts to name and classify them. Yet even though these colonial-invented ethnic categories have now been fully appropriated by Gabonese and are objects of negotiation and manipulation conducted across local political idioms, the original writing down of these terms and their entrance into European textual space denied the prior unwritten significance of clan and lineage membership. A brief examination of an early census serves as an illustration.

In the opening months of 1908, the colonial administrator Bruel had the assignment of facilitating the creation of a new colonial post in the Du Chaillu Massif to the east of Samba as well as determining the exact boundaries of the S.H.O., S.F.N., and S.H.N. concessions. In drawing on the patchy archive of village lists and maps left by his predecessors and concession agents, Bruel cobbled together a census for the region that was computed by multiplying the number of dwellings in a village times a theoretical three inhabitants. In this way, he was able to create a rough map of population density that would allow the colonial administration to make reasonably informed choices as to where to establish the post and what populations to focus on for tax collection and labor recruitment. The five tables he put together were differentiated according to *tribu* (*tribu Bapindji, tribu Mitsogho*, etc.).

It is here that one witnesses the power of the census to impose its abstract categories over a very different and complex existing reality. In the first table providing information on the "Bapindji," it is implied that the fifty villages observed by colonial agents all considered themselves "Bapindji villages" in some fundamental way; the table further implies that the total population estimate of 3700 corresponded to 3700 individuals whose primary identification was "Bapindji." Of course, this was a gross distortion of reality, as the primary identification of the true inhabitants of these villages would have been with their matrilineal clan. Further, each of these villages would have contained inhabitants who resided there due to marriage or dependent exchange and who spoke a different primary language. Concession company agents were probably resident in some of these villages and they were often from Lambaréné or the coast. Indeed, the presence of the S.H.O. in this region had stimulated a series of population movements that made "Bapindji," an abstract ethnic category based principally on language affiliation, even more nonsensical.

Raponda-Walker had traveled in the same region six months earlier and noted that the village of Ngouassa, at the southern limit of a district of Eviya-speaking clans, was a "true tower of Babel" where one could hear the Eviya, Tsogo, Gisir, Nzabi, and Sango languages all spoken at the same time. Thus, though this village was led by Koumoua-Gnondo, a member of the Eviya-speaking Obaï clan, it would have been a serious error to assume all the other inhabitants of Ngouassa were somehow Eviya. But the census, in allowing the colonial government to discuss and administer the populations under its jurisdiction, necessarily imposed this kind of distortion over precolonial reality. As modern territoriality became more effective in Southern Gabon these colonial-invented "empty boxes" came to be filled with meanings by those Gabonese most fully drawn into the workings of the colonial state.[95]

The census, however, usually completed business begun in the textual space of explorers' accounts and maps. How the term "Eshira" came to correspond to an ethnic group made up of Gisir-speaking clans from the Ngosi, Kamba, and Tando districts is an appropriate illustration. The term first appeared in print in Bowdich's early nineteenth-century account as "Asheera," which was said to be a kingdom on the Middle Ogooué. The prefix "A" before the name of a people or clan is particular to what have come to be called the Myènè group of languages (Mpongwe, Orungu, Nkomi, Galwa, Ajumba, and Enenga); Bowdich's informants were most likely Mpongwe-speakers and it is his English transcription of the Mpongwe term that set into motion a politico-linguistic struggle over appropriate prefixes and spellings that continues to this day.[96]

Du Chaillu, whose informants were Nkomi-speakers, furthered the use of the term "Ashira" and was the first European to visit and write about the Ngosi, Kamba, and Tando districts. Though he duly indicated that the "Ashira Kambas consider themselves a distinct people from the . . . Ashira Ngozai" since he could not "detect any difference between them worthy of note" according to physique, customs, and language, Du Chaillu wrongly assumed the existence of a "great Ashira nation" that included the "Otando" (Tando) and the "Apono" (Bapunu). However, in so doing he planted the textual seed for the modern Gisira ethnic identity. Interestingly, on his inaccurate first map he labels the Ngosi district "Ashira Country" and marks the Kamba district simply "Kambas." On his second map, the term "Ashira" does not appear and the districts, "Ngozai," "Kamba," and "Otando," are given equal billing with ethnic group terms like "Ishogo" and "Apingi." The "Ashira nation" had not yet received cartographic reinforcement.[97]

Behind Du Chaillu's notion of an "Ashira nation" was the assumption that at some point in their past the various branches of this "nation" had lived together in a neatly bounded homeland from which they undertook migrations resulting in their dispersion. Yet like Le Testu fifty years later, Du Chaillu had recognized the centrality of clans to the social structures of Southern Gabon:

What struck me in travelling through this great wooded wilderness was the scantiness of the population, and the great number of tribes speaking different languages and dialects. Tribes bearing different names considering themselves different nations, though speaking the same language, and tribes speaking the same language divided from each other by intervening tribes speaking another language. These tribes were divided into a great number of clans, each clan independent of the others, and often at war with one or other of them; in some tribes villages of the same clan were at war with each other.[98]

Yet the assumption of some earlier unity in a shared homeland forced Du Chaillu down the path of sterile speculation: "I have never been able to obtain from the natives a knowledge concerning the splitting of their tribes into clans: they seemed not to know how it happened. . . ."[99] This "splitting" did not happen and thus any attempt to elucidate its circumstances resulted in confusion; there were no historical "tribes" or "nations" called "Ashira," there were only clans that formed fragile alliances within districts. The only reality an "Ashira nation" had ever had in the mid-nineteenth century was in European texts; the path of its realization would be forward into the future not backwards to the past.

A year after Du Chaillu's travels, the trader Walker used a spelling, "Isyira," that rather more approached the local prefix; so did the spelling adopted by Bichet on his 1882 map, "Ishiras." "Gi" is how the prefix for local usage has been rendered with the term "Gisir" usually referring to the language and "Gisira" to the ethnic group.[100] Berton, so keen to set Du Chaillu's errors aright, opted for the not-so-different "Achira" on his 1890 map.[101] The next pivotal figure in the invention of the colonial "Eshira" ethnic identity was Père Buléon, one of the founders of the Sainte-Croix des Eshira mission. The Breton Catholic priest first travelled among the Gisir-speaking clans of the Ngosi district in 1893, and the published account of his experiences serves as a kind of charter for a modern Gisira identity.[102]

Buléon was justly sensitive to the power of naming and the role ethnic names printed on maps played in spreading the particular form of a term:

Numerous maps mention the tribe *Eshira*, and give it the most bizarre names: some put down *Chira*, others *Ichira*, or *Sira*, or finally *Ashira*. This last name is the most widespread and it has good reason to be. It was an Englishman, Mr. Walker, who spelled it the first (sic); and pronounced in the English manner, this term is in effect correct, since in English the "a" commonly corresponds to our "é." . . . French cartographers immediately took possession of this term and transcribed it as such; to the extent that today we find in our parishes few French who have not heard about the *Achiras*.[103]

An interesting irony exists in all this; it seems likely that this invented Eshira ethnic identity had more cognitive reality for French Catholics with access to the maps and texts of the 1890s than for the Gisir-speaking clans to whom it referred but who had little knowledge of these literate instruments.

Buléon presented himself as sincerely wanting "to get it right" and by so doing sought to demonstrate a basic respect for the peoples and customs he was trying to change. Instead of "this mania to overturn all that exists in order to create new names," he urged the learning and adoption of local terms: "Thus, after having obtained information from around the region and even from the mouths of natives, we believed it necessary to correct this error and to write in French the name *Eshira*. . . ."[104] The irony here is that despite the sentiment to reproduce a spelling of the local term, albeit tailored by a motivation to facilitate easier pronunciation for parishioners in France, Buléon was later criticized by Gabonese scholars for having contributed to the deformation of the local term, Gisira.[105]

Buléon further contributed to the invention of a modern ethnic identity by writing down the Gisir dialect spoken in the Ngosi district. After struggling for three years to work out points of grammar and memorize irregular verbs, Buléon had by 1899 prepared in manuscript form a lexicon, a catechism, some prayer books, and a manual for catechists, essentially creating the written Gisir language. His catechism was used at Sainte-Croix, Trois-Épis, and Saint-Martin for more than ten years, and for several decades the Gisira Ngosi dialect was the main linguistic instrument of Catholic religious pedagogy in Southern Gabon. It was employed to teach the catechism to Punu- and Gisira Tando-speakers, whose languages are similar, and to Apindji- and Tsogo-speakers, whose languages are quite different. As late as the 1940s it was being used to teach the catechism to Sango-speakers, another similar language, at the recently opened Dibouangui mission. The experience of Gisira Ngosi becoming a literate language and a vehicle for modern education further cemented the boundaries of a modern Eshira ethnic identity.[106]

The seed of an "Ashira nation" planted by Du Chaillu blossomed in Buléon's text as he constructs a hierarchy of a *race Eshira* corresponding to the inhabitants of the Ngosi District with two related subgroups, the *tribu Nkamba* and the *tribu Tando*. This is clearly depicted on his map and also in the text, where Buléon presents a dialogue between Mbounga, an elderly chief, and the people of his village. This literary device is used to demonstrate the chief's purported desire to have missionaries establish themselves in the district. Mbounga also becomes the mouthpiece for Buléon's invented Eshira identity:

> *Mbounga*: The Eshira race, is it not the greatest nation of these lands?
> *Villagers*: It is.
> *Mbounga*: The Tandos, are they not Eshiras?
> *Villagers*: They are our brothers and we speak the same language.
> *Mbounga*: The Nkambas, are they foreigners for us?
> *Villagers*: It is our blood that flows in their veins, and these three peoples
> form but one.[107]

It is only appropriate that Buléon himself should have become the symbol for this "Eshira race." The Sainte-Croix des Eshira Mission Journal entry for 10 March 1896 reports that Buléon was given the title of *rengondo* by the Eshira.[108] In a letter a year later, he wrote that the Eshira

> have elected me chief of the whole nation, that is to say the three tribes of the Eshira race: Ngori (sic), Kamba and Tando; each tribe presented me with a royal *kendo* bell and they have officially made me a gift of the whole country with the right to reserve for myself all of the palavers over the entire extent of the territory.[109]

There is no need to doubt that some kind of installation did indeed occur. Just what it represented to the parties involved, though, is most certainly a complicated issue. The office of *rengondo* was not one associated with Gisir-speaking clans; it referred to the centralized position of clan mediator prominent among the Nkomi-speaking clans on the Fernan Vaz in the first half of the nineteenth century. For the Gisir-speaking clans the most influential leader within a district was given the title of *mata*. It is thus curious that Buléon would have been named *rengondo*.

A possible explanation is that his abilities to bring the palavers presented to him to satisfactory resolution recalled the main historical function of the *rengondo* among Nkomi-speaking clans. Missionary and colonial administration sources relate that arbitrating disputes was the main activity of the Sainte-Croix priests during the first fifteen years of the mission's existence. Indeed, Buléon's endeavors were reinforced by Brazza, who provided the priest with a case of French flags and allowed him to distribute identity certificates to area chiefs in the name of the colony. Buléon's successor, Père Girod, continued this practice but refused to accept the *rengondo* title when it was offered to him; Girod also indicates that Buléon's influence stretched over an area considerably smaller than that of the Ngosi, Kamba, and Tando districts.[110]

Another possible explanation is that the Gisir-speaking clan leaders who bestowed this title on Buléon had recognized the emergence of a broader ethnic identity and that this was connected to opportunities derived from the colonial and missionary presence. They thus drew from outside their own traditions to name and embody the crystallization of a new identity. François Gaulme suggests something along these lines in the similar installation of Père Bichet as *renima* for the Nkomi-speaking clans at Fernan Vaz. He notes that the ritual might be seen as "an exemplary image of the fixation of a kind of national Nkomi spirit on the person of P. Bichet."[111]

Buléon's writings and the Sainte-Croix des Eshiras mission established in the heart of the Ngosi district from 1895 to 1920 effectively fixed the term "Eshira" in the textual spaces of the colonial world. From 1907, the spelling "Echiras" was used to designate the colonial post in the Ngosi district; with the administrative reorganization of 1909 the spelling became "Eshiras" and the term corresponded to a new unit, the *circonscription*.[112] It is not surprising then that in colonial parlance "Eshira" primarily referred to those Gisir-speaking clans inhabiting the Ngosi district or who had recently established themselves along the Rembo Nkomi and Rembo Ndogo. The Kamba and the Tando were still recognized as distinct, and in colonial reports the Tando were discussed without any reference to their being "Eshira." There was also the Banda district of Gisir-speaking clans not named by Buléon which apparently started to break up just prior to the World War I.[113]

Bruel's mapping project for the Middle Ogooué and Lower Ngounié further clarified the textual boundaries of the modern Eshira ethnic identity, subsuming the Ngosi, Kamba, and Tando districts on a preliminary sketch but at the same time muddling spelling practice by using "Echira." In his own attempt to nail down a standard spelling, Bruel introduced a new application for the term "Echira" as he employed it as an element in a language classification table derived from Avelot; in the table, "Echira" serves as both language and ethnic group and is placed under the heading *Groupe Mpongoué-Okanda*. These classification efforts take a further twist in Poutrin's study and map which also used Avelot's classification. Here "Eshira" is said to be a part of a *Groupe Gabonais* along with "Mpongwé" and "Okandé" as well as forming a *Famille Eshira-Ashango*. On Poutrin's map, which was published by the Anti-Slavery Society of France, an "Eshira" enclave is clearly demarcated for the first time although it is rather confusedly lumped together with the "Iveia"; the Tando and Kamba distinctions have been colored over. The 1911 Delingette map, which incorporated Bruel's data, does not mark out an enclave but simply spreads the term over a loosely defined space; the decision to use either "Eshira" or "Echira" has been sidestepped by employing "Eschira"; the Tando and the Kamba have literally dropped off the map. "Eschira" was the spelling used when the term first appeared as an ethnic (as opposed to an administrative) census category in 1918.[114]

The reissue of Poutrin's unedited classification in 1930 indicates that no new attempts occurred in the 1920s, though Raponda-Walker, a Catholic priest, published an important article, "The Tribes of Gabon," in 1924. In 1932, the Holy Ghost Fathers produced a "A New Map of Gabon" boldly delineating ethnic spaces and indicating linguistic relationships; following their practice since Buléon, the missionaries used the "Eshira" spelling. This colonial tradition of classification culminated with the publications of Soret and Deschamps in the 1950s and 1960s. Interestingly, even Soret does not escape from inconsistent spelling, using "Eshira" in the text and "Echira" on his map.[115]

Though recent efforts to replace "Eshira" with "Gisir" have made some headway in Gabonese scholarly texts, "Eshira" remains the form used on maps.[116] Such is the power of official literacy:

> The printed word possesses an aura of unimpeachableness and codification. Once a name has been established, and once a certain orthography has been chosen, a mapping service will not readily change that orthography, even when it appears incorrect.[117]

By 1920, the term "Eshira" had been effectively established in the colonial spaces of the text and map. The process of its invention outlined above was a small part of the larger European project of ordering and classifying the physical space of Southern Gabon within the textual space of the colonial bureaucracy.[118] The instruments of modern territoriality employed in this task, such as the map and census, were not benign academic undertakings but were meant to be applied to collect tax and control the movements of people. They were integrated with other more brutal instruments of territoriality like the French colonial military units sent from Dakar and the locally recruited Regional Guard. The combination proved lethal as the populations of Southern Gabon experienced unprecedented levels of disease, famine, violence, and general chaos during the first two decades of the twentieth century.

Notes

1. According to Rey, even after a decade of concession company rule, precapitalist modes of production, exchange, and resource exploitation prevailed until 1912 in the districts of Punu- and Lumbu-speaking clans between the Nyanga and Niari Rivers; Rey, *Colonialisme*, 305–6. Vansina suggests that for all of Western Bantu-speaking Africa the equatorial political tradition, though under tremendous pressure, was still functioning at the end of the nineteenth century; Vansina, *Paths*, 239.

2. For the spread of factories in the Fernan Vaz Lagoon, see map in Merlet, *Autour du Loango*, 170–71.

3. See Douglas Wheeler, "A Note on Smallpox in Angola, 1670–1875," *Studia* 13/14 (1964): 351–62; Dauril Alden and Joseph C. Miller, "Unwanted Cargoes: The Origins and Dissemination of Smallpox via the Slave Trade from Africa to Brazil, c. 1560–1830," in *The African Exchange: Toward a Biological History of Black People*, ed. Kenneth F. Kiple (Durham, N.C.: Duke University Press, 1987), 35–109; Rita Headrick (ed. Daniel R. Headrick), *Colonialism, Health and Illness in French Equatorial Africa, 1885–1935* (Atlanta: African Studies Association Press, 1994), 33.

4. Wheeler, "Note on Smallpox," 356–57; Patterson, "Vanishing Mpongwe," 227–28; and Patterson, *Northern Gabon*, 127; M'Bokolo, *Noirs et Blancs*, 182, 191; Metegue N'Nah, "Le Gabon de 1854 à 1886," 12; Bucher, "The Mpongwe," 39; Gaulme, *Le pays de Cama*, 73; Avaro, *Un peuple*, 240.

5. See R. Headrick, *Colonialism, Health and Illness*, 33–43.

6. Du Chaillu, *Journey to Ashango-Land*, 121.

7. Ibid.

8. Ibid., 142–43, 157, 163, 172–73, 178, 199, 232, 248, 251–52, 282, 290, 304.

9. Ibid., 396–401.

10. Ibid., 401.

11. Buléon, *Au pays des Eshiras*, 7–8.

12. Walker, "Relation d'une tentative d'exploration," 72; Aymes, "Voyage d'exploration," 430. Walker was accused by members of Enenga-speaking clans of bringing smallpox to the region; see André Raponda-Walker and Robert Reynard, "Anglais, Espagnols et Nord-Américains au Gabon au XIXᵉ siècle," *BIEC* 12 (1956): 262.

13. Albert Schweitzer, *African Notebook* (Bloomington: Indiana University Press, 1965, orig. 1939), 8. For the 1877 outbreak, see Marche, *Trois voyages*, 327–31, 342; Napoléon Ney, ed., *Conférences et lettres de P. Savorgnan de Brazza sur les trois explorations dans l'Ouest Africain de 1875 à 1886* (Paris: Dreyfous, 1887), 116–17, 127, 132; Brazza, "Rapport," 162–63; Nassau, *My Ogowé*, 177, 227–28, 235, 238; Bonzon, *À Lambaréné*, 44.

14. "Communauté de Sainte-Anne à Fernan-Vaz," *BCSE* 4 (1893–1896), 389; Archives CPSE, Boîte 680, "Journal de la Communauté de Ste. Croix des Eshira du 29 juin 1895 au 3 décembre 1905, entry for 29 novembre 1896"; Raponda-Walker, *Notes d'histoire*, 108.

15. Raponda-Walker, *Notes d'histoire*, 143–44; "Les Tribus," 80.

16. Raponda-Walker provides a list of the different Fang-speaking clans who by 1900 had established villages on the Ngounié between Samba and the confluence with the Ogooué: in and around Samba the "Esendac" ("Esindok") clan had two villages, the "Ebibeng" one and the "Esènzoc" one; the "Ebimvang" had a village at Manga and two villages on the Davo; also with two villages on the Davo were the "Ebimvul" and the "Ebimwène"; the "Ebili" clan had three villages on the Ikoy; and towards the mouth at Nkomadeke and

Abotwé, the "Ebenayal" had two villages and the "Ebindome," the "Esivwé," and the "Ebifanghele" one each; see Archives CPSE, Boîte 1019, Fonds Pouchet, "I. *Notes d'histoires-Walker*."

17. Compiègne, *Okanda-Bangouens-Osyéba*, 225–26.

18. Nassau, *My Ogowe*, 139.

19. Du Chaillu, *Explorations and Adventures*, 10–11; Aymes, "Voyage d'exploration," 433.

20. Nassau, *My Ogowe*, 101; "Lettre de L. Mizon au Commandant du Gabon, Lambaréné, 26 juillet 1882," in Brunschwig, *Brazza explorateur: Les traités Makoko 1880–1882* (Paris: Mouton, 1967), 255; also Lewis, *Trader Horn*, 46–48, 126, 154.

21. Nassau, *My Ogowe*, 500, 632; Coquery-Vidrovitch, *Brazza et la prise de possession du Congo*, 59–61; for the growing Fang influence on the Ogooué and the conflicts resulting from increased trade, see Christopher Chamberlin, "Competition and Conflict: The Development of the Bulk Export Trade in Central Gabon during the Nineteenth Century," (Ph.D. diss., U.C.L.A., 1977).

22. For the impact of Brazza's West African Mission and its contribution to the rise of Fang-speaking clans, see Coquery-Vidrovitch, *Brazza et la prise de possession du Congo*, 203–14; and "Rapport de Brazza au ministère de l'Instruction publique, Madiville, 20 mai 1885," in Coquery-Vidrovitch, *Brazza et la prise de possession du Congo*, 279–84. For the conflicts between the Kele- and Tsogo-speaking clans, Gollnhofer, "*Bokudu*," 252–54; Raponda-Walker, *Essai de grammaire Tsogo* (Brazzaville: Imprimerie du gouvernement, 1937), 4–5; Raponda-Walker, "Au pays des Ishogos," (1910), 177; Raponda-Walker, *Notes d'histoire*, 114.

23. For general comments on Fang and Mpongwe traders, see Coquery-Vidrovitch, *Brazza et la prise de possession du Congo*, 60; for the positive impact of Mpongwe traders on the Ogooué, AOM-AEF (Aix) B 2B 1848–1912, "Resumé de la lettre de M. Koppenfels adressée à M. le Commandant supérieur du Gabon, 29 novembre 1880"; for reference to Ngeza, see Nassau, *My Ogowe*, 212–13; for "Digomi/Dégoma," Compiègne, *Gabonais-Pahouins-Gallois*, 258–59; R. P. Bichet, "Quelques jours dans l'Ogowé," *Les Missions Catholiques* (1882): 582; for Mr. Glass, Kingsley, *Travels in West Africa*, 311. For the spread of the Mpongwe language, see Compiègne, *Gabonais-Pahouins-Gallois*, 107; Compiègne, *Okanda-Bangouens-Osyéba*, 119–21; Lewis, *Trader Horn*, 206; Nassau, *My Ogowé*, 295, 299.

24. For Portuguese and Afro-Portuguese traders on the Nyanga in the 1870s, see "Annexe II: *L'Expédition au Loango (1873–1876): Un récit de voyage en trois parties de Paul Güssfeldt, Julius Falkenstein, Eduard Pechuël-Loesche* (excerpts translated from German of *Die Loango Expedition*)," in Koumba-Manfoumbi, *Les Punu*, 371–72, 384–85; in the 1880s, see Coquery-Vidrovitch, *Brazza et la prise de possession du Congo*, 148, 159.

25. Lewis, *Trader Horn*, 136.

26. For the spread of English on the Rembo Nkomi, see "Rapport du chef de station Henri Delaroche sur le Fernan Vaz, Libreville, 22 juin 1890," in Élizabeth Rabut, *Brazza Commissaire Général: Le Congo français 1886–1897* (Paris: Éditions de l'École des Hautes Études en Sciences Sociales, 1989), 334; for an interesting discussion of the incorporation of Portuguese, English and French words into Gabonese languages, see Raponda-Walker, "Les néologismes dans les idiomes gabonais," *JSA* 3, 2 (1933): 305–14.

27. Patterson, "Vanishing Mpongwe," 227; Fleuriot de Langle, "Croisières à la Côte d'Afrique," *Le Tour du Monde* 31 (1876): 274.

28. Sillans, "L'apport des explorations," 316–17; in the oral traditions of the region, "Kerno" has been saddled with the responsibility of spreading chiggers or "chiques" to Southern Gabon in the mid-1870s following their arrival on the Angolan coast in 1872 in sand ballasts on ships from South America. Marche and Nassau report a great deal of suffering caused by the introduction of this new pest; some Ajumba-speaking clans on Lake Azingo were even forced to abandon their villages; see Marche, *Trois voyages*, 248; Nassau, *My Ogowe*, 36, 57, 95; J. M. Mackaya-Mackanga, "Ethno-histoire des Ajumba," (Mémoire de maîtrise, UOB, 1983), 49; Avaro, *Un peuple*, 157; other references to "Kerno" are found in Fleuriot de Langle, "Croisières," 274; Compiègne, *Okanda-Bangouens-Osyéba*; Marche, *Trois voyages*, 354; Du Quilio, "Voyage," 6. "Youssouf" is mentioned in Compiègne, *Okanda-Bangouens-Osyéba*, 9; Marche, *Trois voyages*, 166; Lewis, *Trader Horn*, 155; 185; "Mané" in Marche, *Trois voyages*, 242; Nassau, *My Ogowe*, 69, 124.

29. In 1883 there were around eighty Senegalese engaged in commerce on the Ogooué for the firms of Hatton and Cookson, John Holt, and Woermann; see Coquery-Vidrovitch, *Brazza et la prise de possession du Congo*, 60. For Brazza's views, see his "Rapport sur le commerce de l'Ogoowé, Madiville, 20 mai 1885," in Coquery-Vidrovitch, *Brazza et la prise de possession du Congo*, 280; for colonial concerns about Senegalese trade, "Note de L. Mizon, chef des stations, en annexe à la lettre de M. de Lesseps du 26 août 1882, Gabon, 13 juillet 1882," in Brunschwig, *Brazza Explorateur, Makoko*, 252–53 and Guiral, *Le Congo Français*, 33; for the role of Senegalese in the slave trade, AOM-AEF (Aix), B 2B 1848–1912, "Commandant du Gabon à M. l'Amiral, Ministre de la Marine, le 31 octobre 1876"; for Senegalese burning of villages, AOM-AEF (Aix), B 2B 1848–1912, "Commandant du Gabon à M. le Ministre de la Marine, le 8 janvier 1881, le 20 juillet 1882"; for conflict with Kele- and Vili-speaking clans, Nassau, *My Ogowe*, 135, 201, 251, 312.

30. Le Testu, *Notes sur les coutumes Bapounou*, 99.

31. Buléon, *Au pays des Eshiras*, 38–40; for a more gritty description of the life of trader in the interior, see Kingsley, *Travels in West Africa*, 308–17.

32. Quoted in Couzens, *Tramp Royal*, 189.

33. Matthew H. Edney, *Mapping an Empire: The Geographical Construction of British India, 1765–1843* (Chicago: University of Chicago Press, 1997), 1, 3.

34. See Harvey, *Condition of Post-Modernity*, 240–59.

35. Mary Louise Pratt, *Imperial Eyes: Travel Writing and Transculturation* (London and New York: Routledge, 1992), 15. Both Harvey and Pratt recognize the influence of Michel Foucault and his reflections on the mutations of power in Western society since the Renaissance; see Michel Foucault, *The Order of Things: An Archaeology of the Human Sciences* (New York: Vintage, 1973); and discussions in Harvey, *Condition of Post-Modernity*, 213–14, 237–38, 252–53; and Pratt, *Imperial Eyes*, 28–29.

36. Harvey, *Condition of Post-Modernity*, 264.

37. The notion of "imperial eyes" is from the title of Pratt's book. For Pratt, Du Chaillu and Brazza would be examples of the "seeing-man," which she describes as "an admittedly unfriendly label for the European male subject of European landscape discourse—he whose imperial eyes passively look out and possess"; Pratt, *Imperial Eyes*, 7. For a fascinating study of the transformation of European vision, see Donald M. Lowe, *History of Bourgeois Perception* (Chicago: U. of Chicago Press, 1982); and for the centrality of vision to the construction of the anthropological "other," Fabian, *Time and the Other*, 105–41.

38. Noyes, *Colonial Space*, 190–91; see also 163–64. I cover much of this material in Christopher Gray, *Modernization and Cultural Identity: The Creation of National Space in*

Rural France and Colonial Space in Rural Gabon Occasional Paper No. 21, MacArthur Scholar Series (Bloomington: Indiana Center on Global Change and World Peace, 1994), 6–13.

39. Du Chaillu, *Explorations*, 445–46. See also further discussion of this point in Gray, *Modernization and Cultural Identity.*

40. Du Chaillu, *Explorations*, 57. Pratt is quick to point out the symbolism of the serpent; see Pratt, *Imperial Eyes*, 209.

41. See Robert Pogue Harrison, *Forests: The Shadow of Civilization* (Chicago: U. of Chicago Press, 1992).

42. The terms are from Pratt, *Imperial Eyes*, 7.

43. Kingsley, *Travels in West Africa*, 102.

44. Bruel, "La boucle de l'Ogooué," *Revue Coloniale* 93 (1910): 642; the forest as obstacle to European vision is a theme Roland Pourtier addresses on several occasions; see Pourtier, *Le Gabon*, 1:35–36, 40–41, 52, 65, 147, 151–52.

45. Pourtier, *Le Gabon*, 1:83; for discussions of Brazza as visionary, see Brunschwig, *Brazza explorateur, Makoko*, 213–14; Rabut, *Brazza Commissaire Général*, 12; Coquery-Vidrovitch, "Les idées économiques de Brazza et les premières tentatives de compagnies de colonisation au Congo Français 1885–1898," *CEA* 5, 1 (1965): 57; and Coquery-Vidrovitch, *Brazza et la prise de possession du Congo*, 214.

46. See Noyes, *Colonial Space*, 75; Pourtier, *Le Gabon*, 1:87–88.

47. Noyes, *Colonial Space*, 136.

48. "Rapport de Brazza au ministère de l'Instruction publique, Madiville, 20 mai 1885," in Coquery-Vidrovitch, *Brazza et la prise de possession du Congo*, 281.

49. Noyes, *Colonial Space*, 196; see also discussion in Gray, *Modernization and Cultural Identity*, 41–58.

50. Map is reproduced in Coquery-Vidrovitch, *Brazza et la prise de possession du Congo*, 172

51. Du Chaillu, *Explorations and Adventures*, 291, 448; Marche, *Trois Voyages*, 271, 338; Ney, *Conférences et lettres de P. Savorgnan de Brazza*, 278, 285; Lewis, *Trader Horn*, 216; Nassau, *My Ogowe*, 50–51, 78; for an interesting discussion of the continued association of writing and power, see Joseph Tonda, "Pouvoirs de guérison, magie et écriture," in *Magie et écriture au Congo* (Paris: Harmattan, 1994), 133–47.

52. Du Chaillu, *Explorations and Adventures*, 440–41.

53. Nassau, *My Ogowe*, 186.

54. Marche, *Trois Voyages*, 242–43.

55. See Gollnhofer, "*Bokudu*," 177–79; also Deschamps, *Traditions orales*, 37. Nzabi traditions assert that blacks lost the ability to write; see Dupré, *Un ordre*, 239.

56. See Pourtier, *Le Gabon*, 2:62–72 for an interesting discussion.

57. Du Chaillu, *Explorations and Adventures*, 258. Du Chaillu never actually saw these rapids which he believed to be an impressive single fall named "Samba Nagoshi"; Robert Bruce Walker pointed out shortly after that the term referred to two different sets of rapids, "Samba" and "Agosyé" ("Magotsi"), neither of which was as large as Du Chaillu believed; see Walker, "Relation d'une tentative d'exploration," 76. "Eugénie Falls" did not catch on and had a relatively brief existence in the textual space of the map; in addition to Du Chaillu's maps, the term appears on "Karte der Gab n-Länder im Äquatoralen Afrika," *Petermann's Geographische Mittheilungen* (1863), tafel 15; and the map to Richard F. Burton, *Two Trips to Gorilla Land and the Cataracts of the Congo*, vol. 1 (London: Sampson Low, Marston Low and Searle, 1876).

58. See Fernandez, *Fang Architectonics*, 3–5, for the lack of a "total overview" among Fang villagers; and Marie-Claude Dupré, "Masques de danse ou cartes géopolitiques? L'invention de Kidumu chez les Téké tsayi au XIXe siècle (République populaire du Congo)," *Cahiers des sciences humaines* 26, 3 (1990): 447–71, for a fascinating attempt to "read" the Kidumu mask of the Téké tsayi for historical information.

59. For local naming practices; see Pourtier, *Le Gabon*, 1:74–75; for examples of local names for falls and rapids on the Upper and Middle Ogooué, see Raponda-Walker, "Chutes, seuils et rapides de l'Ogowe de Franceville à Alembe," *RG* 12 (1961): 39–41; Raponda-Walker is also the source for a list of savannah names along the Middle Ngounié; see Archives CPSE, Boîte 1019, Fonds Pouchet, "I. *Notes d'histoires*-Walker"; for the naming of the Ngounié, see Raponda-Walker, *Notes d'histoire*, 105, 147; Raponda-Walker and Sillans, *Plantes utiles*, 16; Mbigui, "Histoire de Sindara," 18; Du Chaillu, *Explorations and Adventures*, 458, map endpiece; Walker, "Relation d'une tentative d'exploration," 70.

60. Studies on Mitsogo myth and ritual show that these notions are central to the metaphysical conceptions of Tsogo-speaking clans; Gollnhofer, "*Bokudu*," 254; see also Gollnhofer, "Les rites de passage"; and Roger Sillans, "*Motombi*, mythes et énigmes initiatiques des Mitsogho du Gabon central. Route de la vie," (Thèse de doctorat, E.P.H.E., 1967).

61. Du Chaillu, *Journey to Ashango-Land*, x, also vi–ix and map endpiece.

62. J. B. Harley, "The Map and the Development of the History of Cartography," in *The History of Cartography, Volume 1: Cartography in Prehistoric, Ancient and Medieval Europe and the Mediterranean*, ed. J. B. Harley and David Woodward (Chicago: University of Chicago Press, 1987), 1.

63. Harley and Woodward, "Concluding Remarks," in *The History of Cartography, Volume I*, 506.

64. J. B. Harley, "Maps, Knowledge, and Power," in *The Iconography of Landscape*, ed. Denis Cosgrove and Stephen Daniels (Cambridge: Cambridge University Press, 1988), 282; see also Pourtier, *Le Gabon*, 1:41–42.

65. J. B. Harley, "Deconstructing the Map," *Cartographica* 26, 2 (1989): 14.

66. For details, see Pourtier, *Le Gabon*, 1:45–65.

67. Pourtier, *Le Gabon*, 1:60. For early maps, see "Croquis d'une partie du cours inférieur de l'Ogowai fait d'après les données recueillies à bord où pirogue. Juillet, Aout, 1862, par Mr Serval, Lieutenant de Vaisseau, commandant l'Aviso, à vapeur le *Pionnier*, Ministère de la Marine et des Colonies, 1863," in Griffon du Bellay, "Exploration du fleuve Ogo-wai"; "Carte des possessions françaises de l'Afrique Équatoriale dressée par ordre et sous la surveillance de Contre Amiral Vicomte Fleuriot de Langle d'après les officiers de la Marine Française, 1869" in Aymes, "Voyage d'exploration"; "Cours de l'Ogôoué entre Sam-Quita et la Rivière Ivindo, Levé à vue à la boussole par M.M. le Marquis de Compiègne et A. Marche, Janvier-Mars 1874," in Compiègne, *Okanda-Bangouens-Osyéba*; and Brazza's map from his first expedition up the Ogooué (1875–1879), reproduced in Brunschwig, *Brazza explorateur: L'Ogooué*, endpiece.

68. Du Chaillu, *Explorations*, endpiece; *Journey to Ashango-Land*, endpiece; R. P. Bichet, "Quelques jours dans l'Ogowé," *Les Missions Catholiques* (1882): 583.

69. Lewis, *Trader Horn*, 124–25, 137, 193; for a discussion of maps and secrecy, see Harley, "Maps, Knowledge and Power," 284; for a more recent example concerning prospecting maps and the Gabonese timber industry, see Pourtier, *Le Gabon*, 2:151.

70. Note that what has become the accepted spelling "Ngounié" appears on this map (see note 50 above). For the mapping objectives of the West Africa Mission and a list of what was produced, see Coquery-Vidrovitch, *Brazza et la prise de possession du Congo*, 185–87.

71. Jules Berton, "De Lastourville sur l'Ogooué à Samba sur le N'Gounié (septembre et octobre 1890)," *Bulletin de la Société de géographie* 7, 16 (1895): 211–18; "Relation du voyage de Lastourville aux chutes de Samba (Ngunyé) par Godel (extrait), le 1er décembre 1893," in Rabut, *Brazza Commissaire Général,* 182–83; Archives CPSE, Boîte 55, Mgr Le Roy, Croquis; Boîte 62, Mgr Le Roy, Notes et Documents; Boîte 64, Mgr Le Roy, Carnets personnels.

72. Anthony D. Smith, "The Ethnic Sources of Nationalism," in *Ethnic Conflict and International Security,* ed. Michael E. Brown (Princeton: Princeton University Press, 1993), 29.

73. AOM-AEF (Aix), D 4D 4(1)D6 1911, "Résumés des rapports mensuels des chefs de circonscriptions, Circonscription de l'Ofooué-Ngounié, juin-juillet 1911." The first areas to experience dramatic population shifts from colonial labor recruitment were Loango, Mayumba, and their immediate hinterlands. A practice begun during Brazza's West African Mission in 1883, by 1914 virtually all the workers employed by the colony were from these areas, and it was recognized that their population base had been severely depleted; see Coquery-Vidrovitch, *Brazza et la prise de possession du Congo,* 37–38; AOM-AEF (Aix) D 4D 4(1)D11 1914, "Rapports d'ensemble trimestriels, 17 avril 1914, Appendice: Recrutement et utilisation sur place de la main d'oeuvre locale."

74. M. Crawford Young, "Nationalism, Ethnicity, and Class in Africa: A Retrospective," *CEA* 26, 3 (1986): 442.

75. For examples, see Raponda-Walker, "Encore des devises gabonaises, cris de guerre, serments," *RG* 13 (1961): 9–12; for significance and structure of slogans among Kele- and Punu-speakers, see Ngolet, "Dispersion Ongom-Bakele," 37; and Pierre Moundjegou-Magangue, "Littérature orale africaine et problèmes de la traduction: Essai sur la literature des Bajag du Gabon," (Mémoire de maîtrise, Université Paris VIII, 1974), 37–38.

76. Gollnhofer, *"Bokudu,"* 183–92, 197, 271–74; Raponda-Walker, "Les Tribus," 92.

77. Hubert Moukaga, Interview Cassette II, Mouila, June 13, 1991; Le Testu, *Notes sur les coutumes Bapounou,* 17; for the "Bayaka"/"Apounou" distinction, see the map in *Annales des Pères du Saint-Esprit* (1937), 309; for a related discussion regarding the origins of the term "Fang," see Metegue N'Nah, *Lumière,* 13–16.

78. Pourtier, *Le Gabon,* 1:74.

79. Berton, "De Lastourville à Samba," 218.

80. Raponda-Walker, "Essais sur les idiomes," 5.

81. Ibid.

82. The case of the "Eshira" will be discussed below; for an insightful discussion of the history of the colonial census in Gabon, see Sautter, *De l'Atlantique,* 19–51, 86–89; also Raymond Mayer and Michel Voltz, "Dénomination ethno-scientifique des langues et des ethnies du Gabon," *RGSH* 2 (1990): 43–51.

83. See dicussion in Benedict Anderson, *Imagined Communities: Reflections on the Origin and Spread of Nationalism,* rev. ed. (New York: Verso, 1991) 163–78.

84. "Corpus des Traditions Orales, Texte No. 8, François Mbina Moundziegou," in Hygnanga-Koumba, "Canton Ngounié-Centrale," 110. The official is named as "Tito" and probably refers to a certain "Titaux" posted in Mouila during and following World War I; see "Région de la Ngounié, District de Mouila, Calendrier Historique," (Unpublished document, circa 1960); I would like to thank Bodinga-bwa-Bodinga for allowing me to consult a copy of this document.

85. Pourtier, *Le Gabon,* 2:80–81; Gollnhofer, *"Bokudu,"* 170.

86. See "Mission Gendron au Congo Français," *La Géographie* 3 (1901): 181–96; Avelot, "Dans la boucle de l'Ogooué."

87. See Georges Bruel, "Note sur la construction et la rédaction de la carte du Moyen Ogooué et de la Ngounié," *Revue Coloniale* 85 (1910): 209–24, 297–305; this information was then incorporated into G. Delingette, "Carte générale de l'Afrique Équatoriale Française," Échelle au 1/1,000,000, en 5 feuilles, publiée par ordre de M. le Gouverneur général Merlin, Paris, A. Challamel, éditeur (Feuille IV, Gabon et Congo, 1911); I would like to thank Marie-Claude Dupré for providing me with a photocopy of the relevant portions of Feuille IV.

88. Gouverneur-Général Merlin, "Circulaire relative à l'impôt indigène," *Journal Officiel du Congo Français* (27 août 1909).

89. There exists a general reluctance among adults to provide information on the number of children they have, which can be partly understood as a consequence of census/taxation activities.

90. In addition to Anderson's discussion on the role of the census in creating national and ethnic identities, see Bernard S. Cohn, "The Census, Social Structure and Objectification in South Asia," in Bernard S. Cohn, *An Anthropologist among the Historians and Other Essays* (Delhi: Oxford University Press, 1987), 224–54; Charles Hirschman, "The Meaning and Measurement of Ethnicity in Malaysia: An Analysis of Census Classifications," *The Journal of Asian Studies* 46, 3 (1987): 555–82; and Kenneth Dauber, "Bureaucratizing the Ethnographer's Magic," *Current Anthropology* 36, 1 (1995): 75–86.

91. See Le Testu, *Notes sur les coutumes Bapounou,* 27–30; Ibinga-Mbadinga, "L'implantation du pouvoir colonial dans le Sud-Gabon (1880–1910)," (Mémoire de maîtrise, Université de Paris I, 1978), 145–46; Jacques Hubert, "Esquisse de la coutume Bapounou et généralités sur la dégradation des coutumes au Gabon," (Mémoire d'entrée, C.H.E.A.M., Paris, 1951), 10–12; Raponda-Walker, "Les coutumes gabonaises: Noms de mariage," *Liaison* 36 (1953): 44–45; Du Chaillu, *Journey to Ashango-Land,* 429.

92. Adolphe Louis Cureau, *Savage Man in Central Africa: A Study of Primitive Races in the French Congo* (London: T. Fisher Unwin, 1915), 161; the French edition *Les sociétés primitives de l'Afrique Équatoriale* (Paris: Colin, 1912). The book no doubt appealed to the British sense of empiricism as Cureau eschewed "the theorems and classifications of classical sociology" associated with Durkheim and Mauss and vowed to "surrender myself to the facts"; Cureau, *Savage Man,* 15.

93. Le Testu, *Notes sur les coutumes Bapounou,* 30.

94. Ibid., 21–27; AOM-AEF (Aix), D 5D 5D11 1908–1931, "L'Administrateur Bruel à M. le Commissaire Général, Rapport sur la création d'un Cercle des Mitsogho-Nord, Libreville, le 14 mars 1908"; Dr. L. Poutrin, *Enquête sur la famille, la propriété et la justice chez les indigènes des colonies françaises d'Afrique: Esquisse ethnologique des principales populations de l'Afrique Équatoriale Française* (Paris: Masson, 1914), 117ff and map. For Gabon, Poutrin drew from a classification developed by Avelot; even though Poutrin labeled his map "schématique et provisoire" and referred to his "classification anthropogéographique" as "fictive," his study was republished unchanged by Delafosse in 1930; see Poutrin, *Esquisse Ethnologique,* 2–4; M. Delafosse, *Enquête coloniale . . .* (Paris: Société d'Édition Géographique, Maritime et Coloniale, 1930). Cureau, *Savage Man,* 26–32. For examples of early censuses, AOM-AEF (Aix), D 4D 4(1)D6 1911, "Rapport d'ensemble annuel: Tableaux"; 4(1)D16, Gabon, 1918, "Rapport sur la situation de la Colonie pendant l'année 1918"; for developments in the 1930s and 1940s, see Sautter, *De l'Atlantique,*

35–37; see Emmanuelle Sibeud, "La naissance de l'ethnographie africaniste en France avant 1914," *CEA* 34, 4 (1994): 639–58, for some background on Avelot, Poutrin, and Bruel.

95. The tables are in AOM-AEF, D5D 5D11, 1908–1931, "L'Administrateur Bruel à M. Commissaire Général, Rapport sur la création d'un Cercle des Mitsogho-Nord, Libreville, le 14 mars 1908"; Raponda-Walker, "Au pays des Ishogos," (1908), 254; the term "empty boxes" is from Terence Ranger, "The Invention of Tradition Revisited: The Case of Colonial Africa," in *Legitimacy and the State in Twentieth-Century Africa: Essays in Honour of A.H.M. Kirk-Greene,* ed. Terence Ranger and Olufemi Vaughan (London: Macmillan, 1993), 84.

96. Bowdich, *Mission,* 429.

97. Du Chaillu, *Explorations,* map endpiece; *Journey to Ashango-Land,* 95–96, 210, 254, map endpiece.

98. Ibid., 424–25.

99. Ibid., 425.

100. Walker, "Relation d'une tentative d'exploration," 77; Bichet, "Quelques jours dans l'Ogowé," 583. Raponda-Walker first noted "Gisira" as the local term in his 1931 article; see Raponda-Walker, "Essais sur les idiomes," 5; For more recent spellings, see Florent Mbumb-Bwas and Wisi Magang-Ma-Mbuju, *Les Bajag du Gabon (Essai d'Étude Historique et Linguistique)* (Paris: Imprimerie Saint Michel, 1974), 10; N'Dimina Mougala, "Les Gisir," 8; for an "ethnoscientific" spelling, see Mayer and Voltz, "Dénomination ethno-scientifique," 50–51.

101. Berton, "De Lastourville à Samba," map.

102. Buléon, *Au pays des Eshiras.*

103. Ibid., 52.

104. Ibid., 52–53.

105. Mbumb-Bwas and Magang-ma-Buju, *Les Bajag,* 10–11.

106. "Communauté de Sainte-Croix des Eshiras," *BCSE* 5 (1896–1897): 514; 6 (1898–1899), 376; "L'oeuvre linguistique de la Congrégation du Saint-Esprit et du Saint-Coeur de Marie," *Le Messager du Saint-Esprit* (1908): 376; Le Père Joachim Buléon, *Histoire Sainte re mambu ma vaga Nyàmbi gu yi gu kana batu* (Paris: Mission Catholique, 1899); "Communauté de Saint-Martin des Apindjis," *BCSE* 11 (1907–1908): 233; "Résidence de Ste-Croix, Aux Eshiras," *BCSE* 13 (1911–1912): 960; Pouchet, "Vieux Gabon," 227; Hubert Moukaga, Interview Notes XIX, Mouila, June 15, 1989. Missionaries continue to do pioneering work in Gabonese languages; Soeur Gabriel-Marie Le Moine posted in Mandji since the late 1960s, has produced a dictionary of the Gisira Ngosi dialect which differs, she was quick to point out, from the Gisir spoken in Fougamou (Gisira Kamba) and in Guidouma (Gisira Tando); Interview Notes VI, Soeur Gabriel-Marie Le Moine, Mandji, May 30, 1991.

107. Buléon, *Au pays des Eshira,* 58, 24–25 for map.

108. Archives CPSE, Boîte 680, "Journal de la Communauté de Ste. Croix des Eshiras du 29 juin 1895 au 3 décembre 1905."

109. "Nouvelles de la Mission du Gabon," *AA* 12 (1897): 155.

110. Gaulme, *Le pays de Cama,* 219–37; N'Dimina Mougala, "Les Gisir," 47; "Communauté de Ste-Croix des Eshiras," *BCSE* 11 (1907–1908): 200; 12 (1909–1910): 405; "Nouvelles de la Mission du Gabon," *AA* 12 (1897): 155; Archives CPSE, Boîte 680, "Journal de la Communauté de Ste. Croix des Eshiras du 29 juin 1895 au 3 décembre 1905, mai 1900"; "Le Ministère de Sainte-Croix des Eshiras (Lettre de R. P. Girod," *AA* (1900): 203.

111. Gaulme, "Le sacre de P. Bichet," 403.

112. See Pourtier, *Le Gabon,* 2:9–62, for a detailed discussion of French colonial administrative units and terms.

113. AOM-AEF (Aix), D 4D 4(1)D4 1909, "Rapport annuel d'ensemble"; 4(1)D5 1910, "Rapport annuel, Affaires Politiques"; 4(1)D6 1911, "Rapport politique et economique du 3ème trimestre, Rapport politique du 4ème trimestre"; 4(1)D13 1915, "Resumés des rapports mensuels, janvier-février"; 4(1)D14 1916, "Resumés des rapports mensuels, novembre"; 4(1)D15 1917, "Rapports trimestriels d'ensemble, 2ème et 3ème trimestres"; Foret, "Le Lac Fernan-Vaz," 309; M'Bigui, "Histoire de Sindara," 23; Jean-Bruno Soulounganga, Interview Notes XXV, Mouila, June 16, 1991.

114. Bruel, "Carte de Moyen Ogooué et de la Ngounié"; "La boucle de l'Ogooué," (1910), 648; (1911), 124–27; Avelot, "Recherches sur l'histoire," 372–85; Poutrin, *Esquisse ethnologique,* 11–15, map; Delingettes, "Carte Générale," Feuille IV; AOM-AEF (Aix), D 4D 4(1)D16 1918, "Rapport sur la situation de la Colonie du Gabon pendant 1918."

115. Delafosse, *Enquête coloniale*; Raponda-Walker, "Les Tribus"; Mgr Tardy et ses missionnaires, "Une nouvelle carte du Gabon," *AP* (1932): 71; Soret, Introduction, in Raponda-Walker, *Notes d'histoire,* 6–7; Deschamps, *Traditions orales,* 19 for map.

116. See Mbumb-Bwas and Magang-ma-Mbuju, *Les Bajag,* 10–11; N'Dimina, "Les Gisir," 7–8; Mbigui, "Histoire de Sindara," 21–23; Augoueli-Matoka, "Institutions funéraires chez les Gisir"; Goufoura Offiga, "La chefferie indigène Gisira"; Victorien Koumba, "Esquisse phonologique de Gisir (Langue Bantu du Gabon B.41)," (Rapport de license, UOB, Libreville, 1989); Joseph Matsiengui-Boussamba, "Enquête sur le mythe dans la société Gisir 'Mulombi Lendemweli,'" (Rapport de license, UOB, Libreville, 1989). For continued use of "Eshira" on maps, see *Géographie et cartographie du Gabon,* 43.

117. F. J. Ormeling, *Minority Toponyms on Maps: The Rendering of Linguistic Minority Toponyms on Topographic Maps of Western Europe* (Utrecht: University of Utrecht, 1983), 18; see 70–76 for French techniques and practices for naming toponyms.

18. See Christopher Gray, "Territoriality and Colonial 'Enclosure' in Southern Gabon." In *Enfermement, prison et châtiments en Afrique du 19e siècle à nos jours,* ed. Florence Bernault, 101–32 (Paris: Karthala, 1999).

5

COLONIAL TERRITORIALTY'S AMBIGUOUS TRIUMPH IN SOUTHERN GABON, CA.1890–1920

The Colonial State

> Only with the emergence of the state and the associated growth of a specialized political system does society begin to be defined in large part territorially. The polity in state–based societies is a territorial entity charged with the responsibility, among other things, of maintaining its territorial integrity and administratively structuring its internal domain into an integrated set of territorial compartments. No areas are allowed to remain outside the administrative system and at a given functional level no geographical overlapping is permitted. Space must be filled and precise boundaries drawn, for jurisdiction and authority are mainly over pieces of territory and not people.
>
> —Edward Soja[1]

> On one side the work of unification and totalization which belongs to the hegemonic enterprise of governments, and on the other (but indissolubly linked) the deconstruction assured by the scattering of statements: a subtle play of the Full and the Empty, of governmentality itself.
>
> —Jean-François Bayart[2]

The establishment of the colonial state in Southern Gabon was a tortured and ultimately ambiguous process. Though instruments of territoriality employed by the colonial state affected the hegemonic power and breadth described by Soja above, their actual application was a messier affair, less hegemonic than chaotic. Bayart's observation suggests the tensions that existed between the ambitions of the colonial state for control and the frustrated imposition of that control. This chapter traces the evolution of colonial nodal points in Southern Gabon—from factory to Christian mission to concession—holding to outposts of the colonial state—and describes the territorial assumptions of each. It is the concession company/colonial state matrix that developed from around the turn of the century that first affected the totalizing ambitions described by Soja but the results of this imposition of modern territoriality fell more on the side of disruption and ambiguity than control—with dire consequences for the local populations.

Colonial Nodal Points: The Factory

The 1890s witnessed the peak of the accelerating pattern of trade that for several decades had been drawing more and more of Southern Gabon and its inhabitants into its network. The arrival of concession companies to the region in 1898 reflected an ideological shift in European practice, a shift which in just a few short years spelled commercial disaster for many of the network's nodal points. Yet the sometimes strained collusion between the concession companies and the colonial administration did successfully function to undermine those precolonial commercial practices seen as obstacles to capitalist–style commercial exploitation.

Lambaréné continued to be a base of operations for the three most important trading firms—Hatton and Cookson, John Holt and Woermann's—operated from there. However, its preeminent position on the middle Ogooué faced a serious challenge from the colonial post at Ndjolé, founded in 1885 and situated at the center of a dynamic district being established by Fang-speaking clans.[3] Fang-speaking clans were also active in trading with the factories at Samba, and by 1900 they had effectively replaced the Kele-speaking clans on the left bank of the lower Ngounié. They also moved into the networks along the Fernan Vaz where European factories had been active since the 1860s; by 1890 Fang-speaking traders were supplying these factories with ivory and rubber. On the Rembo Nkomi, commerce was still in the hands of Kele- and Gisir-speaking clans who traded with representatives from Holt and Hatton and Cookson, many of whom were "Accras" from the British Gold Coast Colony. The southern-

most extension of Fang-speaking clans—described at the time as a "generally pacific invasion"[4]—was a northern branch of the Setté Cama Lagoon,
where five villages had been created by 1902; commerce in this lagoon
had been flourishing for more than a decade with an important center
established up the Rembo Ndogo at Bongo. A description from 1890
indicates that Bongo was a recent creation resulting from the trade in
rubber:

> Bongo's population is very nomadic. The four tiny villages of Kangala, Nza
> Kouilou, Nvili Mavoungou and Boualabou Nzasi contain so few inhabit-
> ants that it is hardly worth counting. It is principally composed of blacks of
> the trading caravans who, pretty much everyday, carry rubber in the facto-
> ries. The foremen, the leaders of these caravans, are black traders: Accras,
> Sierra-Leonians, Lagos, Gabonese, Loangos or chiefs of the region. They
> arrive with ten, twenty, fifty porters, according to the value of the advances
> they previously received from the managing agent.[5]

Though new nodal points were being created with different clans
and agents becoming more influential in the ever-expanding network of
trade opportunities, the development of factories and the growing number
of outside traders did not fundamentally alter the foundations of precolonial
territoriality or commercial practice, though they did increasingly challenge their capacity to absorb change. European and foreign African traders were obliged to accommodate themselves to the existing practice; they
had to negotiate to set up factories or to establish themselves in a village.
They sought to insert themselves into the complex network of commercial
relations, not to dominate or destroy it. European traders had advantages
in terms of technology, but these were exploited to advance their interests
within the existing network. Romantically depicted by Mary Kingsley, these
were men like the fabled Trader Horn who relished the challenge of negotiating with local figures. Though they might have wanted to do away with
the practice of giving advances or avoid the seeming endless palavers, they
were not in a position to do so.

Their motivations differed from the hegemonic ambitions of the
modern colonial state outlined in the Soja quote above. One finds these
ambitions expressed in the texts of the Christian missionaries and colonial
administrators who proclaimed in their writings that they sought to clear
the ground of existing cultural and territorial practices and then impose
their own. These stated objectives lacked the flexibility and adaptive potential of the nineteenth-century trader and his factory.

Colonial Nodal Points: The Mission

Christian missions had been active in Gabon since the 1840s, American Protestants opening their Baraka mission on the Estuary in 1842 and the French Holy Ghost Fathers opening theirs two years later. Until the 1890s, efforts to create missions in the interior had most often been frustrated and those that had succeeded were established at existing commercial centers in close proximity to the mushrooming number of European factories.[6]

The Christian missions were at pains to distinguish their proselytizing activities as something separate from trade. The task was made doubly difficult when the site of a mission was established in proximity to a commercial center. Such was the case with the Holy Ghost Fathers missions of Saint-François Xavier at Lambaréné and Sainte-Anne at Odimba in the Fernan Vaz, the latter founded in 1887 opposite a Hatton and Cookson factory at the mouth of the Rembo Nkomi. Père Bichet's efforts to create a Christian village community at Odimba and to recruit children to attend the mission school saw him purchasing the bridewealth for one hundred girls over the span of a decade. Food, lodging, and transportation needs for the mission community and school required the priest to enter into the neighboring commercial and labor networks in the fashion of a village clan leader. It is no wonder that Bichet was given the title of *Renima* by the Nkomi-speaking clan leaders of the Fernan Vaz at a ceremony in 1897. Although the significance of this title has been the subject of debate, it does indicate the successful establishment of Odimba as a nodal point and the complexity of the relationships initiated by such a project.[7]

The missionary desire to distance themselves from trade and the moral corruption they believed was brought in its wake[8] no doubt influenced the Holy Ghost Fathers when they founded the missions of Sainte-Croix des Eshira in 1895 and Saint-Martin des Apindji in 1900 at sites removed from the commercial centers on the Rembo Nkomi and the Ngounié.[9] The decision to build Notre-Dame des Trois Épis, founded in 1899, at Sindara near Samba was part of an effort to stop the southern advance of the Protestants from their sphere of activity on the middle Ogooué (always a major concern for the French Catholics) and the wishes of the local Fang-, Eviya-, and Vili-speaking clans to create a European buffer zone between their competing territorial interests (a colonial post was founded a year later). An attempt to create a mission at Aguma, located on the Doubanga which flows into the Rembo Nkomi and which by the 1890s had become a key commercial nodal point for Kele-speaking clans, was abandoned by the turn of the century following the sudden death of the head priest.[10]

Lacking large stocks of European trade goods, the Catholic missions turned to other strategies to carve out a niche in the Southern Gabonese landscape. They sought to build physically imposing missions whose buildings and design would in themselves be attractions to the local population. Père Bichet, who was able to draw on considerable family wealth, constructed a chapel of steel girding ordered from France for Sainte-Anne at Odimba.[11] It was rather more difficult for the missions located in the interior, where obtaining the necessary materials and labor posed problems, to adopt such strategies. In early 1897, the Sainte-Croix mission in the savannah of the Ngosi district of Gisir-speaking clans consisted of two large dwellings and a rather undistinguished chapel. To celebrate the mission's patronal festival the previous year, a monumental cross eleven meters high was erected; this served to attract a considerable crowd, most notably many of the elders in the district. In 1908, a new chapel thirty meters in length was completed and the Vicar Apostolic, Monseigneur Adam, travelled from Libreville for its dedication.

> More than four hundred people came to attend this celebration. From the morning of this splendid day, we saw on all the avenues arriving at the mission long lines of Eshiras [Gisira] dressed for the occasion in their best clothes. . . . At eight o'clock, the ceremony began. The Monseigneur solemnly blessed the chapel between the two bays of spectators while the bells were ringing and gunpowder resounded from all sides. . . . Never had our Eshiras seen such beautiful ceremonies and still today they speak to us with admiration of the Monseigneur's beautiful cloth and his magnificent Chief's cane.[12]

The ritual paraphernalia of the Catholic Church and the extravagance of its celebrations appealed to the peoples of Southern Gabon, as ritual and extravagance were integral elements in their own religious practice.[13]

The missionaries' stated objectives was to bring about an "inauguration of a new social order" by struggling against the enslavement of dependents and women, the two primary sources of precolonial wealth. Recognizing that they were relatively powerless to accomplish this in the final years of the nineteenth century, the French Catholic missions appealed to the almost equally powerless colonial government and to organizations in France such as the Anti-Slavery Society for help.[14]

The establishment of Catholic missions, the construction of imposing buildings, and the organization of religious ceremonies inserted into the landscape of Southern Gabon a completely new kind of space. There now existed European nodal points that were not primarily interested in trade but in talking about "les choses de Dieu," whose calendar of ceremonies was not connected to the rhythms of the planting or trading seasons or to the cycles of birth, maturity, and death that determined the timing of local ritual practices. In this, they were the precursors of the colonial administration's efforts to enforce new conceptions of time and labor.[15] The missions were tolerated because their rites and ceremonies were intriguing to local populations and because they integrated themselves to a greater or lesser degree into the existing commercial and political networks.

For example, Père Buléon, the founder of Sainte-Croix, and his successor, Père Girod, were both active in settling disputes among Gisir-speaking clan leaders in the Ngosi district during the first decade of the mission's existence. In 1907, the priests were concerned that the establishment of a colonial administrative post in the district would undermine their influence but soon realized that:

> due to the continual replacements of our "Chefs de poste" (colonial administrators), and their perfect ignorance of the language of the region, this apprehension was only a propitious illusion, so much so that the Father Superior continues to be the uncontested chief to whom all the Eshiras [Gisira] come to submit their palavers.[16]

Knowledge and the writing down of local languages were crucial activities distinguishing the mission's position from that of the colonial post. At the turn of the century, the mission schools established in Southern Gabon were the sole institutions providing any type of modern education.[17] For the missionaries, reading and writing skills were a means for getting across the message of the Gospel to the young boys who were the focus of their recruitment. However, for the students and their elders the development of literate skills meant gaining access to the knowledge of "whites" and enabled them to engage successfully in trade. Thus there existed a continual tension between the objectives of the teacher and those of the students over how to best make use of "a head that thinks like paper writes."[18]

The three Catholic missions that opened in Southern Gabon between 1895 and 1900 struggled with personnel and resource shortages in the early years of their existence. The limited funds available to the Holy Ghost Fathers for education were reserved for mission schools in Libreville and Lambaréné, where competition with the Protestants was most intense. As a consequence, former students from these schools were able to maintain the dominance of Mpongwe- and Galwa-speakers at commercial and administrative posts requiring literacy.[19] In 1899, Sainte-Croix had difficulty keeping fifteen students enrolled, and the following year the death of a student at the mission resulted in most of the parents withdrawing their children. By 1905 confidence in the mission returned and enrollment was fifty-eight; Saint-Martin and Trois-Épis claimed similar enrollments during this period. The priests at Saint-Martin cited as obstacles to their work the disappointment of the local population when it became apparent that the missionaries had not come to the district for commerce and the belief that the ritual of baptism caused death.[20]

Missionaries were encouraged to travel out into neighboring districts in order to recruit students for their schools. But given their many responsibilities back at the mission station recruitment was delegated to trained catechists drawn from the local populations. Père Lejeune at Saint-François Xavier in Lambaréné was the first to form such a group; the catechists were

> chosen from among our former students who left us knowing how to read and write a bit, desirous to do all they could to avoid the greatest sins but without the privilege of impeccability. Their strength is their regularity in saying prayers and the catechism morning and night in the village where they are based.[21]

Père Buléon boasted in 1898 that at Sainte-Croix he had recruited twelve catechists for work in the Gisir-speaking Ngosi district and had placed three in nearby villages. However by 1905 Buléon's successor reported that:

> All had left their posts, which had become a sinecure. At first, all the peoples of a village, men and women, big and small, had come to attend the catechism. But this fervor very quickly slackened off; and soon it happened that the catechist would ring his bell and no one would answer the call. The moment for placing catechists has not arrived. Thus we will turn our concerns principally toward the children; and we will go ourselves to do the catechism in the villages.[22]

Catechists themselves were often tempted to leave this line of work for more lucrative positions in commerce or the colonial administration. An informant, Hubert Moukaga, who began his association with Saint-Martin as a student in 1916 and was a catechist from 1923, related that he and his colleagues were never well paid, and that a number left to do other things though retaining their Christian beliefs. This was the case with the catechist Edouard from Trois-Épis, who in 1901 profited from his post in the village by purchasing rubber and then selling it to the factories at Samba, much to the chagrin of the missionaries; it is not known whether he maintained his Christian beliefs.[23]

Despite these initial setbacks, catechists did come to play a major role in spreading the influence of the Catholic missions following World War I. As agents of these new nodal points, catechists, and the European missionaries who preceded them, spread some of the rudiments of literacy and modern learning in their recruitment efforts. For as they taught villagers to recite the catechism, they made use of such pedagogical tools as songs, visual reproductions of Christian images, and writing boards. The distribution of religious medals and witnessing the Christian ritual of "talking to God" also served to attract potential converts. It was through observing the prayers of his relative Cyprian Mwanda (among the first catechists from Saint-Martin) that Hubert Moukaga first became interested in Christianity.[24]

The presence of a catechist in a village differed from that of a trader in the same way that the mission differed from that of the factory. The catechist, to the degree that he embodied the message of the missionaries, was not trying to carve out a niche from an existing network in the manner of an outside trader but rather was seeking to replace existing practice. The catechist Moukaga related that by the 1920s the missions were able to demand an end to *mwiri* and *bwiti* initiations in a village as a condition for the posting of catechist.[25] This would not have been possible at the turn of the century.

Simply becoming a catechist was viewed as a direct assault on clan and lineage obligations as indicated in the comments of the Gabonese priest, Florent Mbumb-Bwas:

> For his family, the catechist converted to Christianity appeared as separate, a lost man for the clan. He no longer took part in clan festivities, in festivals of the dead, even if misfortune should strike his family; he could no longer consult diviners: all this because his religion forbade him to do so. What's more, certain laws of the church like that of monogamy, led to the dissolution of the family, for the catechist who must preach and exemplify the Word would never be able to take in the wives of his deceased uncle or brother. Fasting and abstinence add further prohibitions to clan prohibitions linking a Christian to a family of which he does not always grasp the contours. If the close relatives of a catechist were often resigned to the destiny of one of their own, it was not the same for all members of the clan or the local chiefs. In certain cases, the conflict between tradition and the new religion was settled through the poisoning of the catechist.[26]

These clan tensions are reflected in the life experience of Hubert Moukaga. The elders of both his mother's and father's lineages were against

Moukaga's going to Saint-Martin in 1916; his mother, however, was in favor of his decision. Thus, Moukaga left the village for the mission in his father's absence. He was now a "lost man" to his matrilineal clan, and his father was obliged to reimburse Moukaga's maternal uncle with a rifle, some cloth, and some salt. Moukaga noted that he was not present for his parents' deaths but was out working for the mission.[27]

Catechists were, thus, agents of a new type of European nodal point. Missionaries consciously set their activities and their missions apart from those of factories and traders. They employed different strategies and demanded a radical commitment from their catechist agents. The initial impact was slight as their efforts were overwhelmed by the obsession with commerce and the strength of local religious traditions. Catholic religious rituals and celebrations attracted some interest, but as they were separate from the cultural rhythms of the equatorial tradition this initial curiosity was difficult to sustain. Indeed, the message of the missionaries flew in the face of these cultural rhythms and was quickly absorbed by them as the missions had no power to coerce. The clusters of imposing structures that were the mission sites, in the case of Sainte-Croix and Saint-Martin purposely constructed some distance from European factories and colonial posts, were an eccentric kind of nodal point. As the practices of modern territoriality began to ineluctably alter the landscape of Southern Gabon, these missions were forced to abandon their eccentricities and integrate themselves into the territory of the new colonial towns.[28]

Colonial Nodal Points: Concession and Colonial Post

Truly effective colonial nodal points capable of extending the influence of modern territoriality only began to form with the advent of concession companies and the efforts of colonial posts to collect taxes in the closing years of the nineteenth century. The missionary vision for the radical transformation of the cultural practices of Southern Gabon paralleled that of Brazza's for the landscape and employed the same literate instruments to chart its trajectory in textual space.[29] Yet it differed dramatically in the kind and quantity of resources it could draw upon to impose its vision. Even so, the colonial state at the close of the nineteenth century drew upon assets insufficient to meet its modern ambitions. De Brazza, as Commissioner-General of the French Congo colony from 1886 to 1898, squandered the resources made available to him by the French government in trying to conquer Chad and was singularly ineffective in promoting any kind of economic benefit for France. In spite of his efforts to attract French capital, commercial activity in Gabon continued to be dominated by British and German firms, a severe affront to the intensely patriotic colonial servant. By 1898, the French government was frustrated as well and Brazza was recalled to France.[30]

Before his departure Brazza set in motion the project of creating concession companies on the model of those operating in King Leopold's Congo Free State. By 1900 more than seventy percent of the French Congo colony had been divided up into some forty-two different concessions. These concession companies operated from a radically different approach than trading firms like Hatton and Cookson, as they claimed both monopoly control over commerce and ownership rights to land within their concession. Simply put, "all rights of possession and exploitation" accrued to the concession company, this based on a legal argument which posited that:

> Land can only be individual, collective, or public domain property. There is no individual property in the countries of the blacks but only temporary usage and collective property in no case leads to a rental tax for temporary or permanent usage, either within the collectivity or outside of it, nor can it be sold by either one or several members of the collectivity. In law all sales made by the natives are fictive. None are valid legally.[31]

In concluding that all the land of the French Congo was public domain with the local populations having only usage rights, not only were precolonial territorial practices emptied of their significance but so were the accommodations negotiated by the existing European factories.

The most potent symbol of this crucial shift in the European *cognitive* map is the 1900 *cartographic* map published in *La Dépêche Coloniale* illustrating the holdings of the various concession companies (see Map 12).[32] This is a very different product from the tentative mapping efforts of Du Chaillu forty years earlier. The appropriating gaze that first looked out on the physical space of Southern Gabon through the eyes of individual explorers now precisely rendered the perceived chaos of the equatorial forest through the ordered textual space of the cartographic grid. The bold and sharply geometrical lines delimiting the concessions are expressions of an enhanced imperial confidence poised to impose a modern capitalist territoriality over its domain.

Frustrated with the poor economic performance of the French Congo under De Brazza, the metropolitan government in Paris decided to cut its subsidies and require the colony to pay its own way. Thus in 1900 a per capita tax was conceived that would produce the necessary revenue to run the colony. In classic fashion, the local population would be required to collect rubber, ivory, and ebony for the concession companies so as to obtain the monetary sums required to pay the colonial tax. Efforts to obtain taxes from the Fang- and Kele-speaking clans on the middle Ogooué and lower Ngounié in the 1890s had been sporadic and ineffective, but from the turn of the century collecting *les impôts* became an obsession of the French colonial administration in Southern Gabon. In a few short years, this policy, combined with the attempts of French concession companies to enforce their monopolies, brought a halt to commercial activity at many key centers.

On several occasions in 1900, agents in the employ of the Compagnie Française du Congo Occidental (C.F.C.O.) seized rubber collected by British firms along the Nyanga River, claiming monopoly rights over all products gathered in their concession. Seizures also occurred in Setté Cama, where by the middle of 1901 a continual decline in trade due to conflicts between the Société de la Setté Cama and British firms was noted by the colonial administration. After a couple of false starts, the Société du Haut-Ogooué (S.H.O.) started its operations on both banks of the middle and upper Ogooué in 1897 (see Map 13) and began seizing rubber from British firms operating near Samba in 1899. The British advocate E. D. Morel lamented that a decade spent training Tsogo-speaking clans in efficient rubber-gathering techniques was being unjustly appropriated; Mitsogo traditions recall a significant increase in the availability of European cloth from this period. By 1905, the once lively commerce on the Rembo Nkomi had come to a standstill as Hatton and Cookson, Holt, and Woermann's pulled out, leaving behind ten abandoned factory sites. The Compagnie Coloniale du Fernan Vaz concession had claimed rights to all products from the soil but the abusive trading tactics of their agents pushed the leaders of the Gisir- and Nkomi-speaking clans to lodge a complaint with the colonial administration and then finally to move to other districts.[33]

These 1907 observations from the Lieutenant-Governor concerning Mayumba summarize the sentiments found among the inhabitants of other previously active trade centers: "To tell the truth, the blacks despise us and, rightly or wrongly, have considered the departure of the British firms as an act of hostility undertaken against them."[34] Aloysius Smith, in rather more colorful language, captured the frustration of the British trader with the French:

> The biggest stumbling-block to trade ever known to civilized man. The most rapacious nation, consistent with inactivity, the world has ever known. Noth-

Map 13. S.H.O. Concession, ca. 1900.

ing more than funguses sucking life from a healthy tree. Why, they'd change their duties easy as putting a fresh song on the piano desk. Rush the tax off matches and clap it on something else.[35]

The combined obsessions of the colonial administration's pursuit of tax revenue and the efforts of the concession companies to profit from their monopoly claims saw the creation of colonial nodal points that would ultimately introduce modern territorial practices and irreversibly transform the landscape of Southern Gabon. Colonial posts existed at Cap Lopez from 1885 and in Setté Cama and Mayumba from 1887. By 1905 and the arrival of the Brazza Commission to investigate concession company abuses, colonial and concession actions were seen as one and the same by the local populations and were blamed for the decline in commerce. The creation of a post at Agouma in 1904 came on the heels of the commercial collapse on the Rembo Nkomi. The surrounding population at all the above posts simply moved their villages in search of new trade opportunities or to avoid efforts at tax collection by an increasingly brutal colonial militia. The military post of Mouila, also established in 1904, was created in response to the rebellion of the Tsogo-speaking clans in the Kamba and Gésuma districts.[36]

But the colonial/concession tandem was not always a disruption to trade or a stimulus to rebellion. The post at Sindara was created in 1900 shortly after the establishment of the Trois-Épis mission and the arrival of the S.H.O factories. Here at Samba (and downstream at Lambaréné), Christian mission, colonial post, and concession company factories functioned with some degree of coordination to form an efficient colonial nodal point. The S.H.O. was the best-funded and most well-organized of all the concession companies and effectively usurped the role of the colonial administration in the Du Chaillu Massif to the east of Samba through the 1920s. In 1909, colonial officials remarked that the S.H.O appointed village chiefs, levied fines, put together their own militias, and were indeed the main authority in the region. Factories on the Upper Ikoy, the Ikobé, and at Mullerville became centers and were serviced by some forty traders in 1913 the majority of whom were Mpongwe-speakers from Libreville or Galwaspeakers from Lambaréné; there were some Senegalese traders while other Senegalese served in the S.H.O militias. Raponda-Walker toured the immediate hinterland beyond Samba in 1907 and remarked upon the many S.H.O. caravans that crisscrossed the region (rubber and ebony were the primary concerns), the passion of the local Tsogo-, Eviya-, and Gisir-speaking clans for commerce, and the creation of new villages at the most profitable sites along the trade routes.[37]

The S.H.O.'s tight organization and methods of intimidation (Raponda-Walker noted these as well) had resulted in a significant increase in an already active commerce. As previously noted, growing commercial opportunities stimulated further mobility among already mobile populations. From the turn of the century, Tsogo-speaking clans (the Pogéo clan being the first) of the Matèndè district established villages at Samba and for the first time entered into direct contact with European agents. Members of the Nzobe clan appear to have taken particular advantage of these new opportunities. Vili- and Eviya-speaking clans had earlier served as middle-men, but the determination of the S.H.O. to break up this network led to their marginalization; Bwalé, an important village of Eviya-speaking clans, was progressively abandoned, and consequent attempts to establish villages on the trade routes in the Du Chaillu Massif were not very successful.[38]

Meanwhile, a few Tsogo-speaking clan leaders had become quite pow-erful due to gains from the rubber trade and the continuing trade in clan dependents. Mapadi, the founder of the village of Biogo in the Waka dis-trict who died in 1906, was one such leader. An energetic man, he was continually occupied with either iron-working, wood-carving, building huts, clearing trees, planting bananas, or maintaining the village plaza; but more often he was travelling:

> Mapadi had numerous contacts among the Ivilis [Vili], the Ivéas [Eviya] and the Eshiras [Gisira] as well as the Ashangos [Massango] and the Ndjavis [Nzabi]. From the latter two groups, he obtained rubber and especially slaves which he resold to the former, not without a fat profit. . . . Of all the Ishogos [Mitsogo] of the Waka district, it is said that only one other, Magandja of Pingo village, could measure up to Mapadi. It was due to the trade in slaves that Mapadi was able to make Biogo such a large village.[39]

It was the relative prosperity enjoyed by the Tsogo-speaking clans of the Matèndè and Waka districts that influenced their decision not to partici-pate in the rebellion organized by the neighboring districts of Kamba and Gésuma.

The Tsogo-speaking districts of the Du Chaillu massif were able to prosper because the colonial administration was not yet capable of enforc-ing tax collection and the S.H.O realized that they would have to accom-modate themselves to the existing commercial practices associated with the factories. Thus, their agents continued to advance goods for rubber or ebony, though they were quick to make use of the S.H.O. militia if debts were not repaid. Further, S.H.O factories did little to extend the use of colonial currency, preferring instead to exchange local currencies such as "neptunes" for their rubber and ebony purchases. This greatly distressed the colonial administration whose officials were often reduced to collecting the per capita tax in kind. Administrators complained continually about this situation and often blamed concession company practices for their revenue woes.[40]

Though making use of the same instruments of modern territoriality, there were differences between the colonial administration and the conces-sion companies as to how and for whom they were to be employed. The

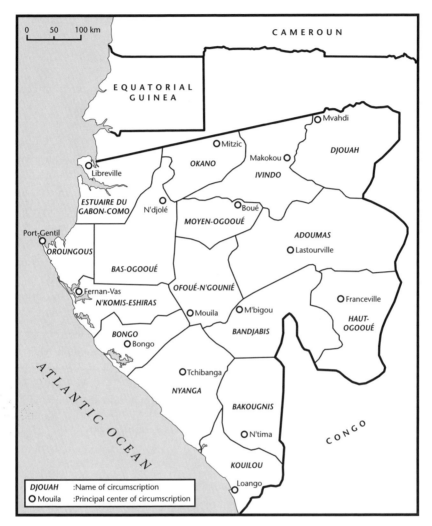

Map 14. Administrative Subdivisions of Gabon, 1916. Based on Colette Dubois, *Le prix d'une guerre* (Aix-en-Provence: Institut d'Histoire des Pays d'Outre-Mer, 1985), p. 322.

boundaries of the S.H.O. concession often intersected or cut across those of the colonial *circonscriptions*.[41] The S.H.O. resented the administration's intrusion on territory they had developed for their own purposes, just as the Catholic missionaries at Sainte-Croix had despaired the establishment of a colonial post on their territory. Yet the advance of the colonial state's modern territoriality was an inexorable, if uneven, process and terribly painful for those populations of Southern Gabon fully drawn into its wake. After nearly a decade of tax collection and concession company activity, the Lieutenant-Governor of Gabon saw more negative than positive results and wrote that the colony suffered from a "mal profond."[42]

Excluding the territory of the S.H.O., commerce at most other centers had severely declined and district structures all but disappeared as villages fled into remote areas to escape tax collection. This was the case of the Gisir-speaking clans of the Banda District who either moved off the Upper Doubandji toward Lake Oguemoué or strategically positioned themselves in the border areas on the Doubigui and Doubandji between the jurisdictions of the colonial posts at Mandji and Sindara. It would seem that all this movement led to the dissolution of Banda as a district.[43] District structures around Samba, long under pressure, effectively collapsed under the weight of the continual flow of new and different clans into the area. With speakers of Fang, Vili, Kele, Gisir, Eviya, and Tsogo all clustered together, the Catholic missionaries found choosing a language with which to teach the gospel a difficult task even though all groups probably knew something of their neighbors' tongues. A priest lamented in 1909:

> If only these peoples lived in clearly distinct regions, one would be able to visit them in turn; but unfortunately this is not the case. Downstream from the Mission one encounters Ivilis [Vili], Pahouins [Fang], and Akélés [Bakele] villages spread out here and there along the Ngounié in no order; meanwhile the Ivéas [Eviya], the Issogos [Mitsogo], and the Eshira [Gisira] Kambas, scattered all over, divide among themselves the mountainous country of the Upper Ngounié.[44]

This perceived disorder of Gabonese space motivated the most energetic of the colonial bureaucrats, Georges Le Testu, to create a modern European order to facilitate their administrative tasks. In one of the few detailed ethnographic studies produced by a French administrator, Le Testu continually criticized the "imprecise" nature of the customs of the Punu-speaking clans around the Nyanga. In noting the "vague" and "poorly defined" terms of local "contracts," Le Testu was in fact delineating the differences between oral and literate practice. He was very clear that the latter must replace the former: "Our task then will be to put some precision into these conventions."[45] Commerce and government rooted in literate bureaucratic practice rarely have much patience for the subtle and complex negotiations of oral cultures.

The activities of the concession companies and the colonial administration in the first decade of the twentieth century might be seen as a continuation of the ever-accelerating pace of commerce that had begun in the mid-nineteenth century. However, the European trader's strategy of integration into existing commercial networks was gradually abandoned with the shift in ideology associated with the concession companies. Their arrival signalled the start of more overt attempts to impose the territoriality required by a modern state. Thus, the earliest efforts at systematic mapping and census-taking were organized to facilitate the collection of tax revenue. Yet these efforts led to a serious commercial decline at many of the centers that had developed around European factories; they also incited a number of districts in the interior to unprecedented levels of rebellion. The chaos thus induced by the end of 1909 caused the colonial governor to assess the French impact in Gabon as largely detrimental to the local populations.[46]

The challenge from a serious external threat to their sources of power and prestige pushed the clan leaders of Tsogo- and Punu-speaking districts to organize in new ways but still within the parameters of the precolonial tradition. The cooperation between the Gésuma and Kamba districts under Mbombé to resist the French no doubt reinforced an identity related to district; the same can be said of the resistance of the Punu-speaking Mokab district under Mavurulu.[47] Yet at the same time those practices that provided the foundation for the functioning of districts in precolonial times— the reciprocal exchange of dependents between the clans residing in the district's villages, the privileges of the first-comer clans, the ritual practice of the *mwiri*-type societies—were being undermined by colonial military expeditions and undisciplined militia who forced entire villages off the main trading routes and deeper into the forest to continue on in splintered fragments. Earlier strategies to maneuver for position along the most active trade routes were reversed as clan leaders sought to distance themselves from colonial territory. Patterns of village settlement and land use were severely disrupted as the populations began to spend more time in seasonal *mpindi* or temporary camps so as to avoid contact with agents of the French administration. This kind of disruption of fragile agricultural and hunting practices could not go on for very long without producing serious food shortages. The physical reality of districts was starting to disappear.

Yet a refined cognitive map was in the making. The experience of active resistance to French colonial rule not only reinforced district identity in Kamba, Gésuma, and Mokab but also provided important kernels around which Mitsogo and Bapunu ethnic identities would later be formed. The figures of Mbombé and Mavurulu are crucial in this regard; though in their lifetimes they could claim allegiance only from some of the districts that would later form the Mitsogo and Bapunu ethnic groups they both became "culture heros" for members of Tsogo- and Punu-speaking clans who later sought to fill in and give meaning to the ethnic categories that emerged from the colonial experience.[48]

Famine And Chaos: A Decade of Disaster, 1910–1920

> *Yi! Mbili mambu me tsotsu tsotsua.*
> (Ah! So many problems have happened here on earth.)
> —Antoinette Guilouba, recalling times of hunger.[49]

In 1910 colonial officials touring the Eshiras *circonscription,* which included the villages of the Gisir-speaking Ngosi district, described the "great misery" in which they found the population:

> The most concrete and prosaic examples are the most eloquent: one daily sees in this region nubile young girls going about their business completely nude whereas elderly Eshira bitterly recall that fifteen years ago all the children were clothed; at present, even when they want to trade they only find worn out merchandise in poor supply at the Agouma and Mbari factories run by traders who are sometimes totally destitute. The only personal wealth that exists in the region is brought there by adults who have gone to work elsewhere and who return after several years of voluntary exile.[50]

From about 1909 labor migration to work in the timber industry started to radically alter the landscape of Southern Gabon. Exports of *okoumé,* the famous "roi *okoumé*" which would dominate economic activity in Gabon throughout the colonial period, had risen from a first few logs in 1889 to 7000 tons in 1905 to 91,000 tons in 1911. The burgeoning timber industry effectively salvaged the economic disaster brought on by the concession companies. Several failed ventures, including the much maligned S.H.N., were reorganized to form the Société Agricole, Forestière et Industrielle pour l'Afrique (S.A.F.I.A.) which focused solely on exploiting its monopoly privileges over the transportation of logs cut on the lower Ogooué and in the Lakes region, the primary sources for *okoumé.* These two areas attracted thousands of "*coupeurs de bois*" (wood-cutters) from surrounding districts, and their activity stimulated the return of Lambaréné as a central nodal point in the colonial commercial network. It had been eclipsed for a time by its upstream rival, Ndjolé; by 1910 continuing unrest in the surrounding Fang-speaking districts had resulted in a commercial decline at Ndjolé.[51]

In this early phase, the exploitation of *okoumé* differed little from the commerce of other forest products: dependent labor of local clan leaders cut down the trees and chopped out the logs which were then floated down creeks and rivers to be sold to agents from European factories. There was no need to recruit labor for work camps in the forest as the *okoumé* trees were sufficiently close to waterways and thus did not require sophisticated extraction techniques. As was the case with the gathering of rubber, ebony, and ivory, the organization of labor for the initial stages of the exploitation of *okoumé* was entirely under the control of local traders and clan leaders; this remained the case up to World War I.[52]

Labor was, however, recruited for the transportation of the logs from the interior waterways down to the coast. Throughout the first decade of concession company activity, the Lumbu-, Vili-, and Punu-speaking districts of the Nyanga *circonscription* were the main sources of this labor. By 1910, the C.F.C.O. concession had become little more than a recruiter for the rest of the colony. The needs of the timber industry accelerated this process, and by 1911 colonial documents report the recruitment of labor from Bongo on the Rembo Ndogo and from villages in the area of Mouila and Ndendé. Most of these workers were employed to move *okoumé* from the lower Ogooué and the Lakes down to the coast, particularly to Port-Gentil on Cape Lopez which became the key port for timber exports.[53]

Complaints from colonial officials and timber industry agents regarding insufficient labor to meet the needs of their various projects were also on the increase. In 1910, the colonial administration decided to organize the construction of a path from the post at Sindara to the rapids at Fougamou in order to better exploit the Ngounié as a means of transportation. Work began in July with a peak of 1000 workers of both sexes employed during the month of August at several work sites along the 32–kilometer stretch of forest. Projects of this scale were not known in the precolonial period, and it is significant that the administration organized the different sites according to their notions of ethnicity. For example, the "Eshira" were responsible for clearing the first ten kilometers heading out of Fougamou; the "Akele" ("Bakele") and "Pahouin" ("Fang") were also grouped into camps, the latter even organizing to demand higher wages (which they did not receive). One cannot underestimate the experience of participating in these kinds of colonial ventures and the consequent push it gave to making these invented ethnic categories more real. The construction of the Sindara-Fougamou path was simply one of the earliest.[54]

Construction continued into 1912 but by this time factory agents at Sindara began to complain that too many workers were being diverted from gathering forest products. This struggle over access to labor would continue throughout the colonial period. But concerns that would have more serious consequences for the populations of Southern Gabon were arising. Beginning in 1911, colonial reports from the Lower Ogooué noted that the rush to participate in the timber industry was resulting in the neglect of village plantations. This was also the case in the Eshiras *circonscription* as Gisir-speaking clans moved out of the Ngosi and Banda districts (Banda virtually ceased to exist) to cut timber on the shores of Lake Oguemoué; Kele-speaking clans abandoned the once active center at Agouma. The consequent shortage of male labor required at the outset of the dry season—when the men prepare the fields for the women farmers—was exacerbated by the ban on the sale of gunpowder in effect since 1908. Imposed to bring the numerous rebellions to an end, the lack of gunpowder led to a decrease in hunting and an ensuing increase in damage done to plantations by wild animals.[55]

The migration of labor to Cape Lopez and Lambaréné assisted the colonial administration's tax collection capability, as timber workers were usually paid in French currency. But this was not always the case as some European agents simply paid their workers in rum; alcohol abuse became a problem in these centers. This was particularly true during the idle dry season as cut logs awaited the rains and the rise in rivers to make the journey down to the coast. Workers far from their home villages with time and money on their hands often spent them drinking. Since those who received wages from timber had little trouble in paying off their taxes, the colonial administration thought it appropriate to raise the rate. This caused serious problems in those parts of the colony not involved in timber.[56]

In 1911 the priests at Saint-Martin reported food shortages and hunger among the Apindji-speaking clans on the Ngounié due to flood damage from the year before:

> Yet, in the middle of famine, we saw the government of the colony raise the per capita tax from 3 to 5 francs in a region where rubber has been more or less exhausted. In order to liberate themselves from the tax, the native of the Apindji region had to carry 100 kilos of palmnuts to Mouila for at the time a kilo was being bought for 0 fr. 05. (Happily since then English competition has upped the price to 0 fr.16.) . . . The result: the natives abandoned their villages to live in the forest with their families under shelters made of branches. And since the tax was not coming in, the military administration began to track them down day and night like wild beasts. The tirailleurs and regional guards arrested and chained all those who were not bearers of the tax badge or the "piece of tin," as the natives call it.[57]

An already dangerous situation reached the critical stage as the climate started to do strange things. The rains that normally follow the long dry season beginning in September fell irregularly, and this disrupted the planting season as well as log transport. Rivers remained too low into April of 1914, and the colonial administration became concerned about the presence of large numbers of unemployed workers at Cape Lopez and Lambaréné. It became possible to move logs in May but the water level went down again in June; European foresters who had advanced credit to local loggers were facing financial ruin. The outbreak of World War I in August brought the timber commerce to a complete halt as the German firms based in Hamburg that had been buying virtually all of the *okoumé* produced in Gabon no longer did so. Thousands of workers who had only just entered into the colonial wage-earning sector were unemployed and obliged to return to their villages in the interior. The initial recruitment had been disruptive enough, but the overnight reversal in fortune led to even greater confusion.[58]

The commercial and economic collapse brought on by the war and the closing down of the timber industry saw the prices of European goods soar; this to the great consternation of traders and clan leaders in the interior. With the market for *okoumé* gone and with low prices paid for forest products (in contrast to the high prices demanded for European goods), there was little motivation to participate in colonial trade networks. The colonial administration now confronted serious revenue shortfalls, which they unwisely tried to meet by doubling the per capita tax from 5 to 10 francs. There were very few inhabitants of Southern Gabon willing or even able to pay this increase; virtually no one could understand why it was being so energetically implemented. From 1915 colonial officials employed the Regional Guard to force the populations in their *circonscriptions* to go out into the forest to harvest rubber or collect palm kernels so as to pay off their tax obligations.[59]

The situation was further exacerbated by the French administration's efforts to recruit porters for the military campaign in German Cameroon. From December 1914 to March 1915, 3000 porters were recruited for the whole colony, primarily from the Bas-Ogooué, Bongo, and Nyanga *circonscriptions*. This pattern continued throughout 1915; 580 were recruited from the Bas-Ogooué in August for a total of 1500 by the end of the year; Bongo supplied the highest percentage during this August drive. Nyanga by December had sent 1100 porters and 500 migrant workers out of the *circonscription*.[60] Le Testu, who at the time was posted to Nyanga, remarked that "the first result of this exodus of young men is a reduction in cultivation" and that village households were "risking a scarcity of food."[61]

Despite these warnings, the colonial administration continued re-cruiting throughout 1916. For the two-year period between December 1914 and the defeat of the German forces in January 1916, the colony of Gabon sent to Cameroon just over 4000 "permanent" porters who stayed for the duration of the war and 56,000 "temporary" porters who were engaged for shorter periods. Given the limitation of recruitment to a few *circonscriptions,* total percentages of those sent to Cameroon may have approached close to half the male population for some districts in Southern Gabon.[62] Though the volume was not nearly so great as those recruited to serve in the other African campaigns (for example, in Belgian Congo 260,000 porters were re-cruited to serve in the East African campaign), historian Michael Crowder's observation that the "sheer numbers involved are mind-boggling" still applies.[63]

Male inhabitants of these *circonscriptions* were encouraged to become porters so that they could earn enough money to pay their tax obligations. The act of recruitment caused resistance, and many simply fled into the forest; many others were almost certainly forcibly conscripted. When the colonial army sought to recruit *tirailleurs* to fight on the European front beginning in 1916, a French captain clearly set the tone for abuses no doubt committed by the Regional Guards: " I cannot regard forced recruit-ment as illegal; to place the native at our side in order to fight for and obtain victory is to enhance the prestige of the black race and not to lessen it."[64]

The recruitment of nearly 60,000 young men over a two-year period from their home districts in Southern Gabon for duty in Cameroon and their return home represented a volume and pattern of population move-ment hitherto unknown to this area. Even the Atlantic slave trade at its height did not approach these figures. With such a large portion of the population making contact with new disease environments and then re-turning home, it is not surprising that the most recent disease scourge that swept equatorial Africa—sleeping sickness—was spread further in the interior.

Sleeping sickness had been noted as the cause of death of a trader on the lower Ngounié as early as 1900. Indeed, its introduction into Southern Gabon was attributed to traders and colonial personnel recruited from Loango and Mayumba, where by 1909 the disease was already a source of administrative concern. The growth of the timber industry and the mix-ture of populations at Lambaréné produced cases of sleeping sickness at this colonial center from 1910. Villages along waterways like the Nyanga River, Rembo Ndogo, and the Iguéla and Setté Cama Lagoons all had docu-mented cases from 1911. By 1913, sleeping sickness was reported in Sindara and laying waste the remaining Vili-speaking clans who had been so hard hit by smallpox fifteen years earlier. In 1914, it was taking casualties among the Apindji-speaking clans on the middle Ngounié and two years later was spreading at a disturbing rate in the heavily recruited Bongo *circonscription*.[65]

If the ban on gunpowder, the recruitment of porters, and the spread of sleeping sickness were not enough to bring on food shortages, the weather continued to play its part as, following the dry spell of 1913–1914, rains were too early and too abundant in 1914–1915, wiping out most of the plantations in the Eshiras *circonscription*. Much of Southern Gabon also experienced food shortages during the long dry season of 1915 with a number of deaths from starvation reported in the Apindji-speaking district near the Saint-Martin mission.[66]

Despite these developments the administration effectively sanctioned the Regional Guard to use increasingly brutal methods to collect revenues and further disrupt cultivation practices. Perhaps the worst abuses occurred in the Eshiras *circonscription* which from 1915 through 1917 was under the command of a colonial administrator named Chamarande; the mere mention of this name continues to provoke an agitated response from those who remember the suffering and humiliation of this period.[67] The colonial administration in Libreville apparently believed that the previous Eshiras administrator had been too lax in collecting revenue and in bringing under control the Gisir-speaking inhabitants of the Tando district. Thus Chamarande was brought in from Dahomey and given considerable leeway to employ his "active" and "energetic" command.[68]

His first move was to arrest two influential Gisir-speaking clan leaders, Ngossi and Babika, from the Ngosi district where the Eshiras post was located. Ngossi, who had previously collaborated with the administration, was accused of being responsible for the deaths of twelve people and for possessing an authority in the district capable of challenging that of the colonial post. Though these actions led to some unrest and an attempt to free Ngossi from his confinement, Gisir-speaking clans were unable to organize around strong district identities such as those found in Tsogo-speaking Kamba or Punu-speaking Mokab. Decades of divisive commercial activity had worn down and splintered their effectiveness for self-defense. Chamarande was apparently able to defuse the situation by meeting with a delegation of nearly 1500 in the village of Tchè in June 1915.[69]

The administrator no doubt used this opportunity to continue his project of a census for the region so as to collect revenue more efficiently. Missionary sources note that it was during this same period that there began the arrest and imprisonment of those unable to meet tax obligations. In July, Chamarande "invited" the Gisir- and Kele-speaking clans near the post to organize themselves into work gangs in order to cut ebony and pay off their taxes. By the end of the year, the priests at Saint-Martin were complaining to Chamarande about the brutality of the Regional Guard and the extortion practices of the post interpreter, Ernest Mondé.[70] Their entreaties went unheeded and were in fact met with hostility. In his reply, Chamarande bluntly outlined his plans to obtain revenue from the hitherto recalcitrant villages of the Tando district: "The Tandos will be mobilized for the collection of rubber, whether they like it or not, and by arms if their insubordination makes this necessary."[71]

By March 1916, work gangs organized by the Regional Guard were collecting rubber in the Tando and Kamba districts. In the Ngosi district, Chamarande claimed that "all able-bodied men are at present mobilized, trained and supervised in the production of rubber in strips or in crepe at collection sites organized by chieftaincy."[72] The Gabonese playwright Vincent de Paul Nyonda, who hailed from this region, recounts in his memoirs that in May 1916 Chamarande, with the aid of his subordinate Cyprien Guipiery, arranged for all those who had not paid their taxes in the Gisir-speaking districts of Tando, Kamba, Banda, and a portion of Ngosi to be sent to Samba to work off their obligation as porters in the employ of the S.H.O. This forced labor absorbed more than 1000 men.[73]

With most of the men coerced to collect rubber and many of the women mobilized to make palm-frond roofing tiles or clear trails, a food shortage at the end of the long dry season of 1916 was unavoidable. Locally this famine is known as *moundala madeka*, the latter term referring to the fact that people had to sift through garbage to find food. Antoinette Guilouba, who lived through this famine, recalled that many children died of hunger and adults died from ingesting spoiled food. People survived by eating raw cassava leaves, palm hearts, palm kernels and wild yams. In the middle of this food shortage, Chamarande continued to recruit porters for the S.H.O. and organize labor teams to cut ebony.[74]

The most powerful memories that emerge from this period center on the brutality of the Regional Guards toward local women. A decade earlier the rape of Punu-speaking women by Senegalese agents of the C.F.C.O. concession was one of the causes of the Mokab revolt. From the perspective of the Regional Guards, these acts of violence were meant to intimidate and humiliate the men of a village as well as to establish their power over the symbols of wealth that female clan members represented in the precolonial equatorial tradition. The abuse of women was certainly part of precolonial practice as female dependents were abducted or killed during skirmishes between clans. What most shocked the populations of Southern

Gabon about the behavior of the Regional Guard, however, was the indiscriminate nature of their violence against women; these were acts that went beyond the "acceptable" norms for violence associated with the resolution of clan disputes.

> The militia respected no one. When they arrived in a village, they caught men, women, children. They beat them with *chicottes* (canes). . . . They caught married women. Whether it was your wife, your sister or your daughter, they took her by force on your own bed.[75]

Other accounts relate that the husband was often tied up and forced under the bed while his wife was being raped on top.[76]

According to Vincent de Paul Nyonda, the abuse during the period of forced rubber collection under Chamarande became particularly depraved:

> When it was time to weigh the rubber, the rule was that the militia men had to ascertain the good quality of the product by pulling it as hard as possible. If the slab broke, the pieces were publicly thrust into the intimate parts of the wife in order to be then plunged into the mouth of the husband. It was rigorously demanded for every weighing that each gatherer be accompanied by his wife and his mother-in-law. Thus, the man with the bad rubber could be forced, according to the humor of the militiaman, to either chew the fragrant rubber or to mate with his mother-in-law at the foot of the flagpole. An ignominious act never imagined in the customs of the black man.[77]

The priests at Saint-Martin reported that at the beginning of 1916 the Regional Guard had imprisoned thirty women in the village of Pemba-Ngéba and had shut them up in a single hut for more than a month. They were no doubt taken hostage to ensure the forced labor of their husbands and were likely victims of rape. The missionaries also mention several violent deaths attributed to a particularly feared Senegalese Regional Guard named Koelmoussa.[78]

The food shortage continued in 1917 with famine reigning in the Eshiras *circonscription* from October until January 1918. The colonial administration squarely placed the blame on Chamarande's obsession with collecting rubber and the consequent neglect of cultivating food. The local population named this second famine *Marandi,* after the administrator; *Marandi* also became a term referring to the swellings of various body parts following the consumption of rotten food. The situation had become so desperate by the beginning of 1918 that an investigation was called for. Chamarande and the members of the Regional Guard were summoned to

Brazzaville, the Eshiras post was temporarily shut down, and the surrounding population took the opportunity to flee from its influence. The investigation continued into 1919 with Gisir-speakers from the region travelling to Brazzaville to present evidence.[79]

However, famine conditions continued through 1919, not only in the Eshiras *circonscription* but in all the *circonscriptions* of Southern Gabon including Kouilou and Bacougnis which are now part of the Republic of Congo. Compounding these dire straits were the appearance of a fungus that blocked the normal maturation of cassava plants and the spread of the Spanish flu epidemic in the region. This latter development occurred at the end of 1918, perhaps the year of greatest suffering for the local populations. The flu virus entered Southern Gabon along the main thoroughfares heading out of Port-Gentil and Mayumba; its spread was facilitated by the efforts to recruit *tirailleurs* for the war effort. It hit hard those populations weakened by several years of food scarcity. In the Bas-Ogooué *circonscription* it claimed 800 casualties from 8000 cases; it was more than likely responsible for several hundred deaths among the Punu-speaking clans of the Nyanga *circonscription*.[80]

Clearly the populations of Southern Gabon were living through a period of chaos and death that was unprecedented in their historical experience. Clan leadership, so contingent on protecting dependent members from sickness and misfortune, was seriously undermined by so much death and disease. Food shortages pushed the different clans within districts to raid each other's plantations. This was the case in the Bongo *circonscription* where hungry members of Vungu- and Varama-speaking clans plundered food from plantations near the colonial post at Malimba. Access to palm trees providing the famine food of palm hearts and kernels led to movements of Vungu-speaking clans into the district of Moabi and to their mixing with the Punu-speaking clans resident there. Famine forced other clans to exchange their dependent children for food. These practices were indicated as occurring among the Sango-, Tsogo-, and Nzabi-speaking districts of the Du Chaillu Massif where early in 1917 colonial officials came across the corpses of porters who had starved to death because they were unable to obtain food from nearby villages.[81]

Famine certainly created a good deal of social tension which was still capable of being expressed through open revolt. This was probably the situation in the districts of Sango-speaking clans who organized to attack S.H.O. caravans at the end of 1917.[82] More often this tension resulted in conflict that led to the splitting apart of villages and the fragmentation of clans and lineages. Indeed, images of the famine such as the destruction of planta-

tions by wild animals and disputes over food entered into the oral traditions from this period. These traditions served to explain the many fissures
in clans and lineages that occurred during this time of crisis.[83]

From about 1912, the Apindji-speaking clans along the Ngounié experienced the ravages of both famine and sleeping sickness; an informant,
Joseph Pombodié, suggested that the story of the split between the Masoto
and Mwabe clans described below dates from this time.[84] The protagonists
and clan ancestors were two sisters:

> A famine ravaging the countryside, the elder sister went into the forest to
> look for anything to be gathered. Discovering some young palm trees (*masoto*)
> full of ripe bunches, she started to cut the bunches of palm kernels. This
> done, she treated herself to some nuts and then filled her basket with them.
> . . . Upon returning to the village, she did not find her younger sister there as
> in the meantime she too had gone out to look for food. Thus in cooking the
> palm kernels, she only gave them to her own children. The younger sister
> returned at that moment and found her own children dying of hunger. . . .
> She reprimanded her elder for her conduct and then gave for food to her
> children some wild fruits (*migabe* from the *mwabe* tree). She then called out
> in great anger to her elder sister: "Nomata kumu dya go *masoto* (From now
> on you will be the clan of young palm trees)". The elder sister retorted: "Any
> nomata mota asi *mwabe* (And you, we will call you those of the *mwabe*
> tree)".[85]

A similar tale exists to explain the split between the Apindji-speaking
Masamba and Ngande clans.[86]

The chaos and disruption of this period most certainly brought a
reconfiguration of clan and lineage relationships with some lineages and
even clans disappearing altogether or establishing special relationships in
order to survive. The Apindji-speaking clans appear to have been particularly hard hit as were the Eviya- and Vili-speaking clans in the area around
Samba.[87]

Precolonial districts were disappearing from the landscape as the unprecedented volume and different kinds of population movement swept
away their loose and fragile structures. Clusters of good-sized villages participating in patterns of exchange over generations were broken up by trade
competition, military campaigns, disease, famine, and flight deep into the
forest away from the well-worn commercial routes so as to escape colonial
tax collection. The "salt route" which had supported the large, neat villages
of the Tsogo-speaking Kamba district encountered by Du Chaillu fifty years
earlier was abandoned by 1916; all that remained of the villages were the

bands of banana and palm trees that had encircled the dwellings. Their former inhabitants had fled into the forest.[88] The colonial military post at the recalcitrant village of Kembélé had been shut down once again in 1914 due to a lack of personnel, but the incessant disruption had left its mark; four years later Kembélé's inhabitants "were dispersed in forest encampments and had not prepared any plantations; they fed themselves on palm kernels and wild fruit."[89] Kele-speaking clans who had established villages on the Ikoy River at the end of the nineteenth century abandoned these sites following numerous deaths from famine. Once relatively prosperous, this stretch of the river was an uninhabited dead zone in the 1930s as the former inhabitants believed the land cursed.[90]

In the forested hills to the east of the Setté Cama Lagoon similar conditions existed among Varama- and Vungu-speaking clans in 1920. Colonial officials attributed this lamentable state to the intrigues of clan leaders who had unwisely pushed their people into rebellion:

> In this way all sense of discipline, of submission to authority has been lost. In order to be more free, numerous individuals have broken community links with the village and have sought isolation: they are dispersed in small groups of four to five, enclosed by links of kinship or friendship and have built small encampments in the forest surrounded by plantations of a few square meters and live off these rudimentary plantations and wild fruits, hidden and forgotten.[91]

Districts had clearly disappeared. Yet, in this same area thirty-five years earlier, the English trader Deemin had painted a strikingly different picture:

> This settlement consisted of five to six large villages situated on the bank of a fairly wide stream. As in other districts visited, the villages consisted of extremely well built huts, constructed with bark sides and roofs thatched with bamboo leaves. They faced a wide main road which was kept absolutely free from grass and weeds, and in fact perfectly clean. . . . The natives themselves were well formed and nourished, and although quite nude they appeared to be happy and contented. Their food plantations of manioc, yams, plantains, and sweet potatoes, covered a wide area, and during our stay we were "in clover" as far as supplies were concerned.[92]

Some colonial officials were reluctant to admit that the French administration in Gabon had been such an unmitigated disaster and preferred to place the whole of the blame on the concession companies or the "laziness" and "poor planning" of local people. However, when Maurice

Lapalud took over as Lieutenant-Governor in May 1919, he minced no words: the metropolitan government in Paris was strongly criticized for not investing in the colony and for setting up the rule of the concession companies. He noted that when the day came for the concessions to depart they "will have left the region much poorer than when they found it and the populations infinitely more miserable."[93] He then outlined the nefarious impact of the forced organization of labor gangs to harvest forest products and their brutal treatment at the hands of the Regional Guard. The recruitment of porters and then *tirailleurs* for the war effort had absented those very young men whose labor was needed to obtain revenue with which households could pay off their taxes. The consequences were

> turmoil, the abandonment of villages, the dispersion of the population into the bush in small encampments or even their departure to other colonies of whom many will not return. It is also the increase in the number hostile or dubious groups. It is equally the abandonment of all the food-producing plantations and food shortages all over the colony.[94]

In 1917, Père Guyader of the Saint-Martin mission, witness to the abuses of the Chamarande period, summed up the first decades of French colonial administration in Southern Gabon in succinct fashion: "We have done nothing for the native and then we hunt him down for a 50 centime piece."[95]

The experience of disease, forced labor, and famine in Southern Gabon during the second decade of the twentieth century has been correctly viewed as a crucial watershed in the imposition of colonial rule. Precolonial territoriality as the predominant practice in the organization of social space effectively ended, the disappearance of the district marked this passing. Districts, though their place and function were not fully recognized, had been noticed, named, and described in the early texts of explorers, missionaries, traders, and colonial administrators. When Le Testu, perhaps the most gifted observer to have served in the colonial administration in Southern Gabon, began work on a census in the Ofooué-Ngounié *circonscription* at the end of 1916, he remarked: "The diverse groupings of the Mouila subdivision—Apindji, Bapounou and Mitsogo—are totally inorganic and as soon as the census is complete it will be necessary to proceed to their division according to land allotments."[96] By this time precolonial district structure was in such a state of disarray that even Le Testu's usually keen powers of observation were not able to recognize it. The chaos and turmoil of the period was effectively erasing the district from the physical space of Southern Gabon thus implementing the textual act of erasure accomplished by colonial cartography some decades earlier.

Notes

1. Edward W. Soja, *The Political Organization of Space* (Washington, D.C.: Association of American Geographers, 1971), 33.

2. Jean-François Bayart, *The State in Africa: The Politics of the Belly* (London: Longman, 1993), 37.

3. See Bonzon, *À Lambaréné*, 10–15; for a discussion of Brazza's policy designed to promote the interests of Fang-speaking clans, see Coquery-Vidrovitch, *Brazza et la prise de possession du Congo*, 83–86; for development of Ndjolé, see Michael C. Reed, "An Ethnohistorical Study of the Political Economy of Ndjolé, Gabon" (Ph.D. diss., University of Washington, 1988), 46–97.

4. As it was labeled in the opening years of the twentieth century by the Protestant missionary Ernest Haug; see Haug, "Le Bas Ogooué: Notice géographique et ethnographique," *Annales de géographie* 12 (1903): 170.

5. A. Ussel, "De Setté-Cama à Bongo (Congo Français)," *AA* (1891): 61; Ussel also mentions the use of children as porters. For the Fang on the Ngounié, see Avelot, "Recherches sur l'histoire," 398; in the Fernan Vaz and Setté Cama, Auguste Foret, "Le Lac Fernan Vaz," 321; R. P. Le Scao, "Setté Cama: Un coin du Congo," *Le Messager du St. Esprit* (1907), 26.

6. The American missionary Nassau established a Protestant mission on the Middle Ogooué in 1874 which he moved to Lambaréné in 1876; in 1881 he built the mission at Talagouga near what was to become four years later the French colonial post of Ndjolé; the French Holy Ghost Fathers created their mission at Lambaréné in 1881 and a second at Lastourville in 1883, two years before it became a colonial post; Nassau, *My Ogowe*, 40–43, 174–75, 368–77; Alexandre Le Roy, "Le Congo Français, Le Gabon," in *Les Missions Catholiques Françaises au 19e siècle*, vol. 5, ed. J. B. Piolet (Paris: Armand Colin, 1902), 228; Gaston Pouchet, *Vieux Gabon, vieilles missions: Histoire et souvenirs* (Unpublished manuscript, 1984), 97–101, 121–27.

7. See François Gaulme, "Un problème d'histoire du Gabon: Le sacre du P. Bichet par les Nkomis en 1897," *Revue française d'histoire d'Outre-Mer* 61, 224 (1974): 395–416; also Pouchet, "Vieux Gabon," 67–69, 103–4.

8. An American Protestant missionary active in Lambaréné in the 1880s stated simply: "Trade is our great enemy"; see Ellen C. Parsons, *A Life for Africa: A Biography of Rev. Adolphus Clemens Goods, Ph.D. (American Missionary in Equatorial Africa)* (New York: Fleming H. Revell, 1897), 41.

9. This distancing is effectively represented in one of the first maps published in *Annales Apostoliques*. It depicts the geographical spread of alcoholism in the Gabon colony; Sainte-Croix and Saint Martin (the latter is erroneously located much further south than it should be) are safely in the white away from the black and gray shading used for those populations in "complete decadence" and touched by alcohol abuse; see G. Stoffel, "À la Côte du Gabon, Une marée d'alcool," *AA* (1914): 165.

10. For the foundation of Trois-Épis, see "Communauté de Sainte-Croix des Eshiras," and "Communauté de N.-D. Trois-Épis à Douanimena," *BCSE* 7 (1899–1900): 373–74, 388–89; and the rather humorous account of Protestant-Catholic mutual antipathy in the mission's journal entry for 27 février 1899, Archives CPSE, Boîte 679 (1), "Journal de la Communauté de Notre-Dame des Trois-Épis, Sindara, 27 février 1899 (Fondation) au 31 décembre 1904"; also Pouchet, "Vieux Gabon," 116.

11. Pouchet, "Vieux Gabon," 102.

12. "Communauté de Sainte-Croix des Eshiras," *BCSE* 5 (1896–1897): 514–16; 12 (1909–1910): 406–7. In an account of the 1900 founding of the Saint-Martin des Apindji mission, Joseph Pombodié relates that it was the strangeness of missionary clothing that caused Mabounda, a Gisir-speaking leader on the Ngounié, to deny the Catholics permission to construct their mission near his village of Mabanga; Joseph Pombodié, Interview Notes XXIV, September 30, 1991. For attitudes toward clothes more generally, see, Phyllis M. Martin, "Contesting Clothes in Colonial Brazzaville," *JAH* 35 (1994): 401–26. By the end of 1909 a chapel and bell tower were completed at Saint-Martin and a chapel completed with plans for a bell tower at Trois-Épis; "Résidence de N.-D. des Trois-Épis de l'Équateur, aux Chutes-Samba," and "Résidence de Saint-Martin des Apindjis (Haute-Ngounyé)," *BCSE* 13 (1911–1912): 977–78. For an account of how a visit made as a boy to Trois-Épis and the subsequent impression left by the mission buildings and missionary clothing influenced the conversion of a Massango chief in the 1930s, see Pouchet, "Vieux Gabon," 270–74; for the general influence of aesthetics and church-building in attracting converts, see Florent Mboumba-Bouassa, "Genèse de l'Église du Gabon: Étude historique et canonique," (Thèse de doctorat, Université de Strasbourg, 1972), 131–33.

13. For the appeal of miracles attributed to Tsogo-speaking ritual specialists, see James W. Fernandez, *Bwiti: An Ethnography of the Religious Imagination in Africa* (Princeton, N.J.: Princeton University Press, 1982), 436–38.

14. See Alexandre Le Roy, "L'antiesclavagisme au Gabon," *AA* 10 (1895): 6–15; R. P. Lejeune, "L'esclavage de la femme au Gabon," *AA* 11 (1896): 87–99; for a missionary criticism of the French colonial administration's inaction, see Le Scao, "Au Pays de Setté Cama," *Le Messager du Saint-Esprit* (1908): 380; (1909): 25; for the creation of "villages de liberté" in Gabon, see Denise Bouche, *Les villages de liberté en Afrique noire française 1887–1910* (Paris: Mouton, 1968).

15. For a discussion of how missionaries prepared the way for modern capitalist perceptions of time and space among the Tswana of South Africa, see Jean and John Comaroff, *Of Revelation and Revolution: Christianity, Colonialism, and Consciousness in South Africa*, vol. 1 (Chicago: University of Chicago Press, 1991). For similar tactics in the capital of AEF, see Phyllis M. Martin, *Leisure and Society in Colonial Brazzaville* (Cambridge: Cambridge University Press, 1995).

16. "Communauté de Ste-Croix des Eshiras," *BCSE* 12 (1909–1910): 405–7; also 5 (1896–1897): 513, and 11 (1907–1908): 200.

17. For a general overview of colonial education, see David Gardinier, "Education in French Equatorial Africa, 1842–1945," *Proceedings of the French Colonial Historical Society* 3 (1978): 121–37; for the situation in Gabon at the turn of the century, see Gardinier, "Les Frères de Saint-Gabriel au Gabon, 1900–1918, et la naissance d'une nouvelle elite africaine," *Mondes et Cultures* 46, 3 (1986): 593–606.

18. Buléon, *De Sainte-Anne d'Auray à Sainte Anne du Fernan Vaz, sous le ciel d'Afrique: Récits d'un missionnaire* (Abbeville: C. Paillart, 1896), 111; Buléon was said to have been described by the old Eshira chief Mbounga as "the man who teaches the things of God and gives the head to Blacks"; see Buléon, *Au pays des Eshiras*, 57.

19. Gardinier, "Les Frères de Saint-Gabriel," 593–94; the Americans handed over their mission and school at Lambaréné to the Société des Missions Evangéliques de Paris in 1892 following the 1883 decision by the French administration in Libreville that all teaching be done in French. Following the wave of anti-clericalism which peaked in France in

1905, the colonial administration's funding of Catholic mission schools in Gabon was discontinued.

20. "Communauté de Ste-Croix des Eshiras," "Communauté de N.D. des Trois-Épis de l'Équateur," "Communauté de St-Martin," *BCSE* 10 (1905–1906): 53–54, 78–85.

21. "Communauté de St.-François-Xavier à Lambaréné," *BCSE* 5 (1896–1897): 493.

22. "Communauté de Ste-Croix des Eshiras," *BCSE* 7 (1899–1900): 374, and 10 (1905–1906): 52–53.

23. See Archives de CPSE, Boîte 679 (1), "Journal de la Communauté de Notre-Dame des Trois-Épis Sindara, 27 février 1899 (fondation) au 31 décembre 1904, entry février 1901"; Hubert Moukaga, Interview Notes XIX, Mouila, June 15, 1989.

24. Hubert Moukaga, Interview Notes XIX, Mouila, June 12, 1991; for pedagogy, June 15, 1989. For interesting accounts of European missionary recruitment efforts, see Raponda-Walker, "Au pays des Ishogos"; Le Scao, "Setté-Cama"; and Père Coignard, "Dans la Haute-Ngunyé: A la recherche des âmes (Lettre du R.P. Coignard au R.P. Fraisse)," *AA* (1908): 173–80; also Pouchet, "Vieux Gabon," 230–38, for the role of catechists in general and the career of Cyprian Mwanda in particular.

25. Hubert Moukaga, Taped Interview II, Mouila, June 13, 1991.

26. Mboumba-Bouassa, "Genèse d l'Église du Gabon," 209. Accounts of the establishment of Christian missions do contain numerous instances of rather sudden and mysterious deaths of African seminarians and personnel; see Pouchet, "Vieux Gabon," 190–91.

27. Hubert Moukaga, Interview Notes XIX, Mouila, June 15, 1989. For a powerful account of the distress of the Abbé Charles Guisinga's mother when she learned of her son's decision to become a priest in 1909, see Charles Rémy, "Nos séminaires indigènes, Saint-Jean de Libreville," *AA* (1922): 189–90.

28. Saint-Martin moved to Mouila in 1958 and though one can still see the chapel bell tower from the Ngounié the site has been overtaken by the forest; Trois-Épis was closed in 1915 but reopened in 1928, and today is more or less abandoned; a large cross marks the former site of Sainte-Croix which was closed in 1920.

29. Pouchet reports that Monseigneur Adam "published a very suggestive map" around 1902 in order to plan for present and future missions; Pouchet, "Vieux Gabon," 115.

30. For this period, see Rabut, *Brazza Commissaire Général*; Marie-Antoinette Menier, "Conceptions politiques et administratives de Brazza, 1885–1898," *CEA* 5, 1 (1965): 83–95; Coquery-Vidrovitch, "Les idées économiques de Brazza," 57–82; and Coquery-Vidrovitch, *Le Congo au temps des grandes compagnies concessionnaires, 1898–1930* (Paris: Mouton, 1972), 25–48.

31. Quoted in Coquery-Vidrovitch, "Les idées économiques de Brazza," 71, from an 1895 correspondence of A. Le Chatelier, a key colonial figure in the initial efforts to establish concessions.

32. Reproduced in Coquery-Vidrovitch, *Le Congo*, 56–57.

33. Edmund D. Morel, *The British Case in French Congo: The Story of a Great Injustice: Its Causes and Its Lessons* (London: Heinemann, 1903), 78–96; AOM-AEF (Aix), B 2B 1848–1912 "Situation économique de la colonie (mai 1901), 28 juin 1901"; D 4D 4(1)D3 1905–1908, "René Ncoma, interprète, à l'Adm. Camus, Poste d'Agouma (Rembo Nkomi), 26 août 1904"; "Adm. Camus, Rapport Général sur le Rembo Nkomi, le 18 juin 1905"; for Mitsogo accounts of collecting rubber for European traders, see Gollnhofer, "*Bokudu*," 295–99.

34. AOM-AEF (Aix), D 4D 4(1)D2 1900–1908, "Lieutenant-Gouverneur du Gabon à Commissaire Général, Rapport du mois d'Avril 1907, 22 juin 1907."

35. Lewis, *Trader Horn,* 50–51; for a more sober analysis, see S.J.S. Cookey, "The Concession Policy in the French Congo and the British Reaction, 1898–1906," *JAH* 7, 2 (1966): 263–78.

36. On this rebellion, see Gray, "Territoriality," 290–320.

37. For a physical description of Samba/Sindara in 1900, see Avelot, "Dans le boucle," 248–49; for an overview and analysis of the S.H.O., Coquery-Vidrovitch, *Le Congo,* 380–400; for S.H.O. activity and number of traders, AOM-AEF (Aix), D 4D 4(1)D4 1909, "Rapport de reconnaissance de Capitaine Thibault au pays Issogho, 31 mars–18 avril 1909"; 4(1)D12, "Rapport Annuel 1914–1915, Carte de la pénétration Commerciale-Année 1913"; Raponda-Walker, "Au pays des Ishogos," (1907), 156–58; 186–89; 352; Maclatchy, "Sub-division de Mimongo," 1; and Albert Schweitzer, *À l'orée de la forêt vierge* (Paris: Albin Michel, 1952), 150–52.

38. Raponda-Walker, "Au pays des Ishogos," (1907), 189, 316; Marcel Mouande Massande, Interview Notes XVI, Sindara, May 14, 1991; Gollnhofer, "*Bokudu,*" 294–95; Mbigui, "Histoire de Sindara," 17; Moutsinga Kebila, "Histoire Eviya," 18–19, map.

39. Raponda-Walker, "Au pays des Ishogos," (1908), 312–13.

40. For a typical complaint from an administrator regarding the S.H.O., AOM-AEF (Aix), D, 4D 4(1)D3 1905–1908, "Le Capitaine Fabiani, Adm. de Région de l'Ogooué à M. Le Gouverneur du Gabon, le 28 septembre 1907."

41. Map found in AOM-AEF (Aix), 4 (1)D12 1914–1915, "Rapport Annuel." "*Circonscription*" was the term adopted by the French beginning in 1909 to refer to the primary administrative units in the Gabon colony; prior to this there had been a confusing of application of the terms "*région,*" "*cercle,*" and "*district.*" Circonscriptions were divided into *subdivisions.* Though the boundaries and names of *circonscriptions* and *subdivisions* were subject to much revision and change, the terms themselves would remain in use until 1934 when *circonscriptions* became known as "*départements*"; see Pourtier, *Le Gabon,* 2:31–51.

42. AOM-AEF (Aix), D 4D 4(1)D4 1909, "Rapport annuel d'ensemble"; for the map 4(1)D12, 1914–1915, "Rapport Annuel 1914–1915."

43. AOM-AEF (Aix), D 4D 4(1)D5 1911, "Rapport Politique du 4ème Trimestre, Circonscription des Eshiras"; 4(1)D9 1912, "Résumés des rapports mensuels, Circonscription des Eshiras, juillet 1912"; the Banda district appeared on maps by the administrator Foret; see Auguste Foret, "Carte: Circonscription de Setté-Cama," *Bulletin de la Société de géographie* 17 (1894); "Le Lac Fernan-Vaz," 309; and Père Le Scao, "Autour de Setté-Cama," *Annales de la Propagation de la Foi* (1903): 382.

44. "Communauté de N.-D. des Trois Épis de l'Équateur," *BCSE* 12 (1909–1910): 427.

45. Le Testu mentions as a long-term goal the "codification of the customs of Gabon" and continually returns to the theme of "precision"; see Le Testu, *Notes sur les coutumes Bapounou,* 4, 127, 142–54; the second part of this book was subsequently published in the *Bulletin de la Société des recherches congolaises* 10 (1929): 3–29; 11 (1930): 33–91.

46. AOM-AEF (Aix), D 4D 4(1)D4 1909, "Rapport annuel d'ensemble."

47. For this rebellion, see Gray, "Territoriality," 308–14.

48. For discussions of Mbombé and Mavurulu as symbolic culture heros, see Ibinga-Mbadinga, "L'implantation du pouvoir colonial," 154; Mounguengui-Nzigou, "Les résistances des populations de la Nyanga," 90; Pascal Mboumba, "Contacts historiques et culturels entre Mitsogo et Fang au Gabon," (Mémoire de maîtrise, Université de Paris I, 1981), 68–69, 80.

49. Antoinette Guilouba, Recorded Interview IV, Fougamou, May 25, 1991.

50. AOM-AEF (Aix), D 4D 4(1)D5 1910, "Tournées administrative effectués 1910 par le personnel civil du Gabon, Circonscription des Eshiras, mai–juin 1910"; "Rapport de politique du 3e trimestre, Circonscription des Eshiras."

51. Guy Lasserre, "Okoumé et chantiers forestiers du Gabon," *Cahiers d'Outre-Mer* 8 (1955): 118; Coquery-Vidrovitch, *Le Congo,* 263–64; for Ndjolé, see Reed, "An Ethnohistorical Study," 86–92, 172–76.

52. Pourtier, *Le Gabon,* 2:152–53.

53. AOM-AEF (Aix), D 4D 4(1)D2 1905–1908, "Rapport Trimestriel et Annuel 1907"; 4(1)D5 1910, "Resumé des rapports politiques des administrateurs Chefs de circonscriptions, Circonscription de la Nyanga, décembre 1910"; 4(1)D6 1911, "Rapport politique et economique, 3e et 4e trimestres 1911."

54. AOM-AEF (Aix), D 4D 4(1)D5 1910, "Rapport annuel 1910"; "Lieutenant-Gouverneur du Gabon à M. le Gouverneur Général d'A.E.F., 11 avril 1910, a.s. tournée dans le Bas-Ogooué"; "Resumé des rapports politiques des administrateurs Chefs de circonscriptions, Circonscription de l'Ofooué-Ngounié, septembre 1910"; "Rapport de 3e trimestre 1910, Circonscription de l'Ofooué-Ngounié."

55. AOM-AEF (Aix), D 4D 4(1)D9 1912, "Resumés des rapports mensuels, Circonscription du Bas-Ogooué, février, mai 1912"; 4(1)D6 1911, "Resumés des rapports mensuels des chefs de circonscriptions, Circonscription du Bas-Ogooué, février 1911, Circonscription de Nyanga, août 1911, Circonscription des Eshiras, septembre 1911," Circonscription du Bongo, novembre 1911; 4(1)D4 1909, "Rapports trimestriels, Rapport sur la situation politique de la Colonie du Gabon pendant le 1er trimestre 1909, 7 mai 1909."

56. AOM-AEF (Aix), D 4D 4(1)D9 1912, "Resumés des rapports mensuels, Circonscription de Bas-Ogooué, décembre 1912"; 4(1)D11 1914, "Rapports d'ensemble trimestriels, 1er trimestre 1914"; 4(1)D6 1911, "Resumés des rapports mensuels des chefs de circonscriptions, Circonscription des Eshiras, Circonscription de Bongo, janvier 1911."

57. "Résidence de Saint-Martin des Apindji (Haute-Ngounyé), juillet 1908–juillet 1912," *BCSE* 13 (1911–1912): 981–82. Beginning in 1910 the colonial administration distributed badges or tokens (*jetons*) to those who met their tax obligations; see AOM-AEF (Aix), D 4D 4(1)D5 1910, "Rapport Annuel, Impôt Indigène."

58. AOM-AEF (Aix), D 4D 4(1)D10 1913, "Resumés des rapports mensuels, Circonscription des Oroungous, Circonscription du Bas-Ogooué, novembre 1913; Circonscription des Nkomis, Circonscription des Eshiras, décembre 1913"; 4(1)D11 1914, "Resumé des Rapports mensuels, Circonscription des Oroungous, Circonscription du Bas-Ogooué, Circonscription des Nkomis, Circonscription des Eshiras, janvier, avril, juin–octobre 1914."

59. AOM-AEF (Aix), D 4D 4(1)D12 1914–1915, "Rapport d'ensemble sur la situation de la colonie et les événements de la Guerre 1914–1915"; 4(1)D13 1915, "Resumés des rapports mensuels, Circonscription des Nkomis, Circonscription des Eshiras, Circonscription de Bongo, Circonscription de la Nyanga, janvier–juin 1915."

60. AOM-AEF (Aix), D 4D 4(1)D13 1915, "Rapport trimestriel—1er trimestre, décembre 1914–mars 1915"; "Resumés des rapports mensuels, Circonscription de Bas-Ogooué, Circonscription de Bongo, Circonscription de la Nyanga, septembre–décembre 1915"; see also "Carte 31: Répartition géographique des porteurs recrutés au Gabon au cours du 1er mois d'août 1915," in Colette Dubois, *Le prix d'une guerre: Deux colonies pendant la Première Guerre mondiale (Gabon-Oubangui-Chari) 1911–1923* (Paris/Aix: Harmattan/I.P.H.O.M., 1985); and the maps reproduced in Marc-Louis Ropivia and Jules Djeki, *Atlas de la formation territoriale du Gabon* (Libreville: Institut National de Cartographie, 1995), 37, 39.

61. AOM-AEF (Aix), D 4D 4(1)D13 1915, "Resumés des rapports mensuels, Circonscription de la Nyanga, décembre 1915."

62. Dubois, "Le double défi de l'A.E.F. en guerre (1914–1918)," *Africa* (Rome) 44, 1 (1989): 29–31; and "Carte 32: Répartition géographique des porteurs recrutés au Gabon au cours du 1er trimestre 1916," in Dubois, *Le prix d'une guerre*; see also Théophile Loungou and Alike Tshinyoka, "Les Gabonais et la Première Guerre Mondiale 1914–1918," in *Les réactions africaines à la colonisation en Afrique Centrale* (Kigali: Université Nationale du Rwanda, 1985), 243–77.

63. Michael Crowder, "The First World War and Its Consequences," in *General History of Africa VII: Africa under Colonial Domination 1880–1935*, ed. A. Adu Boahen (Berkeley/London: U. of California/Heineman/UNESCO, 1985), 295.

64. ANG, Fonds de la Présidence, Gendarmérie et gardes indigènes, Recensement-engagement des tirailleurs, 1914–1918, carton 1711, "Capitaine Sapolin, chargé de l'expédition des affaires, à M. le Lieutenant Gouverneur du Gabon, Libreville, 11 janvier 1911"; see also "Carte 34: Répartition géographique des tirailleurs recrutés au Gabon au cours du 1er trimestre 1916," in Dubois, *Le prix d'une guerre*.

65. Avelot, "Dans la boucle," 253; AOM-AEF (Aix), D 4D 4(1)D4 1909, "Rapport annuel d'ensemble"; 4(1)D5 1910, "Resumé des rapports politiques des administrateurs Chefs de circonscriptions, Circonscription du Bas-Ogooué, décembre 1910"; 4(1)D6 1911, "Resumés des rapports mensuels des chefs de circonscriptions, Circonscription de la Nyanga, Circonscription des Nkomis, Circonscription de Bongo, février–november 1911"; 4(1)D10 1913, "Resumés des rapports mensuels, Circonscription du Bas-Ogooué, mai 1913"; 4(1)D12 1914–1915, "Rapport d'ensemble sur la situation de la colonie et les événements de la Guerre, Santé Publique"; 4(1)D14 1916, "Resumés des rapport mensuels, Circonscription de Bongo, août 1916"; Archives CPSE, Boîte 991 II, "Journal de la Communauté: Saint-Martin des Apindjis, 1 janvier 1913 à 31 décembre 1916, entry mai 1914"; for a detailed discussion of sleeping sickness and its incidence in the A.E.F., see Headrick, *Colonialism, Health and Illness*, 41–43, 67–93.

66. AOM-AEF (Aix), D 4D 4(1)D11 1914, "Resumés des Rapports mensuels, Circonscription des Eshiras, octobre–novembre 1914"; 4(1)D13 1915, "Resumés des Rapports mensuels, Circonscription de l'Ofooué-Ngounié, Circonscription de Bongo, Circonscription de la Nyanga, juillet–octobre 1915."

67. Antoinette Guilouba, Recorded Interview IV, Fougamou, May 25, 1991; Vincent de Paul Nyonda, Recorded Interview III, Libreville, July 24, 1991.

68. As he was described in a May 1916 colonial report; see AOM-AEF (Aix), D 4D 4(1)D14 1916, "Resumés des Rapports mensuels, Circonscriptions des Nkomis-Eshiras, mai 1916"; see also 4(1)D13 1915, "Resumés des rapports mensuels, Circonscription des Eshiras, avril 1915"; "Lieutenant-Gouverneur du Gabon à M. le Chef de la Circonscription des Eshiras, 24 mars 1915"; Nyonda, *Autobiographie*, 104.

69. AOM-AEF (Aix), D 4D 4(1)D13 1915, "Resumés des rapports mensuels, Circonscription des Eshiras, avril–juillet 1915."

70. M'Bigui, "Histoire de Sindara," 87–88; Archives CPSE, Boîte 991 II, "Journal de la Communauté: Saint-Martin des Apindjis, 1 janvier 1913 à 31 décembre 1916, entries novembre–décembre 1915"; AOM-AEF (Aix), D 4D 4(1)D13 1915, "Resumés des rapports mensuels, Circonscription des Eshiras, juillet 1915."

71. Archives CPSE, Boîte 991 II, "Journal de la Communauté: Saint-Martin des Apindjis, entry 13 décembre 1915."

72. AOM-AEF (Aix), D 4D 4(1)D14 1916, "Resumés des rapports mensuels, Circonscription des Nkomis-Eshiras, mars 1916."

73. Nyonda, *Autobiographie,* 105. Cyprien Guipiery went on to become one of the key figures in the creation of a modern Gisira political identity though his reputation among the Gisir-speaking populations of Ngosi, Tando, and Kamba remained ambiguous due to his association with Chamarande. Interestingly Nyonda omitted mention of Guipiery in the published version of his autobiography; see Brian Weinstein, *Gabon: Nation-Building on the Ogooué* (Cambridge, Mass.: M.I.T. Press, 1966), 164; Simon-Pierre Moundouga, Interview Notes XXI, Sindara, May 18, 1991; Soeur Gabriel-Marie Le Moine, Interview Notes VI, Mandji, May 30, 1991.

74. Archives CPSE, Boîte 991 II, "Journal de la Communauté: Saint-Martin des Apindjis, entry 12 janvier 1916"; "Calendrier historique de District de Fougamou et Mandji (Sindara), Région de la Ngounié"; Antoinette Guilouba, Recorded Interview IV; AOM-AEF (Aix), D 4D 4(1)D14 1916, "Resumés des rapports mensuels, Circonscription des Nkomis-Eshiras, août 1916."

75. "Interview with Valère Mourigou and Pototu Mbumb," in Jerôme Nziengui Moukani, "Histoire des implantations Bavungu dans la région du sud-ouest du Gabon: Des origines à 1968," (Mémoire de maîtrise, UOB, Libreville, 1988), 50.

76. Mounguengui-Nzigou, "Les résistances des populations de la Nyanga," 100; Joseph Le Tailleur, Interview Notes X, Sindara, May 14, 1991.

77. Nyonda, *Autobiographie,* 105.

78. Archives CPSE, Boîte 991 II, "Journal de la Communauté: Saint-Martin des Apindjis, entries 12 & 24 janvier 1916."

79. Antoinette Guilouba, Recorded Interview IV; AOM-AEF (Aix), D 4D 4(1)D15 1917, "Rapport d'ensemble sur la situation de la colonie du Gabon en 1917"; 4(1)D16 1918, "Rapport trimestriels d'ensemble, 1e & 4e trimestres 1918"; 4(1)D17 1919, "Rapports d'ensemble trimestriels, 2e trimestre 1919." Documents mention that Chamarande received a "condemnation" in 1921 but I was unable to find any further details; 4(1)D19, "Rapports trimestriels (Gabon), 2e trimestre 1921."

80. AOM-AEF (Aix), D 4D 4(1)D15 1917, "Rapport d'ensemble sur la situation de la colonie du Gabon en 1917"; 4(1)D16, "Rapport sur la situation de la Colonie du Gabon pendant l'année 1918"; Headrick estimates 8000 total deaths from the Spanish flu epidemic for the whole of the Gabon colony; see Headrick, *Colonialism, Health and Illness,* 175.

81. AOM-AEF (Aix) D 4D 4(1)D15 1917, "Resumés des rapports mensuels, Circonscriptions militaires, janvier 1917"; 4(1)D16, 1918 "Rapports trimestriels d'ensemble, 4e trimestre 1918, Circonscription de Bongo"; 5D 5D22 1910–1946, "Rapports divers sur Chefferies 1919–1920"; Nziengui Moukani, "Histoire des implantations Bavungu," 62; Deschamps, *Traditions orales,* 38; B. Guillot, "Le pays Banzabi au nord de Mayoko et les déplacements récents de la population provoquées par l'axe Comilog," *Cahiers de l'ORSTOM, série Sciences Humaines* 4, 3–4 (1967): 40; "Gabon, De Franceville à Saint-Martin, Feuilles de route d'un voyage de Mgr Martrou, vicaire apostolique," *AA* (1924): 154.

82. AOM-AEF (Aix), D 4D 4(1)D15 1917, "Rapports trimestriels d'ensemble, 1e & 4e trimestres 1917."

83. See Joseph Matsiengui-Boussamba, "Enquête sur le mythe dans la société Gisir 'Mulombi Landemweli,'" (Rapport de license, U.O.B., Libreville, 1989), 98–99.

84. Joseph Pombodié, Interview XXIV, Mouila, October 4, 1991.

85. Togo, "La tradition orale des Apindji," 61–62.

86. Ibid., 63.

87. "Le secret de l'Ofoué," *AA* (1923): 58; Bodinga-bwa-Bodinga, Interview Notes I, Fougamou, May 21, 1991; Annexe 34, Germaine Massagui, "Récit sur la regression démographique des Eviya," in Moutsinga Kebila, "Histoire Eviya"; Mbigui, "Histoire de Sindara," 19; Le Testu, in telling the sad story of an Apindji-speaking orphan in Mouila in 1916, notes that some Apindji-speaking clans simply disappeared during this period; Le Testu, "Réflexions sur l'homme-tigre," *BSRC* 25 (1938): 161.

88. "Le secret de l'Ofoué," 58–63.

89. AOM-AEF (Aix), 4(1)D17 1919, "Rapports d'ensemble trimestriels, 1er trimestre 1919"; also D 4D 4(1)D13 1915, "Resumés des rapports mensuels, Circonscription du Bas-Ogooué, mai 1915."

90. Maclatchy, "Sub-division de Mimongo," 3, 23.

91. AOM-AEF (Aix), D 5D 5D22 1910–1946, "Rapports divers sur Chefferies 1919–1920."

92. Deemin, "Autobiography of James Deemin," 130–31.

93. AOM-AEF (Aix), D 4D 4(1)D17 1919, "Le Lieutenant-Gouverneur du Gabon à M. le Gouverneur Général de l'A.E.F., Libreville, 13 mai 1919."

94. Ibid.

95. Archives CPSE, Boîte 991 III, "Journal de la Communauté: Saint-Martin des Apindjis, 1 janvier 1917–31 décembre 1922, entry octobre 1917." The Mission's relationship with the administration was particularly tense during Chamarande's tour of duty; see "Résidence de St-Martin," *BCSE* 17 (1921–1922): 698–99.

96. AOM-AEF (Aix), D 4D 4(1)D14 1916, "Resumés des rapports mensuels, Circonscription de l'Ofooué-Ngounié, décembre 1916."

6

THE IMPOSITION OF AN AMBIGUOUS TERRRITORIALITY: ROADS AND OKOUMÉ, CA. 1920–1940

Communications and Transportation Infrastructure

> Roads, railroads, schools, markets, military service, and the circula-
> tion of money, goods, and printed matter . . . swept away old commit-
> ments, instilled a national of view of things in regional minds, and
> confirmed the power of that view by offering advancement to those
> who adopted it.
>
> —Eugen Weber[1]

The imposition of modern territoriality in rural France in the final decades
of the nineteenth century was accomplished by the same instruments of
change that rearranged the physical space of Southern Gabon from about
1920. Though it is striking to note that these developments occurred within
a generation of each other, the contexts were, of course, very different.[2] The
disorder that resulted from the ordeal of famine and disease left the peoples
of Southern Gabon severely shaken and extremely vulnerable. The "tabula
rasa" that Europeans had thought they had been seeing all along had almost become reality as the equatorial tradition that had for centuries ordered the physical space in this region of Africa was no longer the dominant territorial influence. The forests and savannahs of Southern Gabon
were now fully primed for the imposition of modern territoriality.

170

The hegemony of the French colonial state was dependent upon its ability to create modern communications and transportation infrastructures. The extent to which this was accomplished determined the administration's power to influence people and phenomena by delimiting and asserting control over geographic space; that is, its ability to create territory. The peoples and forest terrain of Southern Gabon presented particular challenges to this project. The penchant for decentralization and the aversion to the consolidation of authority that defined the complex networks of clan and lineage relations ran counter to the requirements of the colonial state. There were no centralized state structures or figures of authority upon which the French could build; there were no formal regions containing a metropolitan center serving a well-defined hinterland over a well-developed system of roads. All of this had to be created.[3]

Many observers note just how little was accomplished in terms of modern infrastructure during the colonial period when Gabon was justifiably considered the classic case of a neglected backwater. The French West Africa federation received considerably more metropolitan attention than its poor relation, the French Equatorial Africa federation, and Gabon was the forgotten colony in the latter. Pourtier cites as evidence the fact that Libreville in 1935, after nearly a century of French colonial rule, remained marginalized from the rest of the colony, as there existed no modern roads connecting it to the interior; this at a time when Brazzaville and Yaounde were already centers in considerably more developed transportation networks.[4]

Yet from the perspective of the peoples who lived through this period the colonial presence was not so slight. Radical transformation occurred and, though the colonial towns and road networks that grew in the decades following World War I pale in comparison to physical changes in other colonial settings, their impact was just as drastic. The concessionary companies and the colonial state shared the all-encompassing assumptions about control over space outlined at the beginning of chapter 5 but were incapable of fully implementing them. The partial imposition of modern territorial practice may have been more destructve than a fully successful process, as the results were neither control nor order but chaos and confusion; they certainly spelled disaster for the local populations.[5]

Roads are the key indicator that modern territoriality has been established in physical space; the geographer Pourtier notes that "only overland roads truly hallmark the appropriation of territory: the material, but also mental, construction of territory relies upon the support of their network."[6] The first road project in Southern Gabon sought to connect the colonial post at Sindara to the cluster of villages that eventually became the post of Fougamou. This would have created a more efficient bypassing of the rapids on the Ngounié and thus have improved communications and transport between Mouila and Lambaréné. As outlined above, the organization of a labor force to undertake this task between 1910 and 1912 represented a public works project on a scale hitherto unknown and served to heighten ethnic awareness as workers were grouped together according to colonial ethnic categories.

The goal at this time was to create an enlarged trail for the transport by porter of palm kernels, the main source of tax revenue in the Middle and Upper Ngounié, to the post and factories at Sindara. The trail fell into a state of disrepair during the period of chaos and food shortages. In 1920, the colonial administration proposed constructing a road capable of handling automobile and truck traffic and duly began organizing work teams. These teams were euphemistically labeled *main d'oeuvre prestataire* (service manual labor) and their creation required coercive tactics from the Regional Guards. The general shortage of labor that existed throughout the colony forced the administration to recruit among Apindji-speaking clans, still reeling from famine and disease, located on the Middle Ngounié some eighty kilometers away from the road site. In October 1920 the priests at Saint-Martin expressed concern that this "huge effort" demanded from the Apindji-speaking clans—an obligatory twelve days of unpaid labor with rudimentary or no tools and an uncertain food supply—would exacerbate a fragile situation.[7]

These efforts failed as two years later the road had yet to be built. The colonial administration recognized that road-building at this level was beyond the competence of the *circonscription* administrator and that the presence of a specialized public works technician was required. A study was duly commissioned at the end of 1924 but the technician was slow in completing his work. In the meantime, porterage traffic along the tortuous thirty-kilometer trail (there were ninety-two bridges between Sindara and Fougamou) continued to increase. In 1923, it was estimated that 60,000 loads were carried up and down the path annually; the local Eviya- and Vili-speaking clans, now decimated, as well as the Gisir- and Fang-speaking clans, who preferred employment in the booming timber industry at Lambaréné and the Lakes region, abhorred this work. Thus, the colonial administration and the S.H.O. were obliged to recruit porters from the Punu- and Nzabi-speaking clans on the Upper Ngounié, 500 of whom were under the charge of the S.H.O. at Sindara in 1923; a total of 720 porters toiled along this route in 1924. The work was grueling—six trips to

Map 15. Road Network, Gabon, 1935–1948. Based on Georges Bruel, *L'Afrique Equatoriale Française* (Paris: Larose, 1935); and Roland Pourtier, *Le Gabon,* vol. 2 (Paris: Editions l'Harmattan, 1989), pp. 220, 222.

be made within twenty-five days—and took its toll on the health of those engaged in it. A road suitable for motor vehicles was viewed as an absolute necessity.[8]

Yet this had been a goal of the colonial administration for five years before serious work was finally undertaken in 1925.[9] The earlier failed efforts to forcibly recruit labor had only served to frustrate the surrounding population by involving them in a seemingly pointless endeavor. The 1925 administrative reorganization which moved the Sindara *subdivision* from the Bas-Ogooué to the Ngounié *circonscription* facilitated the more intense recruitment needed to finally complete the road project. By March of that year, nine hundred workers were stationed at Fougamou, a number deemed excessive by the priests at Saint-Martin who feared food shortages.[10] The Gabonese researcher, Mathias Mbigui, obtained the following account from Vincent de Paul Nyonda:

> The work consisted of first marking out the route and clearing the bush; then leveling and evening out the road. The tools for this work were essentially the machete, the ax, the pick, the hoe and the shovel. The bridges were made of hard-wood logs (*padouk, ozigo*) laid lengthwise. These logs, sometimes weighing more than two tons, were pulled with difficulty with vines by at least forty men who broke their backs all day in order to move the bridge part a mere 100 to 500 meters.[11]

By the end of 1927, the road was completed and motor vehicles were able to make the trip between Sindara and Fougamou; the colonial administration was optimistic that the Ngounié *circonscription* would prosper now that the burden of porterage was lifted and the local populations could focus on exploiting produce from the groves of palm trees found in the area. However, the forced recruitment of labor for the Sindara-Fougamou road—which coincided with recruitment for the less arduous but longer route along the savannah from Mouila to Ndendé (see Map 15)—led to food shortages in several parts of the Ngounié *circonscription* in 1929.[12] Further tempering the optimism from the completion of the Sindara-Fougamou road was the necessity for almost continual maintenance and the considerable drain this made on revenue. The growth anticipated from the exploitation of palm products never materialized as by the mid-1930s low prices paid by the S.H.O. and the high tariffs the concession charged to transport produce from Fougamou to Sindara totally discouraged village producers.[13]

The completion of the Fougamou-Sindara road signalled the decline of Samba Falls as a colonial nodal point. Since 1915 when Chamarande had forcibly recruited Gisir-speaking clans from the Ngosi district to carry rubber and ebony to the S.H.O. factory in Sindara, the cluster of villages at Fougamou had continued to grow; the temporary influx of 900 workers from 1925 to 1927 obliged the colonial administration to construct lodgings, and this led to the creation of a new colonial nodal point. In 1928, the administrative *subdivision* post was moved from Sindara to Fougamou. Though at the time the population around Sindara welcomed the move and the partial relief from colonial harassment it represented, the former post's continuing marginalization in favor of Fougamou became a source of discontent, and continues to be one today.[14]

This move also heralded, however tentatively, the eventual triumph of the road over the river as the dominant means of long-distance transportation in Southern Gabon. Although this would not be fully accomplished until after World War II, the flurry of road construction in the 1930s signalled an end to a precolonial territoriality based on water transport.[15] The contrast between the opening of the decade and its close is revealing not so much in what was completed in terms of suitable roads but in how it was accomplished. In 1929 forced recruitment for the Sindara-Fougamou (30 kilometers) and Mouila-Ndendé (75 kilometers) routes had again led to serious food shortages in much of Southern Gabon. These remained the only roads in the region until the mid-1930s when work was begun on routes connecting Mouila to Fougamou (100 kilometers) and linking Ndendé to Tchibanga and Mayumba (200 kilometers) (see Map 15). The administration was hesitant to forcibly recruit workers, fearing yet another food shortage; furthermore the powerful European timber interests in Gabon frowned upon diverting scarce labor from their camps on the Lower Ogooué.

By 1937, when the administration organized workers for the Mouila-Fougamou route, colonial bureaucratic practice had become more efficient, and work registers were employed to control labor:

> A service register divided according to cantons and villages on which are inscribed the names of each worker and the task to which he is assigned permit a rigorous control of the roll call. . . . Convocations and service notes are addressed to the *canton* chiefs[16] charged with directing the required number of men to the different work sites . . . 13,600 days have been used for construction work on the Fougamou-Mouila route.[17]

The use of such bureaucratic instruments, now implemented by *canton* chiefs in addition to the Regional Guard, allowed officials considerably more control over the people and activities within the physical space of colonial administrative units. For the stretch of the road between the Douya and Doubou Rivers, workers were fed and paid forty francs per month, though on sites further north they received only food.[18]

The administration thus claimed that only "voluntary" labor had been employed in this project; officials further asserted that some elements of the local population saw the benefits of road-building:

The natives worked in great number on the construction of the Fougamou-Mouila road; if the "Mitsogos" hardly understood the importance of this new communication route, it was not the same for the "Eschiras" who appreciate it despite the suffering it caused them. . . .[19]

Indeed, an informant in the village of Mussondji who worked on the road as a young boy recalled receiving brutal treatment at the hands of the Regional Guard.[20]

The Mouila-Fougamou route was completed in 1938; the justification for its construction was to ensure year-round transport, as steamer traffic on the Middle Ngounié was not possible in the low waters of the long dry season. The same problem existed on the Lower Ngounié; thus the Mouila-Fougamou route was useless unless another road was cut over difficult terrain connecting it to the important commercial center at Lambaréné. A fifty-kilometer stretch was built from the village of Fouramwanga between 1940 and 1943; this time there were no food shortages, as laborers from Chad were brought in to do much of the work. The administration also profited from the availability of timber workers idled by the industry's shutdown during World War II. In this way, the Ndendé-Tchibanga-Mayumba route was also finally completed.[21] Neither of these efforts required the degree of coercion seen at the beginning of the 1930s nor did they result in severe food shortages. In just over a decade, the French colonial administration and the timber industry had succeeded in altering the pattern of labor exploitation in Southern Gabon; by the 1940s there existed a "labor market" in French Equatorial Africa sufficiently integrated into the capitalist wage-earning sector and capable of accomplishing infrastructure projects without disastrous consequences for the local population.[22]

"Regroupement" and Revenue-Raising

Modern territoriality, as employed by the colonial or nation state, seeks first to "fix" people and their relationships through the bureaucratic textual space of the map and census (as discussed in chapter 4). This bureaucratic knowledge is then exploited to control and influence people and their relationships in real physical space; the initial goal is to obtain revenue. In Southern Gabon from about 1920, the construction of roads or the improvement of trails provided state-controlled axes along which the local population was forced to move. The bureaucratic term for this was "regroupment" with the goal of "fixing" villages in accessible physical space so that the colonial administration and timber industry could recruit labor. Due to the timber industry's transient exploitation and geographic specificity (the Lower Ogooué and Lakes region), this "fixing" was only momentary, as workers were required to move into temporary lumber camps far from their villages. There thus continued a pattern of fluidity and mobility in terms of settlement and population movement, but under very different conditions than those of the precolonial period. Furthermore, there developed a competition between the colonial administration, which desired access to labor available in its own *circonscriptions* for infrastructure projects, and the timber industry, which recruited throughout the colony with little regard for the needs of areas outside the Lower Ogooué exploitation zone. Yet on other occasions, the administration's desire for infrastructure development was lukewarm, and colonial officials came to assist the timber industry in its attempts to recruit labor.[23]

Attempts to regroup Punu- and Apindji-speaking clans into larger villages in the area of Mouila date from 1910 but concerted regroupment efforts were only undertaken in the 1920s. By the end of 1921, the Apindji-speaking clans of the Mouila *subdivision* were consolidated in thirty-five villages but only "after numerous difficulties and palavers."[24] The administrator had been concerned only with grouping together what he believed was a sufficient number of inhabitants and paid no attention to clan and lineage relations; within a year these settlements no longer existed.[25] In 1922, Kembélé was once again the site of a colonial post, and efforts were made to regroup the clans of the former Kamba district along the abandoned path heading out of Mouila; two villages were established near the Onoy River. Given that labor recruitment possibilities had been exhausted in the Nyanga, Bongo, and Bas-Ogooué *circonscriptions* during World War I, the administration and timber industry started to focus recruitment efforts on the Tsogo-, Sango-, and Nzabi-speaking clans in the relatively populous area around Mbigou; to this end villages were to be grouped along the path connecting Mbigou to Kembélé. However, Tsogo- and Nzabi-speaking clans frustrated administration plans, as a colonial official noted at the end of 1922 that they "still prefer to live in camps and in a state of disgusting dirtiness."[26] The same complaint was made two years later, though the administration now expressed an awareness of the importance of lineage relationships.[27]

In 1918, Le Testu had stressed to colonial officials the importance of obtaining information about clan and lineage relationships; yet his advice was little heeded. As a consequence village regroupments were pell-mell affairs and had to be maintained by force. In a 1924 report, he cited the

Map 16. Administrative Subdivisions of Gabon, ca. 1933. Based on Georges Bruel, *L'Afrique Equatoriale Française.* (Paris: Larose, 1935); and Marc Louis Ropivia and Jules Djeki, *Atlas de la formation territoriale du Gabon* (Libreville: M. L. Ropivia, 1995), p. 45.

attempt to group a number of villages along the trail connecting Mouila to Ndendé as particularly wrong-headed. Not only was the location poorly chosen, but the name of the regrouped village, "Keri," referred to the fear the different lineages felt now that they were obliged to live next to each other. Le Testu thought village regroupment was a poor policy and believed it was easier to administer four villages of twenty-five inhabitants than one of one hundred. These attitudes earned him the animosity of the new Governor-General of the A.E.F., Raphael Antonetti.[28]

Thus throughout the 1920s and 1930s the Regional Guard was continually sent out into the forest to destroy the temporary *mpindi* settlements in which the clans of Southern Gabon distanced themselves from colonial rule. This "passive resistance" was most effectively practiced by peoples ensconced in hilly, thickly forested areas: the Tsogo-speaking clans of the Gésuma district; the Gisir-speaking clans of the Tando district; and the Vungu- and Varama-speaking clans in the hills to the east of the Setté Cama Lagoon. In the latter half of the 1920s, the administration adopted a energetic plan to force recalcitrant Varama-speaking clans to participate in the life of the colony. When it was implemented the *subdivision* commander reported in frustration: "and since then what do the Waramas [Varamas] do? They dance *bouiti* [bwiti]."[29] In the Gisir-speaking Tando district, a chief named Boukouendzi dismantled his village in 1928, destroyed the coffee trees he had been required to grow, and fled with his followers into the forest. The following year the *subdivision* commander ordered the Regional Guard to regroup Boukouendzi's dispersed *mpindi* back into villages.[30]

In 1936, the colonial official Maclatchy described the Tsogo-speaking clans of the Mimongo *subdivision* in the following fashion:

> They put up with our presence more than they accept it and meet the ensuing obligations as if they were executing a chore whose accomplishment is necessary to safeguard their tranquility. But it is certain that our moral influence over them is virtually nil and slips off like water on a rock. . . . Thus villages are built in order to satisfy administration demands but are only lived in incidentally; they serve as a kind of setting for official life. But manifestations of native life take place elsewhere: in the "*pindi*", small sordid camps erected by each lineage far away in the bush in the middle of its plantations and its hunting grounds. The Mitsogo spend the major part of their existence there, outside of all official control thanks to the immensity of the forest. The difference is sharply made by the native who each time clearly specifies if it is a matter concerning the "village for the commander" or the "*pindi*" the "village for the blacks"; plantations give place to an identical distinction.[31]

This double existence represented a creative compromise with modern territoriality, in effect ceding it the spaces of what were once large villages located on active trade routes.

Mwiri's control over public spaces and access to resources was being thrust aside during the regroupment process. *Mwiri* members determined whether the soil and the fauna of a particular habitat were approaching exhaustion and then decided whether or not to move their village. Forced regroupment along colonial trails and roads not only "fixed" settlements in physical space but negated the flexibility of precolonial practice. Villages now remained on the same site even after their surroundings had been depleted. The consequences were already apparent in Mimongo in 1936, as the clearing of trees for peanut cultivation had created a number of small savannahs; Maclatchy noted that "tieing the population to the places that they inhabit certainly increased the devastation."[32] These policies also had the ironic impact of promoting a *mpindi* existence as villagers were often obliged to travel ever greater distances from their regrouped settlements to work plantations or hunt game.

Once a village was subject to colonial territoriality its traditional rhythm was further undermined by forced labor recruitment and production. Disastrous conditions had resulted from the World War I demand for porters and the administration's use of coercion to raise revenue through rubber collection. A number of officials realized that the French colonial presence had a good deal to do with the chaos, food shortages, and declining population that characterized much of Southern Gabon in 1920. Recognizing that the labor needs of the colony required a healthy population and genuinely ashamed of the famines,

> These men try to uplift and moralize the native through work: reunion of dispersed and broken up villages, sound adobe constructions, well-maintained trails, coffee plantations, extensive food plantations, harvesting palm kernels and making oil; one senses that they want to improve the lot of the native pursued for too many years uniquely for taxes.[33]

Each of these activities reflected the growing intervention of modern territoriality.

Attempts to directly control the agricultural production of village plantations date from the period of severe food shortages. These continued in force during the 1920s as the colonial administration sought not only to avoid a repeat of disaster but to commercialize food production to feed the growing conglomerations of labor employed by the timber industry in the Lower Ogooué.[34] Thus *circonscription* officials were exhorted by their superiors to maintain a vigilant watch over village plantations, and this they accomplished by taking measurements of plantation size and sending out the Regional Guard to ensure the work was accomplished.[35] Choosing the location of plantations and determining the claims of different lineages had been the province of male *mwiri* members. Traditionally cultivation itself was the women's work and village women were certainly subject to forced labor on plantations as well as road projects. This sexual division of labor appears to have blurred when it came to cultivating coffee or rice on the largely unsuccessful "plantations for the commander."[36] Tsogo-speaking clans of the Gésuma district dealt with this challenge by creating parallel worlds; yet Tsogo-speaking clans from the Matèndè district at Sindara, traditionally more open to the changes brought by the colonial presence, sought in 1938 to move their villages along the proposed road connecting Fougamou to Lambaréné.[37]

Another attempt by colonial territoriality to leave its mark on the physical space of the village was to insist that the traditional dwelling made of tree bark be abandoned for habitations made of adobe (*pisé*). This became a high priority for several colonial administrators in Southern Gabon in the first half of the 1920s. The idea was that adobe structures were somehow more permanent and that their construction would lead to more permanent villages. Thus numerous reports appear such as that referring to the administrator Daney at Sindara who, in 1922, "began the complete rebuilding of his villages" where the dwellings were to be "done in *pisé* under the direction of specially trained militiamen."[38] The practice of fining or imprisoning village leaders for poorly maintained villages also began at this time. In a classic example of colonial folly, Le Testu, who assumed the head of the new Ngounié *circonscription* in 1924, condemned the *pisé* construction project of the previous three years as impractical and ordered the *subdivision* commanders to rebuild the dwellings in bark. Interestingly, he did not deny the validity of the exercise, perhaps assuming that it was an effective illustration of colonial power. It no doubt contributed to the pattern of parallel colonial and local worlds; the creation of a colonial world for the rural population reached its logical conclusion in 1937 when the administration constructed a model village in the Mimongo *subdivision*[39] (see Map 16).

Lurking behind all these attempts to impose modern territoriality there was the brutality of the Regional Guard. Indeed, it was the members of the Regional Guard who actually did the work of forcing villagers out to their plantations, rounding them up in the forest to be regrouped into larger settlements, and destroying *mpindi*. Colonial reports from the 1920s and 1930s are strewn with complaints by French officials regarding the unruly and undisciplined actions of the Regional Guard. In behavior reminiscent of the abuses committed by concession company agents three decades earlier, these colonial subordinates so consistently abused their authority that by 1933 a French government inspector remarked, "There had developed in the region a kind of tradition which came to consider the wrongdoings committed by our auxiliaries as normal and it is this that explains the silence and resignation of the populations."[40]

Regional Guards used their position to pilfer food and livestock and to obtain sexual favors from village women; male lineage heads often prostituted their dependent females to meet tax obligations. Their position as intermediaries between the village and the post provided numerous opportunities for bribes and the diversion of recruited labor for personal use. The administration complained that the majority of the guards did not grasp what was demanded of them. Though *subdivision* commanders punished guards whose most egregious crimes came to their attention, the administration attempted no real professional training and generally turned a blind eye to the complex daily struggles for power that occurred at the village level. In some instances, such as the 1931 regroupment of villages in the Tchibanga *subdivision,* colonial officials resigned themselves to the "inevitable abuses" committed by the Regional Guard and accepted them as the price to be paid for the desired result of large villages and well-maintained roads and plantations.[41]

Local memory seems to have been most marked by the forced collection of palm kernels in order to meet tax obligations. Dominique Komba, a member of the Eviya-speaking Mobaï clan from the village of Mavono near Fougamou, recalled:

> We cracked palm kernels that we then put into containers. The women filled sometimes two containers and, when they had strong husbands, they sometimes filled three of them. . . . They carried this heavy charge to Sindara which they sold to obtain one franc and a sou for all those palm kernels. . . . In cracking these kernels, we were forced to do so, it was forced labor with militiamen who struck us with whips. In going out in the bush to collect these palm kernels, we had militiamen on our tails, this was not a game, this was true misery. If we did not find three containers of palm kernels, we were thrown in prison.[42]

Flight into the forest was the most effective form of defense. Villages in the Du Chaillu Massif organized surveillance teams that kept watch night and day over the trails running through the area so as to warn inhabitants of the coming of the Regional Guard. When their arrival was imminent, the shouting of a single phrase sufficed to organize the rapid exodus of all the young men and women of a village into the forest, where they would remain for up to several weeks. On occasion, defense became more aggressive with leopard men societies organizing revenge attacks against abusive guards. However, by the 1930s when a small portion of the local population gained access to literacy, written complaints to colonial officials became common. In 1931, for example, young Punu-speakers submitted a petition in the name of Punu clan chiefs regarding systematic patterns of abuse in the Mouila *subdivision* attributed not only to the Regional Guard but to the post interpreters and French commander.[43] The local population had good reason to avoid the colonial administration, and it was not until the late 1930s that a trickle of villages began to see the advantages of establishing themselves on the growing network of roads in Southern Gabon.[44]

The Impact of "King Okoumé"

Though the colonial state's road-building efforts were the most dramatic physical manifestation of a modern territoriality, it was the demand for labor in the booming timber industry that was the most powerful force for change. From 1920, the primary reason for the demarcation of the geographical space of Southern Gabon, and the attempts to control people and relationships within this imposed territory, was to meet the needs of "king *okoumé*." The European market for *okoumé* wood, after disappearing during World War I, returned with new intensity and led to a frenzied decade of exploitation in the Lakes region near Lambaréné (see Map 17). Tens of thousands of men, most of them recruited from the Ngounié *subdivisions,* made the trek to the lumber camps temporarily established in the forests along the complex Ogooué delta network. Here they adapted to a new kind of transience, one whose contours were no longer determined by the equatorial political tradition but by the rhythms and vagaries of modern capitalist territoriality.[45]

Whereas the infrastructure created to service the territorial ambitions of the colonial state was meant to be permanent, that created by the timber industry did not have this goal of persistent hegemony. The roads and dwellings of the lumber camps were constructed solely to fell trees, cut them into logs, cut and transport the logs to waterways, and then send them on for processing in Europe. The lumber camp was a temporary and idiosyncratic nodal point whose location and duration were dependent upon the quantity of exploitable trees. Once a holding was depleted it was abandoned, and the roads and trails simply allowed to return to bush.

Symbolic of this temporary territoriality were the networks of portable *Decauville* rail tracks that were used to transport logs cut in the forest up to forty kilometers away from water transport. This technological inno-

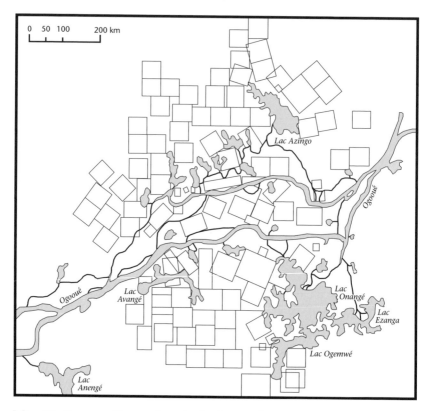

Map 17. Forestry Concessions in the Lower Ogooué Region, 1925. Based on Antonin Fabre, *Le commerce et l'exploitation des bois du Gabon* (Paris: Société d'Editions, 1927), pp. 72–73.

vation, introduced to Gabon in 1913 but not widely used until the 1920s, came to characterize timber exploitation in the interwar period. These tracks could either be moved from site to site or simply left to rust in the forest; a significant portion of the labor recruited by the timber industry was employed in setting up and taking apart these rail networks. The colonial administration sometimes sought to regroup villages along these *Decauville* rail lines. This was the case between 1935 and 1938 when Punu-, Gisir-, and Varama-speaking clans living in *mpindi* near Lake Oguemoué were regrouped into six villages along a *Decauville* line. The idea was that they would provide food to lumber camps belonging to the timber concern of the *Société Agricole et Commerciale du Bas-Ogooué* (S.A.O.). However, in 1939 the S.A.O. pulled out of the region and the villages soon disappeared.[46]

Thus, the territorial practices of the timber industry often ran contrary to the long-term territorial objectives of the colonial state. This became glaringly apparent in terms of the fluid population movement associated with lumber camps and the small urban centers that developed at Port-Gentil and Lambaréné. By 1924, the administration sensed that the furious pace of exploitation and recruitment was getting out of control and heading for a crash. Yet the number of industrial permits grew at a spectacular rate as did the land surface in the Lakes region subject to exploitation. Exports and revenue continued to rise until 1931 when overproduction and the worldwide Depression pushed the Gabonese timber industry into a crisis situation.[47]

The existence of a "floating population" (*population flottante*) had been a colonial concern since the first timber boom prior to World War I. The second boom in the 1920s saw the problem increase dramatically in scale with an estimated four thousand "vagabonds" in the Lower Ogooué in 1927.[48] This segment of the worker population moved from lumber camp to lumber camp in essence selling their labor to the highest bidder.[49] This "floating population" converged on Lambaréné, which took on the airs of a frontier boomtown. In 1927 the Lieutenant-Governor remarked that it had been a "simple post in the bush just three years earlier" but had since become "a very active commercial center where most of the Port-Gentil establishments are represented."[50] Those who fled their jobs in the bush could find refuge in the relative anonymity of the small but growing town; getting caught, though, meant several months in prison.[51]

From 1933 the administration sought to bring this "vagabond" element into the colonial fold by regrouping "foreigners" to the Lower Ogooué into villages according to "race." Thus, out of twenty-three villages plotted on a 1935 map of the Lakes region eight were mixtures of the Ngounié "races," that is, representatives of Punu-, Gisir-, Lumbu-, Vungu-, and Vili-speaking clans.[52] Following another drop in *okoumé* exports in 1938, the administration tried to solve several problems at once by regrouping idled timber workers in model "colonization villages" along the proposed route between Lambaréné and Fougamou. Not only would the "foreign" population of the Lower Ogooué be brought under control but these villages would provide the labor to maintain the new road. Under the watchful eye of the Regional Guard, "the native was thus able, due to the abandonment of the old village, to construct dwellings more in line with the hygiene statutes prescribed unceasingly by the administrative and medical authorities."[53] Yet this population would not stay "fixed": the allure of the lumber camp, now compounded by the existence of gold-mining camps on the Ikoy River and in the Mimongo *subdivision,* and the urban pull of Lambaréné and Port-Gentil, ultimately frustrated these efforts.[54]

The lumber camps served to reinforce and give life to the sense of ethnic identity implied by the categories of the colonial administration. The camps were colonial creations where the rhythms of work and recreation were controlled by European concerns. Though the organizational looseness and the relative freedom to move from employer to employer contrasted with the tight control of the mining compounds of Southern Africa, lumber camps performed the same function, the imposition of a European sense of time and space on African work patterns:

> The manual labor of the camps is certainly trained to perceive time and space in a pointed manner. The indifference to time found in the village is no longer possible. They no longer spend hours according to their whims without a precise schedule moving by inspiration from occupation to another. The notion of space is also clearly defined as the whole forest surface is susceptible to use and exterior constraints control movements. . . . In a way, men find here the obligations that confine women to a regular schedule in the village.[55]

Men recruited to work in lumber camps were thus cut off from the time surplus that women created for them in the conditions of the precolonial village. They were also freed from their obligations to clan elders and their sense of identification with their clan declined. The camps were colonial territory and colonial ethnic identity filled in the vacuum left by the fading influence of the clan.

The experience of Samuel Nzaou is instructive. Working on Lake Gomé at his third lumber camp not long after his arrival in the area in 1928, the young Nzaou was feeling homesick for his village and relatives on the Kouilou River several hundred kilometers to the south in what is today the Republic of Congo. By chance he met Ibadji-I-Leli, "a compatriot," meaning a fellow Punu-speaker, who was also "a brother" because he, too, was a member of the Punu-speaking Mouloulou clan. Nzaou was greatly comforted and through this contact he was able to meet his first wife, Bobenguet, from a Tsogo-speaking clan whose village was near Sindara.[56] Here then was the old precolonial system of clan relations facilitating integration into a new environment as it had for centuries.

However, as the years spent in the colonial milieu of lumber camps and towns passed by, it would appear that Nzaou's identity as a Bapunu became increasingly significant. It was in Lambaréné that he met up with "a group of young people from his (Bapunu) ethnic group" who then made an ill-fated decision to enlist in the military, which led to their imprisonment.[57] Upon his release from detention some time in 1932, Nzaou decided it was time to meet his wife's family and arrange to pay her bridewealth.[58] This in itself was symbolic of Nzaou's freedom from clan obligations, as it was he who was arranging the marriage and paying the bridewealth. Yet when he met with Bobenguet's family and presented them with some gifts and a sum of money, the offer was accepted as reimbursement only for the period of time she had already spent with Nzaou. The family was uncomfortable with the fact that Nzaou was a Bapunu whose clan relations were far away and unknown to them; they feared that he would eventually move away with their daughter and matrilineal kin.[59] The absence of negotiations between clan representatives accentuated Nzaou's identity as a Bapunu, as this was a marriage born of a colonial experience beyond the ken of the precolonial practice of clan leaders and trading friends exchanging dependent women to cement their alliances.

Bobenguet stood firm and went against the wishes of her family, who finally relented but then insisted that the couple reside in the area of Sindara. Thus, Nzaou lived in his wife's village for a time but soon decided to join a group of Bapunu who around 1935 established a village named Biro on the Ngounié just downstream from Sindara.[60] By the mid-thirties, timber concerns had started exploiting holdings in the Sindara area, and Biro was an example of a village that brought together dispersed "foreign" elements residing in the *subdivision.* It was in villages like this that modern Bapunu ethnic identity took root; Biro contained Punu-speakers who hailed from villages near Mouila, Ndendé, and Divénié. In their home regions, clan identity would have taken precedence over the still vague notion of being Bapunu. Yet, in the colonial milieu of the timber industry it was Bapunu ethnic identity that came to the fore.[61]

One hundred years earlier the only way that Nzaou could have made a journey from his home along the Kouilou to a village along the Ngounié would have been if his clan elders had sold him into slavery. In that case, he would have assumed a dependent status within his new clan with his descendants eventually attaining recognition as full clan members. However, in the colonial world of lumber camps, regrouped villages, and developing towns, the integrative functions of the clan were becoming increasingly irrelevant. The empty ethnic categories developed by the colonial administration started to fill in, as between 1920 and 1940 tens of thousands of men like Nzaou felt the ties of clan and lineage loosen through work in the timber industry.[62]

Life in the camps of the 1920s and 1930s was hard. The timber industry did not become mechanized until after World War II, so even though *Decauville* rails and cars had been introduced to facilitate transport, the cutting of trees and sawing of logs was still done by hand. The most arduous task remained the moving of logs over rough forest clearings to reach the *Decauville*. This was still accomplished through the use of *mirombo*, the wood batons that up to seventy men would employ to move a single log. This was dangerous work and accidents were frequent.[63] In the early years, European employers were little concerned with the comfort or diet of their employees. Workers lacked mosquito nets and even blankets to protect themselves from nights of exposure in remote corners of the forest. For rations they were provided with an unfamiliar staple, rice, whose inadequate preparation resulted in numerous outbreaks of beri-beri. Things improved somewhat after 1925 when the colonial administration enacted a number of regulations concerning the treatment of labor in the camps and began to conduct inspection tours.[64]

With an estimated 25,000 workers employed in the timber industry in 1929, disruption was bound to occur in many areas, not just in food production. Since the vast majority of recruits were young males, there developed an imbalance in the sex ratio in both rural areas and the lumber camps. A shortage of husbands was noted in the Eshiras *circonscription* in 1924; a number of women 18 to 20 years old remained unmarried, and many already married had been abandoned. Around 1930, there were three women for every two men in those rural areas that had been subject to heavy recruitment; at the lumber camps there was only one woman for every three men. This situation led to dramatic increases in adultery, prostitution, and sexually transmitted diseases, which resulted in high levels of female sterility and slow demographic recovery. The psychological impact on the culture was devastating given that a woman's worth was largely determined by her ability to bear children.[65]

Life in the lumber camps was traditional existence turned upside down. Since the timber company was legally obligated to provide sustenance for the worker, and later for his wife and children if they accompanied him, women were partially freed from plantation work, as food was generally obtained from surrounding villages or brought in from Lambaréné or Port-Gentil. Men collected firewood, a woman's task in the village. Thus, relatively free from traditional labors, women in lumber camps often obtained revenue by providing sexual favors, sometimes working in collaboration with their husbands to extort adultery fines from unsuspecting workers. Women from neighboring villages engaged in "marriages of convenience" with lumber camp workers from outside the area. These, too, could turn into forms of extortion as the Fang-speaking clans in the Lakes area became notorious for luring Gisir-speaking men into arrangements with their women and then demanding steep bridewealth payments. Unable to pay these debts, many Gisir-speaking men fell into a form of servitude to their wife's clan. Finally, there were many legitimate unions like that of Nzaou and Bobenguet where men freed from obligations to their own lineage married women and paid bridewealth to local clans of their own accord.[66]

There developed a division of labor corresponding to colonial ethnic categories: generally speaking, lower-level clerk positions requiring literacy came to be associated with the Myènè; foremen responsibilities or positions requiring some specialized training became associated with the Fang; and manual labor was associated with workers recruited from Southern Gabon, the Bapunu gaining a reputation as experts in the felling of trees. As occurred in colonial towns, these ethnic differences were reinforced by separate living areas and different kinds of privileges, though there was great variation from camp to camp. Without the presence of clan elders or a heritage of past clan alliances, language and cultural differences that were of secondary importance in the precolonial period came into sharper focus.[67]

The population of camps was generally young and vigorous, so competition between these emerging ethnic groups was infused with the energy of youth. Indeed, European managers often promoted contests between ethnic groups as a form of recreation. In the gold-mining camps that were established at Etéké near Mimongo beginning in 1937,[68] European supervisors organized Saturday dance parties and a major celebration for the 14th of July where ethnic groups sought to outdo one another at both work and entertainment festivities. Thus Mitsogo and Massango workers showed off their *bwiti* and *mwiri*, the Bapunu their *mbwanda* and the Banzabi and the Bakele their *mungala*. Within the colonial context of the camp these dances carried a more pronounced ethnic signet than they would have if performed in the villages of the Du Chaillu massif.[69]

Thus, from the 1920s distinct characteristics and cultural practices started to cluster around colonial ethnic identities as an ever-increasing percentage of the Southern Gabonese population found itself having to live, at least some of the time, in a colonial world imposed through modern territoriality. Yet in this interwar period, these modern Gabonese ethnic identities were similar to the "show" villages created by Tsogo-speaking clans to satisfy the colonial administration. They each existed to meet the demands of the colonial presence but their integration into the cultural practices and everyday existence of these peoples was superficial.

From the perspective of the pretentions outlined in Soja's observations that opened chapter 5, the attempts to impose the physical infrastructure of modern territoriality were, by 1940, equally superficial. Yet, from the perspective of their impact on people's lives, the results of these efforts were drastic and profound. Colonial territoriality did successfully undermine the dominant position of precolonial territoriality; precolonial districts and their historical functions did disappear; a labor force attuned to the practices of wage-earning and the rhythms of capitalist toil had come into being; colonial-imposed ethnic categories did start to take on a lived reality. Ultimately, though, the outcome was not a hegemonic imposition corresponding to the totalizing assumptions behind colonial instruments of power and modern territoriality. The situation in 1940, as Georges Balandier would later describe it, was profoundly "ambiguous."[70]

NOTES

1. Eugen Weber, *Peasants into Frenchmen: The Modernization of Rural France, 1870–1914* (Stanford: Stanford University Press, 1976), 486.

2. See Gray, *Modernization and Cultural Identity.*

3. See discussions in Pourtier, *Le Gabon,* 2:9–14 and Sautter, *De l'Atlantique,* 194–96; also the discussion on "lineage trajectories" in Bayart, *State in Africa,* 133–40.

4. Pourtier, *Le Gabon,* 2:220–21.

5. For an excellent overview, see Pourtier's discussion, ibid., 2:79–122.

6. Ibid., 2:217; see also discussions in Rey, *Colonialisme,* 380–81 and Sautter, *De l'Atlantique,* 1018–20.

7. Archives CPSE, Boîte 991 III, "Journal de la Communauté: St. Martin des Apindjis, 1 janvier 1917 à 31 décembre 1922, entry 22 octobre 1922." For colonial administration plans, see AOM-AEF (Aix), D 4D 4(1)D18 1920, "Rapports trimestriels d'ensemble, Circonscription de Sindara, 3e trimestre"; "Exposé de la situation de la colonie du Gabon."

8. AOM-AEF (Aix), D 4D 4(1)D20 1922, "Rapport annuel 1922"; 4(1)D22 1992, "Rapports mensuels, Circonscription Bas-Ogooué, janvier 1922"; 4(1)D24 1923, "Rapports mensuels, Circonscription Bongo, novembre–décembre 1923"; 4(1)D26 1923, "Rapports mensuels, Circonscription Bas-Ogooué, mars–avril 1923"; 4(1)D29 1924, "Rapports mensuels, Circonscription Ngounié, décembre 1924"; 4(1)D30 1924, "Rapports mensuels, Circonscription Bas-Ogooué, août, novembre 1924"; 4(1)D31 1925, "Rapport trimestriel, Circonscription Bas-Ogooué, 1e trimestre 1925."

9. The administrator Le Testu asked in exasperation at the end of 1924, "When will we finish the Fougamou-Sindara road?"; AOM-AEF (Aix), D 4D 4(1)D29 1924, "Rapports mensuels, Circonscription Ngounié, décembre 1924."

10. Archives CPSE, Boîte 991 IV, "Journal de la Communauté de St. Martin des Apindjis, janvier 1923–13 aout 1927, entry 15 mars 1925."

11. Mbigui, "Histoire de Sindara," 13.

12. In 1928, 10,000 locals had been engaged at work sites along this route; see AOM-AEF (Aix), 5D 5D58 1923–1948, "Dossier Confidentiel au sujet de la situation Vivrière de la Circonscription de la Ngounié, 25 mars 1930."

13. AOM-AEF (Aix), D 4D 4(1)D33 1927, "Rapport du 4e trimestre (Gabon)"; 4(1)D34 1928, "Rapport politique et economique à la fin de l'année 1928"; 4(1)D36 1930, "Lieutenant Gouverneur du Gabon à M. le Gouverneur Général de l'AEF, Rapport de tournée (13 mai au 26 juin 1930)"; "Rapport trimestriel, Circonscription de la Ngounié, 1er trimestre 1930"; 4(1)D38 1932, "Rapport annuel 1932"; 4(1)D43 1936, "Rapport trimestriel, Département de la Ngounié-Nyanga, 1er trimestre 1936"; 5D 5D58 1923–1948, "Dossier Confidentiel au sujet de la situation Vivrière de la Circonscription de la Ngounié, 25 mars 1930"; ANG, Fonds de la Présidence, Carton 99, Rapports Politiques, Département de la Ngounié, 1929–1944, "Rapport trimestriel, 4e trimestre, 1929."

14. Mbigui, "Histoire de Sindara," 82, 87–88; Ikapi-Moutoukoula, "Étude urbaine de Fougamou" (Mémoire de maîtrise, UOB, Libreville, 1986), 29; Field notes, Sindara, May 1991.

15. See Vincent Moulengui-Boukossou, "Une population flottante dans un espace non-maîtrisé: La population de la forêt Gabonaise" (Thèse de doctorat, Université Paul Valery, Montpellier III, 1985), 46.

16. The creation of *canton* chieftaincies is discussed in chapter 7.

17. AOM-AEF (Aix), D 4D 4(1)D45 1937, "Rapport politique, Département de la Ngounié, 1er semestre 1937."

18. Ibid.

19. ANG, Fonds de la Présidence, Carton 35, Politique Générale, Subdivsion de Sindara, 1937–1944, "Rapport politique, Département de la Ngounié, Subdivision de Sindara, 2e semestre 1937."

20. Mussondji/Moulandoufala, Interview Notes XXII, Mussondji, September 19, 1991.

21. Mbigui, "Histoire de Sindara," 15; Pourtier, *Le Gabon,* 2:182.

22. In positing an articulation between lineage, colonial, and capitalist modes of production, Rey emphasizes the construction of the Congo-Océan railroad as the key element in bringing about this shift to a capitalist labor market in the Congo colony between the years 1924 and 1934; he makes reference to a telling 1932 quote from Governor-General Antonetti: "Begun with forced recruitment, the railroad will be completed with voluntary labor"; Rey, *Colonialisme,* 411–12, see also 342–43. Due to the timber industry's need for workers, Southern Gabon was off limits to labor recruitment for the Congo-Océan. However, the railroad's completion and a road connecting Ndendé to Dolisie drew the region into Congo's economic sphere after World War II; see Pourtier, *Le Gabon,* 2:224–25.

23. For a related discussion, see Pourtier, *Le Gabon,* 2:102–9.

24. AOM-AEF (Aix), D 4D 4(1)D19 1921, "Rapports trimestriels, 3e trimestre 1921"; for earlier efforts 4(1)D5 1910, "Resumé des rapports politiques des administrateurs de circonscriptions, Circonscription de l'Ofooué-Ngounié, septembre 1910"; 4(1)D6 1911, "Resumés des rapports mensuels des chefs de circonscriptions, Circonscription de l'Ofooué-Ngounié, aout 1911."

25. AOM-AEF (Aix), D 4D 4(1)D29 1924, "Rapports mensuels-Ngounié, décembre 1924."

26. AOM-AEF (Aix), D 4D 4(1)D20 1922, "Rapport annuel 1922."

27. AOM-AEF (Aix), D 4D 4(1)D29 1924, "Rapports mensuels-Ngounié, mai 1924"; also 4(1)D20 1922, "Rapports mensuels, Circonscription des Bandjabis, aout 1922."

28. Antonetti was responsible for seeing through the construction of the Congo-Océan railroad with a ruthless and wasteful exploitation of African labor; he was very much a proponent of village regroupment; see AOM-AEF (Aix), D 4D 4(1)D31 1925, "Le

Gouverneur Général de l'AEF à M. le Lieutenant-Gouverneur du Gabon, Réponse aux rapports (1925)." See also Sautter, "Notes sur la construction du chemin de fer Congo-Océan 1921–1934," *CEA* 7, 2 (1967): 219–99; Le Testu, *Notes sur les coutumes Bapounou,* 24; AOM-AEF (Aix), D 4D 4(1)D29 1924, "Rapports mensuels-Ngounié, décembre 1924"; and "Texte No. 1, Daniel Baboussa, Corpus de Traditions Orales," in Hygnanga-Koumba, "Villages du Canton Ngounié-Centrale," 92.

29. AOM-AEF (Aix), D 4D 4(1)D37 1931, "Rapport de 2e trimestre 1931, Circonscription des Ouroungous." Another attempt to regroup these Varama-speaking clans was attempted in 1931.

30. ANG, Fonds de la Présidence, Carton 99, Rapports politiques, Département de la Ngounié, 1929–1944, "Rapport trimestriel, 2e trimestre 1929."

31. Maclatchy, "Monographie," 30; for specific references to the passive resistance of the Gésuma district, see AOM-AEF (Aix), D 4D 4(1)D29 1924, "Rapports mensuels-Ngounié, juin 1924"; 4(1)D40 1934, "Rapport trimestriel, Circonscription de la Ngounié, 3e trimestre 1934."

32. Maclatchy, "Monographie," 10; these savannahs have only grown in size and are quite apparent to visitors in Mimongo today.

33. "Haute-Ngounyé, Résidence de St-Martin (1900)," *BCSE* 17 (1921–1922); 700.

34. Rey views these developments in terms of the imposition of a bureaucratic mode of production "whose essential characteristics are the forced recruitment of the forces of labor and the forced commercialization of products obtained according to old modes."; see Rey, *Colonialisme,* 365, also 367–68. For food production for the timber industry in the Lakes region, see Sautter, *De l'Atlantique,* 775–81.

35. AOM-AEF (Aix), D 4D 4(1)D24 1923, "Rapports mensuels-Bongo, juin 1923"; 4(1)D29 1924, "Rapports mensuels-Ngounié, juin 1924"; 4(1)D35 1929, "Rapport annuel (Gabon) 1929."

36. See "Annexe 20, Germaine Massagni, Récit sur l'arrivée des Blancs et ses conséquences," in Moutsinga Kebila, "Histoire Eviya."

37. AOM-AEF (Aix), D 4D 4(1)D46 1938, "Rapport politique, Département de la Ngounié, 1e semestre 1938."

38. AOM-AEF (Aix), D 4D 4(1)D22 1922, "Rapports mensuels, Bas-Ogooué, avril 1922."

39. AOM-AEF (Aix), D 4D 4(1)D29 1924, "Rapports mensuels-Ngounié, décembre 1924"; 4(1)D45 1937, "Rapport politique, Département de la Ngounié, 1er semestre 1937."

40. AOM-AEF (Aix), D 4D 4(1)D39 1933, "Rapport d'ensemble de l'année 1933 (Gabon)."

41. See AOM-AEF (Aix), D 4D 4(1)D37 1931, "Rapport trimestriel, Circonscription de la Nyanga, 2e trimestre 1931"; see also 4(1)D41 1935, "Rapport trimestriel, Ngounié-Nyanga, 2e trimestre 1935"; and Christian Mamfoumbi, "Contribution à l'étude du travail forcé en Afrique Equatoriale Française dans l'entre deux guerres (1919–1939): L'exemple du Gabon," (Thèse de doctorat, Université de Paris I–Panthéon-Sorbonne, 1984), 76.

42. Dominique Komba, "Récit sur les abus de l'administration coloniale en pays Eviya," in Moutsinga Kebila, "Histoire Eviya," 95; see also the testimony of Pauline Mutsinga Ganza in Mombo Maganga, "Histoire Varama," 119; and "Texte No. 6, Augustin Omer Mabila," in Hygnanga-Koumba, "Canton Ngounié-Centrale," 105.

43. See AOM-AEF (Aix), D 4D 4(1)D37 1931, "Reclamation de tous les chefs Bapounous demeurant dans la Subdivision de Mouila, Mouila, le 21 novembre 1931"; for

leopard men revenge attacks, see M'Boukou, *Ethnologie criminelle,* 17; for surveillance techniques, Moulengui-Boukossou, "Une population flottante," 39–40.

44. AOM-AEF (Aix), D 4D 4(1)D46 1938, "Rapport politique, Département de la Ngounié, 2e trimestre 1938." The most dramatic developments in terms of village regroupment occurred after World War II; see Georges Balandier and Jean-Claude Pauvert, *Les villages gabonais: Aspects démographiques, économiques, sociologiques, projets de modernisation* (Brazzaville: Institut d'Études Centrafricaines, 1952), 11–15, 58–79; and Pourtier, *Le Gabon,* 2:102–22.

45. See Christopher Gray and François Ngolet, "Lambaréné, *Okoumé* and the Transformation of Labor along the Middle Ogooué (Gabon) 1870–1945," *JAH* 40 (1999): 87–107.

46. AOM-AEF (Aix), D 4D 4(1)D47 1939, "Rapport politique, Département de l'Ogooué-Maritime, 2e semestre 1939"; for the impact of the *Decauville* rail tracks, see Pourtier, *Le Gabon,* 2:152–60, and Ignace Koumba Pambolt, "L'évolution des procès de travail dans l'industrie du bois au Gabon depuis 1900: Étude de cas de la Compagnie Forestière du Gabon (C.F.G.)" (Thèse de doctorat, Université de Paris V–Réné Descartes, 1984), 127–28.

47. 1924 was the year that timber exports (196,269 tons) topped the pre-World War I peak (150,688 tons in 1913); see AOM-AEF (Aix), D 4D 4(1)D28 1924, "Rapport annuel 1924." 1930 timber exports were 381,000 tons before the sharp dip in 1931; see 4(1)D37 1931, "Rapport annuel d'ensemble 1931," and the export chart in Pourtier, *Le Gabon,* 2:147; also 157–58.

48. AOM-AEF (Aix), D 4D 4(1)D33 1927, "Rapport du 4e trimestre 1927."

49. For an example from Vincent de Paul Nyonda's youth, see Gray and Ngolet, "Lambaréné," 104.

50. AOM-AEF (Aix), D 4D 4(1)D33 1927, "Rapport du 4e trimestre 1927."

51. See the story of Samuel Nzaou in Gray and Ngolet, "Lambaréné," 104–5.

52. See map in Sautter, *De l'Atlantique,* 772–73.

53. AOM-AEF (Aix), D 4D 4(1)D46 1938, "Rapport politique, Département de la Ngounié, 1er trimestre 1938"; also "Rapport politique, Département de l'Ogooué-Maritime, 1er trimestre 1938." It should be pointed out that the French campaign against sleeping sickness and other efforts to improve the health of the population were entirely dependent upon the imposition of modern territoriality. A 1935 medical report complained about the "deplorable mentality" of the rural population and their refusal to cooperate with the Regional Guard and medical personnel come to inspect them; 4(1)D42 1935, "Rapport de 1er trimestre 1935, Département de l'Ogooué-Maritime"; for the colonial health service and the campaign against sleeping sickness in French Equatorial Africa, see Hendrick, *Colonialism,* 191–253, 311–83.

54. Sautter, *De l'Atlantique,* 773; AOM-AEF (Aix), D 4D 4(1)47 1939, "Rapport politique, Département de la Ngounié, 1er semestre 1939"; and Loundou Mounanga, "L'exploitation de l'Or à Etéké de 1937 à 1960 (Esquisse Historico-Economique)" (Mémoire de license, UOB, Libreville, 1981).

55. Jacques Binet, "Notes sur la population du Sud-Ouest, Chantiers forestiers," (Unpublished documents: ORSTOM-Libreville, 1965?), 2. Some sawmills and timber-processing concerns created in Gabon following World War II have focused on hiring Gabonese women as they are seen as more reliable workers; see Pourtier, *Le Gabon,* 2:184, and Bernard Da Costa, Interview Notes IV, Sindara, May 20, 1991.

56. Joseph Nzaou Boubenga, "Histoire de la famille Nzaou: Nzaou Samuel, sa vie et son oeuvre," (Unpublished family document, 1988), 6–7. I would like to thank Samuel Nzaou's son, Simon-Pierre Moundounga, for allowing me to consult this family history while doing fieldwork in Sindara.

57. See Gray and Ngolet, "Lambaréné," 105.

58. Bobenguet had accompanied her older sister, Ngondet, to the lumber camp when the latter married Nzaou's clan brother, Ibadji-I-Leli. It was Ibadji who facilitated the liaison between Nzaou and Bobenguet. Bobenguet accompanied her husband to Ndjolé, where she gave birth to a daughter and waited in Lambaréné during his incarceration. Thus, the couple had already been together several years before making any arrangements with her family.

59. Boubenga, "Famille Nzaou," 7–8.

60. "Biro" is from the French word "*bureau*"; the village was given this name because the French commander at Sindara often spent the night there. Biro broke up sometime in 1938 following the murder of a villager by a European forester; some moved closer to Sindara, others typically went downstream to Lambaréné; Simon-Pierre Moundouga, Interview Notes XXI, Sindara, May 18, 1991.

61. See Boubenga, "Famille Nzaou," 8, and Moundouga, Interview Notes XXI.

62. Rey argues that breaking the hold of the clans and lineages over workers was a key colonial focus in the interwar years: "The task of the colonizers in the Congo from 1920 was then to try to separate the worker as much as possible from this primary community that held him through so many ties." The construction of the Congo-Océan accomplished this in the Congo, while it was the work of the timber industry to bring this about in Gabon; see Rey, *Colonialisme,* 360.

63. For detailed descriptions, see Koumba Pambolt, "Compagnie Forestière du Gabon," 126–28; and Louis Ondénot De Dravo, "L'exploitation forestière au Gabon de 1896 à 1930" (Mémoire de maîtrise, Université de Reims, 1979), 64–70.

64. AOM-AEF (Aix), D 4D 4(1)D31 1925, "Rapports trimestriels, Circonscription Bas-Ogooué, 1er trimestre 1925"; 4(1)D36 1930, "Rapport trimestriel, Circonscription Ouroungou, 2e trimestre 1930."

65. AOM-AEF (Aix), D 4D 4(1)D29 1924, "Rapports mensuels, Ngounié, novembre 1924"; De Dravo, "L'exploitation forestière," 107; Balandier and Pauvert, *Les villages gabonais,* 17–19; Pourtier, *Le Gabon,* 2:173–75.

66. AOM-AEF (Aix), D 4D 4(1)D29 1924, "Rapports mensuels, Ngounié, novembre 1924"; Sautter, *De l'Atlantique,* 772; Binet, "Chantiers forestiers," 4–9; Lasserre, "Okoumé," 143–44.

67. Binet, "Chantiers forestiers," 3, 7–8; Lasserre, "Okoumé," 141.

68. These represented a certain refinement when compared to the earlier lumber camps as greater control was imposed over worker movements to counter the risk of theft; bureaucratic controls such as identification cards and leave passes were made use of in a rigorous manner; see Mounanga, "L'Or à Etéké," 19–20; for a description of life on these camps in the 1950s, see Russell Warren Howe, *Theirs the Darkness* (London: Herbert Jenkins, 1956), 65–66.

69. Mounanga, "L'Or à Etéké," 32–33.

70. Georges Balandier, *Afrique ambiguë* (Paris: Plon, 1957).

7

DEATH OF THE EQUATORIAL TRADITION? OF LEOPARD MEN, CANTON CHIEFS, AND WOMEN HEALERS

In the introduction to her study of political culture in Gabon and Congo-Brazzaville between 1940 and 1965, Florence Bernault places Vansina's deep-time study, *Paths in the Rainforest,* at one end a of a chain of possible scholarly approaches to the colonial experience of equatorial Africa and the work of French political scientist Jean-François Bayart on the nature of the African state at the other; she then asks whether it is "possible to establish a continuity between the two approaches"; whether one can write a history that incorporates the remnants of equatorial tradition and the "human, economic and political disruption linked to colonization."[1] It is a useful juxtaposition as it opposes Vansina's strong statements on the "death of tradition" to Bayart's insistence on African continuities in precolonial, colonial, and post-colonial political practice.

Vansina posits that after some forty years of challenges "[t]he equatorial tradition finally died in the 1920s."[2] Modern territoriality, though not fully imposed, had pushed precolonial territorial practice to the margins and destroyed the functioning of districts. All that remained of equatorial tradition was "some cultural flotsam and jetsam" and colonial-created "customary law."[3] In his classic study, *The State in Africa: The Politics of the Belly,* Bayart concurs that in lineage societies such as those found in Southern Gabon: "the changes that took place during the colonial period, as well as the dynamics of incorporation, had more deleterious consequences for acephalous societies than for centralised societies."[4] Yet, he subsequently suggests that "it is important not to underestimate the capacity of the lineage to reappropriate the preserves of the contemporary state. However violent they may be, the 'tremors' caused by incorporation should not permit the exclusion, a priori, of the hypothesis that there is a fundamental continuity from past to present. . . ."[5] He then goes on to support this notion of continuity by drawing on studies of lineage societies from Cameroon and Congo-Brazzaville.[6]

Bayart's discussion emphasizes the continuing importance of the realm of the "invisible" to the practice of political power in countries like Gabon, and access to esoteric powers certainly played an important role in the development of the post-1945 modern Gabonese political class. In fact, one might argue that given the "disenchantment of the world" associated with modernity and modern territoriality, this was the one area of the precolonial cognitive map that remained subject to the control of lineage elders who did all they could to exercise their authority in this realm.

This chapter analyzes three "moments" in the colonial experience of Southern Gabon in terms of the death or continuity of equatorial tradition. The spate of leopard-men killings in the 1910s and 1920s are discussed as final desperate acts of clan elders witnessing the decline of the *mwiri* initiation society and the destruction of equatorial tradition. The creation of canton chieftaincies in the 1920s and 1930s are discussed as institutions almost entirely dependent upon colonial power. Unable to effectively draw upon the remaining "flotsam and jetsam" of tradition, chiefs quickly become marginal figures in the post-1945 world of Gabonese politics. The third "moment" is the spread of new kinds of healing societies in the 1930s. This development is seen as representing the most significant survival of equatorial tradition as this rich area of the precolonial cognitive map was tapped to bring a sense of control back to a physical world torn asunder.

Leopard Men and The Decline of Mwiri

The influx of trade opportunities in Southern Gabon had begun to undermine the power of the various *mwiri*-type male initiation societies, but the chaos of famine and resistance further eroded their position and the imposition of colonial administrative structures subverted their territorial practices. The first two decades of this century and the onset of the concession/ colonial administration collusion witnessed the collapse of *mwiri* societies.[7] The cognitive map that had served the populations of Southern Gabon for centuries proved increasingly ineffective as a guide to the sometimes horrific developments occurring in material space.[8] Instead, confusion and the sense of social disintegration resulted in the rising prominence of pathological practices in the precolonial tradition such as poison ordeals and, most spectacularly, the ritual murders committed by so-called *hommes-léopards* (leopard men).[9]

The leopard is, of course, a real animal whose predatory habits are a cause of fear and concern among all the peoples of Southern Gabon. But the leopard also provides the most dreaded and powerful symbol in the cognitive world of myth and lore in this part of the world, comparable to the role played by the wolf in premodern Europe.[10] Local beliefs supposed that a man could either turn himself into a leopard or that his spirit could enter into a leopard or that a leopard could do the bidding of someone practicing sorcery. Thus, for the colonial administrator trying to determine the responsibility of actual attacks upon domestic animals and on people, this was an extremely difficult area.[11]

There existed the real damage done by leopards but there also existed the equally real violence perpetrated by individual leopard men. The actions of leopard men and the terror they inspired among the local populations were described in the texts of the first Europeans to visit Southern Gabon.[12] There exist conflicting interpretations as to whether the murders attributed to leopard men were the work of isolated individuals or organized by secret initiation societies. Raponda-Walker reports that during his many years in the Ngounié region he had never heard of any organized societies but only, and this quite rarely, of individual cases of leopard men attacks. He further argues that "leopard men were generally slaves whom their master—a chief or notable—charged with executing a personal vengeance upon the wife of an adversary or competitor."[13]

However, accounts exist which claim that organized societies of leopard men were formed in the Nyanga *circonscription* in the opening decades of this century.[14] In discussing these groups, the Gabonese magistrate, Jean-Hubert M'Boukou, makes a distinction between temporary bands of leopard men brought together for economic goals and those societies whose practices were primarily political or religious:

> The former, due to their flexible recruitment criteria and the occasional character of the association, did not practice human sacrifice. United exclusively

for a particular operation—the looting of a caravan, the capture of slaves, the abduction of women, theft or slaughter of livestock in time of famine— the members reassume their total independence after accomplishing their mission. The secret character of their participation ceases after the operation because the whole community benefits from its fruits. In a way, they form the mutual assistance brigade of a village.[15]

Only the clan elders who led these temporary associations were members of the more permanent societies that practiced human sacrifice and the consumption of certain body parts. According to M'Boukou, these acts of ritual sacrifice and anthropophagy by clan elders

> generally took place at the beginning or at the end of the principal seasons or on the occasion of certain calamities or other exceptional events. . . . [Thus] from time to time, the members of the ruling class entered into contact with the supernatural powers that they represented and in this way obtained from them either the appeasement of their anger or the abundance necessary for the survival of the population, or the maintenance and reinforcement of the power permitting them to perpetuate traditional institutions without inter-ruption.[16]

The sustained aggressions of Kele-speaking clans against the districts of Tsogo-speaking clans in the last decade of the nineteenth century would certainly have been an example of "exceptional events." It is interesting to note that the various Tsogo-speaking clans turned to the sacrifice of female clan dependents in order to make their war charms effective. It is claimed that the Nzobe clan created a charm that served as the basis for the *kono* warrior society. This *kono* society then became a higher grade of *ya-mwei* (the term for *mwiri* among Tsogo-speaking clans) as one had to be a mem-ber of *ya-mwei* before entering *kono. Kono* then served as the enforcement wing of *ya-mwei.*[17] Given the overlapping functions and shared symbols within the various initiation societies, the suggestion made by Sillans and Raponda-Walker that there may be a correlation between *mwiri* and leop-ard men becomes quite plausible.[18]

In more stable times, the fear and actions of leopard men would have been deployed to enforce the edicts of *mwiri* regarding village upkeep and the control of female dependents by male elders. Ritual sacrifice was prac-ticed periodically to ensure the continuation and renewal of traditional institutions. An accelerating increase of leopard men killings for economic motives no doubt developed with the growing trade and increase in cara-van traffic during the latter half of the nineteenth century. A further increase occurred during the periods of food scarcity starting around 1910 as livestock became prey to those clans experiencing hunger. The sense of crisis left by disease, famine, and colonial aggression must certainly have pushed clan leaders into more desperate action, which was expressed through pathological acts of ritual murder. The victims were almost always women and children, the symbols of precolonial wealth, a wealth that was seen to be slipping from the control of the clan leaders.[19]

In April 1904 during a tense period in the early stages of the nearby Kamba district's rebellion, the priests at Saint-Martin, already familiar with leopard charms and attacks on livestock, first learned of ritual murder by leopard men when a woman was killed and mutilated in the forest close to the mission. The men involved, members of Apindji-speaking clans, were captured, but the mission priests convinced the local population not to kill them and gave the accused asylum.[20] Regular mention of leopard man attacks start appearing in administration reports only from about 1913, a period of food scarcity in several districts of Southern Gabon. In Nyanga, where recruitment for service in Cameroon was particularly heavy and the famine especially severe, colonial officials linked the increase in leopard men attacks to food scarcity and consequent social tension.[21]

It was also in Nyanga that the administrator Hippolyte Charbonnier was able to discover a number of secret associations of leopard men connected to the three most powerful Punu-speaking clans in the area, the "Bouyala" (Bujala), the "Boumouellé," (Bumwele) and the "Dibamba." His influential report is unique for the detail it provides on the structure of these societies and for the grim accounts of mutilation. It came to be published in both missionary and administration journals and forced colonial observers to consider the implications of the existence of clandestine groups organized solely for the purpose of ritual killing.[22] Interestingly, Charbonnier was able to obtain his information through an intriguing combination of colonial gaze and census-taking. He noted that "the members of these societies have neither watchwords, signs, nor rallying marks." He claimed that leopard men recognized each other "by their gaze." Indeed, the administrator further declared that he himself had been able to recognize six leopard men by simply staring at them while out gathering census data. Charbonnier had these men arrested; in subsequent inquiries with the prisoners he was able to obtain the information later published in his article.[23]

Colonial administrators were primarily concerned in finding ways to punish and bring a halt to these killings. Le Testu remarked that when faced with a corpse it was not a question of confirming a superstition or justifying a preconceived opinion but of conducting an investigation. Thus administrators were not inclined to see in these murders dramatic evidence that the societies of Southern Gabon were in terrible distress.[24] The hinter- land between Mayumba and the Nyanga River had been the main labor reserve for the colony since the days of Brazza, and young men had become accustomed to travelling far from their home districts and to freeing them- selves from the influence of their clan leaders. By 1920, a ban was imposed on labor recruitment in the Nyanga as the villages in this *circonscription* had been virtually emptied of their productive labor force.[25] The clan el- ders, left alone in the villages with their remaining female dependents, had lost control over the labor and tribute of their absent dependents.

One might then view the rash of ritual murders which continued well into the 1920s as a last desperate effort by clan leaders to regain con- trol over their dependents. A 1923 account of an attack on a ten-year-old girl named Moumbou N'Djimbi in the village of Loubomo near Mayumba is revealing. The man accused of the attack, a certain Bouiti N'Souami, claimed that he had indeed come to visit the girl, his clan relative, on the day of the crime but that unbeknownst to him his clan elder, Gouli Bouanga, had sent with him a leopard. Bouiti N'Souami claimed that it was the leopard of Gouli Bouanga that was responsible for the attack. It seems that the mother of the young Moumbou N'Djimbi had been a slave in the lineage of Gouli Bouanga and the latter claimed rights over the girl but she had refused to live with him. The leopard man attack could then be inter- preted as a final frustrated effort of waning clan authority to assert control over its members.[26]

These motivations were clearly stated in the case of a certain Bouala accused of organizing the murder of his nephew Loundou on the road between Mbigou and Kembélé in 1924. The unfortunate Loundou, said to be "an excellent worker as well as a good hunter," refused to live with his uncle. Bouala, extremely jealous that the fruits of his nephew's labor were being enjoyed by other relatives, decided to kill Loundou and organized his murder. These insights regarding the deteriorating power of clan lead- ers would not, however, have been much use to the administrator on the spot trying to determine culpability according to European statutes.[27]

The increasing incidence of leopard men attacks might also be seen as stemming from the constraints applied to the movements of dependents between clans, which were in turn a consequence of the colonial administration's growing capacity to impose its territoriality. The close con- nection between the salt trade and dependent exchange pushed the conces- sion companies and colonial administration to shut down the salt hangars on the coast in the first decade of this century.[28] This severely disrupted the movement of dependents from clan to clan and in rather quick fashion blocked the most tried and true way of ridding a clan or village of undesirable members. Marcel Guebende, an Eviya informant for Moutsinga Kebila, noted that: "When we no longer wanted to see someone around, we sold him."[29] It is interesting that those accused of leopard men killings sometimes gave as their motivation the desire "to get rid of relatives with whom we have problems."[30]

Concrete information on leopard men was hard to obtain from informants, as there continues to be a general reluctance to discuss these kinds of activities. One informant claimed that he knew a great deal about leopard men activities in the Nyanga region but as some of those involved were still alive he was reluctant to stir up old problems.[31] The fear generated by these killings and their connection to such a powerful symbol created a strong sense of paranoia that is still felt today. Strong leaders such as Mbombé were able to exploit this paranoia by accusing rivals of leopard men activities and then obliging them to appear before his *mangonde* charm, which then often sentenced them to death. He was accused of doing away with his brother-in-law Opongo in this fashion just prior to his capture in 1913.[32]

The climate of fear created by leopard men was another reason for the numerous population movements that occurred between 1914 and 1925. In 1922 and 1923 a number of villages in the Tsogo-speaking Waka district moved closer to the colonial post at Sindara citing the ravages of leopard men as their motivation. During the same period a number of Nzabi-speaking clans fled the districts around the colonial post of Mbigou to escape "the man-killers and the leopard who killed many people" and established themselves among the Punu-speaking villages of the Ngounié savannah. The fear of leopard men attacks also kept women throughout Southern Gabon from properly tending their plantations and thus contributed to the ongoing food scarcity.[33]

Charbonnier's arrest of twenty-nine men purported to have participated in leopard men killings in the Nyanga *circonscription* at the end of 1916 marked the colonial administration's first real crackdown on these activities. Several of the accused were found guilty of murder and sentenced to death. The executions of leopard men left a deep impression on the local population but more often than not confusion was the result. This was due to a delay in imposing death sentences while waiting for approval from Libreville. Thus, an accused killer was often arrested and fed and lodged at the colonial post for a period of one or two months. Then, well after passions about the crimes had settled, the accused was taken out and shot. The trees behind the *sous-préfecture* in the town of Mandji, colonial post for the

Eshiras *circonscription,* are quickly pointed out to the visitor today as the site of leopard men executions.[34]

The first half of the 1920s appears to have been a peak of known leopard men activity, as ritual murders spread for the first time to the Fang-speaking clans of the Middle Ogooué just when the effects of famine were being felt.[35] Following concerns about the food supply, the colonial administration considered leopard men killings the biggest problem they had to face in the Tsogo-, Sango-, and Nzabi-speaking villages between the posts of Kembélé and Mbigou. Some forty arrests of purported leopard men were made by the military administrator in Mbigou in 1923, of whom thirty-six died in custody. The administrator speculated that they had either been poisoned by their leaders or had poisoned themselves so as not to divulge information about their activities or be killed at the hand of the white man.[36]

In the area around Kembélé, it was thought that each village had its own *"marmite"* or "ritual cooking vessel" around which as few as four to five leopard men organized for ritual murder. It was estimated that a pattern of killing and reprisals between villages had already resulted in hundreds if not one thousand deaths. This is most certainly an exaggerated figure influenced by the spectacular nature of leopard men crimes. A more level-headed analysis in 1924 suggested that the actual numbers of leopard men were quite small and that more serious damage was coming from the widespread use of the *mbundu* poison ordeal resorted to in virtually all attempts to determine cause of death.[37]

It is very seductive to view this period of intense leopard men activity as a final desperate attempt of the violent segments of the *mwiri*-type of initiation societies to regain control over the people who represented wealth in the precolonial equatorial tradition. It was by accumulating male and female clan dependents (and the objects that could be potentially turned into clan dependents) that precolonial clan leaders became capable of exploiting the territorial opportunities available within precolonial districts. By the 1920s all of these precolonial practices were becoming increasingly irrelevant within a physical space more and more under the sway of the modern territoriality exercised by the French colonial state. Power and influence in the material world recognized by modern European territoriality would now have to be obtained by other means.

Yet there remained those parts of the precolonial cognitive map where the modern European did not travel and which it labeled supernatural. It was in the continued appropriation of these relationships, relegated to the sphere of magic by colonial administrators and missionaries, that clan elders were able to maintain an authority and identity separate from those imposed and constructed in the modern colonial world. With their authority over people and objects in the material world rapidly diminishing in the opening decades of the twentieth century, there occurred a related decline in *mwiri*-types of societies, which were primarily concerned with control over people, objects, and phenomena in physical space. This was accompanied by the growing importance of the *bwiti* initiation society, which, though it assumed some of the functions of *mwiri,* promised esoteric insights into the workings of the universe through an hallucinatory initiation experience and the performance of spectacular miracles.

Already in 1913, Gisir-speaking clan leaders of the Ngosi district, concerned by bizarre weather and ravaged plantations stemming from an extended dry season as well as by the younger generation's obsession with gaining money through migrant labor in the timber industry, organized an important gathering at the village of Mwao to discuss these alarming developments. Clan ancestors had related to various leaders through dreams that the misfortune experienced by their people was due to their neglect of various charms associated with *mwiri* and other practices.[38] Three of those who had such dreams, two men and a woman, spoke of their concerns with Père Girod of the Sainte-Croix des Eshiras mission:

> We no longer respect *Mwiri*. Women and uninitiated children dare to utter in mocking fashion the sacred cry. . . . What's more, all tribute goes to *Bwiti*, which is not right. . . . Those young people faithful to *Bwiti* are far too demanding; when we kill an antelope in the village, the haunches, the shoulders, the filets are always reserved for *Bwiti*.[39]

Indeed, it was in the growing importance of *bwiti* and a panoply of healing societies organized by women that the populations of Southern Gabon negotiated the full impact of modern territoriality in the 1920s and 1930s.

Colonial Flotsam and Jetsam: The Creation of Chieftaincies

The appointment of chiefs by the colonial administration began in the early years of the twentieth century as auxiliaries were sought to collect the new per capita income tax.[40] These initial efforts were unsuccessful as administration officials did not understand the nature of clan authority and were unable to coopt influential clan leaders who still exercised control over trade and labor; indeed, the most powerful clans in Southern Gabon were in a state of rebellion during these years. The period of hunger and famine undermined the power of the clan heads, and by 1920 they had been sufficiently marginalized for the administration to embark upon a more systematic policy of chief appointments.

Thus, chiefs were appointed for the Orungu, Nkomi, and Ngowe "tribes" of the Ouroungous *circonscription*. In the Bongo *circonscription* precise boundaries were drawn up for the two chiefs appointed: Colo Pele, whose jurisdiction included the islands and villages settled along the Setté Cama Lagoon, and Moundango Lamou, who was given the area from the lagoon to the Nyanga delta to administer. The Gisir- and Varama-speaking clans in the interior to the east were in 1920 considered too disorganized for the appointment of a chief. In the Bas-Ogooué *circonscription*, twenty-one *cantons* were created but due to the heterogeneous mixture of peoples the administration postponed chief appointments.[41] In the Mouila *subdivision*, four chieftaincies were created, each corresponding to an ethnic category: Mitsogo, Apindji, Bapunu, and Gisira. This latter action was in response to Le Testu's 1916 call to bring some order to the "inorganic" groupings of these peoples.[42]

The *canton* was the new territorial innovation associated with the creation of chieftaincies in 1920. In a clear illustration of the logic of the colonial state's modern territoriality, the administration, using maps and censuses, first delimited geographical space and then sought to appoint Africans with sufficient authority to serve as their auxiliaries. The fact that these practices were so fundamentally different from precolonial territoriality and notions of authority resulted in administrative confusion, as chiefs were appointed to head not only *cantons* but *terres* and *tribus*. At first, the distinctions were not clear but they eventually evolved into a hierarchical system with the *canton* chief at the top enjoying better compensation and more privileges than his counterparts at the *tribu* and *terre* levels. Yet all three administrative units implied territoriality as a 1923 colonial report clearly indicated: "The *terre*, the *canton* or the *tribu* are composed of a group of villages and the territories dependent on them."[43]

This description recalls the precolonial district which also served to group together villages. However, the colonial administration had failed to fully recognize the existence and functions of districts in precolonial Southern Gabon; by the 1920s they were on the verge of disappearing. These functions contrasted drastically with those of the colonial *canton, terre,* or *tribu.* The precolonial district was a loose decentralized grouping that developed from patterns of marital exchange and trade. There was generally no single leader or central village, and member villages were fluid settlements whose constituent clans came and went as they pleased. A colonial *canton* was made up of villages that were bureaucratically fixed and physically regrouped in space. A *canton* chief was supposed to exercise territorial power unknown to his precolonial counterparts. In February of 1920 colonial officials in the Bongo *circonscription* outlined the functions of their appointed chiefs in the following fashion:

> The *terre* chiefs are going to set about forcing out from the forest those who have sought refuge there and then make them construct large villages like in the past, three or four for each *terre* will be sufficient. If by the first of July they have not succeeded, a sufficient number of militiamen will be sent to Bongo in order to proceed with the cleaning out of the forest and the grouping of natives into large villages under the command of chiefs who will be chosen in place of those who have shown themselves incapable. . . . Chiefs will make sure taxes are paid at the beginning of the year and they will organize service labor at the moment desired. For all services rendered, they will have the right to 5% of the tax. They will have the right to imprison—punishment under the *indigénat*[44]—whoever refuses to obey them. They will have badges that will distinguish them from the common people and bring them respect.[45]

Colonial-appointed chiefs in Southern Gabon during the interwar period were agents of the French and thus had to rely on the administration to enforce their legitimacy, as they had little or no authority to undertake the tasks expected of them. Chieftaincies and their constituents were more often than not invented without reference to traditional structures of authority or territoriality.[46] All parties were soon frustrated (or worse) by this state of affairs. Throughout the 1920s and into the 1930s, colonial officials lamented the ineffectiveness of the *canton* chiefs. Those who were appointed often feared, with good reason, the populations they were supposed to administer: at Kembélé in 1922 two chiefs loyal to the administration were poisoned. Two years later in Ngoguina, a village of Apindji-speaking clans near Mouila, no one wanted to be chief and the entire village population agreed not to accept anyone imposed by the administration.[47]

Colonial-appointed chiefs were expected to exercise considerable coercion over the population of their *canton* but they were not given the means to do so. They were denied access to the bureaucratic instruments of modern territoriality and thus often had to rely on the brute force of the Regional Guard to accomplish their colonial duties.[48]

Indeed, colonial auxiliaries such as former members of the Regional Guard, *tirailleurs,* and post interpreters served as a pool for *canton* chief appointments, this despite instructions from the Lieutenant-Governor discouraging this practice as early as 1922.[49] Thus, Joseph Mouanga, an interpreter for the post at Sindara from 1929, became chief of the Mitsogo *canton* in that *subdivision* in 1938. At Mayumba in 1937, the *canton* chiefs were a former *tirailleur* and a former domestic servant. Interestingly, three years earlier the nomination of Jerôme Njimbi, an interpreter who had served at posts in the Ngounié area for twenty-five years, to a *canton* chief position in his native Mayumba was denied, the Lieutenant-Governor citing the need to appoint someone who enjoyed local clan authority.[50] Colonial officials clearly expressed a desire to appoint chiefs who were important clan leaders as far back as 1923 but clan authority had by then been severely undermined. In an interesting juxtaposition of the conflicting territorialities, this report concluded: "In a word, it would be desirable that we administer less through villages and more through families."[51] Yet even at its precolonial height, the power exercised by clan heads would not have been sufficient to meet modern colonial obligations like tax collection and labor recruitment.

The failure to find appropriate chiefs did not slow down the administration's project of further delimiting space. The 1929 Annual Report noted: "These difficulties will not hold up the methodical pursuit of efforts to organize native groups into *terres, cantons,* and *tribus* nor will they prevent their application over the whole of Gabon."[52] Territory was duly demarcated but in the Mimongo *subdivision* of Tsogo-, Sango-, Kele-, and Simba-speaking clans creating effective units of administration was particularly difficult. Maclatchy described the situation in 1936:

> The *subdivision* is divided administratively into five *cantons* each corresponding to an ethnic group (the Simba group being incorporated in the North *canton*). . . . Each of these *cantons* is itself subdivided into *terres*; although not officially recognized, this latter division is the only one accepted by the native as it corresponds to a real ethnic group. In his eyes, the *canton* is but a fictive and purely administrative link between the diverse *terres*.[53]

The colonial terms for the different *terres* generally referred to placement on rivers; villages were now grouped together on administrative charts and given the cachet of belonging to either a Massango or Mitsogo ethnic category. The next step was to appoint *canton* chiefs to personify these new ethnic identities, a particularly difficult task among these traditionally recalcitrant clans.[54]

The South *canton* of Tsogo-speaking clans included the precolonial district of Gésuma that produced the rebel leader Mbombé. Well into the

1930s, the remnants of the Gésuma district identity served as a rallying point for passive resistance to the colonial regime. The Gésuma villages were the only ones in the whole of the Ngounié *circonscription* not to participate in an agricultural fair that attracted close to five thousand people to Mouila in September 1934. This act triggered a bureaucratic outburst from the colonial official in charge who went on about the "inertia," "passive resistance," and "bad attitude" of these "Mitsogos Issoumas"; regarding the chiefs, he noted: "the chiefs named by us have no authority, I have already changed the *terre* chief and this had no impact which clearly proves that we do not yet know who the true chiefs are . . . "[55] In May 1935 another change was made with Nzambi appointed *canton* chief to replace Ivounga though neither was particularly effective in colonial eyes.[56]

The precolonial Diboa district also maintained an existence within colonial West *canton*; the appointed chief here was Matiba, who aided the French during the military occupation of the 1920s. He was considered to possess real authority among the local population; as a result the French turned a blind eye to his manipulations of the tax roll in 1934. Indeed, the official tax register had mysteriously disappeared during this time; what is more, the Mimongo post caught fire in May 1935 and all bureaucratic records, the source of European power, were destroyed. It was only with the establishment of gold mines at nearby Etéké beginning in 1937 that the Mimongo *subdivision* fully experienced modern territoriality through the building of roads, systematic village regroupment, and rigidly supervised labor at the gold-mining camps. Though gold-mining was more organized and tightly controlled than the timber industry, it was still a temporary affair, as by 1959 the European technicians had abandoned the region and the considerable infrastructure they had put in place. Today Mimongo is a forgotten corner. Diboa, now virtually empty and containing no roads, has become a symbol of the esoteric powers of the forest in the contemporary Gabonese imagination.[57]

Chief appointments among the Gisir-speaking clans were somewhat more successful. Here the heritage of the precolonial districts of Kamba, Ngosi, and Tando provided the administration with some structure and these were eventually coopted as colonial institutions.[58] The 1920s represented a somewhat confused period as officials in Sindara rescinded their predecessors' appointments and created tension by grouping some Kele-speaking clans under a Gisir-speaking chief, Mourambo Ngungu.[59] Following the opening of the Sindara-Fougamou road and the move of the colonial post to Fougamou at decade's end, there came an administrative reorganization in 1932 that resulted in the creation of eight *canton* chieftaincies. Here the *cantons* were named after the individuals appointed to lead them, thus facilitating identification of the actual village groupings with a person.[60] This was further aided by the lengthy tenures of such chiefs as Kenguelé Mbini, Makoulouba, and Mourambo Ngungu, the latter serving the colonial administration from 1915 to his death in 1951. A significant aspect of these 1932 appointments was that each *canton* chief would be assisted by a secretary who would submit trimester reports to the administration.[61]

Another administrative reorganization was implemented in 1937 following a major rethinking of the *canton* chieftaincy structures the preceding year. For the *tribu Eshira* there were now three *canton* chieftaincies corresponding to the Ngosi, Kamba and Tando precolonial districts, which were labeled *familles* in French. Mourambo was the Ngosi *canton* chief with three *terres* chiefs under his authority; Kenguelé was the Kamba *canton* chief with two *terres* subordinates; Mounombi, a younger man who had a difficult relationship with the colonial authorities, was the Tando *canton* chief and had three *terres* subordinates.[62]

This arrangement served to crystalize Gisira ethnic identity and effectively marginalize the other budding ethnic identities in the *subdivision*. Thus, the Bakele were limited to an "autonomous *terre*" in the Ngosi *canton* and a *canton* of their own under the chief Lepende located near the declining center of Sindara. Sindara's fall and Fougamou's rise left the newly appointed Mouanga and his Mitsogo *canton* (which included the precolonial Matèndè, Waka and Ikobey districts) on the margins. The once important presence of Fang- and Vili-speaking clans was now reduced to a single village for each and placed under Lepende's Bakele *canton*.[63] The Bakele, whose clans had been such aggressive participants in the nineteenth-century trade networks, were unable to make a successful transition to a modern ethnic group. Dispersed throughout the colony and unable to lay claim to any of the developing colonial towns, the Bakele were destined to merge with more successful ethnic groups. By the 1960s, a Bakele intellectual ruefully reflected upon this situation:

> I am no longer surprised but instead feel confused and upset about witnessing, sooner or later, the poignant spectacle of the slow absorption of a people by an insidious colony. I will see this people disappear without warning, without war or even treaty.[64]

The Eviya were allotted a *terre* chieftaincy; the chief was Bodinga-bwa-Dimbombi, the father of informant Bodinga-bwa-Bodinga. This *terre* contained but eight villages at the time of its creation of which one remains today. The younger Bodinga has made it his task to preserve through his writings the language and traditions of this disappearing ethnic group. This disappearance, as we have seen, was a consequence of population loss from disease but also due to the absorption of potential ethnic Eviya by the more dominant Gisira ethnic category. One way that this occurred was through patterns of intermarriage between Gisir- and Eviya-speaking clans; as the importance of clan identity decreased and that of colonial ethnic identity crystallized, children having one Gisira parent and one Eviya parent would opt to recognize their Gisira side since it opened more doors in the colonial world. In my encounters with Bodinga, he was quick to point out that a Catholic brother at the mission in Fougamou passed himself off as Gisira but was really Eviya. Bodinga also noted that language became politicized in ways that it had not been before; he claimed that Gisir-speakers from his father's generation also spoke Eviya and did so without hesitation; likewise Eviya-speakers spoke Gisir. However, following the creation of the three Gisira *canton* chieftaincies, Eviya-speakers continued to speak Gisir as language and took on a central role in formulating the dominant Gisira ethnic identity. But Gisir-speakers no longer spoke Eviya or even admitted that they were capable of doing so.[65]

The migration of labor to the growing centers of Port-Gentil and Lambaréné provided other contexts in which one could assume the ethnic identity most likely to open colonial doors. Bodinga cited the independence-era politician, Réné-Paul Soussatte, as an example of someone who claimed to be Gisira to advance his career but who was really from the Bavarama group.[66] In his autobiography, Vincent de Paul Nyonda describes his youth among the Vungu-speaking clans of his mother's family, but in 1956 when he was put on an electoral list representing Fougamou he claimed the Gisira ethnic identity of his father. It is not without significance that he learned to read Gisir when preparing the catechism as a boy.[67]

The urbanizing center of Lambaréné with its diverse mixture of peoples posed particularly delicate problems when it came to appointing chiefs. On the one hand, the local Galwa formed a singularly effective ethnic bloc as they claimed a strong contingent of educated clerks and traders much despised by the colonial administration for their use of anonymous tracts critical of the regime and their adoption of European lifestyles. The 1930s saw a number of elites attempt to assume the ethnic mantle of chief for all Galwa, harkening back to the rule of Nkombé in the 1870s as a precedent. Notable in this regard were the efforts of Auguste Renagho but the struggle produced no clearcut victor.[68] The Galwa were in the process of forming a broader alliance with the Nkomi of Fernan Vaz, the Orungu of Cap Lopez, and the Mpongwe of Libreville that became the powerful Myènè ethnic bloc of post-1945 party politics.[69]

The Fang were to provide the main challenge to the Myènè, and by the 1930s the battle between Fang and Mpongwe interests in Libreville was well underway. Though not as intense, Fang and Galwa ethnic competition also marked life in Lambaréné. The boom years of the timber industry allowed the *canton* chiefs near Lambaréné to accumulate wealth and power unattainable in less dynamic areas. They were thus often targets for criticism from their constituents who were quick to present the administration with written complaints. In 1935, the mostly Fang population in the village of Junckville protested that their *canton* chief was abusing his position by taking married women for wives and confiscating tax revenue.[70]

Similar accusations in 1937 brought the downfall of Vincent Poaty, who was the *canton* chief of the "vagabond" population in Lambaréné. Poaty's career was an illustration of the new kinds of opportunities provided by a growing urban center. Originally from the Loango coast, he worked as an interpreter and trader for more than two decades before he was elected chief by the members of the immigrant "Loango"[71] community of Lambaréné in 1932. In 1935, the administrator Gamon praised Poaty's energy in assisting with the implementation of a very ambitious plan to regroup the growing vagabond population into neatly ordered villages. Yet it was the changing nature of this immigrant community that led to his departure, as increasing numbers of Bapunu and Gisira settled in Lambaréné following the 1931 slowdown in the timber industry. The signatories of the 1937 complaint outlining Poaty's pattern of abuse appear to have been either Bapunu or Gisira. The developing ethnic consciousness of the Bapunu in particular coalesced around a distrust of Loango colonial auxiliaries. An earlier expression of this antipathy occurred in Mouila where in 1931 a complaint addressed to the Governor-General demanded that young, mission-educated Bapunu replace the Loango interpreters employed by the colonial administration.[72]

The experience of labor in the camps or residence in Lambaréné and Port-Gentil facilitated the contact of tens of thousands of men and women from Southern Gabon with the different populations and institutions that formed the life of the colony of Gabon. The colony was a new French-imposed creation and it required the imagination of a different kind of "we," one that was larger and based on a different set of criteria than the traditional clan.[73] Thus was spread the consciousness of belonging to a colonial ethnic group such as the Bapunu or the Gisira; ethnic groups that were continually defining themselves in reference to colonial structures.

This occurred at the level of the *subdivision* where the distribution of *canton* chieftaincies determined which ethnic entity would control colonial nodal points like Fougamou, which became a Gisira fief, and Mouila, which developed into a center for the Bapunu.

The creation of *canton, terre,* and *tribu* administrative units and the appointment of individuals to head them were largely accomplished by the end of the 1930s. The reforms of 1936 provided chiefs with an allowance so that they could properly entertain visitors and pay a small security force. Knowing that their authority rested on the colonial administration and that they could not effectively draw upon traditional symbols of power, colonial chiefs in 1939 requested that the Lieutenant-Governor provide them with insignias appropriate to their command. Thus, it was recommended that *canton* chiefs wear uniforms and carry canes as symbols of authority and *terre* chiefs sport a badge and a sabre. The cost of these items was to be deducted from the chiefs' allowances.[74]

However, the most significant development for the crystallization of the colonial ethnic identities through the figures of chiefs was the creation of *Conseils des notables* (Councils of notables) in 1937. Here, for the first time, representatives of these colonial-invented ethnic groups spoke in a modern administrative context for the interests of their emerging constituency. Ethnic groups now assumed a real political existence in the life of the colony. Indeed, the production of the ethnic groups and regional blocs that define the contemporary Gabonese political scene first took form in these obscure regional councils, the minutes and summary accounts of these meetings providing an early glimpse of modern ethnic identity at work.[75]

A 1937 meeting in Mouila of the Ngounié *département* council brought together colonial officials and *canton* chiefs from the Mouila, Sindara, Mimongo, and Mbigou *subdivisions* to discuss tax, labor-service, and road construction policies. Kenguelé was a representative for the Gisira, and Matiba one of two chiefs who spoke for the Mitsogo. Interestingly, the notables were against raising the per capita tax though they did agree to a hike the following year, presumably since they were now receiving a portion of the receipts. Chiefs from Mbigou and Mimongo expressed the desire for roads to be built in their *subdivisions*.[76] Chief N'Gokelele representing developing Nzabi interests was quoted as saying:

It's necessary to open up our region of Mbigou, just as it was done for Mouila. . . . Our men will do the service labor for the roads but once this work is completed, funds should be supplied so that the men can be paid and the work continued.[77]

The peoples of Southern Gabon had begun a fuller, more cooperative participation in the workings of the colonial state and henceforth ethnic group interests were adopted as the idiom of expression at this level.

Integral actors in this developing drama were the members of the Western-educated elite whose ranks continued to grow in the 1930s. Most of the key political figures representing Southern Gabon during the period of party politics prior to independence received their education from Catholic Missions, whether in the region, in Libreville, or even in Brazzaville.[78] Indeed, the 1930s witnessed the peak of Saint-Martin's importance as a colonial nodal point as the mission essentially abandoned recruitment among the decimated and recalcitrant Apindji and moved further afield to recruit among the more numerous Bapunu; these efforts were greatly aided by the construction of roads.[79] Canton chiefs, though not usually Christians themselves, made sure to send some of their children to study at the missions. Nyama-Bika, an Gisira *terre* chief under Kenguelé, was a member of Bwiti and an accomplished player of the *ngombé* harp central to Bwiti rites; indeed he was called upon to perform in dances organized in villages throughout the area. Even so, Nyama sent all but one of his children to study at Saint-Martin.[80]

Mission-educated elites were quick to recognize the convergence of their interests and the opportunities presented by a colonial chieftaincy. Thus in January 1932, Hilaire Mougala, residing at the Sainte-Croix des Eshiras mission site (the mission had been closed in 1920), petitioned Governor-General Antonetti in Brazzaville to be named chief of the "Christian Eshiras." Antonetti deemed that such an appointment would lead to confusion and refused to accept the nomination.[81] Just two months earlier, the Governor-General received a complaint concerning abuses by the Mouila *subdivision* commander and interpreters purportedly sent by the Bapunu chiefs but, as the lines below indicate, composed by young mission-educated Bapunu:

> M. Governor-General, we request that the interpreters, who are from the Mayoumba race, should be replaced by our young people who leave the mission knowing quite well how to read, write and speak French correctly. . . .[82]

By 1937, mission-educated Gisira in Fougamou had adopted the tactic of distributing anonymous tracts criticizing the various aspects of colonial rule. In April of that year "young people of the Eshira race" addressed a list of complaints to the Governor-General regarding forced labor, tax collection, and Regional Guard abuse. They also requested that a hospital and quality school be built in Fougamou. They further suggested that, "the functions of *canton* chief be exercised by young people rather than the elders of the region since the latter do not conform to French laws."[83] Thus was announced the generational split that became so apparent in the post-1945 era of party politics. This split led to the marginalization of the *canton* chieftaincies not much more than a decade following their creation. The dramatic shift in French colonial policy after World War II and the political opportunities it afforded were the sole province of a small circle of Western-educated elites.[84]

Women and Healing Societies

The 1930s witnessed the crystallization of modern Gabonese ethnic identities around the figures of the *canton* chiefs. The decade also saw the growing significance of ethnicity in the everyday life of the lumber camps and colonial towns. Colonial rule had stabilized and the traumatic experiences of famine and disease were no longer serious threats. But their memory was vivid and powerful, reminders that the precolonial world of the equatorial tradition had collapsed. The disruptive influence of labor recruitment for the lumber camps and administration efforts to control life in the villages had created a deep malaise among the peoples of Southern Gabon. The shrinking population indicated by colonial statistics was only too apparent to the inhabitants themselves who lived in the tiny dispersed villages. Women, who in increasing numbers became infertile as a result of gonorrheal infections,[85] suffered acute agonies. There were very deep sociological and psychological wounds that needed healing; no longer able to rely on the clan or lineage chief to assure their health and well-being, the population at large, and women in particular, devoted much of their creative cultural energy to the formation of healing cults.

There was considerable work to be done as the *canton* chiefs in the 1930s were viewed quite rightly as colonial authorities in opposition to traditional clan leaders. These clan leaders had lashed out violently in the 1920s at their growing powerlessness with leopard-men attacks on the symbols of precolonial wealth, women, and dependents. Leopard-men assaults were less-frequent in the next decade, though an extreme state of paranoia continued to mark local populations (colonial-appointed chiefs included), as clan leaders were still very much capable of inflicting harm through acts of sorcery. Rey cites the case of the Kuni *tribu* chief Aloïse Mbungu, appointed by the colonial administration at Mossendjo (Congo) though a member of a dependent lineage, who from 1940 was the target of acts of sorcery from Bumwele clan leaders, his traditional masters. Guy-Joseph Mboundou described similar traditional opposition faced by his father, the Gisira *terre* chief Nyama-Bika, who obtained his position following service in the military. Both men held positions for more than two decades and thus developed reputations as powerful sorcerers themselves.[86] The growing recourse to the "invisible" was a poignant illustration of the weakened position of clan leaders no longer able to impose their will by means of precolonial territoriality. Both men and women sought protection through participation in anti-sorcery movements or healing societies. Rey notes the presence of sorcery is always an indication of crisis but that it was only during the colonial period, and this due to the economic disruption of labor recruitment, that there "appeared a generalized sorcery necessitating a global response."[87] This response took the form of syncretic religious movements—often integrating elements from Christianity—which sought to end acts of sorcery and destroy its paraphernalia.

In the 1930s the cultural energies of a considerable portion of the Southern Gabonese population were focused on healing the deep ruptures brought about by the experience of colonialism and modern territoriality. At the popular level, there existed the sense of a widespread malaise between men and women. This has been particularly well documented for the Fang, but it was also mentioned in colonial reports as both a consequence of and contribution to the decline of traditional lineage structure among the Massango and the Bapunu.[88] The perspective presented was generally a male one that voiced complaints about having lost control over women. Colonial influences, particularly those of Christian missionaries, garnered much of the responsibility for these developments.

The phenomenon was certainly real. Just as the constraints of clan obligation had loosened for those male dependents who migrated to lumber camps so had they also loosened for female clan dependents. Marriage in the precolonial context had been an exchange of women to cement clan alliances. With the authority of the clan and its leaders now on the wane, it is not surprising that marriage in the towns and lumber camps became an affair one could easily enter into or exit from. The models of Christian and civil matrimony proposed by the missions and colonial administration were foreign impositions whose meanings, like those of colonial ethnic categories, remained to be negotiated once their hegemony became firmly established.

In the meantime, the pervasive sense that things had fallen apart pushed men and women to seek ritual reconciliation through healing cults. The precolonial context that had justified the strict separation of the men's *mwiri* initiation society from the women's *njembe* counterpart was becoming increasingly less relevant.[89] Thus, though it is difficult to be precise, at some point during the interwar years radical innovations in ritual practice were adopted in Southern Gabon. These involved the creation of healing societies open to both men and women but whose predominant membership was female. Initiation generally involved possession by an ancestor or spirit and was undertaken as part of a therapeutic agenda to cure afflictions like infertility.

These societies seem to have first developed among the Nkomi of the Fernan Vaz and from there spread throughout Southern Gabon as well as to the north among the Fang.[90] The French sociologist André Mary notes:

> The principle of cult mixing that saw the parallel introduction of Nkomi *elombo* and Fang *bwiti* during this epoch translated a desire for openness stemming from the novelty of the social roles imposed by colonization and missionary pressure, notably the evolution of the status of women. The separation was no longer clear, the boundaries which guaranteed the respect of spheres of influence had burst; globally, however, the symbolic definition of roles and positions of power were maintained.[91]

A man named Nango Y'Apandji (also rendered "Nango yi Vandji") from the island of Nengé Sika which faces the mouth of the Rembo Mkomi in the Fernan Vaz Lagoon and his disciple, Ntchandi Barthélemy, are credited with the founding of the *elombo* healing society in 1935. Nango Y'Apandji lived a life of adventure and travel before his death at Port-Gentil in 1965. He had resided among the Apindji and the Gisira, and, while with the latter, had contacts with an *nganga* (healer) named Okuti. Thus, his own movements facilitated the spread of *elombo* to the peoples of the Ngounié region. Though *elombo* was founded by men, women became its most accomplished practitioners; this further aided its dissemination. For example, Mitsogo women who left the interior for Port-Gentil to accompany Mitsogo men working in the timber industry became initiated into *elombo* during their stay. When they returned to their home villages near Sindara and Mimongo they brought with them *elombo*-related healing practices that have come to be known as *ombudi*.[92]

Elombo, ombudi, and another variation known as *mabandji* are each organized around a different cluster of spirits (*ombwiri*). Sallée notes that healing practices invoking possession from the *abandji* spirits were in vogue in Libreville in 1918 and then spread to the Orungu and Nkomi; *mabandji* is the dance of preference today among the Balumbu and the Gisira.[93] Yet these healing societies are similar in form and function and during the interwar years shared many of the same innovations. Perhaps the most important was the joint participation of men and women, but also very significant was the ritual use of the hallucinogen *iboga* to facilitate contact with these spirits and thus gain insight into the causes of an affliction. Prior to the creation of these healing cults, ritual use of *iboga* seems to have been the sole province of the male initiation society, *bwiti* (*bwété* in Tsogo). These innovations were part of a turning to traditional therapeutic practices to negotiate what had been a brutal encounter with modernity and an effort to mend the perceived rift that had opened up between men and women.

Spirit possession had long been a part of the therapeutic process; indeed, *elombo* borrowed a great deal from an earlier Nkomi practice known as *elenge*. The exchange of ritual ideas and dances was a fluid process that allowed for considerable variation and creativity among the individual women healers who led these societies. However, the transformation of *elenge* into *elombo* revealed some specific adjustments to the growing power of colonial territoriality. First, the *nwombi* (or *ngombe*) harp took a more prominent place in the newer society as, according to local tradition, two successive colonial administrators posted to the Fernan Vaz between 1930 and 1942 discouraged the playing of drums. Also, those wishing to practice *elenge* were obliged to do so at their *mpindi*.[94]

One of the reasons for the success of *elombo* was that Nango Y'Apandji had been able to find a method and the necessary medicinal plants to reduce the initiation ceremony from two seances for *elenge* to one for *elombo*.[95] The temporal collapsing of all ritual initiations in Southern Gabon occurred during the colonial period as European conceptions of time and patterns of labor imposed themselves upon daily life. Indeed, when colonial officials reported on *bwiti* activity, they were more concerned about the lost time and wasted labor that resulted from all-night dance ceremonies than any potential political resistance. A report from the Bongo *circonscription* in 1923 noted an upswing in *bwiti* ceremonies and complained that the ingestion of large quantities of *iboga* during the nocturnal rites resulted in "an excessive laziness" and the "neglect of plantation upkeep" for days thereafter. It was decided to impose fines on those caught dancing *bwiti*. That same year a number of Tsogo-speaking *bwété* members from Kembélé were sentenced to eight days in jail for organizing a dance ceremony instead of clearing trails as they had been ordered to do by the administration.[96]

A 1939 colonial report from the Ogooué-Maritime *département* categorically stated that "there are no reports anywhere of political activity with serious quasi-religious or even fetish origins."⁹⁷ And yet the decade had witnessed major transformations in religious and healing practice. The politics of healing groups and initiation societies such as *bwiti* had by this time taken the path of avoidance and were not directly linked to the kinds of political action that concerned the colonial administration. Though Fang *bwiti*, a syncretic religion incorporating elements of Christianity, was deftly exploited by Léon Mba, the first president of Gabon, in his attempts to forge a modern Fang political constituency in Libreville,⁹⁸ the situation in Southern Gabon was different. Here the several different variations of *bwiti* served as an alternative to the colonial world, a ritual flight into the forest where one could find comfort among the remnants of precolonial tradition. Thus, *bwiti's* importance continued to grow vis-à-vis *mwiri* and even incorporated some of its functions and rituals.

It has been observed on a number occasions that those who are most knowledgeable and respected in the worlds of *bwiti* in Southern Gabon are men for whom success in the modern world means little. This is a testament to the power and vision provided by the esoteric knowledge one gains upon initiation into the society. A *bwiti* member named Jean Michonet, whose grandfather, Jean-Marie Isaac, was one of the most successful French foresters of the interwar years (and was initiated into *bwiti*), and whose grandmother, Esonguérigo, was the daughter of an Orungu chief, observed that in the years since Gabonese independence in 1960 many *bwiti*

> initiates stopped their children from entering the sect when it was their turn. There one sees the uselessness of everything in this world: the danger is to no longer react. If he does not overcome the shock, the adept will no longer have any ambition.⁹⁹

In Southern Gabon, the transformation of healing practices and the turn to the esoteric associated with the growing importance of *bwiti* represented the most effective efforts of the equatorial tradition to adapt to the radical change of colonial rule. Though Vansina rightly points out that "in the realm of physical reality, the conquest prevented the tradition from inventing new structures to cope with a new situation,"¹⁰⁰ new structures were developed in those realms of the precolonial cognitive map not recognized by modern territoriality. The realms of "the invisible" were beyond the influence of the colonial administration and provided the strongest points of continuity between the precolonial, colonial, and post-colonial cognitive maps of the peoples of Southern Gabon. Yet, as Jean Michonet's observations above indicate, there is a devious irony involved and a price to be paid for partial integration into modernity. Vansina argues that the peoples of the rain forests "turned into cultural schizophrenics" during the colonial period.[101] The same schizophrenic tendencies are found in the territorial practices of the Gabonese colonial state and its post-colonial successor.

Notes

1. Florence Bernault, *Démocraties ambiguës en Afrique centrale, Congo-Brazzaville, Gabon: 1940–1965* (Paris: Karthala, 1996), 11–12.

2. Vansina, *Paths*, 247.

3. Ibid., 239.

4. Bayart, *State in Africa*, 137.

5. Ibid., 138.

6. For Cameroon, Bayart cites material from Peter Geschiere, "Hegemonic Regimes and Popular Protest—Bayart, Gramsci and the State in Cameroon," *Les Cahiers de CEDAF* (July 1986): 309–47; and for Congo, Georges Dupré, *Les naissances d'une société: Espace et historicité chez les Beembé du Congo*; Pierre Bonnafé, *Histoire sociale d'un peuple congolais. Livre I: La terre et le ciel* (Paris: ORSTOM, 1987); and Rey, *Colonialisme*.

7. Koumba-Manfoumbi, "Les Punu," 285–86; Mamfoumbi, "Évolution des sociétés secrètes," 148–52; Hubert, "Esquisse de la coutume Bapounou," 21.

8. Vansina makes a similar point about "a tragic chasm between physical and cognitive realities"; see Vansina, *Paths*, 245.

9. Sometimes referred to as "hommes-tigres" or "hommes-panthères" in European texts—neither tigers nor panthers are found in Southern Gabon; the terms for Mpongwe-, Galwa-, Nkomi-, Orungu-, Ajumba-, and Enenga-speakers are *mongi-ndjegó* or *kuya*; for Apindji-speakers *oma-a-di-ndjègó* or *wasi-ekóngó*; for Tsogo-speakers *asi-ekóngó*; for Vili-speakers *banga-mapivi*; for Punu-speakers *mimbènga* or *bapuni*; for Eshira-, Varama-, Vungu- and Lumbu-speakers *puni*; for Nzabi-speakers *matsókó*; and for Sango-speakers *matsóku*; see Raponda-Walker and Sillans, *Rites*, 178. For overviews of these kind of societies in Africa south of the Sahara, see Paul-Ernest Joset, *Les sociétés secrètes des hommes-léopards en Afrique noire* (Paris: Payot, 1955) and Birger Lindskog, *African Leopard Men* (Uppsala: Almquist & Wiksells Boktryckeri AB, 1954).

10. For a related discussion of the lion as symbol among the Turu people in the Singida District of Tanzania, see Harold K. Schneider, "Male-Female Conflict and the Lion Men of Singida," in *African Religious Groups and Beliefs: Papers in Honor of William R. Bascom*, ed. Simon Ottenberg (Meerut, India: Folklore Institute, 1982), 105–6.

11. For a summary of the leopard man issue in Southern Gabon, see Le Testu, "Réflexions sur l'homme tigre," 147–68; for a succinct statement of local knowledge of the natural world, Auguste Chevalier, "Les rapports des noirs avec la nature: Sur l'utilisation par les indigènes du Gabon d'une fougère pour piègage et d'un champignon pour la fabrication des ceintures de parure," *JSA* 4 (1934): 123–27.

12. Du Chaillu, *Journey to Ashango-Land*, 50–52; Griffon du Bellay, "Le Gabon 1861–1864," *Le Tour du Monde* 7 (1865): 365; Nassau, *Fetishism*, 200–203.

13. Raponda-Walker and Sillans, *Rites*, 179–81.

14. H. Charbonnier, "Congo Français, L'Homme-Tigre," *AA* (1921): 50–58.

15. Jean-Hubert M'Boukou, *Ethnologie criminelle du Gabon* (Le Vesinet: Ediena, 1984), 18–19.

16. Ibid., 19.

17. Gollnhofer, "*Bokudu,*" 97–100, 255–58.

18. Raponda-Walker and Sillans, *Rites,* 236. Le Testu, searching for the clarity of a literate culture, saw this overlapping as lack of "precise doctrine." As indicated earlier this lack of precision is not experienced by those participating in the creation and development of these initiation societies; Le Testu, "Réflexions," 152.

19. The link between chaos and leopard men is made by the Gabonese historian, C. Felix Pambo-Loueya, "La colonie du Gabon de 1914 à 1939: Étude économique et sociale" (Thèse de doctorat, Université Paris VII, 1980), 76–78; see also Allen F. Roberts, "'Like a Roaring Lion': Tabwa Terrorism in the Late Nineteenth Century," *Banditry, Rebellion and Social Protest,* ed. Donald Crummey (London/Portsmouth: James Currey/Heinemann, 1986), 66–69; and Schneider, "Male-Female Conflict," 107.

20. Pouchet, "Vieux Gabon," 139–42.

21. ANG, Fonds de la Présidence, Politique Générale, carton 522 dossier 5989, "Rapport Trimestriel, Subdivision de Mimongo, mars–mai 1914"; AOM-AEF (Aix), D 4D 4(1)D11 1914, "Resumés des rapports mensuels, Circonscription de Bongo, avril–mai 1914"; "Rapport d'ensemble trimestriels, 4e trimestre 1913"; 4(1)D13 1915, "Resumés des rapports mensuels, Circonscription de la Nyanga, août, décembre 1915."

22. Charbonnier's report was originally written at the end of November 1916 and first published in *Annales Apostoliques* in 1921; it later appeared in the *BSRC* 6 (1925): 171–81.

23. Charbonnier, "Notre enquête sur les Sociétés secrètes," *BSRC* 6 (1925): 174; the corresponding paragraph in the *Annales Apostoliques* version omits the reference to census-taking.

24. Le Testu, "Réflexions," 167; Le Testu's inability to assess the negative impact of French colonial rule is discussed in Rey, *Colonialisme,* 172–75.

25. AOM-AEF (Aix), D 4D 4(1)D18 1920, "Rapport d'ensemble sur la situation de la Colonie du Gabon pendant l'année 1920."

26. AOM-AEF (Aix), D 4D 4(1)D26 1923, "Rapports Mensuels (Nyanga), août–septembre 1923."

27. "Assassinat par le feu: Hommes panthères—Anthropophagie—Race Bandjabis," *BSRC* 10 (1929) 133–34; for further complaints regarding the difficulty of investigating and determining guilt in leopard men attacks, see AOM-AEF (Aix), D 4D 4(1)D19 1921, "Rapport Mensuel (Nyanga), décembre 1921." For similar developments in colonial Nigeria, see Geoffrey I. Nwaka, "The 'Leopard' Killings of Southern Annang, Nigeria, 1943–48," *Africa* 56, 4 (1986): 417–45.

28. See Gray, "Territoriality," 290–320.

29. See Annexe 1, Marcel Guebende, "Récit sur l'esclavage et ses origines," in Moutsinga Kebila, "Histoire Eviya."

30. See the "Procès-verbal d'interrogation du nommé Moulélé" in Mariani, "Assassinat par le feu," 138.

31. Robert-Marie Djyoni, Interview Notes V, Mouila, July 11, 1991.

32. AOM-AEF (Aix), D 5D 5D13 1910–1913, "Le Lieutenant-Gouverneur du Gabon à M. le Gouverneur-Général d'A.E.F., le 28 août 1913, A.S. de l'internement de Bombi et de la Mission confiée à l'interprète du poste de Mouila"; "Interrogatoire de Bombi,

Mouila, 21 mars 1913"; "Procès-Verbal d'audition de témoins, déposition de Masandi Mondadi, Mouila, 1 avril 1913."

33. AOM-AEF (Aix), D 4D 4(1)D22 1922, "Rapports mensuels (Bas-Ogooué), juin 1922"; 4(1)D24, Rapports mensuels (Bongo), août 1923"; "Annexe I, Texte No. 6, Jean Ibassa-Makanda," in Koumba-Mamfoumbi, "Les Punu," 297.

34. AOM-AEF (Aix), D 4D 4(1)D14 1916, "Resumés des rapports mensuels, Circonscription de la Nyanga, novembre 1916"; 4(1)D24, "Rapports mensuels (Banjabis), mars 1923"; "Appendice No. 10, Documentation judiciaire concernant la criminalité, la sorcellerie et l'anthropophagie en Afrique Équatoriale Française," in Joset, *Les sociétés secrètes,* 239–46; Interview Notes IX & Field Notes, Mandji, May 31, 1991.

35. See "Agression des hommes-tigres," *Journal des Missions Evangéliques* 97, 1 (1922): 65–68; "Encore les hommes-tigres," *Journal des Missions Evangéliques* 98, 2 (1923): 106–7; AOM-AEF (Aix), D 4D 4(1)D19 1921, "Rapport mensuel-Circonscription du Bas-Ogooué, décembre 1921."

36. AOM-AEF (Aix), D 4D 4(1)D24 1923, "Rapports mensuels (Banjabis), mars–août 1923"; "Rapport trimestriels, 3e trimestre 1923."

37. AOM-AEF (Aix), D 4D 4(1)D24 1923, "Rapports mensuels (Banjabis), août 1923"; 4(1)D29 1924, "Rapports mensuels-Ngounié, novembre 1924."

38. "Gabon: Un congrès des gauches au pays Eshira," *AA* (1913): 149–51.

39. Ibid., 152.

40. AOM-AEF (Aix), D 4D 4(1)D3 1905–1908, "Rapport général sur le Rembo N'Comi, le 18 juin 1905," for colonial-appointed chiefs among Gisir-speaking clans in 1904.

41. AOM-AEF (Aix), D 4D 4(1)D18 1920, "Exposé de la situation de la colonie du Gabon (1920)."

42. AOM-AEF (Aix), D 4D 4(1)D18 1920, "Rapport d'ensemble sur la situation de la Colonie du Gabon pendant l'année 1920"; 4(1)D14 1916, "Resumés des rapports mensuels, Circonscription de l'Ofoué-Ngounié, décembre 1916."

43. Quoted in Pourtier, *Le Gabon,* 2:55–56.

44. The colonial legal code instituted in 1910 for the administration of the local Gabonese population.

45. AOM-AEF (Aix), D 5D 5D22 1910–1946, "Lieutenant-Gouverneur du Gabon à M. l'Administrateur de la Circonscription du Bongo, Libreville, le 25 février 1920."

46. For a pertinent discussion on the creation of chiefs among the Maka people in Southeast Cameroon, see Peter Geschiere, "Chiefs and Colonial Rule in Cameroon: Inventing Chieftaincy, French and British Style," *Africa* 63, 2 (1993): 153–57.

47. AOM-AEF (Aix), D 4D 4(1)D19 1921, "Rapports trimestriels, Circonscription de Bongo, 3e trimestre 1921"; 4(1)D24 1923, "Rapports mensuels, Circonscription de Banjabis, mai 1923"; 4(1)D29 1924, "Rapports mensuels, Circonscription de la Ngounié, septembre, novembre 1924."

48. Pourtier, *Le Gabon,* 2:54.

49. AOM-AEF (Aix), D 4D 4(1)D20 1922, "Rapports mensuels, Circonscription des Banjabis, juin 1922"; see Mbigui, "Histoire de Sindara," 82, for the different categories from which *canton* chiefs were chosen.

50. ANG, Fonds de la Présidence, Carton 99, Rapports politiques, Département de la Ngounié, 1929–1944, "Rapport trimestriel, 1er trimestre 1929"; AOM-AEF (Aix), D 4D 4(1)D47 1939, "Rapport politique semestriel, Départment de la Ngounié, 1er semestre 1939"; 4(1)D45 1937, "Rapport politique, Département de la Nyanga, 2e semestre 1937"; 4(1)D40 1934, "Rapport du 3e trimestre 1934, Circonscription de la Nyanga."

51. AOM-AEF (Aix), 4(1)D24 1923, "Rapports mensuels, Circonscription de Bongo, janvier–mars 1923."

52. AOM-AEF (Aix), D 4D 4(1)D35 1929, "Rapport annuel 1929."

53. Maclatchy, "Monographie," 19.

54. Ibid., 20; AOM-AEF (Aix), D 4D 4(1)D40 1934, "Rapport trimestriel, Circonscription de la Ngounié, 3e trimestre 1934."

55. AOM-AEF (Aix), D 4D 4(1)D40 1934, "Rapport trimestriel, Circonscription de la Ngounié, 3e trimestre 1934."

56. AOM-AEF (Aix), D 4D 4(1)D41 1935, "Rapport trimestriel, Département de la Ngounié-Nyanga, 1er and 4e trimestres 1935."

57. AOM-AEF (Aix), D 4D 4(1)D41 1935, "Rapport trimestriel, Département de la Ngounié-Nyanga, 2e, 4e trimestres 1935." In 1951 Vincent de Paul Nyonda witnessed a systematic search of mine employees at a camp near Etéké where women were stripped and their sexual organs examined for hidden packets of gold dust; see Nyonda, *Autobiographie,* 107; see also Mounanga, "L'or à Etéké," 19–46, for camp life and gold-mining's impact. For a description of the Diboa just following a village regroupment by the Gabonese government in 1968, see Pierre Sallée, "L'Arc et la Harpe: Contribution à l'histoire de la musique du Gabon" (Thèse de doctorat, Université de Paris X, 1985), 9–10.

58. See Christopher Gray, "The Disappearing District? Territorial Transformation in Southern Gabon 1850–1960," in *Space, Time, and Culture in Africa,* ed. Allen M. Howard and Richard M. Shain.

59. AOM-AEF (Aix), D 4D 4(1)D29 1924, "Rapports mensuels, Circonscription de la Ngounié, juin, novembre 1924."

60. Thus the *canton* of Tsogo-speaking clans near Sindara was named after its chief, Mouembo; the *canton* encompassing the Gisir-speaking Kamba district was named after its chief, Kenguelé Mbini, who, according to informant Guy-Joseph Mboundou, was descended from a dependent lineage (this was not uncommon with colonial-appointed chiefs); under Kenguelé's tutelage was the *terre* chief for the Eviya-speaking clans, Bodinga. The Tando district had two *cantons* named after chiefs Mounombi and Doulégou; the latter was soon succeeded by his son, Bimbounza, and the *canton* took his name. The Ngosi district was represented by Mourambo, Komodiambe and Makoulouba; Komodiambe claimed clan relatives among both Kele- and Gisir-speakers and thus was appointed to resolve the earlier tension; the Sounénè *canton* grouped together *terres* chiefs for the remaining Fang-speaking clans (Chief Ndongo), and Kele-speaking clans (Chief Lepende) resident near Sindara. In Makoulouba's *canton,* a woman from the Mussanda clan named Koumba Moungueka was *terre* chief until her death in 1936; Makoulouba himself had succeeded the influential Ngossi Guitsola who had been arrested by Chamarande. See Mbigui, "Histoire de Sindara," 81–83; Goufoura Offiga, "La chefferie indigène Gisira," 44; Raponda-Walker, *Notes d'histoire,* 22–23; Nyonda, *Autobiographie,* 175; Guy-Joseph Mboundou, Interview Notes XVIII, Libreville, March 30, 1991; for a portrait of Makoulouba, see Christian Dedet, *La mémoire du fleuve: L'Afrique aventureuse de Jean Michonet* (Paris: Éditions Phebus, 1984), 164–69.

61. Mbigui, "Histoire de Sindara," 83; Goufoura Offiga, "La chefferie indigène Gisira," 44.

62. AOM-AEF (Aix), D 4D 4(1)D46 1938, "Organisation des chefferies dans la Région du Gabon, 13 novembre 1937"; for Mounombi's conflicts with the administration, see Nyonda, *Autobiographie,* 109–11.

63. Ibid.

64. Marc-Aurélien Tonjokove, "La famille, son aspect juridique chez les Bakélé" (Mémoire de stage, Institut des Hautes-Études d'Outre-Mer, Paris, 1964), 30.

65. Bodinga-bwa-Bodinga, Interview Notes I, Fougamou, May 21, 22, 28, 1991; see also Weinstein, *Nation-Building*, 91. For similar conditions among the Bakele, Tonjokove, "La famille," 28–31.

66. Bodinga-bwa-Bodinga, Interview Notes I, Fougamou, May 22, 1991.

67. Nyonda, *Autobiographie*, 7, 19, 72.

68. See AOM-AEF (Aix), D 4D 4(1)D42 1935, "Rapports trimestriels, Département de l'Ogooué-Maritime, 4e trimestre 1934"; for administration views of the Galwa elite, 4(1)D19 1921, "Rapports mensuels, Circonscription du Bas-Ogooué, décembre 1921"; 4(1)D22 1922, "Rapports mensuels, Circonscription du Bas-Ogooué, avril 1922"; see Ogoula-M'Beye, *Galwa*, xxxi-xxxv, 199–202, for insight regarding the incorporation of the Galwa into the Myènè and the importance of Nkombé as culture hero.

69. "Myènè" means "I say" in the Galwa, Mpongwe, Orungu, Nkomi, Ajumba, and Enenga languages. It has become not only an ethnic term but also a linguistic one indicating the increasing politicization of language. Other regional groupings have adopted similar labels; for example "Mérié" is used by Nyonda to refer to all the peoples of the South and "Mbere" for the peoples of the Haut-Ogooué; see Nyonda, *Autobiographie*, 10; and Martin Alihanga, "Structures communautaires traditionnelles et perspectives coopératives dans la Société Altogovéenne (Gabon)" (Dissertatio ad doctoratum, Pontificium Universtatem S. Thomae de Urbe, Rome, 1976), 11, 593–606.

70. AOM-AEF (Aix), D 4D 4(1)D42 1935, "Rapport trimestriel, Département de l'Ogooué-Maritime, 3e trimestre 1935"; for differences between Fang and Galwa, see "Lambaréné," *BCSE* 20 (1927–1928): 958.

71. The place term "Loango" came to refer to an ethnic grouping of all those from the Loango coast region who worked in Gabon, thus ignoring whether the individual was a member of a Vili- or a Lumbu-speaking clan.

72. AOM-AEF (Aix), D 4D 4(1)D45 1937, "Plaintes indigènes, Inspections Gabon 1937, Les populations flottantes faisant partie du Groupement dit 'Étrangers' à Lambaréné à M. le Gouverneur-Général de l'AEF, 12 janvier 1937; Vincent de Paul Poaty, Déclaration de sa durée au Gabon, juillet 1937"; 4(1)D47 1939, "Rapport politique, Département de l'Ogooué-Maritime, 2e semestre 1939"; 4(1)D42 1935, "Rapport trimestriel, Département de l'Ogooué-Maritime, 3e trimestre 1935"; 4(1)D37 1931, "Reclamation de tous les chefs Bapounous demeurant dans la Subdivision de Mouila, Mouila, 21 décembre 1931."

73. In referring to the transformation of rural peasants into Frenchmen, historian Eugen Weber remarked: "Another 'we' appeared, another *pays* took shape; and both were larger"; see Eugen Weber, "*Comment la politique vint aux paysans*: A Second Look at Peasant Politization," *American Historical Review* 87 (1982): 387.

74. AOM-AEF (Aix), D 5D 5D22 1910–1946, "Chefferies Indigènes dans l'AEF, Uniformes des chefs, Propositions Gabon-1939"; 4(1)D43 1936, "Rapport trimestriel, Département de la Ngounié-Nyanga, 2e trimestre 1936."

75. See discussion in Pourtier, *Le Gabon*, 2:76.

76. AOM-AEF (Aix), D 4D 4(1)D46 1938, "Rapport politique, Département de la Ngounié, 2e semestre 1938"; AGG-AEF (Brazzaville), III GG182, Conseils des notables dans des départements du Gabon 1936–1941, "Conseil des notables du Département de la Ngounié, réunion du 6 septembre 1937."

77. AGG-AEF (Brazzaville), III GG182, Conseils des notables dans des départements du Gabon 1936–1941, "Conseil des notables du Département de la Ngounié, réunion du 6 septembre 1937."

78. Vincent de Paul Nyonda studied at missions in all three places; Nyonda, *Autobiographie*, 17–61.

79. See Père Joseph Coignard, "Gabon: Routes nouvelles dans l'extrême-sud," *AP* (1937): 306–11; "Vicariat apostolique du Gabon," *Chronique des Missions confiées à la Congrégation du Saint-Esprit* (1931–1933): 113.

80. Guy-Joseph Mboundou, Interview Notes XVIII, Libreville, March 30, 1991; Nyama-Bika was the late Mr. Mboundou's father.

81. AGG-AEF (Brazzaville), IV GG348, Plaintes, requêtes et réclamations indigènes 1922–1938, "M. le Gouverneur-Général de l'AEF à M. le Lieutenant-Gouverneur du Gabon, 8 janvier 1932, Nomination du chef."

82. AOM-AEF (Aix), D 4D 4(1)D37 1931, "Reclamation de tous les chefs Bapounous demeurant dans la subdivision de Mouila, Mouila, le 21 novembre 1931."

83. AGG-AEF (Brazzaville), II GG98, Gabon: Requête des jeunes Eschiras après la mort du Chef Mwendingui, 1937–1938, "Les jeunes gens de la race Eschiras à M. le Gouverneur-Général de l'AEF, Fougamou, 12 avril 1937."

84. For a recent analysis, see Bernault, *Démocraties*.

85. See Headrick, *Colonialism, Health and Illness*, 125–30.

86. Rey, *Colonialisme*, 191–92, 455–56; Guy-Joseph Mboundou, Interview Notes XVIII, Libreville, March 30, 1991.

87. Rey, *Colonialisme*, 458; see also Vansina, *Paths*, 246.

88. See Maclatchy, "Monographie," 28, 54; Balandier and Pauvert, *Les villages gabonais*, 10, 27; for the Fang, see Fernandez, *Bwiti*, 150–69; and Georges Balandier, *Sociologie actuelle de l'Afrique noire: Dynamique sociale en Afrique centrale* (Paris: PUF, 1982, orig. pub. 1955), 185–97.

89. For a discussion of the changing role of *niembé* (*njembe*) among the Nzabi, see Annie Dupuis, "Etre ou ne pas être, quelques sociétés de femmes du Gabon," *Objets et Mondes* 23, 1–2 (1983): 79–80.

90. Fernandez notes that *mbiri* was largely a female healing society among the Fang during the interwar years which complemented the male-dominated Fang version of *bwiti*. It was only following World War II that women began to play an important role in Fang *bwiti* and men assumed more of a presence in *mbiri*; see Fernandez, *Bwiti*, 599; also Stanislaw Swiderski, "L'Ombwiri, société d'initiation et de guérison au Gabon," *Studi e Materiali di Storia delle Religioni* 40–41 (1972): 125–204; and Michel Fromaget, "Aperçu sur la thérapeutique du conjoint invisible chez les Myéné du Gabon," *Journal des africanistes* 56, 1 (1986): 105–12.

91. André Mary, "L'alternative de la vision et de la possession dans les sociétés religieuses et thérapeutiques du Gabon," *CEA* 23, 3 (1983): 305.

92. See Pierre-Claver Akendengue, "Religion et education traditionnelles en pays Nkomi au 19e siècle" (Thèse de doctorat, Université Paris V, 1986), 652–53, 661–62; François Gaulme, "Le Bwiti chez les Nkomi: Association culturelles et évolution historique sur le littoral gabonais," *JA* 49, 2 (1979): 49–54; Gollnhofer et Sillans, "Phénoménologie de la posséssion chez les Mitsogho," 187–209; Sallée, "L'Arc et la harpe," 146–47; Marcel Massande Mouanga, Interview Notes XVI, Sindara, May 16, 1991.

93. Sallée, "L'Arc et la harpe," 152–54; Mary, "L'alternative de la vision," 295; Maroundou Annie-Joëlle, Interview Notes XV, Libreville, September 14, 1991.

94. Akendengue, "Religion et education," 405–15, 653.

95. Ibid., 652.

96. AOM-AEF (Aix), D 4D 4(1)D24 1923, "Rapports mensuels, Circonscription de Bongo, janvier–mai 1923; Circonscription des Banjabis, mars 1923."

97. AOM-AEF (Aix), D 4D 4(1)D47 1939, "Rapport politique, Département de l'Ogooué-Maritime, 1er semestre 1939."

98. See John A. Ballard, "The Development of Political Parties in French Equatorial Africa" (Ph.D. thesis, Fletcher School of Law and Diplomacy, 1963), 125–26; Balandier, *Sociologie actuelle,* 219–32, 262–63; Mary, "L'alternative de la vision," 298, 307.

99. Dedet, *La mémoire du fleuve,* 483; for a detailed exposition of Mitsogo *bwiti* rituals and symbolism, see Gollnhofer, "Les rites de passages"; and Sillans, *"Motombi."*

100. Vansina, *Paths,* 247.

101. Ibid.

CONCLUSION

Centering on struggles over space and employing the theory of terrritoriality allow new insights into the cognitive, spiritual, and physical world of the peoples who inhabited the equatorial regions of Southern Gabon. The historical analysis of the colonial experience becomes more complex, tortuous, and ambiguous, as it was for Africans who faced the crisis of the times.

In the second half of the nineteenth century, two very different cognitive maps confronted each other in Southern Gabon. Clan and lineage relationships shaped the local cognitive map and the management of kinship relations was crucial in controlling people and things. Territory was socially defined. The European perspective involved a territorial definition of society, one shaped by the rise of the nation-state and by industrial capitalism and employing such tools as maps and censuses, bureaucratic instruments previously unknown to the peoples of equatorial Africa. Order and clan identity for the people of Southern Gabon involved flexibility and nonterritorial conceptions of space— "the clan knows no boundary"; Europeans named and categorized people to a European logic and to meet the needs of colonial rule.

In the early period of colonial conquest, before around 1920, colonial agents—traders, missionaries, administrators, and militia—began to realize their territorial ambitions and reorder space through constructing new centers and communication networks. Their power for injecting disruption and chaos was demonstrated in the food shortages, famine, and disease experienced by local people. The subsequent building of roads and the development of a timber industry helped in the transformation of Southern Gabon as a functional region. A spate of "leopard men" killings in the

1910s and 1920s gave expression to the predicaments of clan elders as they witnessed a decline in their power. In the 1930s, a proliferation of healing societies in which women played predominant roles also represented the survival of traditional means of mediating crisis. A more nuanced view of the "death of tradition" seems called for.

Such responses to rapid social transformation occupied the cultural energies of a considerable portion of the Southern Gabonese population faced with healing the deep ruptures brought about by the experience of colonialism and modern territoriality. At the same time, by the 1920s, a tiny elite was occupied with the business of negotiating the cultural significance of broader ethnic identities. Colonial-appointed chiefs were ultimately sidelined by educated elites trained by Catholic missionaries and by workers who appropriated new opportunities provided by growing urban centers and in labor camps. In such new colonial centers, employers and colonial administrators attempted to regroup populations in settlements ordered after imagined ethnic categories. Ethnic categories and institutions started to become "real" as cultural elites negotiated their meanings in reference to their own traditions and colonial structures. New "ethnically based" cultural associations and politics, especially in the 1940s and 1950s, were the vehicle for the emergence of these new and often politicized identities.

By around 1940 when this study ends, modern territoriality had obtained an ambiguous triumph in Southern Gabon. The physical space of the region was now effectively delimited so that the agents of the colonial presence could influence and control people, phenomena, and relationships in a more or less hegemonic fashion. The transition, occurring within the span of a single generation, was radical. In the conclusion to his masterful study on the spatial development of the Gabonese nation-state, Roland Pourtier describes a historical process where "the fluid and mobile space of the past was hardened and ossified by its retraction onto a restricted number of places."[1] In Southern Gabon, these "places" were colonial nodal points with names like Lambaréné, Mouila, or Fougamou. Pourtier further proposes that "space crystallized around these fixed cores."[2] This "crystallized space" is the outcome of the imposition of modern territoriality.

One need only glance at the pattern of village settlement along the network of roads to sense modern territoriality's impact on the physical space of Southern Gabon. What I have suggested is that the imposition of modern territoriality in physical space necessarily implies a parallel transformation in the cultural identities of the peoples inhabiting these new territories. In the same way that bureaucratic instruments like the map and census or the brute force of the Regional Guard facilitated the crystallization of space so that workers could migrate to lumber camps and villages be regrouped along roads, cultural identity was also crystallized into ethnic groups. Just as the fluid precolonial conceptions of space had to be destroyed to make room for modern bureaucratic territory, so did the fluid and aterritorial system of clan and lineage identity have to give way to ethnic categories that made sense in a culture where a territorial definition of society was predominant. To reverse a bit the Nzabi proverb, the visible boundaries of the field were now applied to the prior boundlessness of the clan.

Map 18, the "Peoples of Gabon," is an apt illustration of the distance that has been covered in this study. Most survey texts will carry for reference

Map 18. Peoples of Gabon. Redrawn from David Gardinier, *Historical Dictionary of Gabon,* 2nd ed. (Metuchen, N.J.: Scarecrow Press, 1994), p. xii.

purposes such a map with ethnic categories plotted in cartographic space. The simple appearance of a term such as "Mitsogo" on a map implies that "Mitsogo" ethnicity is defined by its relationship to a corresponding territoriality. But in considering the transformation of cultural identity in Southern Gabon, I have shown that considerable ambiguity exists in this relationship and will continue to do so. These ethnic terms have only imperfectly papered over a different relationship to territory that existed in the precolonial era.

The effective appropriation of modern ethnic identities in Southern Gabon (and in other parts of the country) by the mass of the people has been an ongoing process under the independent Gabonese nation-state.[3] As the life of the nation-state steadily increases its influence over the population through schooling, single-party organization, and the distribution of the fruits of Gabon's incredible post-independence economic boom, ethnic categories continue to be filled out with meaning and take on new shapes. Radical changes in the physical space of independent Gabon brought about by the mining and petroleum industries have accelerated rural exodus and formed national space defined by nodal regions centered at Libreville, Port-Gentil, and Franceville. For example, Omar Bongo's long term in office and the construction of the Transgabonais railroad to Franceville have seen the rise of the Haut-Ogooué province. Inhabitants of this region have become increasingly prominent in government positions and have been able to group together under an *Altogovéen* regional identity.[4]

Southern Gabon, sensing its growing marginalisation at the national level, has sought to strengthen its regional solidarity. As in other regions of the country, this has been a project for intellectuals, students, and cultural organizations who make imagined ethnic identity real to the population at large through religious activity, art, literature, popular music, and sporting events. As regional identities continue to crystallize and Gabonese assume greater control over modern instruments of territoriality, one can imagine a continuing evolution in the kind of ethnic categories that will appear on maps. The process is part of the long, continuing, and contested history of territoriality.

Notes

1. Pourtier, *Le Gabon*, 2:308.

2. Ibid.

3. See also, for example, "Carte des peuples Gabonais" in François Gaulme, *Le Gabon et son ombre* (Paris: Karthala, 1988), 45, based on the map in Hubert Deschamps, *Traditions orales et archives au Gabon: Contribution à l'ethno-histoire* (Paris: Berger-Levrault, 1962).

4. See Pourtier, *Le Gabon*, 2:237–64; Alihanga, "Structures communautaires," 11–12.

SOURCES AND BIBLIOGRAPHY

I. Informants

Interviews were carried out during two field trips to Southern Gabon in 1989 and 1991. Most interviews were conducted in French. Respecting the wishes of my informants, our conversations were not generally recorded. Instead I took notes which were later fleshed out into fuller accounts. I studied the Tsogo and Gisir languages and used a research assistant to help with translations when my proficiency was not at the required level of fluency. I was also able to make use of an interesting number of mémoires de maîtrise done by Gabonese students at the Université Omar Bongo in Libreville (see "Unpublished Works" below). These provided local language transcriptions of informant interviews along with French translations.

Information given after each name is as follows: Approximate age in 1991; Ethnic Group; Clan (if applicable).

Bodinga-bwa-Bodinga, Sebastien; 65; Eviya; Mobai
A retired civil servant, he has published a short book on the traditions of the Eviya ethnic group. His father was a colonial canton chief; interviewed in Fougamou on May 21, 22, and 28, 1991.

Da Costa, Bernard; 50; French national
A forester active in the timber industry in Gabon for more than thirty years; also a collector of Gabonese art and rare books on Gabon; interviewed in Sindara on May 19 and 20, 1991.

Djyoni, Robert-Marie; 45; Balumbu; Badumbi
A former Catholic monk and a Catholic lay worker in Mouila, he is a local historian who has compiled several Balumbu clan genealogies and is a specialist in the history of the Nyanga region; interviewed in Mouila on July 11 and September 27, 1991.

Guilouba, Antoinette; 90; Eviya/Eshira; Bululu
A mother and a farmer during her long life, she lived through the period of famine and food shortage from 1915 to 1918 in the area around Sindara; interviewed with Bodinga as interpreter in Fougamou on May 25, 1991.

Le Moine, Marie (Soeur Gabriel); 75; French national
A Catholic nun, she has spent more than fifty years at numerous missions throughout Gabon. She knew many of the first generation of Southern Gabonese elite trained in Catholic schools. She compiled a dictionary of the Eshira Ngosi dialect; interviewed in Mandji on May 30, 1991.

Le Tailleur, Joseph; 45; Bapunu; not known
Formerly a worker in the timber industry, he was a driver, carpenter and a palm wine tapper in Sindara; interviewed in Sindara May 14 and 18, 1991.

Mabende, Jean-Christophe; 40; Massango; Sima
Formerly a worker in the timber industry, he trapped game for a living. I spent a week with him in the forest not far from the former site of the Saint-Martin Catholic mission; source of information for forest material culture; interviewed between June 17 and 25, 1991.

Makady, Jeremy; 50; Mitsogo; not known
A Protestant Christian trained by the American Christian and Missionary Alliance, he has worked on translating the Bible into Tsogo and in the 1960s was a translator for the ethnographer Otto Gollnhofer; interviewed in Seka-Seka on July 4, 1991.

Mangari, Marcel; 44; Eshira; not known
A cook who worked for a French Catholic priest and a Gabonese *préfet*, he is one of the most respected members of *Bwiti* in Fougamou; interviewed in Fougamou on July 6, 1989, and May 28, 1991.

Maroundou, Annie-Joëlle; 26; Eshira; Minanga
A former student from my days as a Peace Corps English teacher in Mouila, Annie has been initiated into two healing societies, *mabanji*

and *mugulu*. She provided me with information about the different rituals involved; interviewed in Libreville on June 4 and 5, 1989, and September 14, 1991.

Massande, Marcel Mouanga; 33; Mitsogo; Motoka
A nurse running the infirmary in Sindara, he was a source for timber industry activity in the area and Mitsogo arrival at Samba; interviewed in Sindara May 14 and 15, 1991.

Mayassa, Jean-Claude; 37; Massango/Mirsogo; Osembe
A nurse running an infirmary near Mimongo, he is a member of the founding clan of the regrouped village of Seka-Seka inhabited by Mitsogo and Bakele; source on Mitsogo/Bakele relations; interviewed in Seka-Seka July 3, 5, and 6, 1991.

Mboundou, Guy-Joseph; 59; Eshira; not known
A carpenter who worked in the timber industry, he was the son of Nyama-Bika, an Eshira *terre* chief during the colonial period. He attended the mission school at Saint-Martin in the 1940s; interviewed in Libreville on March 14, April 22, and May 5, 1991. M. Mboundou died in 1994.

Moukaga, Hubert; 88; Bapunu; Dijaba
A catechist and Catholic school inspector from 1923 until his retirement, he served as an informant to the Gabonese Catholic priest and historian André Raponda-Walker. A local historian specializing in the origin tales of the Bapunu clans; interviewed in Mouila on June 15, 1989, and June 12 and 13, 1991.

Moukandja, Joseph; 55; Mitsogo; not known
A *chef de quartier* in Mimongo, his father was a colonial *canton* chief. He provided information on the creation of the colonial post at Mimongo; interviewed in Mimongo on June 6, 1991.

Moundouga, Simon-Pierre; 51; Bapunu/Mitsogo; Moghene
A primary school teacher in Sindara, he attended the Trois-Épis mission in the 1940s. His father was Nzaou Samuel, a Bapunu who came to the area to work in the timber industry. He kindly allowed me to copy a family document produced by his brother, Nzaou Joseph; interviewed in Sindara on May 13 and 18, 1991.

Mwanda, Père Ghislain; 40; Bapunu; Mitsimba
A Catholic priest who once wrote a study on Bapunu clans, he was very
knowledgeable concerning the local history of the Ngounié and Nyanga
regions; interviewed in Mouila on September 27, 1991.

Nyonda, Vincent de Paul; 73; Eshira/Bavungu; Mussanda
Employed in lumber camps as a small boy, he studied in Catholic schools
until seminary. He was a key political figure in Southern Gabon until independence, and a minister in early Gabonese government. A playwright who
created modern Gabonese theater, M. Nyonda was one of the preeminent
figures of the independence generation; interviewed in Libreville on July
24, 1991. M. Nyonda died in January 1995.

Peron, Père Zacherie: 60: French national
Père Zacherie had served in Gabon for more than thirty years; a good source
for mission history and the role of the missionary priest; interviewed in
Fougamou on May 24, 1991.

Pombodie, Joseph Frère; 75; Apindji; Geboyi
A Catholic brother associated with the Saint-Martin mission, he was
an informant for the ethnographer Stanislaw Swiderski in the 1960s
and for several university students interested in the Church and Apindji
history. Uncle of the historian and one-time Minister of Culture, Lazare
Digombe; interviewed in Mouila on September 30, October 2 and 4,
1991.

Prudhomme, Tom; 41; American national
A former teaching colleague who has lived in Gabon since 1979, he is
married to a Mitsogo woman, Mogoula Therese (Motoka clan): and has
written an unpublished novel detailing Mitsogo traditions. Tom is also an
accomplished sculptor. We had daily discussions during my time in Mouila
in 1991.

Soulounganga, Jean-Bruno; 60; Bakele/Eshira; Boudiegui
A retired laborer, he is the father of Maroundou Annie-Joëlle and a veteran
of the French war in Indochina. He attended the Trois-Épis mission in the
1940s. He provided some information about Bakele/Eshira relations near
the village of Yombi.

II. Archives

A. *France*

Archives Nationales, Centre des Archives d'Outre-Mer, Aix-en-Provence
Archives d'Outre-Mer—Afrique Equatoriale Française (AOM-AEF)
    Série D, Politique et Administration Générale
    sous-serie 4(1)D, Rapports politiques-Gabon
    4(1)D1–4(1)D36 (1894–1930)
    sous-serie 5D, Dossiers divers des Affaires Politiques
    5D 58 Situation vivrière en AEF (1923–1948)
    5D 64 Fétichisme, sociétés secrètes en AEF (1925–1953)
Archives de la Congrégation des Pères du Saint-Esprit, (CPSE) Chevilly-Larue
Deux Guinées/Gabon 6A
    Boîte 273–A (Gabon)
    Boîte 991 I-IV, Journal de la Communauté de Saint-Martin des Apindjis (1899–1927)
    Boîte 679 I-III, Journal de la Communauté de Notre Dame des Trois-Épis, Sindara
        (1899–1911, 1928–1934)
    Boîte 680, Journal de la Communauté de Sainte Croix des Eshiras (1895–1905)
    Boîte 1019 (Fonds Pouchet)
    Boîte 1010 (Fonds Pouchet)

B. *Gabon*

Archives Nationales du Gabon (ANG): Libreville
Archives d'Outre-Mer—Afrique Equatorial Française (AOM-AEF) MICROFILM
    Série B, Correspondance Générale
    Sous-Série 2B, correspondance ancienne (1848–1912)
    61–Mi-1 (2B 1 A8)—61–Mi-28 (2B 108–111)
    Série D, Politique et Administration Générale
    Sous-Série 4(1)D, Rapports politiques-Gabon
    51–Mi-56 (4(1)D48) (1930–1940)
    Sous-Série 5D, Dossiers divers des Affaires Politiques
    51–Mi-69 (5D 7) Gabon: Région du littoral (1907–1908)
    51–Mi-70 (5D 11) Organisation administrative (1908–1931)
    51–Mi-72 (5D 13) Pouvoirs répressifs de l'administration en matière de l'indigénat
        (1909–1913)
    51–Mi-71 (5D 22) Chefferies indigènes en AEF (1910–1946)
    51–Mi-73 (5D 27) L'enseignement public et privé en AEF (1911–1952)
Fonds de la Présidence:
    Politique Générale:
        Carton 99, Rapports politiques, Départment de la Ngounié (1929–1944)
        Carton 344, Rapports politiques, Région de la Ngounié (1936–1950)
        Carton 418, Rapports politiques, Région de la Ngounié (1937–1959)
        Carton 35, Rapports politiques, Subdivision de Sindara (1937–1944)
    Carton 517, Rapports politiques, Région du Bas-Ogooué/Mimongo (1932–1961).

Carton 522, Rapports politiques, Subdivision de Mimongo/Eshiras (1914).
Personnel Militaire:
Carton 10, Recrutement de tirailleurs indigènes (1916)
Santé et Assistance/Services Sanitaires:
Carton 675, Service de santé (1916)
Gendarmerie et gardes indigènes:
Carton 1711, Recensement-engagement des tirailleurs (1914–1918).

C. Congo

Archives Nationales du Congo (ANC): Brazzaville
Archives du Gouvernement Général de l'Afrique Equatoriale Française (AGG-AEF)
Rubrique II: Affaires Politiques et Administration Générale (1886–1959)
  GG 98 Gabon: requête des jeunes Eschiras après la mort du Chef Mwendingui (1937–
    1938)
Rubrique IV: Justice, Etat Civil et Curatelle, Police Générale
  GG 334: Traite des esclaves (1894–1943)
  GG 348: Plaintes, requêtes et réclamations indigènes (1922–1938)
  GG 340: Justice européene
  GG 363: Requêtes et plaintes des indigènes (1931–1938)
  GG 365: Plaintes, jugements et réclamations des indigènes (1931–1939)
  GG 178: Conseil contentieux du Gabon (1913–1936)
  GG 182: Conseils locaux (1936–1941)
  GG 185: Conseils locaux (1938–1947)

III. Unpublished Works

Agondjo-Okawe, Pierre-Louis. "Structures parentales gabonaises et développement." Thèse
  de doctorat, Faculté de Droit et des Sciences Economiques de Paris, 1967.
Akendengue, Pierre-Claver. "Religion et éducation traditionnelles en pays Nkomi au 19^e
  siècle." Thèse de doctorat, Université Paris V, 1986.
Alihanga, Martin. "Structures communautaires traditionnelles et perspectives coopératives
  dans la Société Altogovéene (Gabon)." Dissertatio ad doctoratum, Pontificium
  Universtatem S. Thomae de Urbe, Rome, 1976.
Ango, Florentin. "Des relations juridiques chez les Gisiras du Gabon." Mémoire de Stage,
  Institut des Hautes Études d'Outre-Mer, Paris, 1963.
Assoko Ndong, Alain. "Archéologie du peuple holocene de la réserve de faune de la Lopé,
  Gabon." Thèse de doctorat, Université Libre de Bruxelles, 2000.
Augoueli-Matoka, Simon. "Sur les institutions funéraires chez les Gisir du Gabon." Mémoire
  de maîtrise, Université de Caen, 1979.
Ballard, John Addison. "The Development of Political Parties in French Equatorial Africa."
  Ph.D. thesis, Fletcher School of Law and Diplomacy, Tufts University, 1963.
Balouki-Moussa-Manzanz, Cécile. "Tradition et modernité chez les Punu du Gabon: La
  santé de la femme enceinte et celle du nouveau-né de l'ère coloniale à nos jours."
  Mémoire du diplôme, École des Hautes Études en Sciences Sociales, Paris, 1983.

Berre, Robert. "L'extension du pouvoir colonial français à l'intérieur du Gabon (1883–1914)." Thèse de doctorat, Université Paris I, 1979.

Binet, Jaques. "Notes sur la population du sud-ouest (Gabon)." Unpublished document, ORSTOM, Libreville, n.d.

Biwawou-Koumba, Manonza. "Histoire, ethnologie et clans des peuples du Sud Gabon." Unpublished document, n.d.

Bucher, Henry Hale. "The Mpongwe of the Gabon Estuary: A History to 1860." Ph.D. diss., University of Wisconsin, 1977.

"Calendrier Historique: Région de la Ngounié." Unpublished document in possession of M. Bodinga-bwa-Bodinga, n.d.

Chamberlin, Christopher. "Competition and Conflict: The Development of Bulk Export Trade in Central Gabon during the Nineteenth Century." Ph.D. diss., University of California at Los Angeles, 1977.

Cinnamon, John. "The Long March of the Fang: Anthropology and History in Equatorial Africa." Ph.D. diss., Yale University, 1998.

————. "The Marriage of Crampel: Colonial Penetration and Social Landscapes in Equatorial Africa." Paper presented at the American Society for Environmental History, Annual Meetings, Tacoma, March 2000.

De Dravo, Louis Ondenot. "L'exploitation forestière au Gabon de 1896 à 1930." Mémoire de maîtrise, Université de Reims, 1979.

Denbow, James. "The Archaeology of the Congo Coast: Report on Reconnaissances and Excavations in the Bas Kouilou Region of the Congo and Recommendations for Further Work." Unpublished report, 1991.

————. "Progress report on the Congo Archaeology Project: 1991." Unpublished report, 1991.

Dissa Foundou, Jacques. "La présence française (pénétration, occupation et pacification) dans le sud-ouest du Gabon de 1898 a 1919." Mémoire de maîtrise, Université de Provence–Aix, 1979.

Eckendorf, J. J. "Une curiosité ethnographique: Les O-Kota du Bas-Ogooué." Unpublished document, n.d.

Frey, Roger. "L'ami Pouchet." Unpublished document, 1987.

Gaulme, François. "La terre des Bramas: Recherches sur la formation des sociétés gabonaises et des sociétés voisines." Thèse d'état, Université de Paris I (Sorbonne): 1999.

Giles-Vernick, Tamara Lynn. "A Dead People? Migrants, Land and History in the Rainforests of the Central African Republic (Mpiemu)." Ph.D. diss., The Johns Hopkins University, 1996.

Gollnhofer, Otto. "*Bokudu* ethno-histoire Ghetsogo: Essai sur l'histoire générale de la tribu d'après la tradition orale." Mémoire de l'École Pratique des Hautes Études, Paris, 1967.

———— "Les rites de passage de la société initiatique du *Bwete* chez les Mitsogho: La manducation de l'*iboga*." Thèse de doctorat, Université Paris V, 1974.

Goufoura Offiga, Antoinette. "Recherches sur le rôle de la chefferie indigène Gisira dans l'administration coloniale française de la Ngounié 1909–1960." Mémoire de maîtrise, Université Omar Bongo, Libreville, 1985.

Gray, Christopher J. "Mapping and the Making of Colonial Space in Southern Gabon." Conference paper presented at the African Studies Association 36th Annual Meeting, Boston, 1993.

————. "Territoriality, Ethnicity, and Colonial Rule in Southern Gabon, 1850–1960."
    Ph.D. diss., Indiana University, 1995.

Hamilton, Benjamin Arthur. "The Environment, Establishment and Expansion of Protes-
    tant Missions in French Equatorial Africa." Ph.D. diss., Grace Theological Semi-
    nary, Goshen, Indiana, 1959.

Hubert, Jaques. "L'évolution des sociétés secrètes au Gabon." Unpublished Document, Centre
    Hautes Études d'Administration Musulmane, Paris, 1951.

————. "Esquisse de la coutume Bapounou et généralités sur la dégradation des coutumes
    au Gabon." Mémoire d'entrée, Centre Haute Études d'Administration Musulmane,
    Paris, 1951.

Hygnanga-Koumba, Francis-Bernadin César. "Recherches sur l'histoire des villages du Canton
    Ngounié Centrale du début du 18ᵉ s. au milieu de 20ᵉ s." Mémoire de maîtrise,
    Université Omar Bongo, Libreville, 1989.

Ibinga-Mbadinga. "L'implantation du pouvoir colonial dans le sud-Gabon (1880–1910)."
    Mémoire de maîtrise, Université Paris I, 1978.

Ikapi-Moutoukoula. "Étude urbaine de Fougamou." Mémoire de maîtrise, Université Omar
    Bongo, 1986.

Ivala, Clotaire Christian. "Structures monétaires et changements économiques et sociaux au
    Gabon (1914–1960)." Thèse de doctorat, Université de Reims, 1985.

Jean, Suzanne. "Organisation sociale et familiale et problèmes fonciers des populations
    Bandjabi et Bapunu de la Ngounié-Nyanga: Étude préliminaire." Unpublished
    report, Bureau pour le Développement de la production Agricole, 1960.

Kombila, Oscar. "Approche sémiotique du récit *Mbwang* (épopée Punu)." Mémoire de
    maîtrise, Université Omar Bongo, Libreville, 1989.

Koumba, Micheline. "Le Dibur-Simbu et la naissance de Mwil-Bapunu." Rapport de li-
    cence, Université Omar Bongo, Libreville,1985.

Koumba, Victorien. "Esquisse phonologique du Gisir (langue Bantu du Gabon B. 41)."
    Rapport de licence, Université Omar Bongo, Libreville, 1989.

Koumba-Manfoumbi, Monique. "Les Punu du Gabon, des origines à 1899: Essai d'étude
    historique." Thèse de doctorat, Université Paris I, 1987.

Koumba Pambolt, Ignace. "L'évolution des procès de travail dans l'industrie du bois au
    Gabon depuis 1900: Étude de cas de la Compagnie Forestière du Gabon (C.F.G.)."
    Thèse de doctorat, Université de Paris V, 1984.

Loubamono-Bessacque, Guy-Claver. "L'armée coloniale au Gabon de 1910 à 1930." Mémoire
    de maîtrise, Université Omar Bongo, Libreville, 1984.

Loungou-Mouele, Theophile. "Le Gabon de 1910 à 1925: Les incidences de le Première
    Guerre Mondiale sur l'évolution politique, économique et sociale." Thèse de
    doctorat, Université de Provence–Aix, 1984.

Mackaya, Hilaire. "Contribution à l'étude de la santé en A.E.F.: Médecines Traditionnelle
    et occidentale, le cas du Gabon." Thèse de doctorat, Université de Reims, 1984.

Mackaya Mackanga, J.-M. Thiery. "Ethno-histoire des Adyumba: Essai sur l'implantation
    des peuples du Gabon, des origines à l'independence." Mémoire de maîtrise,
    Université Omar Bongo, Libreville, 1982.

Maclatchy, Alain. "Monographie de la subdivision de Mimongo." Unpublished document,
    Layoule, 1936.

Mamfoumbi, Christian. "Evolution des sociétés secrètes chez les Gisir du Gabon." Mémoire
    de maîtrise, Paris, Val-de-Marne, 1981.

————. "Contribution à l'étude du travail forcé en Afrique Equatoriale Française dans l'entre-deux guerres (1919–1939)." Thèse de doctorat, Université Paris I, 1984.

Mamoundou-Mounguengui, Sebastian. "*Mugulu:* Aspects psychopathologiques." Thèse de doctorat, Université Paris XIII, 1984.

Matsiengui-Boussamba, Joseph. "Enquête sur le mythe dans la société Gisir: *Mulombi Landemweli.*" Rapport de licence, Université Omar Bongo, Libreville, 1989.

Mayer, Raymond. "Contribution à une explication des nomenclatures de parenté Gabonaise." Unpublished document, Département de Sociologie, Université Omar Bongo, Libreville, 1977.

Mbigui, Mathias. "Recherche sur l'histoire de Sindara (1858–1946)." Mémoire de maîtrise, Université Omar Bongo, Libreville,1984.

Mboumba, Pascal. "Contacts historiques et culturels entre Mitsogo et Fang au Gabon." Mémoire de maîtrise, Université Paris I, 1981.

Mboumba-Bouassa (Mbumb-Bwas) Florent. "Genèse de l'Eglise du Gabon: Étude historique et canonique." Thèse de doctorat, Université de Strasbourg, 1972.

Metegue N'Nah, Nicolas. "Le Gabon de 1854 à 1886: 'Présence' française et peuples autochtones." Thèse de doctorat, Université Paris I, 1974.

Meyer, R. P. "Hiérarchie des clans (*bifumba*): ethnies (*malongo*): tribus, peuples." Unpublished document, n.d. (circa 1960).

Mombo Maganga, Charles. "Un siècle d'histoire varama: Seconde moitié du 19ᵉ s., première moitie du 20ᵉ s." Mémoire de maîtrise, Université Omar Bongo, Libreville, 1986.

————. "Naissance et développement du pouvoir *gimondu* chez les Varama au 15ᵉ siècle." Rapport de DEA, Université Paul Valery, Montpellier III, 1987.

Mouketou-Mouketou, Olivier. "Étude du système traditionnel de communication chez Les Bapunu du Gabon." Mémoire de maîtrise, Université Omar Bongo, Libreville, 1985.

Moulengui-Boukossou, Vincent. "Une population flottante dans un espace non-maîtrisé: La population de la forêt gabonaise." Thèse de doctorat, Université Paul Valery, Montpellier III, 1985.

Moulengui-Mouele. "Esquisse d'étude monographique sur une ethnie gabonaise: Le Cas des Sangu dans la première moitié du 19ᵉ siècle." Mémoire de maîtrise, Université Omar Bongo, Libreville, 1983.

Mounanga, Loundou. "L'exploitation de l'or à Etéké (Gabon) de 1937 à 1960: Esquisse historico-économique. Mémoire de licence, Université Omar Bongo, Libreville, 1981.

Moundjegou-Magangue, Pierre. "Littérature orale africaine et problèmes de la traduction: Essai sur la littérature des Bajag du Gabon." Mémoire de maîtrise, Université Paris VIII, 1974.

Mounga Mouloungui, Eugénie. "Contribution à l'histoire de Mouila des origines à 1971." Mémoire de maîtrise, Université Omar Bongo, Libreville, 1984.

Mounguengui-Nzigou, Faustin. "Les résistances des populations de la Nyanga (Sud- Gabon) contre l'implantation coloniale française 1844–1911." Mémoire de maîtrise, Université Omar Bongo, Libreville, 1983.

Moutsinga Kebila, Léonard Diderot. "Contribution à l'histoire Eviya." Mémoire de maîtrise, Université Omar Bongo, Libreville, 1989.

N'Dimina Mougala, Antoine Denis. "Monographie d'une ethnie gabonaise: Les Gisir de 1855 à 1900." Mémoire de maîtrise, Université Omar Bongo, Libreville, 1983.

Ndombet, Wilson André. "Histoires des Adjumba." Mémoire de maîtrise, Université Omar Bongo, Libreville, 1984.

Ndong Alloghe, Raphaël. "L'exploitation forestière entre les deux guerres 1920–1940 au Gabon." Mémoire de maîtrise, Université Paris VII, 1979.

Ndonga Imbibi, Fabien. "Impact de la civilisation occidentale sur le groupe ethnolinguistique Nzebi du Haut-Ngunié (1895–1965)." Mémoire de licence, Université Omar Bongo, Libreville, 1981.

Ngolet, François. "La dispersion Ongom-Bakele en Afrique Centrale: Esquisse d'anthropologie historique (origines–vers 1900)." Thèse de doctorat, Université Paul Valéry, Montpellier III, 1994.

Ntsoumbourou, Pierre. "Les villages Apindji de 1900 à 1955." Rapport de licence, Université Omar Bongo, Libreville, 1985.

Nzaou Boubenga, Joseph. "Histoire de la famille Nzaou: Nzaou Samuel, sa vie et son Œuvre." Unpublished family document, 1988.

Nzengui-Mihindou. "Le *Dindzambu*: Rite initiatique, impact sur la société Balumbu de l'embouchure du fleuve Nyanga." Mémoire de DUEL, Université Omar Bongo, Libreville, 1990.

Nziengui Moukani, Jerôme. "Histoire des implantations Bavungu dans la région sud -ouest du Gabon: Des origines à 1968." Mémoire de maîtrise, Université Omar Bongo, Libreville, 1984.

Ogowet, Thérèse. "Histoire des chefs Adjumba." Rapport de licence, Université Omar Bongo, Libreville, 1984.

Orendo Sossa, Anselme-Moise. "Recherches sur l'histoire des Pové: De la période ante-coloniale à l'aube de la colonisation." Rapport de licence, Université Omar Bongo, Libreville, 1985.

Pambo-Loueya, C. Felix. "La colonie du Gabon de 1914 à 1939: Étude économique et Sociale." Thèse de doctorat, Université Paris VII, 1980.

Pouchet, R. P. Gaston, "Vieux Gabon, vieilles missions: Histoires et souvenirs." Unpublished manuscript, 1984.

Ratanga-Atoz, Anges. "Les résistances gabonaises à l'impérialisme de 1870 à 1914." Thèse de doctorat, École Pratique des Hautes Études, Paris, 1973.

Read, Michael Charles. "An Ethnohistorical Study of the Political Economy of Ndjolé, Gabon." Ph.D. diss., University of Washington, 1988.

Sallée, Pierre. "Le Département de la Ngounié: Culture et histoire." Unpublished report, ORSTOM, Libreville, n.d.

———. "L'arc et la harpe: Contribution à l'histoire de la musique du Gabon." Thèse de doctorat, Université Paris X, 1985.

Schrag, Norm. "Mboma and the Lower Zaire: A Socio-Economic Study of a Kongo Trading Community, ca.1785–1885." Ph.D. diss., Indiana University, 1984.

Shank, Floyd A. "Nzabi Kinship: A Cognitive Approach." Ph.D. diss., Indiana University, 1974.

Sillans, Roger. "L'apport des explorations à la connaissance du milieu naturel gabonais de 1843 à 1893: La rencontre de deux civilisations." Thèse de Doctorat d'état, Université Paris I, 1987.

———. "L'apport des explorations à la connaissance du milieu naturel gabonais de 1843 à 1893." Thèse de doctorat, Université Bordeaux III, 1981.

———. "*Motombi* mythes et énigmes initiatiques des Mitsogho du Gabon central: Route de la vie." Thèse de doctorat, École Pratique des Hautes Études, Paris, 1967.

Togo, Hortense. "La tradition orale des Apindji (Ngounié, Gabon): Origines de peuple, mode de vie, médecine, religion et ethique." Mémoire de maîtrise, Université Omar Bongo, Libreville, 1988.

Tonjokoue, Marc-Aurelien. "La famille: Son aspect juridique chez les Bakélé." Mémoire de stage, Institut des Hautes Études d'Outre-Mer, Paris, 1964.

IV. Journals

Annales Apostoliques de la Congrégation du Saint-Esprit/ Annales des Pères du Saint-Esprit (AA/AP) (1884–1940)
Annales de la Propagation de la Foi (1891–1910)
Bulletin de la Congrégation du Saint-Esprit (BCSE) (1893–1936)
Bulletin de la Société des Recherches Congolaise (BSRC)
Bulletin de l'Institut d'Études Centrafricaines (BIEC)
Bulletin du Comite de l'Afrique Française with supplement *Renseignements Coloniaux*; from 1909 *Bulletin de l'Afrique Française*
Cahiers d'Études Africaines (CEA)
Chronique des Missions confiées a la Congrégation du Saint-Esprit (1932–1936)
International Journal of African Historical Studies (IJAHS)
Journal de la Société des Africanistes/Journal des Africanistes (JSA/JA)
Journal des Missions Evangéliques
Journal Officiel du Congo Français
Journal Officiel de l'Afrique Equatorial Française (from 1911)
Journal of African History (JAH)
Liaison: Organe des cercles culturels en A.E.F.
Le Messager du Saint-Esprit (1906–1910)
Les Missions Catholiques (1872–1932)
Muntu: Revue scientifique et culturelle du CICIBA Pholia
Réalités Gabonaise (RG)
Revue Gabonaise des Sciences de l'Homme (RGSH)
La Revue Indigène

V. Books and Articles—Nineteenth Century

Aymes, Lieutenant A. "Résumé du voyage d'exploration de l'Ogooué entrepris par le *Pionnier* en 1867 et 1868." *Bulletin de la Société de Géographie* 5, 17 (1869): 417–33.

Berton, Jules. "De Lastourville sur l'Ogooué à Samba sur le Ngounié (septembre et octobre 1890.)" *Bulletin de la Société de Géographie* 7, 16 (1895): 211–18.

Bichet, R. P. "Quelques jours dans l'Ogowé (Afrique Occidentale)." *Les Missions Catholiques* (1882): 581–85.

Bonzon, Charles. *À Lambaréné: Lettres et souvenirs de Charles Bonzon, missionnaire au Congo-Français, 16 juillet 1893–20 juillet 1894.* Nancy: Berger-Levrault, 1897.

Bouët-Willaumez, Louis-Edouard. *Commerce et traite des noirs aux côtes occidentales d'Afrique.* Paris: Imprimerie Nationale, 1848; reprint Genève: Slatkine Reprints, 1978.

Bowdich, T. Edward. *Mission from Cape Coast Castle to Ashantee.* London: John Murray, 1819; reprint London: Frank Cass, 1966.

Buléon, R. P. Joachim. *De Sainte-Anne d'Auray à Sainte-Anne du Fernan-Vaz, Sous le ciel d'Afrique: Récits d'un missionnaire.* Abbeville: C. Paillart, 1896.

———. *Histoire Sainte re mambu ma vaga Nzambi gu ei gu kana batu.* Libreville: Vicariat Apostolique du Gabon, 1899.

———. *Voyage d'exploration au pays des Eshiras.* Lyon: Bureaux des *Missions Catholiques,* 1895.

Burton, Richard F. *Two Trips to Gorilla Land and the Cataracts of the Congo.* Volume 1. London: Sampson Low, Marston Low, and Searle, 1876; reprint London: Johnson Reprint Editions, 1967.

Compiègne, Le Marquis de. *L'Afrique équatoriale: Gabonais-Pahouins-Gallois.* Paris: Plon, 1875.

———. *L'Afrique équatoriale: Okanda-Bangouens-Osyéba.* Paris: Plon, 1875.

Du Chaillu, Paul B. *Explorations and Adventures in Equatorial Africa.* London: T. Werner Laurie, 1861; reprint, London: Live Books Resurrected, 1945.

———. "The Great Equatorial Forest of Africa." *The Fortnightly Review* n.s. 47 (1890): 777–90.

———. *A Journey to Ashango-Land.* New York: D. Appleton, 1867.

———. "Second Journey into Equatorial Western Africa." *Journal of the Royal Geographical Society* 36 (1866): 64–76.

Du Quilio, Contre-Amiral. "Voyage dans l'Ogoway." *Revue Maritime et Coloniale* 41 (1874): 5–26.

Fleuriot de Langle, M. le Vice-Amiral. "Croisières à la côte d'Afrique." *Le Tour du Monde* 31 (1876): 241–304.

Forêt, Auguste. "Le Lac Fernan-Vaz (Congo Français)." *Bulletin de la Société de Géographie* 7, 19 (1898): 308–27.

———. "Les rivières N'Dogo et N'Gové." *Comptes rendus des séances de la Société de Géographie et de la Commission Centrale* (1894): 417–20.

Griffon du Bellay, M. T. "Exploration du fleuve Ogo-wai, côte occidentale d'Afrique (juillet et août 1862)." *Revue Maritime et Coloniale* 9 (1863): 66–89, 296–309.

———. "Le Gabon 1861–1864" *Le Tour du Monde* 12 (1865): 273–320.

Guiral, Léon. *Le Congo Français du Gabon à Brazzaville.* Paris: Plon, 1889.

Kingsley, Mary H. *Travels in West Africa: Congo Français, Corisco and Cameroons.* London: MacMillan, 1897.

Lejeune, R. P. "L'esclavage au Gabon." *Annales de la Propagation de la Foi.* (1891): 299–311; 339–40.

Marche, Alfred. *Trois voyages dans l'Afrique occidentale: Senegal-Gambie Casamance-Gabon-Ogooué.* London: MacMillan, 1897.

Neuville, D., and Ch. Bréard. *Les voyages de Savorgnan de Brazza: Ogooué et Congo (1875–1882).* Paris: Berger Levrault, 1884.

Ney, Napoléon, ed. *Conférences et lettres de P. Savorgnan de Brazza sur ses trois explorations dans l'ouest africain de 1875 à 1886.* Paris: Dreyfus, 1887; reprint, Heidelberg/ Brazzaville: P. Kivouvou Verlag/Editions Bantoues, 1984.

Parsons, Ellen C. *A Life for Africa: A Biography of Rev. Adolphus Clemens Good, Ph.D. (American Missionary in Equatorial Africa).* New York: Fleming H. Revell, 1897.

Payeur-Didelot. *Trente mois au continent mystérieux: Gabon-Congo et côte occidentale d'Afrique.* Paris: Berger Levrault, 1899.

Proyart, Abbé. *Histoire de Loango, Kakongo et autres royaumes d'Afrique*. Paris: C. P. Berton, 1776, reprint, Farnsborough: Gregg International Publishers, 1968.

Reade, W. Winwood. *Savage Africa: Being the Narrative of a Tour of Equatorial, Southwestern and Northwestern Africa*. New York: Harpers, 1864.

Reading, Joseph H. *The Ogowe Band: A Narrative of African Travel*. Philadelphia: Reading, 1890.

Ussel, A. "De Setté-Cama à Bongo." *AA* (1891): 52–62.

Walker, R.B.N. "Letter of a Journey up the Ogowe." *Proceedings of the Royal Geographical Society* 17 (1873): 354–55.

———. "M. Du Chaillu and his Book." *The Annals and Magazine of Natural History* 3, 46 (1861): 346–49.

———. "Relation d'une tentative d'exploration en 1886 de la rivière de l'Ogowé et de la recherche d'un grand lac devant se trouver dans l'Afrique centrale." *Annales des Voyages de la Géographie, de l'Histoire et de l'Archéologie* 1 (1870): 59–80, 120–44.

Wilson, J. Leighton. *Western Africa: Its History, Condition and Prospects*. New York: Harper & Brothers, 1856; reprint, Westport: Negro Universities Press, 1970.

VI. Books—Twentieth Century

Aba, Ngoua, Bonjean, Abdoulaye Sokhna Diop, Michel-Marie Dufeil, Théophile Loungou-Mouélé, Jean Boex Mbega Ossa, and François-Charles Meye M'Atome, eds. *Millenaire de Mulundu, Centenaire de Lastourville*. Libreville: Multipress Gabon, 1986.

Adjanohoun, E. J., and Jean-Noël Gassita, eds. *Médecine traditionelle et pharmacopée: Contribution aux études ethnobotaniques et floristiques au Gabon*. Paris: ACCT, 1984.

Aicardi de Saint-Paul, Marc. *Le Gabon: Du Roi Denis à Omar Bongo*. Paris: Albatross, 1987.

Ambouroue-Avaro, Joseph. *Un peuple gabonais à l'aube de la colonisation: Le Bas Ogowé au 19e siècle*. Paris: Karthala/C.R.A., 1981.

Amselle, Jean-Loup., and Elikia M'Bokolo, eds. *Au coeur de l'ethnie: Ethnies, tribalisme et état en Afrique*. Paris: Éditions de la découverte, 1985.

Anderson, Benedict. *Imagined Communities: Reflections on the Origin and Spread of Nationalism*. Rev. ed. New York: Verso, 1991.

Annuaire de l'Archdiocèse de Libreville et du Diocèse de Mouila. Libreville: Privately printed, 1964.

Ardener, Shirley, ed. *Women and Space: Ground Rules and Social Maps*. London: Croon Helm, 1981.

Aubréville, A. *Étude sur les forêts de l'Afrique Equatoriale Française et du Cameroun*. Nogent-sur-Marne: Ministère de la France d'Outre-Mer, 1948.

Augé, Marc, ed. *Les domaines de la parenté: Filiation, alliance, résidence*. Paris: Maspero, 1975.

Auracher, Tim. *Le Gabon, une démocratie bloquée? Reculs et avancées d'une décennie de lutte*. Paris: l'Harmattan, 2001.

Balandier, Georges, and Jean-Claude Pauvert. *Les villages gabonais: Aspects démographiques, économiques, sociologiques, projets de modernisation*. Montpellier: Imprimerie Charité for the Institut d'Études Centrafricaines, 1952.

Balandier, Georges. *Sociologie actuelle de l'Afrique noire: Dynamique sociale en Afrique centrale.* 4th ed. Paris: Quadrige/PUF, 1982 (1st ed. 1955).

———. *Afrique ambiguë.* Paris: Plon, 1957.

Barnes, James F. *Gabon: Beyond the Colonial Legacy.* Boulder, Colo.: Westview, 1992.

Bates, Robert H., V. Y. Mudimbe, and Jean O'Barr, ed. *Africa and the Disciplines: The Contributions of Research in Africa to the Social Sciences and Humanities.* Chicago: University of Chicago Press, 1993.

Bayart, Jean-François. *The State in Africa: The Politics of the Belly.* London: Longman, 1993.

Bernault, Florence. *Démocraties ambiguës en Afrique centrale: Congo Brazzaville, Gabon, 1940–1965.* Paris: Karthala, 1996.

———, ed.. *Enfermement, prison et châtiments en Afrique du 19e siècle à nos jours.* Paris: Khartala,1999.

Bertin, A. *Les bois coloniaux.* Paris: Ministère des colonies, 1921.

Birinda, Prince. *La Bible secrète des noirs selon le Bouity (Doctrine initiatique de l'Afrique Équatoriale).* Paris: Omnium littéraire, 1952.

Birmingham, David, and Phyllis M. Martin, eds. *History of Central Africa.* 3 volumes. London: Longman, 1983, 1997.

Bodinga-bwa-Bodinga, Sebastien. *Traditions orales de la race Eviya.* Paris: T.M.T., 1969.

Bonnafé, Pierre. *Histoire sociale d'un peuple congolais.* Vol. 1: *La terre et le ciel,* vol. 2: *Posséder et gouverner.* Paris: ORSTOM, 1987/1988.

Bouche, Denise. *Les villages de liberté en Afrique noire française, 1887–1910.* Paris: Mouton, 1968.

Bouquerel, Jacqueline. *Le Gabon.* 2nd ed. Paris: PUF, 1976.

Bouquiaux, Luc, ed. *L'expansion bantoue.* 2 vols. Paris: SELAF, 1980.

Bourdieu, Pierre. *Outline of a Theory of Practice.* Translated by Richard Nice. Cambridge: Cambridge University Press, 1977.

Brewer, Anthony. *Marxist Theories of Imperialism: A Critical Survey.* London/New York: Routledge & Kegan Paul, 1980.

Briault, R. P. Maurice. *Dans la forêt du Gabon: Études et scènes africaines.* Paris: Bernard Grasset, 1930.

———. *Sur les pistes de l'A.E.F.* Paris: Éditions Alsatia, 1945.

Bruel, Georges. *L'Afrique Équatoriale Française.* Paris: Larose, 1935.

Brunschwig, Henri, ed. *Brazza explorateur: Les traités Makoko 1880–1882.* Paris: Mouton, 1972.

———, ed. *Brazza explorateur: L'Ogooué 1875–1879.* Paris: Mouton, 1966.

Casimir, Michael J., and Aparna Rao, eds. *Mobility and Territoriality: Social and Spatial Boundaries among Foragers, Fishers, Pastoralists and Peripatetics.* Oxford: Berg, 1992.

Charbonnier, François. *Gabon: Terre d'avenir.* Paris: Encyclopédie d'Outre-Mer, 1957.

Chavannes, Charles D. *Le Congo Français: Ma collaboration avec Brazza (1886–1894): Nos relations jusqu'a sa mort (1905).* Paris: Plon, 1937.

Chevalier, Auguste. *La forêt et les bois du Gabon.* Paris: A. Challamel, 1916.

Clark, John F., and David E. Gardinier. *Political Reform in Francophone Africa.* Boulder, Colo.: Westview, 1997.

Clavel, Paul. *Espace et pouvoir.* Paris: PUF, 1978.

Clist, Bernard. *Gabon: 100,000 ans d'histoire.* Sepia-Centre Culturel Français Saint- Exupery (Gabon): 1995.

Cohn, Paul. *An Anthropologist among the Historians and Other Essays.* Delhi: Oxford University Press, 1987.

Comaroff, John., and Jean Camaroff, eds. *Ethnography and the Historical Imagination.* Boulder: Westview, 1992.

———. *Of Revelation and Revolution.* Vol. 1: *Christianity, Colonialism and Consciousness in South Africa.* Chicago: University of Chircago Press, 1991.

———. *Of Revelation and Revolution.* Vol. 2: *The Dialectics of Modernity on a Southern African Frontier.* Chicago: University of Chicago Press, 1997.

Cooper, Frederick, and Ann Laura Stoler. *Tensions of Empire: Colonial Cultures in a Bourgeois World.* Berkeley: University of California Press, 1997.

Coquery-Vidrovitch, Catherine. *Brazza et la prise de possession du Congo: La Mission de l'Ouest Africain, 1883–1885.* Paris: Mouton, 1969.

———. *Le Congo au temps des grandes compagnies concessionnaires, 1898–1930.* Paris: Mouton, 1972.

Couzens, Tim. *Tramp Royal: The True Story of Trader Horn.* Johannesburg: Raven Press 1992.

Crummey, Donald., and C. C. Stewart, eds. *Modes of Production in Africa: The Precolonial Era.* London/Beverly Hills: Sage Publications, 1981.

Cureau, Adolphe Louis. *Savage Man in Central Africa: A Study of the Primitive Races in the French Congo.* Translated by E. Andrews. London: T. Fisher Unwin, 1915 (French ed., 1912).

Davies, P. N., ed. *Trading in West Africa, 1840–1920.* London: Croom Helm, 1976.

Dedet, Christian. *La mémoire du fleuve: L'Afrique aventureuse de Jean Michonet.* Paris: 1984.

Delcourt, J. *Au Congo Français: Monseigneur Carrie, 1842–1904.* Paris: By the author, n.d.

Denis, Commandant M. *Histoire militaire de l'Afrique Equatoriale Française.* Paris: Imprimerie Nationale, 1931.

Deschamps, Hubert. *Quinze ans de Gabon: Les débuts de l'établissement français 1839–1853.* Paris: Société Française d'Histoire d'Outre-Mer, 1965.

———. *Traditions orales et archives au Gabon: Contribution à l'ethno-histoire.* Paris: Berger Levrault, 1962.

Dubois, Collette. *Le prix d'une guerre: Deux colonies pendent la première guerre mondiale (Gabon-Oubangui-Chari).* Aix-en-Provence: Institut d'Histoire des Pays d'Outre-Mer, 1985.

Dupré, George. *La naissance d'une société: Espace et historicité chez les Beembé du Congo.* Paris: ORSTOM, 1985.

———. *Un ordre et sa destruction.* Paris: ORSTOM, 1982.

Eliade, Mircea. *The Myth of the Eternal Return or, Cosmos and History.* Translated by William R. Trask. Bollingen paperback edition. Princeton, N.J.: Princeton University Press, 1974.

Fabian, Johannes. *Language and Colonial Power: The Appropiation of Swahili in the Former Belgian Congo, 1880–1938.* Berkeley: University of California Press, 1986.

———. *Out of Our Minds: Reason and Madness in the Exploration of Central Africa.* Berkeley: University of California Press, 2000.

Feierman, Steven. *Peasant Intellectuals: Anthropology and History in Tanzania.* Madison: University of Wisconsin Press, 1990.

Fernandez, James W. *Bwiti: An Ethnography of the Religious Imagination in Africa.* Princeton, N.J.: Princeton University Press, 1982.

Foucault, Michel. *The Order of Things: An Archeology of the Human Sciences*. New York: Vintage, 1973.

Gardinier, David E. *Historical Dictionary of Gabon*. Metuchen, N.J.: Scarecrow Press, 1981.

———. *Historical Dictionary of Gabon*. 2nd ed. Metuchen, N.J.: Scarecrow Press, 1994.

Gaulme, François. *Le Gabon et son ombre*. Paris: Karthala, 1988.

———. *Le pays de Cama: Un ancien état côtier du Gabon et ses origines*. Paris: Karthala/ C.R.A., 1981.

Gauthier, R. P. *Étude historique sur les Mpongoués et tribus avoisinantes*. Montpellier: Imprimerie Charité for the Institut d'Études Centrafricaines, 1950.

Giles-Vernick. *Cutting the Vines of the Past: Environmental Histories of Death and Loss in the Sangha River Basin Rainforest, Central African Republic, 1900–1994*. Charlottesville: University of Virginia Press, forthcoming.

Gollnhofer, Otto, Pierre Sallée, and Roger Sillans. *Art et artisant tsogho*. Paris: ORSTOM, 1975.

Gollnhoffer, Otto, and Roger Sillans. *La mémoire d'un peuple: Ethno-histoire d'un peuple: Mitsogho, ethnie du Gabon central*. Paris: Présence Africaine, 1997.

Gray, Christopher. *Modernization and Culture Identity: The Creation of National Space in Rural France and Colonial Space in Rural Gabon*. Occasional paper, no. 21, MacArthur Scholar Series. Bloomington: Indiana Center on Global Change and World Peace, 1994.

Grébert, F. *Au Gabon (Afrique Équatoriale Française)*. 3rd ed. Paris: Société des Missions Evangéliques de Paris, 1948..

Groffier, Valérin. *Héros trop oubliés de notre épopée coloniale: Afrique occidentale, centrale et orientale*. Lyon: Librairie Catholique Emmanuel Vitte, 1928.

Guernier, Eugène, ed. *L'Encyclopédie coloniale et maritime: Afrique Équatoriale Française*. Paris: Encyclopédie coloniale maritime, 1950.

Guillemot, Marcel. *Notice sur le Congo Français*. Paris: J. André, 1900.

Guthrie, Malcolm. *The Bantu Languages of Western Equatorial Africa*. London: Oxford University Press, 1953.

Hagenbucher-Sacripanti, Frank. *Les fondements spirituals du pouvoir au Royaume de Loango: République populaire du Congo*. Paris: ORSTOM, 1973.

Hallpike, C. R. *The Foundation of Primitive Thought*. Oxford: Clarendon, 1979.

Harley, J. B., and David Woodwoard, eds. *The History of Cartography*, vol. 1: *Cartography in Prehistoric, Ancient and Medieval Europe and the Mediterranean*. Chicago: Chicago University Press, 1987.

Harms, Robert. *Games against Nature: An Eco-Cultural History of the Nunu of Equatorial Africa*. Cambridge: Cambridge University Press, 1987.

———. *River of Wealth, River of Sorrow: The Central Zaire Basin in the Era of the Slave and Ivory Trade, 1550–1891*. New Haven, Conn.: Yale University Press, 1981.

Harrison, Robert Pogue. *Forests: The Shadow of Civilization*. Chicago: University of Chicago Press, 1992.

Harvey, David. *The Condition of Post Modernity: An Enquiry into the Origins of Cultural Change*. Oxford: Basil Blackwell, 1989.

Headrick, Rita. *Colonialism, Health and Illness in French Equatorial Africa, 1885–1935*. Edited by Daniel R. Headrick. Atlanta: African Studies Association, 1994.

Henige, David. *Oral Historiography*. London: Longman, 1982.

Hobsbawm, Eric, and Terence Ranger, eds. *The Invention of Tradition*. Cambridge: Cambridge University Press, 1983.

Howe, Russell Warren. *Theirs the Darkness.* London: Herbert Jenkins, 1956.

Hunt, Nancy Rose. *A Colonial Lexicon of Birth Ritual, Medicalization, and Mobility in the Congo.* Durham, N.C.: Duke University Press, 1999.

Janzen, John M. *Lemba, 1650–1930: A Drum of Affliction in Africa and the New World.* New York: Garland Publishing, 1982.

Jean, Suzanne. *Les jachères en Afrique tropicale: Interprétation technique et foncière.* Paris: Institut d'ethnologie, 1975.

Joset, Paul-Ernest. *Les sociétés secrètes des hommes léopards en Afrique noire.* Paris: Payot, 1955.

Kassa Mouiri, Romain. *Les contes Bapunu.* Libreville: Impriga, 1986.

Kopytoff, Igor, and Suzanne Miers, eds. *African Slavery: Historical and Anthropological Perspectives.* Madison: University of Wisconsin Press, 1977.

Kuper, Adam. *The Invention of Primitive Society: Transformations of an Illusion.* London: Routledge, 1988.

Larkin, Robert P., and Gary L. Peters, eds. *Dictionary of Concepts in Human Geography.* Westport: Greenwood Press, 1983.

Lasserre, Guy. *Libreville: La ville et sa region.* Paris: Armand Colin, 1958.

Laszio, Ervin, and Ignazio Masulli, eds. *The Evolution of Cognitive Maps: New Paradigms for the Twenty-First Century.* New York: Gordon & Breach Science Publishers, 1993.

Lefebvre, Henri. *La production de l'espace.* Paris: Anthropos, 1974.

Le Roy, Mgr. Alexandre. *La religion des primitifs.* Paris: Gabriel Beauchesne, 1910.

Le Testu, Georges. *Notes sur les coutumes Bapounou dans la circonscription de la Nyanga.* Caen: J. Haulard la Brière, 1918.

Lewis, Etherelda, ed. *Trader Horn: Being the Life and Works of Alfred Aloyius Horn.* New York: Simon and Schuster, 1927.

Lindskog, Birger. *African Leopard Men.* Uppsala: Almquist & Wiksells Boktryckeri, 1954.

Lowe, Donald M. *History of Bourgeois Perception.* Chicago: Unversity of Chicago Press, 1982.

MacGaffey, Wyatt. *Kongo Political Culture: the Conceptual Challenge of the Particular.* Bloomington: Indiana University Press, 2000.

———. *Religion and Society in Central Africa: The Bakongo of Lower Zaire.* Chicago: University of Chicago Press, 1982.

Magang-Ma-Mbuju, W., and F. Mbumb Bwas, *Les Bajag du Gabon: Essai sur l'étude historique et linguistique.* Paris: Imprimerie Saint-Michel, 1974.

Maran, Réné. *Brazza et la fondation de l'A.E.F.* Paris: Gallimard, 1941.

Martin, Phyllis M. *The External Trade of the Loango Coast, 1576–1870: The Effects of Changing Commercial Relations on the Vili Kingdom of Loango.* Oxford: The Clarendon Press, 1972.

———. *Leisure and Society in Colonial Brazzaville.* Cambridge: Cambridge University Press, 1995.

Mayer, Raymond. *Histoire de la famille gabonaise.* Paris/Libreville: Sépia/Centre Culturel Français Saint-Exupéry, 1992.

Mbah, Jean-Ferdinand. *La recherche en sciences sociales au Gabon.* Paris: L'Harmattan, 1987.

M'Bokolo, Elikia. *Noirs et blancs en Afrique Équatoriale: Les sociétés côtières et la pénétration française (vers 1820–1874).* Paris: Éditions de l'École des Hautes Études en Sciences Sociales, 1981.

Mbot, J. E. *Un siécle d'histoire du Gabon raconté par l'iconographie.* Libreville: Ministère de la Culture et des Arts, 1977.

M'Boukou, Jean-Hubert. *Ethnologie criminelle du Gabon.* Le Vesinet: Ediena, 1984.

M'Bou -Yembi, Léon. *Essai d'analyse des mécanismes de fonctionnement de la démocratie dans la société précoloniale des Bavoungous du Gabon.* Ivry: Ateliers Silex, 1986.

Meillassoux, Claude, ed. *L'esclavage en Afrique précoloniale.* Paris: Maspero, 1975.

Merlet, Annie, ed. *Autour de Loango (14ᵉ–19ᵉ siècles): Histoire des Peuples du Sud-Ouest Gabon au temps du royaume de Loango et de "Congo Français".* Paris/Libreville: Sépia/Centre Culturel Français Saint-Exupéry, 1991.

———. *Légendes et histoires des Myènè de l'Ogooué.* Paris/Libreville: Sépia/Centre Culturel Français Saint-Exupéry, 1989.

———. *Vers les plateaux de Masuku (1866–1890). Histoire des peuples du bassin de l'Ogooué, de Lambaréné au Congo, au temps de Brazza et des factoreries.* Paris/Libreville: Sépia/ Centre Culturel Français Saint-Exupéry, 1990.

Metegue N'Nah, Nicolas. . *Domination coloniale au Gabon: La résistance d'un peuple (1839– 1960).* Paris: L'Harmattan, 1981.

———. *Économies et sociétés au Gabon dans la première moitié du 19ᵉ siècle.* Paris: L'Harmattan, 1979.

———. *Lumière sur points d'ombre: Contribution à la connaissance de la société gabonaise.* Langres: Imprimerie Guéniot, 1984.

Miller, Joseph C., ed. *The African Past Speaks: Essays on Oral Tradition and History.* Folkestone: Dawson, 1980.

———, *Way of Death: Merchant Capitalism and the Angolan Slave Trade, 1730–1830.* Madison: University of Wisconsin, 1988.

Ministère de l'Education Nationale de la République Gabonaise, Institut Pédagogique National. *Géographie et cartographie du Gabon: Atlas illustré.* Paris: EDICEF, 1983.

Moore, Henrietta L. *Space, Text and Gender: An Anthropological Study of the Marakwet of Kenya.* Cambridge: Cambridge University Press, 1986.

Morel, Edmund D. *The British Case in French Congo: The Story of a Great Injustice, Its Causes and Its Lessons.* London: Heinmann, 1903.

Morel, Gérard., and Maria Rohrer. *Soeur Hyacynthe Antini: Première religieuse gabonaise.* Libreville: Centre Appels, 1990.

Nassau, Robert Hamill. *Fetishism in West Africa: Forty Years' Observation of Native Customs and Superstitions.* New York: Neale, 1914.

———. *My Ogowe: Being a Narrative of Daily Incidents during Sixteen Years in Equatorial West Africa.* New York: Neale, 1915.

Nidzgorski, Denis. *Arts du spectacle africain: Contributions du Gabon.* Bandundu: CEEBA, 1980.

Noyes, John K. *Colonial Space: Spatiality in the Discourse of German South West Africa 1884– 1915.* Philadelphia: Harwood Academic Publishers, 1992.

Nyonda, Vincent de Paul. *Autobiographie d'un Gabonais: Du villageois au ministre.* Paris: L'Harmattan, 1994.

———, ed. *Épopée Mulombi.* Libreville: by the author, 1985.

Obenga, Théophile, ed. *Les peuples Bantu: Migrations, expansion et identité culturelle.* 2 vols. Libreville/Paris: CICIBA/L'Harmattan, 1989.

Ogoula-M'Beye, Pasteur. *Galwa ou Edongo d'antan.* Translated by Paul-Vincent Pounah. Fontenay-le-Comte, Imprimerie Loriou, 1978.

Ormeling, F. J. *Minority Toponyms on Maps: The Rending of Linguistic Minority Toponyms on Topographic Maps of Western Europe.* Utrecht: University of Utrecht, 1983.

Patterson, K. David. *The Northern Gabon Coast to 1875.* Oxford: Oxford University Press, 1975.

Pepper, Herbert. *Anthologie de la vie africaine: Congo-Gabon.* Libreville/Brazzaville: ORSTOM, 1958.

Perrier, André. *Gabon: Un rével religieux, 1935–1937.* Paris: L'Harmattan, 1988.

Perrois, Louis. *Arts du Gabon: Les arts plastiques du bassin de l'Ogooué.* Arnouville/Paris: Arts d'Afrique noire/ORSTOM, 1979.

Peyro, Bernard., and Richard Oslisly. *Les gravures rupestres de la vallée de l'Ogooué (Gabon).* Paris: Sépia, 1993.

Piolet, Père J. B., ed. *Les missions catholiques françaises au 19ᵉ siécle. V. Missions d'Afrique.* Paris: Armand Colin, 1902.

P.-Lévy, Françoise, and Marion Segaud, eds. *Anthropologie de l'espace.* Paris: Centre Georges Pompidou, 1983.

Pounah, Paul-Vincent. *Carrefour de la discussion.* Coulonges sur l'Antize: Imprimerie Reynaud, 1971.

———. *Concept gabonais.* Monoco: Société des Éditions Paul Bory, 1968.

———. *Notre passé: Étude historique.* Paris: Société d'Impressions Techniques, 1970.

Pourtier, Roland. *Le Gabon,* Tome 1: *Espace—histoire—société,* Tome 2: *État et développement.* Paris: L'Harmattan, 1989.

Poutrin, Dr. L. *Enquête sur la famille, la propriété et la justice chez les indigènes des colonies françaises d'Afrique: Esquisse ethnologique des principales populations de l'Afrique Équatorial Française.* Paris: Masson, 1914.

Pratt, Mary Louise. *Imperial Eyes: Travel, Writing and Transculturation.* London/New York: Routledge, 1992.

Rabut, Elisabeth, ed. *Brazza Commissaire Général: Le Congo Français 1886–1897.* Paris: Éditions de l'École des Hautes Études en Sciences Sociales, 1989.

Ramphele, Mamphela. *A Bed Called Home: Life in the Migrant Labour Hostels of Capetown.* Athens: Ohio University Press, 1992.

Raponda-Walker, André. *Contes Gabonais.* Paris: Présence Africaine, 1967.

———. *Essai de grammaire Tsogo.* Brazzaville: Imprimerie du Gouvernement, 1937.

———. *Notes d'histoire du Gabon,* avec une introduction, des cartes et des notes de Marcel Soret. Montpellier: Imprimerie Charité for the Institut d'Études Centrafricaines, 1960.

———, and Roger Sillans. *Les plantes utiles du Gabon.* Paris: Éditions Paul le Chevalier, 1961.

———, and Roger Sillans. *Rites et croyances des peuples du Gabon: Essai sur les pratiques religieuses d'autrefois et d'aujourd'hui.* Paris: Présence Africaine, 1962 ; reprint, Paris: Agence de Coopération Culturelle et Technique, 1983.

Ratanga-Atoz, Anges. *Histoire du Gabon des migrations historiques à la République 15ᵉ–20ᵉ siècle.* Paris: Les Nouvelles Éditions Africaines, 1985.

———. *Les peuples du Gabon occidental: Ng'omyènè, Shekiani, Bakélé, Benga, Ngubi, Gisire, Varama, Lumbu, Vili, Fang pendant la première période coloniale (1839–1914).* Libreville: Editions Raponda Walker, 1999.

Ravenstein, E. G., ed. *The Strange Adventures of Andrew Battell of Leigh in Angola and the adjoining Regions.* London: Hakluyt Society, 1901.

Reed, Michael C., and James F. Barnes, eds. *Culture, Ecology and Politics in Gabon's Rainforest.* Boulder, Colo.: Westview Press, forthcoming.

Renourd, G. *L'Ouest africain et les Missions Catholiques: Congo et Oubanghi*. Paris: H. Oudin, 1905.

Retel-Laurentin, Anne. *Sorcellerie et ordalies, l'épreuve du poison en Afrique noire: Essai sur le concept de négritude*. Paris: Éditions Anthropos, 1974.

Rey, Pierre-Phillippe. *Colonialisme, néo-colonialisme et transition au capitalisme: Exemple de la "Comilog" au Congo-Brazzaville*. Paris: Maspero, 1971.

Rouget, Fernand. *L'expansion coloniale au Congo Français*. Paris: Emile Larose, 1906.

Sack, Robert David. *Conceptions of Space in Social Thought: A Geographic Perspective*. Minneapolis: University on Minnesota Press, 1980.

———. *Human Territoriality: Its Theory and History*. Cambridge: Cambridge University Press, 1986.

Saint-Aubin, G. de. *La forêt du Gabon*. Nogent-sur-Marne: Centre Technique Forestier Tropical, 1963.

Sautter, Gilles. *De l'Atlantique au fleuve Congo: Une géographie du sous-peuplement*. 2 vols. Paris: Mouton, 1966.

Schweitzer, Albert. *À l'orée de la forêt vierge: Récits et réflexions d'un médicin en Afrique Équatoriale Française*. Nouvelle édition. Paris: Albin Michel, 1962. (orig. English pub. *On the Edge of the Primeval Forest*. 1926).

———. *African Notebook*. New York: Henry Holt, 1939.

———. *The Forest Hospital at Lambaréné*. New York: Henry Holt, 1931.

Soja, Edward W. *The Political Organization of Space*. Washington, D.C.: Association of American Geographers, 1971.

Spear, Thomas., and Richard Waller. *Being Maasai: Ethnicity and Identity in East Africa*. London: James Currey, 1993.

Swiderski, Stanislaw. *Histoire de le religion Bouiti*. Saarbrücken: Forschungen zur Anthropologie und Religionsgeschichte, 1978.

———. *La religion Bouiti*, vol. 1: *Histoire I & II*. Ottawa: Lagas, 1970.

———, and Marie-Laure Girou-Swiderski. *La poésie populaire et les chants religieux du Gabon*. Ottawa: Éditions de l'Université d'Ottawa, 1981.

Thompson, Virginia., and Richard Aldoff. *The Emerging States of French Equatorial Africa*. Stanford: Stanford University Press, 1960.

Thornton, John. *Africa and African in the Making of the Atlantic World 1400–1680*. Cambridge: Cambridge University Press, 1992.

Tuan, Yi-Fu. *Space, Time and Culture among the Iraqw of Tanzania*. Minneapolis: University of Minnesota Press, 1977.

Vacquier, Raymond. *Au temps des factoreries (1900–1950)*. Paris: Karthala, 1986.

Vail, Leroy, ed. *The Creation of Tribalism in Southern Africa*. Berkeley: University of California Press, 1989.

Valdi, François. *Le Gabon: L'homme contre la forêt*. Paris: Librairie de la Revue Française, 1931.

Vansina, Jan. *Oral Tradition as History*. London: James Currey, 1985.

———. *Habitat, Economy and Society in the Central African Rain Forest*. Providence: Berg, 1992.

———. *Living with Africa*. Madison: University of Wisconsin Press, 1994.

———. *Paths in the Rainforests: Toward a History of Political Tradition in Equatorial Africa*. Madison: University of Wisconsin Press, 1990.

Veistroffer, Albert. *Vingt ans dans la brousse africaine: Souvenirs d'un ancien membre de la Mission Savorgnan de Brazza dans l'Ouest Africain (1883–1903)*. Lille: Mercure de Flandre, 1931.

Weber, Eugen. *Peasants into Frenchmen: The Modernization of Rural France, 1870–1914.* Stanford: Stanford University Press, 1976.

Weinstein, Brian. *Gabon: Nation-Building on the Ogooué.* Cambridge, Mass.: M.I.T. Press, 1966.

White, Luise. *Speaking with Vampires: Rumor and History in Colonial Africa.* Berkeley: University of California Press, 2000.

Yates, Douglas A. *The Rentier State in Africa: Oil Rent and Neocolonialism in the Republic of Gabon.* Trenton, N.J.: Africa World Press, 1996.

VII. Articles—Twentieth Century

"L'Afrique: Un autre espace historique." *Annales ESC* 40, 6 (1985): 1245–1406.

Agondjo-Okawe, Pierre-Louis. "Les droits fonciers coutumiers au Gabon (Société Nkomi, Groupe Myene)." *Rural Africana* 22 (1973): 15–29.

———. "Représentations et organisations endogènes de l'espace chez les Myene du Gabon (Nkomi et Mpongwe)." In *Enjeux fonciers en Afrique noire*, ed. E. Le Bris, E. Le Roy, F. Leimdorfer, and E. Grégoire, 101–14. Paris: ORSTOM/Karthala, 1982.

Akelaguelo, Aganga. "Esquisse d'histoire ethnique du Gabon." *Présence Africaine* 132, 4 (1984): 3–32.

Aleko, Hillaire, and Gilbert Puech. "Note sur la langue Ngové et les Ngubi." *Pholia* 3 (1988): 257–71.

Anon. "Le Bouiti." *BSRC* 4 (1924): 3–7.

Avelot, René. "Dans la boucle de l'Ogooué: Conférences sur les opérations de la Brigade Topographique de l'Ogooué-Ngounié." *Bulletin de la Société de Géographie de Lille* (1901): 225–56.

———. "Ethnogénie des peuplades habitant le bassin de l'Ogooué." *Bulletins et Mémoires de la Société d'Anthropologie de Paris* 5, 7 (1906): 132–38.

———. "Notes sur les pratiques religieuses des Ba-Kalé." *L'Anthropologie* 24 (1913): 197–243.

———. "Notice historique sur les Ba-kalé." *L'Anthropologie* 24 (1913): 197–243.

———. "Recherches sur l'histoire des migrations dans le bassin de l'Ogooué et la région littorale adjacente." *Bulletin de Géographie Historique et Descriptive* (1905): 357–412.

Barberet, J. "Les Issogho." *Revue d'Ethnographie* 15 (1923): 271–76.

Bernault-Boswell, Florence. "Le rôle des milieux coloniaux dans la décolonisation du Gabon et du Congo-Brazzaville (1945–1964)." In *L'Afrique noire française: L'heure des indépendances*, ed. Charles-Robert Ageron and Marc Michel, 285. Paris: CNRS Éditions, 1992.

Bourdieu, Pierre. "The Social Space and the Genesis of Groups." *Theory and Society* 14, 6 (1985): 723–44.

Bruel, Georges. "La boucle de l'Ogooué." *Revue Coloniale* 93 (1910): 641–51; 94 (1911): 1–12; 95 (1911): 122–28; 96 (1911): 185–92; 97 (1911): 235–43.

———. "Note sur la construction et la rédaction de la carte du Moyen Ogooué et de la Ngounié." *Revue Coloniale* 85 (1910): 209–24; 86 (1910): 297–303.

Brunschwig, Henri. "Expéditions punitives au Gabon (1875–1877)." *CEA* 2, 3 (1962): 347–61.

————. "Les factures de Brazza 1875–1878." *CEA* 4, 1 (1963): 14–21.

Bucher, Henry H. "The Atlantic Slave Trade and the Gabon Estuary: The Mpongwe to 1860." In *Africans in Bondage,* ed. Paul Lovejoy, 136–54. Madison: University of Wisconsin Press, 1986.

————. "Canonization by Repetition: Paul De Chaillu in Historiography." *Revue Française d'Histoire d'Outre-Mer* 66 (1979): 15–31.

————. "Mpongwe Origins: Historiographical Perspectives." *History in Africa* 2 (1975): 59–89.

Chamberlin, Christopher. "The Migration of the Fang into Central Gabon during the Nineteenth Century: A New Interpretation." *IJAHS* 11, 3 (1978): 429–56.

Charbonnier, Hippolyte. "Congo-Français: L'homme-tigre." *AA* (1921): 50–58.

————. "Notre enquête sur les sociétés secrètes (Extrait d'une lettre de M. Charbonnier, adjoint des Services civils, datée de Tchibanga, le 26 novembre 1916)." *BSRC* 6 (1925): 171–80.

Chevalier, Auguste. "Les rapports des noires avec la nature: Sur l'utilisation par les Indigènes du Gabon d'une fougère pour piégeage et d'un champignon pour la fabrication des ceintures de parure." *JSA* 4 (1934): 123–27.

Cinnamon, John. "Of Mice and Big-Men: Women, Warfare, and Stories in Equatorial Africa." *Yale Graduate Journal of Anthropology* 6 (1994–95): 62–77.

Clist, Bernard. "Archeological Fieldwork and Labwork in Gabon during 1992." *Nyame Akuma* 39 (1993): 26–32.

————. "Archeology in Gabon, 1886–1988." *The African Archeological Review* 7 (1989): 59–95.

Collomb, Gérard. "Fragments d'une cosmologie Banzèbi." *JA* 53, 1/2 (1983): 107–18.

————. "Métallurgie du cuivre et circulation des biens dans le Gabon précoloniale." *Objets et Mondes* 18, 1/2 (1978): 59–68.

————. "Quelques aspects techniques de la forge dans le bassin de l'Ogooué (Gabon)." *Anthropos* 76, 1/2 (1981): 50–66.

————. "Les sept fils de Nzèbi: Un mythe cosmogonique des Banzèbi du Gabon." *JA* 49, 2 (1979): 89–134.

Cookey, S.J.S. "The Concession Policy in the French Congo and the British Reaction 1898–1906." *JAH* 7, 2 (1966): 263–78.

Coquery-Vidrovitch, Catherine. "Les idées économiques de de Brazza et les premières tentatives de colonisation au Congo-Français, 1885–1898." *CEA* 5, 1 (1965): 57–81.

————. "Recherches sur un mode de production africain." *La Pensée* 114 (1969): 61–78.

Crowder, Michael. "The First World War and Its Consequences." In *General History of Africa,* vol. 7: *Africa under Colonial Domination, 1880–1935,* ed. A. Adu Boahen, 284–311. Berkeley/London: University of California Press/Heineman/UNESCO, 1985.

Daney, Pierre. "Sur les croyances des indigènes de la subdivision de Sindara (Gabon, AEF)." *Revue Anthropologique* 34 (1924): 272–82.

Dauber, Kenneth. "Bureaucratizing the Ethnographer's Magic." *Current Anthropology* 36, 1 (1995): 75–86.

De Craemer, Willy, Renée Fox, and Jan Vansina. "Religious Movements in Central Africa: A Theoretical Study." *Comparative Studies in Society and History* 18 (1976): 458–75.

Denbow, James, Amié Manima-Moubouha, and Nicole Sanviti. "Archeological Excavation along the Loango Coast, Congo." *Nsi* 3 (1988): 37–42.

Dubois, Collette. "Le double défi de l'AEF en guerre (1914–1918)." *Africa* (Rome) 44, 1 (1972): 616–58.

Dupré, Georges. "Le commerce entre sociétés lignagères: Les Nzabi dans la traite à la fin du 19ᵉ siècle (Gabon-Congo)." *CEA* 12, 4 (1972): 616–58.

———. "Une mise en perspective." *Canadian Journal of African Studies* 19, 1 (1985): 46–50.

Dupré, Georges, and Pierre-Philippe Rey. "Réflexions sur la pertinence d'une théorie de l'histoire des échanges." *Cahiers Internationaux de Sociologie* 46 (1969): 133–62.

Dupré, Marie-Claude. "Une catastrophe démographique au Moyen Congo: La guerre de l'impôt chez les Téké Tsaayi, 1913–1920." *History in Africa* 17 (1990): 59–76.

———. "La guerre de l'impôt dans les Monts Du Chaillu: Gabon, Moyen Congo (1909–1920)." *Revue Française d'Histoire d'Outre-Mer* 80 (1993): 409–23.

———. "Masques de danse ou cartes géopolitiques? L'invention de Kidumu chez les Téké Tsaayi au 19ᵉ siècle (République populaire du Congo)." *Cahiers des Sciences Humaines* 26, 3 (1990): 447–71.

Dupuis, Annie. "Être ou ne pas être: Quelques sociétés de femmes du Gabon." *Objets et Mondes* 23, 1/2 (1983): 79–93.

———. "Quelques représentations relatives à l'enfant de la conception au sevrage chez les Nzébi du Gabon." *JA* 51 (1981): 117–32.

Ebiatsa-Hopiel, and François Ngolet. "Histoire: Hommage au Professeur Michel-Marie Dufeil." *RAFIA* (mars 1992): 4–19.

Ekarga Mba, Emmanuel. "Régime foncier et structures agraires dans le Moyen-Ogooué (Gabon)." *Muntu* 8 (1988): 74–101.

Esparre, Paul-Louis. "Quelques aspects métaphysiques du 'Bouiti Mitsogo.'" *Genève Afrique* 7, 1 (1968): 53–57.

Foucault, Michel. "Of Other Spaces." *Diacritics* 16 (1986): 22–27.

———. "Questions on Geography." In *Power/Knowledge: Selected Interviews and Other Writings,* ed. Colin Gordon, 63–77. Brighton: Harvester, 1976.

———. "Space, Knowledge and Power." In *The Foucault Reader,* ed. Paul Rabinow, 239–56. New York: Pantheon, 1984.

Fuglested, Finn. "The Trevor-Roper Trap or the Imperialism of History: An Essay." *History in Africa* 19 (1992): 309–26.

Furon, Raymond. "Au Gabon: De la Nyanga à l'Ogooué (Notes géologiques et ethnographiques)." *La Terre et la Vie* 2, 3 (1932): 145–55.

Gardinier, David E. "The Beginnings of French Catholic Evangelization in Gabon and African Responses, 1844–1883." *French Colonial Studies* 2 (1978): 49–74.

———. "Education in French Equatorial Africa, 1842–1945." *Proceedings of the French Colonial Historical Society* 3 (1978): 121–37.

———. "Les Frères de Saint-Gabriel au Gabon, 1900–1918, et la naissance d'une nouvelle élite africaine." *Mondes et Cultures* 46, 3 (1986): 593–606.

Gassita, Jean-Noël. "Iboga et toxicomanie." *Bulletin Médical d'Owendo* 1, 5 (1979): 4–9.

Gaulme, François. "Le Bwiti chez les Nkomi: Associations culturelles et évolution historique sur le littoral gabonais." *JA* 49, 2 (1979): 37–87.

———. "Un problème d'histoire du Gabon: Le sacre de P. Bichet par les Nkomi en 1897." *Revue Française d'Histoire d'Outre-Mer* 61 (1974): 395–416.

Geschiere, Peter. "Chiefs and Colonial Rule in Cameroon: Inventing Chieftaincy, French and British Style." *Africa* 63, 2 (1993): 151–75.

————. "Imposing Capitalist Dominance through the State: The Multifarious Role of the Colonial State in Africa." In *Old Modes of Production and Capitalist Encroachment,* ed. Wim van Binsbergen and Peter Geschiere, 94–143. London: Kegan Paul, 1984.

Giles-Vernick, Tamara. "Doli: Translating an African Environmental History of Loss in the Sangha River Basin of Equatorial Africa." *JAH* 41, 3 (2000): 373–96.

————. "Leaving a Person Behind: History, Personhood, and Struggle over Forest Resources in the Sangha Basin of Equatorial Africa." *IJAHS* 32, 2/3 (1999): 311–38.

————. "Na lege li guirira (On the Road of History): Mapping Out the Past and Present in M'Bres Region, Central African Republic." *Ethnohistory,* 43, 2 (1996): 245–75.

Godelier, Maurice. "Territory and Property in Primitive Society." *Social Science Information* 17, 3 (1978): 399–426.

Gollnhofer, Otto, and Roger Sillans. " Aperçu sur les pratiques sacrificielles chez les Mitsogho: Mythes et rites initiatiques." *Systèmes de Pensée* 5 (1979): 167–74.

————. "Aspects du phénomène de consensus dans la psychothérapie ghetsogho." In *La notion de personne en Afrique noire: Colloques Internationaux du C.N.R.S., No. 544,* 545–63. Paris: C.N.R.S., 1981.

————. "Aspects phénoménologiques et initiatiques de l'état de déconstructuration temporaire de la conscience habituelle chez les Mitsogho du Gabon." *Psychopathologie Africaine* 12, 1 (1976): 45–75.

————. "Cadre, éléments et techniques de la médecine traditionnelle Tsogho: Aspects psychothérapiques." *Psychopathologie Africaine* 11, 3 (1975): 285–321.

————. "Le mythe de la découverte des génie de l'eau chez les Mitsogho." *L'Ethnographie* 1 (1981): 37–46.

————. "Phénoménologie de la possession chez les Mitsogho: Aspects psycho-sociaux." *Psychopathologie Africaine* 10, 2 (1974): 187–209.

————. "Phénoménologie de la possession chez les Mitsogho (Gabon): Rites et techniques." *Anthropos* 74 (1979): 737–51.

————. "Pratiques sacrificielles chez les Mitsogho du Gabon." *Systèmes de Pensée* 7 (1984): 175–86.

————. "Recherches sur le mysticisme des Mitsogo peuple de montagnards du Gabon central (Afrique équatoriale)." In *Réincarnation et vie mystique en Afrique noire: Colloque de Strasbourg 16–18 mai 1963,* by the Centre d'études supérieures spécialisé d'histoire des religions de Strasbourg, 143–73. Paris: PUF, 1965.

————. "Le symbolisme chez les Mitsogho: Aspects de l'anthropomorphisme dans la société initiatique du Bwete." In *Systèmes de signes: Textes réunis en hommage à Germaine Dieterlan,* 223–41. Paris: Hermann, 1978.

————. "Symbolisme et prophylaxie chez les Mitsogho (Gabon)." *Anthropos* 73 (1978): 449–60.

————. "Théâtre de marionnettes au Gabon: Représentation rituelle d'entités spirituelles chez les ethnies du Gabon central." *Le Courrier du Musée de l'Homme* 1 (1977).

————. "Tsâmbo: Texte rituel de guérison chez les Mitsogho." *L'Ethnographie* 1 (1978): 45–53.

Gray, Christopher J. "Chiefs and Their Discontents: the Politics of Modernization in Lambaréné." *Canadian Journal of African Studies,* forthcoming.

———. "Cultivating Citizenship through Xenophobia, 1960–1995." *Africa Today* 45, 3/4 (1998): 389–410.

———. "In the Shadow of the Rainforest: What History for Which Gabon?" In *Culture, Ecology, and Politics in Gabon's Rainforest,* ed. J. F. Barnes and M. C. Reed. Boulder, Colo.: Westview Press, forthcoming.

———. "Missionaries, Masonry, and Male Initiation Societies: The Legacy of French Colonial Interpretation of Gabonese Religious Practice." In *Proceedings of the French Colonial Historical Society's Annual Meeting, Midland, Ontario, 1997.* Forthcoming.

———. "Territoriality and Colonial 'Enclosure' in Southern Gabon." In *Enfermement, prison et châtiments en Afrique du 19e à nos jours,* ed. Florence Bernault, 102–13, Paris: Khartala, 1999.

———. "Who Does Historical Research in Gabon? Obstacles to the Development of a Scholarly Tradition." *History in Africa* 21 (1994): 413–33.

———, and François Ngolet. "Lambaréné, *Okoumé* and the Transformation of Labor along the Middle Ogooué (Gabon): 1870–1945," *JAH* 40, 1 (1999): 87–107.

Guillot, B. "Le pays Banzabi au nord de Mayoko et les déplacements récents de la population provoquées par l'axe Comilog." *Cahiers de l'ORSTOM (série Sciences Humaines)* 4, 3/4 (1967): 37–56.

Guyer, Jane. "Household and Community in African Studies." *African Studies Review* 24, 2/3 (1981): 87–137.

———. "Wealth in People and Self-Realization in Equatorial Africa." *Man* 28 (1993): 243–65.

———. "Wealth in People, Wealth in Things—Introduction." *JAH* 36 (1995): 83–90.

———, and Samuel M. Eno Belinga. "Wealth in People as Wealth in Knowledge: Accumulation and Composition in Equatorial Africa." *JAH* 36 (1995): 91–120.

Harley, J. B. "Deconstructing the Map." *Cartographica* 26, 2 (1989): 1–20.

———. "Maps, Knowledge and Power." In *The Iconography of Landscape,* ed. Denis Cosgrove and Stephen Daniels, 277–312. Cambridge: Cambridge University Press, 1988.

Haug, Ernest. "Le Bas-Ogooué: Notice géographique et ethnographique." *Annales de Géographie* 12 (1903): 159–71.

Hauser, André. "Notes sur les Omyéné du Bas Gabon." *Bulletin de l'IFAN* 17, 3/4 (1954): 402–15.

Hilton, Anne. "The Jaga Reconsidered." *JAH* 22 (1981): 191–202.

Hirschman, Charles. "The Meaning and Measurment of Ethnicity in Malaysia: An Analysis of Census Classifications." *Journal of Asian Studies* 46, 3 (1987): 555–82.

Ilougou, Bernadin. "'Iboga': Arbre de science." *Liaison* 23 (1952): 27–28.

Jameson, Frederic. "Cognitive Mapping." In *Marxism and the Interpretation of Culture,* ed. Cary Nelson and Lawrence Grossberg, 347–57. Urbana and Chicago: University of Illinois Press, 1988.

Janzen, John M. "The Tradition of Renewal in Kongo Religion." In *African Religions: A Symposium,* ed. Newell S. Booth Jr., 69–115. New York: NOK Publishers, 1977.

Jobit, E. "Mission Gendron au Congo-Français: Explorations de la brigade Jobit." *La Géographie* 3 (1901): 181–92.

Kristof, K. D. "The Nature of Frontiers and Boundaries." *Annals of the Association of American Geographers* 49 (1959): 269–82.

Kuper, Adam. "Lineage Theory: A Critical Retrospect." *Annual Review of Anthropology* 11 (1982): 71–95.

Kwenzi Mikala, Jérôme Tangu. "Contribution à l'inventaire des parlés Bantu du Gabon." *Pholia* 2 (1987): 103–10.

Lasserre, Guy. "Okoumé et chantiers forestiers du Gabon." *Cahiers d'Outre-Mer* 8 (1955): 118–60.

Law, Robin. "In Search of a Marxist Perspective on Precolonial Africa." *JAH* 19, 3 (1978): 441–52.

Le Bourhis, L. "Du matriarcat dans le Niari-Ogooué: Tribus Bakougnis, Bakambas, Batékés, Bassoundis, Bayakas, Ballalis, Batchanguis, Bapounous, Bayombés." *BSRC* 21 (1935): 93–98.

Leroux, M. "Les croyances religieuses des indigènes de la region de Sindara (Gabon)." *Revue Anthropologique* 35 (1925): 320–22.

Le Scao, R. P. "Autour de Setté-Cama." *Annales de la Propagation de la Foi* (1903): 382–90.

———. "Setté-Cama: Un coin du Congo." *Le Messager du Saint-Esprit* (1906): 179–82, 207–11, 240–44, 277–80, 305–8; (1907): 23–26, 85–88, 282–85, 309–11, 374– 77; (1908): 21–23, 86–90, 253–56, 277–81, 308–10, 347–49, 377–80; (1909): 25–28.

Le Testu, Georges. "Les coutumes indigènes de la circonscription de la Nyanga (Gabon)." *BSRC* 10 (1929): 3–29; 11 (1930): 33–91.

———. "Études sur le fétiche N'Gwéma." *BSRC* 12 (1930): 73–76.

———. "Notes sur les cultures indigènes de l'intérieur du Gabon." *Revue de Botanique Appliquée et d'Agriculture Tropicale* 20 (1940): 540–56.

———. "Réflexions sur l'homme-tigre." *BSRC* 25 (1938): 147–68.

Locko, Michel. "La recherche archéologique à l'Université Omar Bongo: Bilan scientifique." *Muntu* 8 (1988): 26–44.

Loeffler, Ch. "Mission Gendron au Congo-Français: Exploration du Lieutenant Loeffler (23 août–18 octobre 1899): Note sur la région comprise entre le Ngounié et l'Alima." *La Géographie* 3 (1901): 193–96.

Loungou, Théophile, and Alike Tshinyoka. "Les Gabonais et la Première Guerre Mondiale, 1914–1918." In *Les réactions africaines à la colonization en Afrique Centrale: Actes de Colloque international d'histoire, Kigali, 6–10 mai 1985,* 243–77. Kigali: Publication de la Faculté des Lettres de l'Université Nationale de Rwanda, 1985.

Mabogunje, Akin L., and Paul Richards. "Land and People: Models of Spatial and Ecological Processes in West African History." In *History of West Africa,* vol. 1. 3rd edition, ed. J. F. Ade Ajayi and Michael Crowder, 5–46. London: Longman, 1985.

Maclatchy, Alain. "L'organisation sociale des populations de la région de Mimongo (Gabon)." *BIEC* 1 (1945): 53–86.

———. "Quelques motifs ornementaux utilisés par les indigènes de la Ngounié (Gabon)." *La Terre et la Vie* 2, 11 (1932): 668–72.

———. "Le territoire forestier de Mimongo (Gabon)." *Bulletin de l'Association des Géographes Français* 105 (1937): 65–71.

Mariani. "Assassinat par le feu, hommes panthères anthropologie: Race Bandjabis." *BSRC* 1 (1929): 133–48.

Martin, Phyllis M. "Contesting Clothes in Colonial Brazzaville." *JAH* 35 (1994): 401–26.

———. "Family Strategies in Nineteenth Century Cabinda." *JAH* 28 (1987): 65–86.

———. "Power, Cloth and Currency on the Loango Coast." *Muntu* 9 (1987), 135–48.

————. "The Violence of Empire." In *History of Central Africa,* vol. 2, ed. David Birmingham and Phyllis M. Martin, 1–26. London: Longman, 1983.

Mayer, Raymond. "Histoire de l'écriture des langues du Gabon." *RGSH* 2 (1990): 65–91.

————. "Inventaire et recension de 130 récits migratoires originaux du Gabon." *Pholia* 4 (1989): 171–216.

————. "Mariages préférentiels dans les sociétés matrilinéaires du Gabon." *Annales de l'Université Nationale du Gabon* 5 (1984): 67–71.

————, and Michel Voltz. "Dénomination ethno-scientifique des langues et des ethnies du Gabon." *RGSH* 2 (1990): 43–53.

Mayilas, Augustin. " Une séance de Bouiti." *RG* 14 (1961): 17–20.

Menier, Marie-Antoinette. "Conceptions politiques et administratives de de Brazza 1885–1898." *CEA* 5, 1 (1965): 83–95.

"Mode of Production: The Challenge of Africa." *Canadian Journal of African Studies* 19, 1 (1985): 1–171.

Miller, Joseph. "Requiem for the 'Jaga.'" *CEA* 8, 1 (1973): 121–49.

————. "Thanatopsis." *CEA* 18, 1/2 (1978): 229–31.

————, and Dauril Alden. "Unwanted Cargoes: The Origins and Dissemination of Smallpox via the Slave Trade from Africa to Brazil, c. 1560–1830." In *The African Exchange: Toward a Biological History of Black People,* ed. Kenneth F. Kiple, 35–109. Durham: Duke University Press, 1987.

Nast, Heidi J. "The Impact of British Imperialism on the Landscape of Female Slavery in the Kano Palace, Northern Nigeria." *Africa* 64, 1 (1994): 35–73.

Ndombet, Marie-Augustine. "La femme et la pratique du droit coutumier au Gabon (baptême, mariage, décès)." In *La civilisation de la femme dans la tradition africaine: Rencontre organisée par la Société Africaine de Culture, Abidjan, 3–8 juillet 1972,* 328–36. Paris: Présence Africaine, 1975.

Ngolet, François. "Cohabitation ambiguë entre conscience nationale et conscience ethnique: l'exemple des Bakele." In *Frontières plurielles, frontières conflictuelles en Afrique subsaharienne,* ed. C. Dubois, M. Michel, and P. Soumille, 335–46. Paris: l'Harmattan, 2000.

————. "Ideological Manipulations and Political Longevity: The Power of Omar Bongo in Gabon since 1967." *African Studies Review* 43, 2 (2000): 55–71.

————. "Inventing Ethnicity and Identities in Gabon: The Case of the Ongom (Bakélé)." *Revue Française d'Histoire d'Outre-Mer* 85, 321 (1998): 5–26.

Nyama, Louis-Bernard. "Les jumeaux chez les Bapounous." *RG* 33 (1968): 22–25.

Nzaou-Makiba, Jeanne. "Initiative et pouvoir créateur de la femme: L'exemple du Gabon." In *La civilisation de la femme dans la tradition africaine: Rencontre organisée par la Société Africaine de Culture, Abidjan, 3–8 juillet 1972,* 286–95. Paris: Présence Africaine, 1975.

Oslisly, Richard. "The Neolithic/Iron Age Transition in the Middle Reaches of the Ogodue [*sic*] Valley in Gabon: Chronology and Cultural Change." *Nyame Akuma* 40 (1993): 17–21.

Patterson, David K. "Early Knowledge of the Ogowe River and the American Exploration of 1854." *IJAHS* 5, 1 (1972): 75–90.

————. "Paul B. Du Chaillu and the Exploration of Gabon 1855–1865." *IJAHS* 7, 4 (1974): 647–67.

————. "The Vanishing Mpongwe: European Contact and Demographic Change in the Gabon River." *JAH* 17, 2 (1975): 217–38.

Peyrot, Bernard, and Richard Oslisly. "Recherches récentes sur le paléoenvironnement et l'archéologie au Gabon, 1982–1985." *L'Anthropologie* 90, 2 (1986): 201–16.

———. "L'arrivée des premiers métallurgistes sur l'Ogooué, Gabon." *The African Archeological Review* 10 (1992): 129–38.

Pope, Harrison G. "*Tabernanthe iboga*: An African Narcotic Plant of Social Importance." *Economic Botany* 23 (1969): 174–84.

Ranger, Terence. "The Invention of Tradition Revisited: The Case of Colonial Africa." In *Legitimacy and the State in Twentieth Century Africa: Essays in Honour of A.H.M. Kirk-Greene,* ed. Terence Ranger and Olufemi Vaughan, 62–111. London: Macmillan, 1993.

Raponda-Walker, André. "L'alphabet des idiomes gabonais." *JSA* 2, 2 (1932): 139–46.

———. "Au Gabon d'autrefois." *RG* 20 (1963): 12–14.

———. "Au Gabon: Gestes de compte." *RG* 17 (1962): 7–9.

———. "Au pays des Ishogos." *Le Messager du Saint-Esprit* (1909): 156–59, 186–89, 217–20, 250–52, 279–84, 314–16, 350–52, 379–81; (1910): 22–24, 58–60, 86–88, 115–17, 153–56, 177–81, 222–23, 252–54, 286–88, 312–17.

———. "Le bananier (variétés, usages)." *BSRC* 12 (1930): 131–43.

———. "Chutes, seuils et rapides de l'Ogowé de Franceville à Alembé." *RG* 12 (1961): 39–41.

———. "Les cimetières de familles au Gabon." *RG* 4 (1959): 5–9; 5 (1960): 7–10.

———. "Conte Tsogo: Recueilli à Sindara (rivière Ngounié, Gabon)." *JSA* 9, 2 (1939): 153–57.

———. "Contes Eshira." *BSRC* 7 (1925): 188–90.

———. "Les coutumes gabonaises: Noms de mariage." *Liaison* 36 (1953): 44–45.

———. "Une curieuse coutume gabonaise: La parenté entre clans familiaux de tribus différentes." *Liaison* 69 (1959): 45–48.

———. "Dénominations astrales au Gabon." *BSRC* 24 (1937): 191–209.

———. "En l'honneur du fétiche N'déa." *Liaison* 55 (1957): 42–43.

———. "Encore des devises gabonaises, cris de guerre, serments." *RG* 13 (1961): 9–12.

———. "Un enterrement chez les Ishogos; Coutumes Ishogos; Le Galago (Conte Ishogo)." *BSRC* 9 (1928): 134–46.

———. "Essais: Sur les idiomes du Gabon." *BSRC* 14(1931): 3–66.

———. "Feuilles potagères." *BSRC* 10 (1929): 100–121.

———. "Initiation à l'*Ébongwè* (language des Négrilles)." *BSRC* 23 (1937): 129–55.

———. "Invitation à payer sa contribution au Bouiti." *Liaison* 46 (1955): 47.

———. "Poisons de pêche." *BSRC* 9 (1928): 39–48.

———. "Proverbes gabonais en 12 dialectes différents." *Liaison* 73 (1960): 43–46.

———. "Proverbes Ivilis." *BSRC* 11 (1930): 145–47.

———. "Les néologismes dans les idiomes gabonais." *JSA* 3, 2 (1933): 305–14.

———. "Les tatouages au Gabon." *Liaison* 65 (1958): 34–39.

———. "La tribu des Ishogo ou Mitsogo; Le caméléon tue sa mère pour une affaire de champignons (conte Mitsogo)." *BSRC* 18 (1933): 87–96 ; 115–17.

———. "Les tribus du Gabon." *BSRC* 4 (1924): 55–99.

———, and Robert Reynard. "Anglais, Espagnols, et Nord-Américains au Gabon au XIXᵉ siècle." *BIEC* 12 (1956): 253–79.

Ratanga-Atoz, Anges. "L'immigration Fang: Ses origines et ses conséquences." *Afrika Zamani* 14/15 (1984): 73–81.

Rey, Pierre-Philippe. "Articulation des modes de dépendance et des modes de reproduction dans deux sociétés lignagères (Punu et Kunyi du Congo Brazzaville)." *CEA* 9, 3 (1969): 415–40.

———. "L'esclavage lignager chez les Tsangui, les Punu et les Kuni du Congo Brazzaville: Sa place dans le système d'ensemble des rapports de production." In *L'esclavage en Afrique précoloniale,* ed. Claude Meillassoux, 509–28. Paris: Maspero, 1975.

———. "Guerres et politiques lignagères." In *Guerres de lignages et guerres d'États en Afrique,* ed. Jean Bazin and Emmanuel Terray, 33–72. Paris: Éditions des Archives Contemporaines, 1982.

Roberts, Allen F. "'Like a Roaring Lion': Tabwa Terrorism in the Late Nineteenth Century." In *Banditry, Rebellion and Social Protest in Africa,* ed. Donald Crummey, 65–86. London: James Currey, 1986.

Schneider, Harold K. "Male-Female Conflict and Lion Men of Singida." In *African Religious Groups and Beliefs: Papers in Honor of William R. Bascom,* ed. Simon Ottenberg, 95–109. Meerut: Archana for Folklore Institute, 1982.

Sibeud, Emmanuelle. "La naissance de l'ethnographie africaniste en France avant 1914." *CEA* 34, 4 (1994): 639–58.

Smith, Anthony D. "The Ethnic Sources of Nationalism." In *Ethnic Conflict and International Security,* ed. Michael E. Brown, 27–41. Princeton, N.J.: Princeton University Press, 1993.

Soret, Marcel. "Carte ethno-démographique de l'Afrique Équatoriale Française: Note préliminaire." *BIEC* 11 (1956): 27–52.

Swiderski, Stanislaw. "Les agents éducatifs traditionnels chez les Apindji." *Revue de Psychologie des Peuples* 2 (1966): 193–220.

———. "Le Bwiti: Société d'initiation chez les Apindji au Gabon." *Anthropos* 60 (1965): 541–76.

———. "Les chants rituels et les chansons populaires chez les Apindji." *Cahiers du Musée National d'Ethnographie à Varsovie* 4/5 (1966): 164–80.

———. "Histoire des Apindji d'après la tradition." *Anthropologica* n.s. 17, 1 (1975): 85–124.

———. "L'Ombwiri: Société d'initiation et de guérison au Gabon." *Studi e Materiali di Storia delle Religioni* 40–41 (1972): 125–204.

Thornton, John K. "A Resurrection for the Jaga." *CEA* 18, 1/2 (1978): 223–27.

Tonda, Joseph. "Pouvoirs de guérison, magie et écriture." In *Magie et écriture au Congo,* 133–47. Paris: L'Harmattan, 1994.

Vansina, Jan. "The Bells of Kings." *JAH* 10, 2 (1969): 187–97.

———. "Comment: Traditions of Genesis." *JAH* 15, 2 (1974): 317–22.

———. "Deep-Down Time: Political Tradition in Central Africa." *History in Africa* 16 (1989): 341–62.

———. "Do Pygmies Have a History?" *Sprache und Geschichte in Afrika* 7, 1 (1986): 431–45.

———. "Esquisse historique de l'agriculture en milieu forestier (Afrique Équatoriale)." *Muntu* 2 (1985): 5–34.

———. "The Ethnographic Account as Genre in Central Africa." *Paideuma* 33 (1987): 433–44.

———. " L'homme, les forêts et le passé en Afrique." *Annales ESC* 6 (1985): 1307–34.

———. "Lignage, idéologie et histoire en Afrique Équatoriale." *Enquêtes et Documents d'Histoire Africaine* 4 (1980): 133–55.

————. "The Peoples of the Forest." In *History of Central Africa,* vol. 1, ed. David Birmingham and Phyllis M. Martin, 75–117. London: Longman, 1983.

————. "The Power of Systematic Doubt in Historical Enquiry." *History in Africa* 1 (1974): 109–28.

————. "Towards a History of Lost Corners in the World." *The Economic History Review* 35, 2 (1982): 165–78.

————. "Western Bantu Expansion." *JAH* 25 (1984): 129–45.

Wheeler, Douglas. "A Note on Smallpox in Angola 1670–1875." *Studia* 13/14 (1964): 351–62.

Young, M. Crawford. "Nationalism, Ethnicity, and Class in Africa: A Retrospective." *CEA* 26, 3 (1983): 421–95.

INDEX

CHRISTOPHER J. GRAY

Curriculum Vitae

Education:

Ph.D., History, Indiana University, Bloomington, 1995; Dissertation: "Territoriality, Ethnicity, and Colonial Rule in Southern Gabon, 1850–1960"
M.A., Area Studies (Africa), School of Oriental and African Studies, University of London (UK), 1987
B.A., History, University of Massachusetts, Amherst, 1980

Teaching Experience & Employment:

1995–2000	Assistant Professor / History Department / Florida International University
1992–1994	Instructor / Independent Study Program / Indiana University / "African History, 1750–present"
1992–1994	Associate Instructor/ History Department/ Indiana University Visiting Lecturer / History Department / Indiana University / "Creating Ethnicity & Nationalism"
Winter 1987–88	Translator (French to English) / School of Oriental & African Studies / Papers from West African politics conference, June 1987 (pub. In Cruise-O'Brien, Dunn & Rathbone eds. *Contemporary West African States,* Cambridge, 1989)
1984–1986	Educational Consultant / U.S. Peace Corps & Ministry of Education, Republic of Senegal
1982–1984	English Language Teacher / U.S. Peace Corps & Ministry of Education, Republic of Gabon
1981–1982	Bookseller / Waldenbooks / Seattle, WA
1980–1981	Substitute Teacher / Public Schools / Medway, MA

Fellowships & Honors:

1999	Fulbright Senior Scholar Award, University of Natal, Durban, South Africa (Declined)

Summer 1998	Florida International University Foundation / Provost's Office Research Award
Summer 1996	American Council of Learned Societies Grant for Travel to International Meetings Abroad
Fall 1996	Academy for the Art of Teaching Minigrant (w/ Dr. Mitchell & Dr. Erika Rappaport) / FIU
1994–1995	John H. Edwards Fellowship / Indiana University
Fall 1993	Travel Award to Present Conference Paper / Indiana Center on Global Change and World Peace / Indiana
1992–1993	MacArthur Scholar / Indiana Center on Global Change and World Peace / Indiana University
1990–1991	Fulbright-Hays Doctoral Dissertation Research Abroad Grant / Ph.D. research in France and Gabon
Summer 1989	Social Science Research Council Predissertation Fellowship / Preliminary Ph.D. research in Gabon
1988–1990	Title VI Foreign Language and Area Studies Fellowships / Study of Lingala at Indiana University
1987	Awarded a "Mark of Distinction" for M.A. degree work at the School of Oriental and African Studies, University of London, England.
1980	Graduate Cum Laude from University of Massachusetts-Amherst

Publications:

Forthcoming	*Colonial Rule and Crisis in Equatorial Africa: Southern Gabon, ca. 1850–1940.* Rochester: University of Rochester Press.
Forthcoming	"Missionaries, Masonry, and Male Initiation Societies: The Legacy of French Colonial Interpretations of Gabonese Religious Practice." In *Proceedings of the Annual Meeting of the French Colonial Historical Society, Midland, Ontario, 1997.*
Forthcoming	"In the Shadow of the Rainforest: What History for Which Gabon?" In *Culture, Ecology, and Politics in Gabon's Rainforests,* ed. J. F. Barnes and M. C. Reed. Boulder, Colo.: Westview Press.
Forthcoming	(co-authored with François Ngolet), "Chiefs and their Discontents: The Politics of Modernization in Lambaréné," *Canadian Journal of African Studies.*
1999	(co-authored with François Ngolet) "Okoumé and the Transformation of Labor along the Middle Ogooué (Gabon), 1870–1945." *Journal of African History* 40, 1: 87–107.
1999	"Territoriality and Colonial 'Enclosure' in Southern Gabon," in *Enfermement, prison et châtiments en Afrique, du 19e siècle à nos jours,* ed. Florence Bernault. Paris: Karthala, 101–32.
1998	"Cultivating Citizenship through Xenophobia in Gabon, 1960–1995," *Africa Today* 45, 3/4: 389–409.

1998	"Diop, Cheikh Anta." In *Encyclopedia of Historians and Historical Writing.* London: Fitzroy Dearborn.
1998	"Film Reviews, Africa: Le grand blanc de Lambaréné; Rouch in Reverse," *American Historical Review* 103, 1: 311–12.
1996	"Film Reviews, Africa: Keïta: The Heritage of the Griot; Rocking Popenguine; The Blue Eyes of Yonta," *American Historical Review* 101, 4: 1144–46.
1994	*Modernization and Cultural Identity: The Creation of National Space in Rural France and Colonial Space in Rural Gabon.* Indiana Center on Global Change and World Peace, MacArthur Scholar Series, Occasional Paper #21, Indiana University.
1994	"Who does Historical Research in Gabon? Obstacles to the Development of a Scholarly Tradition," *History in Africa* 21: 413–33.
1989	*Conceptions of History in the Works of Cheikh Anta Diop and Théophile.* Obenga. London: Karnak House.
1988	"The Rise of the Niassène Tijaniyya, 1875 to the Present." *Islam et Société au Sud du Sahara* (Paris) 2: 34–60.

Book Reviews:

La recherche en histoire et l'enseignement de l'histoire en Afrique francophone. In *Journal of African History* 40, 2 (1999): 346–47.

D. Cordell, J. Gregory, and V. Piché, *Hoe and Wage: A Social History of a Circular Migration Sysytem in West Africa,* in *Journal of Asian & African Studies* 34, 2 (1999), 246–48.

S. Weigert, *Traditional Religion and Guerilla Warfare in Modern Africa,* in *Journal of Third World Studies* 16, 1 (1999): 234–36.

F. Bernault, *Démocraties ambiguës en Afrique centrale: Congo-Brazzaville, Gabon 1940–1965,* in *Journal of African History* 39, 2 (1998): 336–38.

T. Lumumba-Kasongo, *The Rise of Multipartyism and Democracy in the Context of Global Change,* in *The International Journal of African Historical Studies* 31, 3 (1998): 660.

M. Liniger-Goumaz, *Les USA et la France face à la Guinée Equatoriale à la fin du XXe siècle: La continuité de l'Histoire; Etats-Unis, France et Guinée Equatoriale: Les 'amitiés' douteuses, Trois synopsis historiques—Quatres bibliographes (trilingue),* in *Journal of African History,* 39, 3 (1998): 504–5.

A. Jalloh and S. Maizlich, eds., *The African Diaspora,* in *Hispanic American Historical Review* (1998).

R. Werbner and T. Ranger, eds., *Postcolonial Identities in Africa,* in *American Anthropologist* 100, 2 (1998): 548–49.

L. Malkki, *Purity and Exile: Violence, Memory, and National Cosmology among Hutu Refugees in Tanzania,* in *Journal of Third World Studies* 15, 1 (1998): 282–83.

O. Likaka, *Rural Society and Cotton in Colonial Zaire,* in *Choice* 35, 5 (1998).

M. Azevedo and E. Nnadozie, *Chad: A Nation in Search of Its Future,* in *Choice* 35, 9 (1998).

A. Disney, ed., *Historiography of Europeans in Africa and Asia, 1450–1800,* in *Hispanic American Historical Review* 77, 2 (1997).

A. Kirk-Greene and D. Bach, eds., *State and Society in Francophone Africa since Independence,* in *Journal of Third World Studies* 14, 1 (1997): 190–95.

E. Ardener, *Kingdom on Mount Cameroon: Studies in the History of the Cameroon Coast, 1500–1970,* in *Choice* 34, 5 (1997).

H. Muoria, *I, the Gikuyu, and the White Fury,* in *Choice* 33, 3 (1995).

J. Vansina, *Living with Africa,* in *Choice* 32, 5 (1995): 530.

G. Westfall, *French Colonial Africa: A Guide to Sources,* in *African Studies Review* 37, 2 (1994): 186–87.

D. Gardinier, *Gabon,* in *Journal of African History* 35, 1 (1994): 176–77.

C. Carozzi and M. Tiepolo, *Congo Brazzaville. Bibliografia generale. Bibliographie générale,* in *The International Journal of African Historical Studies* 26, 2 (1993): 400–401.

V. Y. Mudimbe, *The Invention of Africa,* in *The International Journal of African Historical Studies* 22, 2 (1989): 324–25.

Conference Papers:

"'The Clan Knows No Boundary': Practices of Territoriality in Southern Gabon, c.1800–1940," University of Liberia, Monrovia, Liberia, December 1999.

"L'enfermement de l'espace: Territoriality and Colonial 'Enclosure' in southern Gabon," African Studies Association 42nd Annual Meeting, Philadelphia, PA, November 1999.

"Multinationals and Human Rights Promotion: A Role for Mining Companies in the Democratic Republic of Congo? African Studies Association 41st Annual Meeting, Chicago, IL, November 1998.

"The Disappearing District: The Decline of Precolonial Space in Southern Gabon 1850–1940," American Historical Association 112th Annual Meeting, Seattle, WA, January 1998.

"In the Shadow of the Rainforest: What History for Which Gabon?," African Studies Association 40th Annual Meeting, Columbus, OH, November 1997.

"Regional Identity in Congo (ex-Zaire) and Gabon: From Colonial Invention to African Imagination," International Studies Association (South) Annual Conference, North Miami Beach, FL, October 1997.

"Missionaries, Masonry, and Male Initiation Societies: The Legacy of French Colonial Interpretations of Gabonese Religious Practice," French Colonial Historical Society Annual Meetings, Midland, Ontario, May 1997.

"Who are the Banyamulenge? Inventing Ethnicity and the Rebellion in Eastern Zaire," African Studies Forum, Florida International University, February 1997.

"The Transformation of a Men's Initiation Society: Mwiri in Southern Gabon,

1850 to the Present," African Studies Association 39th Annual Meeting, San Francisco, November 1996.

(with François Ngolet) "The Fickleness of the 'King': Okoumé and Arrested Urbanization in Lambaréné, Gabon," Africa's Urban Past, Centre of African Studies, School of Oriental and African Studies, University of London, June 1996.

"Inventing and Imagining a Modern Gabonese Political Identity: The Case of the Gisira (Eshira)," African Studies Association 38th Annual Meeting, Orlando, FL, December 1995.

"The Disappearing District: The Decline of Precolonial Space in Southern Gabon 1850–1940," African Studies Association 37th Annual Meeting, Toronto, Canada, November 1994.

"Regional Identity in Zaire and Gabon: From Colonial Invention to African Imagination," Global Change and World Peace toward the Year 2000, Indiana University, Bloomington, IN, May 1994.

"Ethnic Conflict in Zaire," African Studies Program Noon Talks, Indiana University, Bloomington, IN, January 1994.

"Mapping and the Making of Colonial Space in Southern Gabon," African Studies Association 36th Annual Meeting, Boston, December 1993.

"The Works of Théophile Obenga and Their Contribution to Contemporary Afrocentric Thought," The 10th Annual Pan-African Studies Conference, Indiana State University, Terre Haute, IN, April 1993.

"Imposing Bourgeois Space: Culture and Modernization in 19th-Century Rural France and Colonial Gabon," A Workshop on Global Change and World Peace, Indiana University, Bloomington, IN, April 1993.

"Colonial Resistance and the Creation of Ethnic Identity: The Case of Bombi Mondjo (Gabon)," African Studies Program Noon Talks, Indiana University, Bloomington, IN, April 1992.

"Religious Change in Gabon under French Colonialism," African Studies Program Noon Talks, Indiana University, Bloomington, IN, March 1990.

"The Legacy of Cheikh Anta Diop," African Studies Program Noon Talks, Indiana University, Bloomington, IN, February 1989.

Teaching Interests:

African History; African and African-American Sociocultural History; Imperialism; Colonial History; Modern European History; World History; Historiography; History of Religions.

University and Public Service:

Florida International University

1997–1998   Member History Department Search Committee, American History

1997–1998	History Department Library Representative
1996–1998	History Department Steward, United Faculty of Florida
1996–1997	Member History Department Search Committee, American History
1996–2000	Member Steering Committee, African Studies Forum
1996–2000	Faculty Advisor, Amnesty International Student Group; Association of People of African Ancestry and Culture
1995–2000	Member Graduate Program Committee, Department of History
1995–2000	Member Coordinating Committee, African-New World Studies Program
1995–1996	Member History Department Search Committee, African-American History

Indiana University

| 1993–1995 | Member Working Group on Ethnicity and Nationalism, Indiana Center on Global Change and World Peace. |
| 1989–1990 | Member African Studies Program Student Advisory Committee, Indiana University |

Other

October 1998	Member/Consultant on International Foundation for Election Systems team to conduct "Pre-Election Technical Assessment" in Gabon
1995–2000	Member Fulbright Association, South Florida
1995–2000	Member Returned Peace Corps Volunteers of South Florida
1989–2000	Member Association of Concerned Africa Scholars
1989–2000	Member Friends of Gabon, National Council of Returned Peace Corps Volunteers.
1987–2000	Member Amnesty International–USA
1992–2000	Congo (ex-Zaire) & Gabon Coordinator, Central Africa Coordination Group, Amnesty International–USA.
1989–1990	Senegal & Mauritania Coordinator, West Africa Coordination Group, AI–USA
Spring-Summer 1990 & 1994–1995	Acting Coordinator, Amnesty International, Local Group 328, Bloomington, Indiana
1982–1986	Volunteer Service with the United States Peace Corps in Gabon & Senegal (English Teacher)

Professional Organizations:

| 1988–2000 | African Studies Association (USA) |
| 1992–2000 | American Historical Association |

1994–2000	French Colonial Historical Society
1994–2000	Francophone Africa Research Group
1996–2000	Association of Third World Studies
1996–1999	World History Association

Travel:

Dec. 1999	Visit to Liberia as Thesis Advisor to William Allen, Recipient of Rockefeller Foundation Grant.
Oct. 1998	Member/Consultant on team organized by the International Foundation for Election Systems to conduct a "Pre-Election Technical Assessment" in Gabon; travel to Libreville & Franceville.
Feb. 1998	Part of delegation from Amnesty International-USA attending an Amnesty International Regional Strategy Conference in London.
Dec. 1996	Represented Amnesty International-USA at an international conference organized in Paris by the French Section of AI concerning the situation in the former Zaire.
1990	Research travel to France and Gabon; personal travel to Congo, Zaire, and Burundi.
Fall 1990	Research travel to France.
Summer 1989	Research travel to Gabon.
1986–1987	Study in London, England; travel to France.
1984–1986	Lived and worked in Senegal as Peace Corps Volunteer; travel to Gambia, Canary Islands, Mali, Côte d'Ivoire, and Gabon.
1982–1984	Lived and worked in Gabon as Peace Corps Volunteer.
1979–1980	Year Abroad study in Lancaster, England; travel throughout United Kingdom and Ireland; France, Switzerland, Austria, Yugoslavia, Greece, Italy, Netherlands, Denmark, and Norway.
Summer 1975	Rotary Club Summer Exchange to France.

DEMCO